CATALOOCHEE

Cataloochee

Lost Settlement of the Smokies

BY

Elizabeth D. Powers with Mark E. Hannah

Western Carolina University
Hunter Library

Original copyright © 1982, Elizabeth D. Powers and Mark E. Hannah. Foreword to the New Edition copyright © 2025, Mark E. Hannah II. Introduction to the New Edition by Jim Casada copyright © 2025, Western Carolina University Hunter Library.

This work is licensed under a Creative Commons CC BY-NC-ND license. To view a copy of the license, visit http://creativecommons.org/licenses.

Suggested citation: Powers, Elizabeth and Mark Hannah. *Cataloochee: Lost Settlement of the Smokies*. Cullowhee: Western Carolina University Hunter Library, 2025.

DOI: https://doi.org/10.5149/9781469687933_Powers

ISBN 978-1-4696-8792-6 (paperback)
ISBN 978-1-4696-8793-3 (open access EPUB ebook)
ISBN 978-1-4696-8794-0 (open access PDF ebook)

Published by the Hunter Library at Western Carolina University

Distributed by the University of North Carolina Press

CONTENTS

Foreword to the New Edition by Mark E. Hannah II viii

Foreword to the Original Edition by Elizabeth D. Powers xi

Timeline xiii

Introduction to the New Edition by Jim Casada 1

PART 1
Times Past 9

CHAPTER ONE
The Buzzard's Wing 11

CHAPTER TWO
Paradise: A Point of View 19

CHAPTER THREE
Dirt Captains and Land Pirates 24

CHAPTER FOUR
The Life Line 33

CHAPTER FIVE
Mt. Sterling: The Last Bastion 38

CHAPTER SIX
Blockade: Another Rebellion 50

CHAPTER SEVEN
Lost! 59

PART 2
The People 69

CHAPTER EIGHT
A Rose, a Snake, and a Dove 71

CHAPTER NINE
As Cataloochee Goes... 83

CHAPTER TEN
The Long Arm 87

CHAPTER ELEVEN
The Hickory Stick 95

CHAPTER TWELVE
The Best Days of All 103

CHAPTER THIRTEEN
Two by Two 118

CHAPTER FOURTEEN
Running with the Pack 133

CHAPTER FIFTEEN
The Blooming of the Beelzebubs 146

CHAPTER SIXTEEN
Hiram's Fixation 164

CHAPTER SEVENTEEN
The Compleat Cataloochan 178

CHAPTER EIGHTEEN
Shelter 189

CHAPTER NINTEEN
Plenty 200

CHAPTER TWENTY
The Food of Love 208

CHAPTER TWENTY-ONE
Tom-Walker-Nation-on-the-Devil! 218

PART 3
The Place 233

CHAPTER TWENTY-TWO
Once an Inland Sea 235

CHAPTER TWENTY-THREE
About as Far as New York to California 239

CHAPTER TWENTY-FOUR
Herrycanes and Sech 244

CHAPTER TWENTY-FIVE
Flora's Ark 254

CHAPTER TWENTY-SIX
Klandaghi and Other Lords 265

Epilogue 287

References and Acknowledgments 291

Images from the Original 1982 Book 312

About the Authors 318

FOREWORD TO THE NEW EDITION

On June 7, 2020, a little over 180 years after their great-great-great grandparents had settled here, two men parked their vehicle at the Double Gap gate which leads into the Cataloochee Valley. The first Sunday in June, Decoration Day, had been a Little Cataloochee tradition since the 1930s. It was a day meant for fellowship, music, and reunion of families who had once lived there, but also a time meant for honoring the ones whose remains would forever lie in what was once the community of Ola in the Little Cataloochee part of the valley.

This year, however, that tradition was at risk of being missed, due to the worldwide pandemic known as Covid. All the Park gates were locked, and therefore inaccessible to driving visitors. While there would be no food or music, the two men were determined to decorate the graves of their ancestors, so they started the 14-mile round trip hike, carrying two backpacks filled with flowers.

It was a beautiful late-spring day, and hiking into the Valley allowed them time to share their memories of past Decoration Days and enjoy the many wildflowers in bloom—galax, summer bluets, flame azalea, and mountain laurel were all in spectacular form. They talked about how hard life must have been not only for the earliest settlers, but also the families who lived in the established community during the thriving times in the early 1900s. As they entered the Little Cataloochee trailhead and crossed Correll Branch, they saw that recent heavy rains had washed out the roads and fallen trees covered the trail, which surely would have been a source of constant work in those days. Now, the road is only cleared once a year by National Park maintenance crews when the Decoration festivities come around.

The two men arrived at the Little Cataloochee Baptist Church at noon, just in time to ring the church bell, decorate all the gravesites, and uphold a lost mountain communities' tradition that is dear to so many. Ironically, they noted, some of the gravesites decorated were those that passed almost exactly a century ago, during another worldwide pandemic.

The two men, myself (named for my grandfather, Mark Hannah) and my nephew, Will Mooney, (named for his great-great grandfather, Will Messer) hiked through the lands owned by our forefathers, and wondered what the community must have been like when it was at the height of its short existence. What did the Messer and

Hannah farms look like back then? What would it be like now, if the Park had not been established?

While the first question can be explored, at least to some extent, through existing photographs, the latter question will never be known. It will always be left to the eye of the beholder, or to the imagination of whomever visits the Cataloochee Valley now.

To drive or hike through what was once the community of Ola in Little Cataloochee or over Davidson Gap into Nellie in Big Cataloochee, one can barely imagine that people ever lived here. All that remains of these communities are two churches, a schoolhouse, and a few restored homeplaces of the families that lived in Cataloochee. Today, the valley is lush and thriving with plant life, elk, wild turkey and bear, with only a few reminders of the thriving homesteads that once occupied the valley.

My father, Harold, was one of the last people still living who was born in Little Cataloochee and intended to write this foreword, but unfortunately passed away before he could write down his thoughts. However, we did have many conversations about what he thought Cataloochee might look like today. He and my grandfather Mark (co-author of this book) had also discussed that topic at length over the last years of Mark's life.

Mark Hannah was convinced that the valley had, to a certain extent, reached its peak and would struggle to continue to thrive. The main reason he stated was that there was not enough fertile land in the valley to support farming—or to use his phrase the land was "used up". While the residents had adapted to maintain an income stream from apple production and the later efforts to develop tourism businesses to attract visitors to enjoy the pleasures of trout fishing, the valley remained quite remote and difficult to travel in and out of—as it remains even today. Of course, in today's world, most of which is accustomed to paved roads and grocery stores within easy driving distance, the valley communities could have once again adapted, but that would have also meant (at least to a certain extent) the loss of isolation. The seclusion of the Cataloochee Valley was one of the things that drew many of them to the valley originally.

Harold took a more scientific approach to the question of why the valley was "used up" and focused mostly on the geology of the valley. He remembered large storm events which washed what little good topsoil for agriculture away at regular intervals, forcing the farm production to go "further up the mountain" on a routine basis. The geology of most of the Cataloochee Valley was simply not able to support an agricultural community for the long term, in Harold's opinion, because of the presence of large amounts of sandstone and quartz, and the absence of large amounts of limestone, which would have been able to help support maintaining a fertile ground in which to plant crops.

The intention of this book was to preserve the history and lifestyles of the communities which once existed in the Cataloochee Valley. It does so through first-person accounts of what life was like in Cataloochee before it became a National Park. Today, the descendants of those families still congregate on two Sundays every year to celebrate their family memories and stories, remember their family history through sharing of food and music, and remember their loved ones who will always remain in our hearts. If those traditions continue, the Lost Settlement of the Smokies will, in fact, survive!

Mark E. Hannah II
September 2024

FOREWORD TO THE ORIGINAL EDITION

Above Maggie Valley, North Carolina, a theme park called Ghost Town, patterned after a Wild West mining community, sprawls over the bull-dozed top of Buck Mountain. In season, this honkytonk, touristy attraction reverberates night and day with the sound of mock gun battles outside the Red Dog Saloon.

Not many miles further, as the crow flies, over the rim of the Cataloochee Divide in the heart of the Great Smoky Mountains National Park lies a true ghost town, Cataloochee, reluctantly abandoned by seven hundred people in the thirties when the National Park Service pressured them to sell out and move from the splendid isolation of their valley.

Under the guise of returning Cataloochee to its former state of wilderness, the Park Service regrettably burned most of the fine old log buildings, thus destroying nearly all traces of this hundred-year-old pioneer settlement. Fortunately, today an enlightened Park Service has completely reversed this trend and tries to preserve both old buildings <u>and</u> the land.

This book, often told in the actual words of former inhabitants, attempts to recreate the civilization of a beautiful Cataloochee that was, in their eyes, an ideal way of life. Because of its extreme isolation, it was like a womb, a small untouched world all to itself.

The author has merely been the transmitter of the flame, with the collaboration of Mark E. Hannah, a native of Little Cataloochee who remained behind as Chief Ranger for thirty-one years after the settlement was deserted. They were encouraged by Dr. Doris Hammett, of the Haywood Trail Riders, to write a short history of the valley, from which this book grew.

Intrigued by Cataloochee through stories handed down in the family by a great-grandfather, Colonel Allen T. Davidson, the author wished to discover what drew her ancestor to this spot.

Though Allen Davidson seems a peripheral figure in Cataloochee (he never lived there, though he owned land on the Long Bunk), he had herded his father's cattle on its pastures, a scene which remained vivid all his life. His father, too, William Mitchell Davidson, had owned Cataloochee land long before it was settled, as had the author's great-great-great-grandfather, Reuben Moody, whose grand-daughter, Adeline Howell, married Allen. Some of her Howell kin eventually settled in Cataloochee.

Davidson Gap and Davidson Branch in Cataloochee were named for these, early cattlemen, though none of the descendants interviewed knew the connection, as the Davidsons were long gone by 1840 when they followed Sam Houston down to settle Texas. Only young Allen remained behind to become a colonel in the local militia, a circuit-riding mountain lawyer, a delegate to the Confederate Congress, as well as legal counsel to the Cherokee Nation and a life-long devotee of Cataloochee territory.

This book is dedicated to the memory of those ten informants, and perhaps others, who died even as this book was being completed:

Tom Alexander
Iva Hannah Bennett
'Tine Bennett
Floyd Burgess
Eldridge Caldwell
Flora Palmer Medford
Fred Hannah
Glenn Palmer
Floyd Woody
Jonathan Woody

Elizabeth D. Powers
The Cataloochee Divide
September 1982

TIMELINE

The events in *Cataloochee: Lost Settlement of the Smokies* are not presented in chronological order. This timeline is intended to help the reader gain a better understanding of the history of the Cataloochee Valley and how it became a national park.

1776
Earthquake on the Balsam Range, recorded by Revolutionary soldiers

1790
Eastern elk considered extinct in North Carolina

1791
Treaty of Holston ended Cherokee/American wars and gave the U. S. Government control of the lands in the Cataloochee Valley

1796
Two of the largest land grants west of the Blue Ridge made to John Gray Blount and David Allison, totaling 570,880 acres, including all of Cataloochee

1798
Four treaties of Tellico – Cherokee had to cede Cataloochee territory

1806
William Mitchell Davidson deeded land on eastern frontier of Cataloochee – began summering his cattle there – Davidson Branch and Davidson Gap so-named

1810
Bishop Francis Asbury rode through Cataloochee

1814
Earliest known land entry for Cataloochee, Henry Colwell (later Caldwell), a hunting cabin, not a permanent settlement

1815–1817
Last remaining buffalo seen in surrounding areas

1819
Cherokees relinquish the last of the lands in the Smoky Mountains

1819
Colonel Allen T. Davidson (Elizabeth Powers' great grandfather) born in Jonathan Creek

1825
Stock drivers' road into Cataloochee authorized by Haywood County

1832
Two tracts entered by Feldred Davis. Also John L. and Jacob Smith, and Neddy McFalls entered 100 acres on Little Cataloochee. Reuben Moody entered 880 acres. No permanent settlers but a real cattle track had begun

1834
Blount lands to Colonel Robert Love who becomes owner of huge Cataloochee tract

1835
Treaties of New Echota – ceded all Indian land east of the Mississippi

1838
Trail of Tears – Oconaluftee Cherokee hid out in Cataloochee

1839
Evan and Elizabeth Noland Hannah (Mark Hannah's great grandparents), their sons, John Jackson and Benjamin and Elizabeth's father, William Noland, first permanent settlers in Cataloochee

1839
Agreement between Will Thomas and the Secretary of War, Joel R. Poinsett, allowed the Oconaluftee Cherokee to stay

1841
Levi B. Colwell (Caldwell) and his father James Colwell settled in Big Cataloochee as well as the Bennetts. Allen "Twitty" Davidson entered 300 acres but did not settle permanently

1848
George Palmer arrived with his family to settle in Big Cataloochee
Allen Davidson, attorney, helped Cherokee with claims to land

1849
Cataloochee was made a voting precinct

1850s
Dan and Harriett Cook cabin built in Little Cataloochee

1851
Jonathan Woody family settled in Cataloochee. Creation of road into Cataloochee started

1860
"Cataloochee Turnpike" completed which allowed Civil War troops entry into the valley

1861
Start of Civil War. North Carolina joined the Confederacy; Cataloochee was neutral

1865
The Love Speculation – 375,000 acres. End of Civil War

1872
Congress established Yellowstone National Park in the territories of Montana and Wyoming "as a public park or pleasuring-ground for the benefit and enjoyment of the people"

1886
Earthquake in Charleston SC (August 31), felt in Cataloochee during a revival

1890
Cataloochee Baptist Church (chartered in 1855) built in Little Cataloochee

1896
Forty-two inch snowfall in Cataloochee

1898
Hurricane made landfall in Georgia and passed through Cataloochee

1899
Palmer United Methodist Chapel built in Big Cataloochee

1899–1905
The Appalachian National Park Association (later called the Southern Forest Reserve Association) advocated for conservation of the region's vital forests

Late 1800s through early 1900s
Cataloochee – grew as a self-sustaining community. Commerce included logging, moonshine, and tourism

1900
764 residents in Cataloochee

1909
North Carolina imposed statewide prohibition

1910

Rainbow trout first introduced to Cataloochee Creek

1910

Population of Big and Little Cataloochee was 1,251, making it the largest community in the Smokies

1910

Will and Rachel Cook Messer house completed on Little Cataloochee Creek. It had 11 rooms, hot and cold running water, and an acetylene lighting system

1913

Snow fell in Cataloochee on June 10

1914

Apples were the major cash crop in Cataloochee

1916

First wedding at Little Cataloochee Baptist Church, Flora Messer (daughter of Will and Rachel Cook Messer) and Charles Morrow

1916

President Woodrow Wilson signed the "Organic Act" creating the National Park Service, a federal bureau in the Department of the Interior responsible for maintaining national parks and monuments

1918–20

Spanish flu epidemic took the lives of three of Will and Rachel Messer's daughters (Vanalee, Ollie, Loretta)

1918–1930

Jarvis Palmer had tourist fishing cabins above his house in Cataloochee

1919

18th Amendment to the U. S. Constitution established nationwide prohibition

1920

Last panther (*Puma concolor cougar*) killed in Great Smoky Mountains National Park (near present day Fontana Village)

1920s

Horace Kephart (writer) and George Masa (photographer) began a vigorous campaign to save the Smoky Mountains from logging

1921
Concept of the Appalachian Trail proposed by Benton MacKaye

1924
Rockefeller Foundation funded a study that led to the creation of the Great Smoky Mountains and Shenandoah National Parks. North Carolina Park Commission established

1925–1930
Carolina Power & Light built the Waterville Plant. The plant is at Waterville, TN but the water comes from the mouth of Big Cataloochee through a tunnel which was bored through the mountains of Cataloochee

1925–1940
Chestnut blight wiped out all the American Chestnut trees which accounted for approximately a third of all the trees in the Smokies

1926
President Calvin Coolidge signed legislation creating the Great Smoky Mountains National Park with both local citizens and the legislatures of NC and TN contributing $5 million dollars

1926
John D. Rockefeller, Jr. donated the remaining $5 million to help purchase land for the Great Smoky Mountains National Park

1927–28
First inkling in Cataloochee that the Federal Government was planning to buy all of their land for a national park. It was announced in church

1929
Stock market crash, beginning of the Great Depression

1930s
The federal government purchased lands through the 1930s, acquiring tracts from residents and timber companies

1933
Prohibition repealed by the 21st Amendment to the U.S. Constituion

1933
Over the next decade, twenty-two functioning CCC camps would be established in what would become the Great Smoky Mountains National Park, as many as 4,300

men worked in these camps, reforesting the area and building fire towers, trails, bridges and fire roads

1934
Great Smoky Mountains National Park officially chartered by the U.S. Congress on June 15

1936
The last significant logging operations in the Smokies finally cease. Cataloochee was, for the most part, spared. Over 500,000 acres were clear-cut before the timber companies were stopped

1937
The Appalachian Trail, a 2,198.4-mile trail going through 14 states was completed from Georgia to Maine

1937
Little Cataloochee Decoration and Big Cataloochee Homecoming – reunions for the former residents and their descendants – officially begin. Unofficial gatherings in remaining residents' homes began in the early 1930s

1939
End of the Great Depression

1940
Franklin D. Roosevelt dedicated the Great Smoky Mountains National Park on September 2 at Newfound Gap, "for the permanent enjoyment of the people"

1941
Pearl Harbor, beginning of U.S. involvement WWII

1942
Last permanent settler moved out of Cataloochee, other than a few who stayed on as National Park Service employees

1942, 1943, and 1945
Cataloochee Decoration and Homecoming reunions cancelled due to the war and gas rationing

1943
Mark Hannah became ranger for Cataloochee and Big Creek sections of the park

1946
Cataloochee Homecoming was reconvened with over 1,000 people in attendance

1965 to 1973
U. S. involvement in Vietnam War

1973
Endangered Species Act signed into law by President Richard Nixon

1975
Confirmed panther (*Puma concolor cougar*) sighting in Cataloochee

1975
Dan Cook cabin dismantled and stored in barn near Big Cataloochee

1978
Estimated to be approximately 300 black bears in Great Smoky Mountains National Park

1979
Wedding of Flora Messer Morrow's great niece, Donna Hannah (daughter of Harold and granddaughter of Mark Hannah) to Glenn Mooney, the second wedding at Little Cataloochee First Baptist Church

1999
Dan Cook cabin restored using stored and new components through a joint project between Aurora Foods, Inc. (maker of Log Cabin Syrup), Friends of the Smokies, and Great Smoky Mountains National Park

2001
Fifty-two elk were reintroduced into Cataloochee after being exterminated more than 200 years earlier

2017
Dan Cook cabin was reworked again through a joint project between the Friends of the Smokies, The Hands of Sean Perry (donated all the labor), and Great Smoky Mountains National Park

2020
Cataloochee Decoration and Homecoming reunions cancelled due to the global pandemic known as COVID-19

2021
Great Smoky Mountains National Park sets new attendance record with over 14 million visitors, making it, by far, the most visited national park in the U.S.

2022
Elk population in Western North Carolina estimated at 240. Black bear population estimated to be around 1,960 in Great Smoky Mountains National Park

INTRODUCTION TO THE NEW EDITION

by Jim Casada

ALTHOUGH NATIVE AMERICANS KNEW well the surpassing beauty of the hidden valley they called, in their wonderfully rhythmic and vowel-filled language, Gadalutsi, there is no evidence they ever had a permanent settlement there. Cherokee towns and villages tended to be in wide valleys along larger streams such as the Oconaluftee, Tuckasegee, and Little Tennessee rivers. However, the sprawling valley with its many feeder streams and surrounding mountains offered prime hunting territory. The game-rich environment, along with trout-filled streams, would continue to be of considerable importance after the arrival of white settlers who made the semantic place name change and called the land of wonder Cataloochee.

A rough translation for the word Gadalutsi is "fringe standing erect," likely a reference to the tree-lined ridges surrounding the vast bowl of gently sloping land which forms the heart of Cataloochee Valley. One can only imagine the reactions of the first Europeans to view the valley or the delight of those hardy souls who first settled in this place of striking beauty, majestic trees, and so many foods from nature. There is no place quite like it anywhere in the Smokies. While there are similarities to Cades Cove on the Tennessee side of the Great Smoky Mountains National Park and, to a lesser degree to the Enloe-Floyd bottomlands in the area where Raven Fork pours its waters into the Oconaluftee River, neither place quite matches the sheer majesty of Cataloochee Valley.

That is at least in part because Cataloochee is such a surprise. The earliest European explorers climbed steep ridges surrounding it to be greeted by the unexpected sight of a sprawling place of beauty where myriad creeks and branches, like so many laughter lines on an old man's face, came together in wondrous fashion. Even today, as vehicular passengers make the steep climb up Cove Creek Road, the primary access to Cataloochee, then top Cove Creek Gap and start their steep downward journey into the valley, first glimpses of the panorama unfolding before them are breathtaking. You don't get the same suddenness of scenic change when using the other means of road access, State Road 32 from the Tennessee side of the Park at Cosby (closed as this is being written) or the approach from Exit 451 on Interstate 40 at Waterville. Both involve slow passage through woodlands along graveled, seldom used roads. Even so, once into Cataloochee Valley proper first-time visitors have the same visceral reaction. It is one of sheer awe.

Regardless of the approach, contemporary visitors are experiencing hints of the grandeur, a scintilla of the sensation, that Cataloochee assuredly inspired in those who first visited and later settled here. To visit Cataloochee is to go back to simpler days and ways and a lifestyle of closeness to the earth belonging to a world we have largely lost. That world is one captured in the pages of this book, and its reprinting is of surpassing importance for anyone who wants to understand concepts such as a deep sense of a place and abiding love for that place, the importance of family and friends, and recognition of the timeless wisdom found in the historian's adage, "You can't know where you are going if you don't know where you've been."

There's no more powerful or poignant testament to the enduring nature of the manner in which Cataloochee enthralled those who settled and lived there than the manner in which their descendants harken back to their roots. There may be bigger family gatherings across the country than those held on Decoration Day and Homecoming annually at Little Cataloochee and Big Cataloochee, but few if any match the enduring draw this special place exerts. The better part of a century, embracing four generations, has come and gone since those living in the Valley learned that their highland homeland was to be forever lost. Matchless apple orchards lining hillsides; carefully crafted and lovingly constructed houses, barns, root cellars, and other outbuildings; fields cleared with laborious efforts involving crosscut saws, grubbing hoes, oxen and mules, and many a drop of honest sweat from honest brows—all had to be abandoned thanks to what must have been almost universally viewed in the Valley as a diktat from a remote, heartless government. Everyone had to leave.

The same forced exodus happened elsewhere across the half million acres that would become the nation's most visited national park, but arguably nowhere was it quite as gut-wrenching, quite as devastating, as in Cataloochee. It left abiding bitterness, although most folks in the contemporary world would reckon that the mandated diaspora was, on balance, eventually for the greater good. From today's perspective, at least if you have a fairly solid sense of the times when this all transpired, it's truly a wonder there wasn't violence. Had it not been for a number of influential ministers devoted to peaceful ways who found heedful ears in their congregations, there almost certainly would have been.

Even so, there was consuming anger in abundance. The colorful character who was "Boogerman" Palmer took what the government offered (with him, as with virtually everyone, it was far less than they should have received) and left never to return. Men who had never known any way of life except working on and living off the land found themselves without places to farm and without jobs of any kind to fill. It says a great deal about the collective character of those who called this place home that they somehow weathered all of this and still, in most cases, managed to pass on to future generations an abiding sense of what they had lost.

That abiding love for Cataloochee should be kept firmly in mind as the pages that follow are read. This book is by no stretch of the imagination a chronicle of doom and gloom. Rather, it is a work of love, crafted by writers who deeply understood their subject thanks to what is sometimes described as "connectedness"—a tangible linkage to place—that anyone who cares about what can be fairly described as being "purt nigh" an idyllic agrarian life should read. This volume is about a specific place, but it also serves as a clarion literary call, pure and powerful as the bell at Little Cataloochee Church, sure to move almost anyone. It is a book filled with countless threads that, when woven together, offer a quilt of lives and a depiction of a lifestyle we can only envy. It is a distant cry indeed from avenues of asphalt and technology running so rampant as to threaten everything that is placid, pure, and sustaining for the inner man in our modern world. To visit Cataloochee in person is to wander down a delightful road into the past; to read the pages of this book is to gain a deep and defining appreciation of just what it was like.

Originally published in 1982, WorldCat.org, an on-line source offering information on books' physical nature, libraries holding them, and more, *Cataloochee: Lost Settlement of the Smokies*, is described as being in a "large softcover" format printed on "lightweight stock." Translated to practical realities, this means the book was printed in a manner mitigating against longevity when it came to the wear and tear any book faces when pitted against the ravages of time and use. That's unsurprising, because the first (and to this point, only) printing was self-published. Self-publication is commonplace in today's world of books, but that was not the case in the early 1980s. At that juncture computers were in their infancy and things such as proper formatting, professional layout and design, and scores of printers from which to choose lay rather far down the road.

There's probably no way of knowing for sure, but it's reasonable to surmise that no more than a thousand copies of this book were printed; there's every likelihood the number was appreciably less. One thing is certain—you can't launch an Internet search using any of the many engines available for locating out-of-print books for sale and expect to locate a copy. Over the course of more than a half century as a devoted collector, sometime bookseller, and constant peruser of catalogs, this writer has never seen a single copy offered for sale and precisely one copy, outside of library holdings, at all. The book is that rare, and the WorldCat.org list of libraries anywhere in the country holding copies totals exactly a baker's dozen. There are likely a few small local libraries, primarily if not exclusively in Western North Carolina, also holding copies, but there certainly aren't many of them. In other words, *Cataloochee* is scarce as proverbial hen's teeth.

Most of the individuals who acquired copies when the book originally appeared would have had some type of familial link to Cataloochee. Those folks, or their offspring, likely consider the book a veritable treasure. They are right. My studied estimate of the value of a copy in fine condition would place it somewhere in the $2000+ range. Sheer scarcity and/or collectability offer at least moderately persuasive arguments for reprinting, but the nature of the actual book provides the primary justification for this edition. Simply put, it is an invaluable resource.

There's little question that one key consideration weighing on the minds of the co-authors when *Cataloochee* originally appeared focused on the same thought underlying lyrics from the Canadian songwriter, Ian Tyson, in his tribute to Charlie Russell. In "The Gift" Tyson offers this recurrent refrain: "Get her all down before she goes. You gotta get her all down, 'cause she's bound to go." Russell captured timeless images of the vanishing world of the Western frontier on canvas; Elizabeth D. Powers and Mark Hannah did this for Cataloochee on the printed page. Posterity owes them a deep, enduring debt of gratitude for having done so.

Internal evidence clearly indicates that Elizabeth Davidson Powers was the primary author of the book, although in the Foreword she chooses to describe herself as "merely . . . the transmitter of the flame." Powers had family connections to Cataloochee, mainly through her great-grandfather, Allen Turner Davidson. While he was born in Haywood County and owned land in Cataloochee (Davidson Branch carries the family name), as had his father before him, Colonel Davidson never resided in the Valley. Instead, he became a regionally prominent figure in legal circles and was well to the forefront among North Carolinians during the Civil War. He had been a colonel in the North Carolina State Militia for a full two decades prior to that conflict, was a member of the state's Secession Convention, and served first in the Confederacy's Provisional Congress and subsequently was elected to the Confederate Congress. Davidson then became a prominent criminal lawyer in Asheville, where he lived until his death in 1905. He is buried in Asheville's Riverside Cemetery. While Davidson spent almost the entirety of his four score plus years living in close geographical proximity to Cataloochee, there is scant evidence, other than Powers' mention of him herding cattle there during his early manhood, of any meaningful connection to the Valley in terms of day-to-day affairs.

In her Foreword Powers also notes a second familial link to Cataloochee, this one through her great-great-great grandfather, Reuben Moody, who also owned land there in pre-settlement days. Precisely what drew Powers to undertake the background research and literary effort leading to this work's creation remains something of a mystery, but clearly multiple ties to Cataloochee through her ancestors loomed large. It also explains why she was able to gain ready access when it came to interviewing former inhabitants and obtaining meaningful insights and useful quotations from them. As anyone intimately familiar with traditional mountain folkways realizes, seldom does an "outlander" manage to get old-timers to open up in a full and frank conversational manner (although Joseph Hall, who made recordings of interviews with scores of former residents of the Park, among them Mark Hannah, is a noteworthy exception). Powers may not have been a direct descendant of folks who lived in Cataloochee, but she was the next best thing—an individual with blood ties to land ownership there.

Elizabeth "Betty" Dixon Powers had a fascinating life. According to her obituary notice in the *Asheville Citizen-Times*, she was a native of the Asheville area who studied at prestigious and expensive institutions of higher education for women, Hollins College in Virginia, before transferring and earning an undergraduate degree from even more prestigious Wellesley College. She would do postgraduate study at American University and the Corcoran Gallery of Art. Drawing on this variegated formal training, Powers would serve for a time as director for Adams, Davidson, and Company gallery and as a conservator of paintings for H. Stewart Treviranus Laboratory, both in Washington, D.C. In addition, she dabbled extensively in literary endeavors including the authorship of plays as a college student, completion of a number of novels, and similar endeavors.

A 1978 feature story on her by Kay Cusack in *The Charlotte Observer*, "You Go Home Again," by that point in her life she reckoned "My professional writing career is just beginning." However, other than a fine article, "Cataloochee – A Sense of Place," in the December 1974 edition of *National Parks and Conservation Magazine*, there seems to be no evidence of published material being a part of her resume.

All this would soon change as she began her research and writing on "Cataloochee" soon after from her residence in the high country of Haywood County in a place called Pinch Gut. Her research work on this book may have spanned decades, but most of the actual writing would have taken place while she was "Home Again," working from a home about as close, physically speaking, as she could get to the Cataloochee Valley.

Two factors connected to the admirable endeavor of this project stand out with great clarity. The first of these is that this book far transcends an emotional or romantic treatment intended to pay homage to a slice of the past involving family and those close to her ancestors. Instead, as the "References and Acknowledgements" at the conclusion of the book indicate, hers was research, in primary and secondary printed sources, amply supported by interviews, worthy of a scholar. At some point during the research or writing process she began to interact with Mark Hannah, and that is the second key consideration in the book's creation. Simply put, it was a stroke of sheer genius. Powers' work with Hannah saw him function a sort of jack-of-all-trades on the literary front—consultant, flowing font of local information and personal knowledge, interviewee, and as the title page words "With Mark Hannah" indicate, in essence a co-author.

At the time the book was being written, arguably no one had greater knowledge of Cataloochee, its people, its past, and its lore, than Hannah. Also, in contrast to

Powers, there is an extensive corpus of material on Hannah. It takes a variety of forms including dozens of descendants, many of whom have been intimately involved in this reprint, recorded interviews (some of which have been transcribed), magazine and newspaper articles, and records connected with his many years as a Park ranger. Hannah was recognized by *Smokies Life* magazine and the Great Smoky Mountains Association, deservedly and unequivocally so as one of the "Top 100 Most Influential People in GSMNP History."

Mark Elmer Hannah was born on May 14, 1906, to Mack and Fannie Hannah. He spent most of a long and what must be reckoned an exceptionally well lived life, first dwelling and later working in his beloved Cataloochee. The son of farming parents, he would, in early adulthood, pursue farming as well. The 1930 census lists him, along with his wife, nee Verda Faye Messer and two children, living in a home they owned (valued at $4000, although it is not completely clear from the records whether this included the farmland as well). Eventually the couple would have seven children. Census records are not always fully reliable—this one, for example, states he had never attended school yet Joseph Hall, in notes on an interview with Hannah many years later, says he had some college. His death certificate indicates he finished nine years of school. Whatever the precise details of Mark's education, there are multiple indications in census records and elsewhere suggesting he was, from early adulthood and marriage onward, an individual of substance possessed of a fine work ethic. While that is certainly noteworthy, the same could have been said of many, if not most, of his Cataloochee neighbors.

A talented musician from a family of folks who were musically gifted, Mark was involved in traditional mountain music and ballad singing throughout virtually all his life. For many years he led a group, known as the Cataloochee Ballad Singers, who performed frequently at local festivals, reunions, and other events. He was also recognized for his expertise as a student of local history.

He was an exemplar as a ranger-- initially in his first years of service on Big Creek and then, from the middle of World War II until his retirement in the early 1970s, on Cataloochee. Over the course of more than three decades he was a staunch link to the Cataloochee past, a sane and soothing voice in what could have been a time of turbulent transition, and someone who managed to weather the storms of Cataloochee change in a fashion that can only evoke deep admiration and even wonder.

Hannah continued to be active on the local scene for many years after his retirement. His smiling face was often seen at Haywood County pickin' and grinnin' gatherings, he was a fixture at annual Cataloochee Decoration Day and Homecoming, students of area history and genealogists found him a flowing font of wisdom, and newspapermen knew he was always good for a fine tale or interesting anecdote. He lived almost three decades after retirement, with all but the last few years, which were spent in Abingdon, Virginia where one of his sons, Harold, resided, finding him in his beloved mountains. When he died on February 11, 2001 in Abingdon, his remains returned to Haywood County for final rest in the Garrett-Hillcrest Cemetery where the remains of many of those with blood connections to the man also repose.

Taken in the contextual frame outlined above and given the circumstances of his background, there could have been no finer choice than Mark Hannah to oversee Cataloochee's inaugural years as part of the newly created national park. Similarly he was the perfect man to empathize with people had been removed from their beloved homeland in gut-wrenching fashion. Like them, his roots were there, deep in the Little Cataloochee soil, and through family ties and marriage, linked to that of Big Cataloochee as well. Hannah's was, in short, the perfect voice—compassionate when needed, ever vigilant and protective of land he and others had lost that now belonged to the nation he served as a caretaker with the title of Park ranger, and a man who knew and understood how to communicate with those who had been uprooted. In his February 14, 2001 "Mountain Folkways" column for the *Asheville Citizen-Times*, Geoffrey Cantrell nicely summed up what was arguably the most significant aspect of Mark's multi-faceted career as a ranger: "Mark Hannah was among those men who served as the best ambassadors for the park in its formative years, a vital connection between a sometimes disenfranchised local populace and a national bureaucracy." To that insightful thought might well be added that the man managed, with admirable diplomatic skill, to ease deep-rooted angst between displaced, disaffected Cataloocheeans and local park authorities.

He was also the perfect choice to guide and inform Elizabeth Powers as this book took shape. In this regard theirs was a truly fortuitous partnership. The product of that partnership stands as an enduring, endearing memorial to a lost world, one now enveloped in the mists of history much as the mists of the mountains greeted Mark Hannah day after day, year after year, through his boyhood and the prime of his manhood. Yet in these pages we can travel, borne on the gentle breezes of yesteryear, to a special time in an even more special place—Cataloochee.

PART I

Times Past

The Cherokee used Ga-da-lu-tsi (Cataloochee) as a hunting and fishing grounds but did not settle here. Their path into the valley was the access point for the original settlers of the valley. Artwork by Keisha Lambert.

CHAPTER I

The Buzzard's Wing

(Indians in Cataloochee)

The Cherokee have been making pottery for over 3000 years and were among the first to make pottery in North America. Their pottery was hand-built using coiling and pinch methods. Elizabeth French Smith is shown here creating a pinch pot using the traditional method. Photograph used with permission of the Terry Smith family.

WHEN THE GREAT Buzzard first flew over the soft flat earth it lagged one tired wing downward, creating a valley in its wake, raising a mountain in the subsequent upthrust of its wing. So said the Indians about the creation of Cataloochee.

Later there were to be explanations by the white man as to how the valley was formed by this and that mass shifting, exploding, boiling up, being worn away by swift torrents.

Though the geologic past may still be open to conjecture, it is not hard to prefer this Cherokee legend as one regards the huge buzzards hanging indolently on the updrafts over Cataloochee, casting ominous shadows over the valley.

Then, as now, the valley lay shielded from those who sought it by a fine fortress of steep mountain walls. Because of this inaccessibility, the actual civilization of Cataloochee had a very brief span, perhaps only one hundred years all told, before it was dismantled. When it became part of the Great Smoky Mountains National Park it was allowed to revert to wilderness again, as though all of this had never been.

From its vantage point, the prehistoric buzzard saw more of the life of the valley in the beginning than any living creature. It saw the massive looming head of the first buffalo peering into the Valley of No-Name—for the Indians had not yet come this way—crushing the bushes of the lowest mountain passes to make the first trails into this Cataloochee-Yet-To-Be-Found, grunting, pawing, and bellowing its pleasure at discovering the sweetness of grass on the mountain balds. Where white men yet fail to agree, the Indians had an explanation for these balds: Old Field Mountain in the Balsams, or Mt. Sterling in Cataloochee, was known as the Devil's Bedchamber. The old Indian fields, or balds, were thought to be his huge footprints.

Then came the Indians themselves, out of a murky, mysterious past into a cloudier future. Asian migrants, of 15,000 years before, they were said to have crossed the Bering Straits in canoes, making their way down the west coast of America to Mexico and thence to the land east of the Mississippi, some eventually settling in the land of the Great Smokies.

Here the Cherokees, as they were later called, moved slowly, cautiously, afraid of what they would see, remembering the superstitions of their ancestors and their worship of all things in nature.

Finally, they gathered up enough courage, when they needed further game, to leave the safety of the ridges where they could see clearly on either side, to follow the buffalo trail through the low gap into the unknown, into the Valley of No-Name.

Who came first? A Mongoloid-featured ancestor of mischievous Mollie Runningwolf who played tricks in later years on the storekeeper in Nellie? Or a forebear of Swimmer, the famous shaman who practiced his magic at the Raven's Place in Big Cove on the rim of Cataloochee? Whoever it was, the first hardy individual who was venturous enough to follow the blaze of the strong-scented buffalo, returned to his people... mirabile dictu... to tell of the wonders of this hunting paradise, to tell of the fish flashing in the dazzle of deep green waters, of the roaring of cascades, the running of the deer, the crashing of the bear and the ponderous elk, the skulking of the wary wolf and the merry otter, and the circling of the golden eagle over crags as high as the Star People, in company with the Great Buzzard himself.

"Ga-da-lu-tsi", the old Cherokees called the area, translated as "standing up in a row", according to the ethnologist, James Mooney, referring either to the high mountain peaks which surrounded the valley, or to row upon row of stark, pointed firs and balsams on the ridges. Later the white man, stuttering over the Cherokee syllables, mouthing them over cornmeal mush or fierce firewater, corrupted them to Cataluche, Cattalooch, Cattyloochy, Cataloocha, Catalouche, or Catalucha, and finally Cataloochee, as it is known today.

There was never a permanent Indian settlement in the valley. The Cherokees used it only for game, so deduced Hiram Wilburn, a surveyor employed by the Great Smoky Mountains National Park in the 1920s. Borne out by the discovery of artifacts and tools of the hunt, he made copious notes on his archaeological finds. These left him with no doubt that the ancient Cherokee had often left the aboriginal trail to come down and explore, hunt, and fish in Cataloochee. His finds excited him so much that he eventually became the self-designated historian of the Park.

HIRAM WILBURN: "Cultural material that has been picked up in various places along the streams is evidence of campsites, and scattered finds along the ridgetops and in the gap mark this as a notable hunting ground long before the coming of the white man."

The aboriginal Indian trail of Cataloochee was well known to Mark Hannah, too. Born and bred in Little Catalooch', he was for thirty-one years the park ranger in that area. Together, he and the indefatigable Wilburn, had painstakingly pieced out the whole trail, following it in its entirety. About six miles of the prehistoric trail was within the borders of Cataloochee, between Cove Creek and Mt. Sterling Gap.

MARK HANNAH: "There's an Indian grave on that trail. Large mound of rocks about thirty feet across 'em. It was a mound like a cone at one time. We had a man come in, by the name of Indian John, back when I was a boy about 1915. He went up there and dug into that, threw rocks out of that mound. And it has a cavity in the top of it where he said he was huntin' for gold. We've talked to the Indians about why there'd be a mound of rocks, and they said it was a chief buried there, and they honored the chief by throwing a rock on the grave every time they passed."

MACK HANNAH (Mark's late father): "A big Indian chief had been killed and buried there. 'Tine Woody and William Bennett opened the grave about 1900."

Cataloochans referred to the Indian Chief's grave rather prosaically as the Rockpile. It is located beside the old Cataloochee trail, south and east of Mt. Sterling Gap, near a spring which gives rise to Indian Grave branch. There were considerable numbers of Indian relics nearby, such as chips and broken arrow heads.

Along the hunter's trail on the ridge of Mt. Sterling, early settlers found a small clearing of about an acre, with Indian campsites and fireplaces. Under a rock shelter of Indian Knob on Indian Ridge of Mt. Sterling Ridge someone discovered a tomahawk and a handful of arrowheads. Similarly, arrowheads were also picked up by young Robert Hilliard Woody in Little Cataloochee. And flint chips left over from the making of arrowheads were found in abundance next to what was probably a time-honored camp site on a slightly elevated flat beside a trail which cuts off from the main trail at Hogland (or Hoglen) Gap, near a small stream leading down to Hogland Branch.

There was also a good campsite known as Indian Flats on Indian Creek (renamed Palmer Creek) at the mouth of Pretty Hollow Creek, just above Turkey George Palmer's house. When Turkey George first came upon this site before 1875, thinking to build there, he found what had been a small, cleared field with an old fireplace, stones and pottery pieces.

FLORA PALMER MEDFORD (daughter of Turkey George): "My father ploughed up arrowheads and flints near our house. The old campground is near the bench mark near the ford in the creek. (There) may be a flat log there crossing Pretty Hollow Creek to go to Indian Creek. He also found a rock bowl, used for grinding corn, and he put it under a downspout to water the horses."

Centuries of recorded history passed the carefree Indians by as they hunted in Cataloochee. Then the Spanish conquistadores, under the command of DeSoto, came in the sixteenth century hunting for gold. They came all too close, within a day's march of the great domain. In the short space of two hundred years the French, then the English, followed. The Indians hid from these interlopers within the confines of Cataloochee and the Great Smokies. But it was soon all over for them through the four treaties of Tellico on October 2, 1798, when they finally had to cede Cataloochee territory, among others, with the Balsam Mountains designated as their Eastern boundary. Here they clung tenaciously when land was dissolving all around them in the treaties of New Echota in 1835 which ceded all Indian land east of the Mississippi. And here they cling today on the Western rim of Cataloochee still, a much diminished but stubborn band.

That they finally did not lose this piece of land where the present Indian Territory stands, they owe almost entirely to their friendship with a quixotic white man, Colonel Will Thomas, who eventually became their Chief.

Except for that, the Cherokees were natural losers, aiding the hapless Spaniards in 1540 in a fruitless search for gold. They sided with the French and lost during the French and Indian Wars, and lost with the British during the American Revolution. After 1812 they were betrayed by Andrew Jackson, with whom they had fought at Horseshoe Bend. He later ordered them out of their present territory on the edge of Cataloochee. They were even persuaded to fight for the Confederacy during the Civil War, guarding the high passes of the Cataloochee which had once been theirs!

When all other Cherokees were forced by Andrew Jackson to march West to Arkansas and Oklahoma on the infamous Trail of Tears in 1838, many of the Oconaluftee Indians hid out in Cataloochee and other parts of the Smokies, later being allowed to stay through an agreement made in 1839 between Will Thomas and the

Secretary of War, Joel R. Poinsett. Thomas fed and clothed the remaining Cherokees for two years, and spent an equivalent of seven years in Washington between 1836-1848 attending to the claims of the North Carolina Cherokee.

By 1848, Allen Davidson supplemented Thomas by serving as attorney for Cherokee land claims, perhaps because of his early association with the Cherokee through his cattle herding days on the Cataloochee bald mountains which were much frequented for the same purpose by the Big Cove Indians of Oconaluftee.

Big Cove was one of the five districts, or towns, laid out by Will Thomas for the Cherokees. It lies directly against the Western boundary of Cataloochee, hiding under the high peaks of the Balsams on the Raven Fork where it meets with the Straight Fork of the Oconalufty River.

Much has been made of the fact that out of the whole Indian nation only Big Cove still retains the aboriginal flavor of tribal life. Michael Frome, an author of a book about the Smokies, made his way there in 1966 to see for himself, and found that the beliefs or practices relating to medicine were still alive, and so was conjuring. The great shaman, Swimmer, once practiced in Big Cove. This, and the fact that Big Cove was so isolated, and still is today, probably accounts for the vestigial remains of these arts. Swimmer, once a scout in Cataloochee during the Civil War, died in the last part of the last century, but not before preserving, together with James Mooney of the Smithsonian's Bureau of American Ethnology, "the great majority of Cherokee history, tradition, and folklore, and, in particular, the sacred formulas."

One wonders how much of this richness of Indian life on the Western side of Cataloochee seeped in. Certainly, Allen Davidson absorbed as much Indian lore as anyone connected with Cataloochee. He was born in 1819 in Jonathan's Creek on the outer Eastern rim of Cataloochee before the area was settled. An old Indian trail ran through the family property. His entire boyhood was spent hunting and herding cattle in the summer pastures of Cataloochee on the old Indian fields of Mt. Sterling. Once his imagination was captured, he was to spend a large part of his life writing in a romantic vein about the Indians, as their lawyer and champion of their rights.

He had grown up, partly in Cataloochee, in close proximity with these primitive peoples and was fascinated by their wisdom and beauty and wild shy ways to the end of his days.

ALLEN DAVIDSON: "The little children of the Indians were as wild and skittish as wild turkeys or partridges, and it was almost as impossible to come upon them unawares as it was to come upon a fox. These Indian children do not cry like white children do, but merely whimper. Also, if one happened to catch sight of one or more of them before they did of you, they had the strange and mysterious faculty of disappearing from sight in a most singular and noiseless manner."

"The most beautiful Indian squaw I think I ever saw... was of rather low stature, and wore a loose gown fastened about her neck and shoulders and dropping thence to her bare feet. She had an immense head of hair, which was entirely innocent of any adornment or dressing of any kind. It was as glossy and as black as a raven's wing. Her face was a beautiful oval, as regular and perfect as if chiseled. Its expression was benign and soft. The dew and the fog of morning had settled on her hair, making a perfect picture of innocence and unaffectation."

"The sister of Eunoguskee (the great Cherokee chief) was still living and residing then with Wauchesa (Eunoguskee's grandson). She said that she was nearly one hundred years old, though her faculties seemed unimpaired. Her name was Nanie-Katata-Hah... we stopped there several days, and I spent much of my time talking with her and listening to Indian tradition."

Allen, who spoke Cherokee, as did his uncle and one of his sons, sometimes playfully called his children by Cherokee names. One was nicknamed Wauchesa, meaning "Little Grasshopper". The Indians, too, had a special down-to-earth name for Allen Davidson. Because of his propensity for feeding lots of beans to the Indians he hired to clear his forest lands, Allen was known simply as "Beans" by the magnificent Chief Bushyhead of Valley River who often came to dine with him. His son, Theodore, was known as "Bean's Boy", or "Littley Beans".

The Cherokee sense of humor was sometimes hard to take, though. Once, an Indian squaw, as a joke, swept into Allen Davidson's house and substituted her own papoose for his sleeping daughter, Addie, in her crib, running off down the road laughing, with Allen's wife, Adeline, in hot pursuit. Addie, who had a fine straight "Indian" nose, was teased in later life by her grandchildren who asked: "How do you know the babies were changed back properly?"

The companion of Allen Davidson's boyhood was Ned McFalls, his father's factotum, with whom he used to go to the range in Cataloochee to salt the stock. This legendary Scots hunter had a lifelong grudge against the Indians as a result of his father's having been scalped by them. He got his revenge in a most curious fashion one day in Cataloochee which was his major stamping ground. One day Neddy and Sam McGaha saw an Indian sitting on a log. Neddy told Sam to take a good aim with his Gillespie rifle at the unsuspecting Indian just to scare him, telling him beforehand that the triggers were "set" or locked. Poor McGaha merely touched the hairtrigger of the gun, only to see the Indian fall off the log as dead as Ned's father. Neddy had "sprung" the trigger and tricked Sam McGaha into wreaking his own revenge, somehow salving his own conscience in that he himself had not actually pulled the trigger. But Sam was sore wrathful, according to the story, and stormed after Neddy who had to run for his life.

Despite Ned's vengeance, the nearby Big Cove Indians, who had largely adapted themselves to the white man's ways were peaceable to their new neighbors over the back fence of Cataloochee. They had long ago put aside their murderous tomahawks, blowguns, and bows, and had become farmers and cattlemen, chasing wild hogs and grazing cattle together with the new settlers on the balds of Cataloochee, particularly along The Ledge Bald, which was the nearest.

FLOYD WOODY: "We got acquainted with this Indian friend of ours a-rangin' cattle. They'd call it the Indian Nation. We'd go over there and maybe spend the night with this Indian. Big Cove, up there in Big Cove, Jess Swayney. Our cattle would get gone in that country. He'd come and pick the banjer and spend the night. He's clean and dressed... clean, y'know. And he'd a great banjer-picker. And come over there and stay and then go back 'cross the mountain, home through the woods... 'bout, I don't know how far. There was a trail for miles to the Indian Nation."

Jess, who carried an owlhead pistol and had a working knowledge of blowguns, used to play pranks with the Woody boys, getting them all into trouble. Mollie Runningwolf, an ancient Indian who still lives in Big Cove, was full of mischief, too, and once sold Mrs. Will Palmer at the Nellie store in Cataloochee a basketload of precious ginseng which was later found to be dried poke roots. Her son, Ammoneeta Sequoyah, may be the sole surviving medicine man among his people.

Though he often found arrowheads, Robert Hilliard Woody scarcely ever saw Indians in Little Cataloochee, but Flora Palmer (Medford), over in Big Catalooch' said that Indian traders sometimes walked past her house from the Indian Nation down Beech Ridge and Indian Creek through Spanish Oak Gap (renamed Pin Oak Gap) with their woven baskets for sale. They were only about twenty-five cents then, as opposed to the twenty-five or more dollars they bring in craft shops today. Every Cataloochee child had an Indian lunch basket at school laden with huge provisions.

ELDRIDGE CALDWELL: "We played some Indian Ball, too. It's like the Indians play... we played the same game, but didn't have the ball sticks."

One doubts, however, that any of the rites of the Cherokee ballplay were invoked when the Cataloochans played... no enforced fasts, no herbal concoctions, no shaman's magic of scratching the players with bear teeth to make them strong, rattlesnake fangs to make them unrelenting, deer antlers to make them fleet, or fox claws to make them wily. The ancient Cherokee often used this game to settle major disputes. They were sometimes called "The Little Wars", and games were played to the death. The Indians still play this lacrosse-type of game so roughly that players are sometimes carried off the field with broken collarbones and dislocated shoulders.

Once at a reunion for the descendants of the settlers of old Cataloochee, now in the Great Smoky Mountains National Park, a photographer's eye roved the crowd, hunting for someone who might epitomize the stalwart pioneer. He finally photographed a strikingly handsome young man, whose rugged good looks, as he stood gravely with his arms folded, seemed to personify this image. When the picture was shown to Mark Hannah, the photographer was astonished to hear him say: "Why, that's my Cherokee son-in-law, Sam Smith!"

Unwittingly the photographer had picked a descendent of the aboriginal hunters of Cataloochee. His ancestor had been the great chief, Nimrod Jarrett Smith, who had served in Cataloochee as one of the Thomas Legion during the Civil War.

It all seemed very proper and fitting.

CHAPTER 2

Paradise: A Point of View

(White Hunters, Herders, and Evangelists)

The Cataloochee encountered by the original settlers was heavily forested with American chestnuts, conifers, poplars, and maples. The settlers cleared fields and built barns such as this to raise crops and earn a living. When the Park came in, most of these fields were allowed to return to their original state. Only a few remain to show how Cataloochee appeared in its heyday. Courtesy Great Smoky Mountains National Park Archives.

"THEY WAS RASPBERRIES and strawberries and June apples and all sorts of fruit, and it was more like livin' in the Garden of Eden than anything I can think of."

So said Charlie Palmer wistfully of Cataloochee Valley after he had been turned out of this paradise by the advent of the Great Smoky Mountains National Park.

Small wonder that the old Indian archaeological finds were mainly arrowheads and tools of the hunt. At one time there was more game than a man could fathom. The early white hunters, too, would have agreed with Charlie Palmer who was describing the Cataloochee of his childhood. By word of mouth, they described the valley as a land where grouse, turkeys, fish, and an extraordinary mast of nuts and wild berries all but rained on the sleeping mortals under the great Cataloochee dream tree, like Pieter Breughel's painting, The Land of Cockaigne. And the elk, deer, and bear, if you could believe their tales, stood nearby as docile as the creatures in the primitive painting of The Peaceable Kingdom.

In spite of this untamed splendor and abundance of game, however, there was very little activity in the trans-Allegheny area before 1776. Only the Cherokee foragers, a few explorers, Indian traders, and some white long-hunters ventured into Cataloochee prior to the Revolution. This was partly because of Indian domination and the Anglo-French rivalry, and partly because of the sparseness of population. Land expansion was not really needed in North Carolina at that time.

Ned McFalls, that same avenging Indian hunter, eventually came out of the Rabbit Skin section to take up claims in the virgin Cataloochee country because he was told the hunting surpassed that of the wildest imagination. Rabbit Skin was just what its name implied—a poor area by comparison. Others soon followed.

MARK HANNAH: "Tobe Phillips, Tom Barnes, and Maston Hall came into this area and located because of the great hunting grounds. There were turkey, bears, deer, coon, squirrels, and other wild life all over the woods, the streams were full of native speckle trout. These men and their families were in need of food, so the men decided to leave their families in Tennessee and just erect a camp in the center of this wonderful hunting area, and they could send the meat home every two weeks... (then) the wives would saddle the old oxen and leave their children home, start for Hollow Log Camp in Cataloochee."

"They would come through the Indian trails on Big Creek to Mt. Sterling Gap, then up the ridge one quarter mile and turn South down a hollow and through a small gap into the Bearwallow. This is a mudhole that gets full of water when it rains, and the bears wallow in it to cool themselves in summer weather. The trail then turned southwest and then only one half mile to camp. I have followed this trail many times to feed and check Dad's hogs when I was ten or so years old."

"The Hollow Log Camp was located on the ridge between the little branch from Hollow Maple Gap (on Long Bunk Mountain) and Dude Creek (north of that watershed where cattle ranging used to be). It is about three hundred yards from the forks of those two branches, and about four hundred yards west of the Pig Pen Flats (between the Flats of the Bunk and Mt. Sterling), on the north side of Long Bunk Mountain."

"After spending the night at Hollow Log Camp, the wife would load the oxen with large leather bags full of the choice meat, deer, turkey and squirrels, and leave early on the return trip home. It is believed that the Tobe Phillips place on Tobe's Creek (in Tennessee) was the storage place for these trips, and the other families mentioned would come there to get their share."

"My father (Mack Hannah) gave me these stories. He stated that Tom Barnes and Tobe Phillips were the best hunters of their day, and Maston Hall was a blacksmith. He made the bear traps to get his third of the meat. There is a bear trap around here that Maston Hall made."

Nearer to saintliness than most of his contemporaries, Bishop Francis Asbury, traversing much of the same path in 1810, might have likened Cataloochee to a beartrap rather than to Paradise. No doubt his views were partly colored by age, infirmity, and his hair shirt of asceticism. Sent to America by John Wesley, this great Methodist circuit rider logged over 200,000 miles before he died, much of it in the Appalachians. He eschewed carriages, rode a horse, sometimes walked, carried no tent, and suffered all his long life from tuberculosis. It is not surprising, therefore, to hear him speak sourly of the so-called heavenly reaches of these mountains.

FRANCIS ASBURY: "I rode, I walked, I sweat, I trembled, and my old knees failed; here are gullies, and rocks, and precipices... Once more have I escaped from filth, fleas, rattlesnakes, hills, mountains, rocks, and rivers; farewell, western world... for awhile."

But his proselytizing spirit drove him on, physically wretched and miserable, and at the same time, ecstatic, as the messenger of the Lord. At age sixty-five, he came into Cataloochee on a cold day, on November 30, 1810, following part of the old aboriginal Indian trail.

FRANCIS ASBURY: "Friday our troubles began at the foaming, roaring stream which hid the rocks. At Catahouche (Cataloochee Creek) I walked over a log. But oh, the mountains... height after height, and five miles over! After crossing other streams, and losing ourselves in the woods, we came in about nine o'clock at night to Vater Shucks (Shook's). What an awful day. Saturday, December 1. Last night I was strongly afflicted with pain."

One of his faithful companions, the Reverend Henry Boehm, confirmed the Bishop's darkest views on Cataloochee.

HENRY BOEHM: "After crossing we had to toil several hours over high mountains and then came to Catalouche Creek... This was a deep and rapid stream. After we had refreshed both man and beast we prepared to cross. There was no bridge. Brother M'Gee rode through and we drove our horses after him, then the bishops and myself walked over the rapid stream on a tree, and were thankful to get across in safety. The next thing was to climb the Catalouche Mountain. No wonder the bishop wrote 'But, oh, the mountain, height after height and five miles over.', and to add to our troubles, we got lost in the wilderness and crossed other streams, wandering hour after hour in the home of wild beasts. Seventeen miles we went in a dreary wilderness. We came to a gate which we entered and passed through the settlements of Jonathan's and Richland Creeks, and came in at Brother Jacob Schunk's (Shook's) at nine o'clock in the evening, long after dark, weary, cold and hungry."

MARK HANNAH: "The Asbury Crossing was where I got it marked just below the lower bridge there on Cataloochee Creek. We have a signboard there... just below the mouth of Little Cataloochee Creek. My father said that they could remember seeing the log that was over the creek where Asbury was supposed to have crossed from one side to the other, because it was the narriest place in that creek, see. And then I found the original Indian trail leading right off down through there on both sides."

Along with the white hunters who replaced the Indians, and with the long-suffering Bishop, came the early cattle herders whose view of Cataloochee was tempered by better weather than Asbury experienced, as they free-ranged their stock on the lush green balds only in spring and summer. Since William Mitchell Davidson, coming in from Bee Tree and Swannanoa in the eastern Blue Ridge, was deeded land on the eastern frontier of Cataloochee in 1806 at the junction of Jonathan's Creek and Cove Creek and began simmering his cattle in Cataloochee soon thereafter, he preceded the Bishop into the valley by a few years, as did other early cattle herders coming up from Jonathan's Creek, such as Reuben Moody, Bill Boyd, the Allisons, and Davises.

HIRAM WILBURN: "Davidson Branch and Davidson Gap in Cataloochee were so-named by reason of the hunting and cattleranging activities of William Mitchell Davidson and his sons. Shanty Mountain and Shanty Branch were called so because of a very early shanty's being built on that branch by Old Smart, a Negro slave who herded for Mitchell Davidson in the very early part of the nineteenth century."

What would an African slave do up there in that wilderness, lonely as any Basque sheepherder, listening to the screams of the panther and wondering how many pairs of strange Indian eyes peered through the vast darkness of the Smokies. It is impossible to imagine what he might have thought. How did he pass the time? Had he friends, other Africans, back in Jonathan's Creek? Did he live off the land; was he allowed to carry a gun? So many slaves were not. Did he have herding dogs for company and discuss the day's plans with them? Did he call the cattle by name, as friends? Or did he feel so desolate that he wailed far-off melancholy chants in a Gullah tongue to remind himself of his own people and his own lost land?

There was no doubt, however, that lazing in green pastures, with time left over for hunting and fishing, was a heavenly pursuit for Mitchell's young son, Allen. He was allowed to go with his father's cattleman, Ned McFalls, when they had to salt the stock up in The Cataloochee Range.

ALLEN DAVIDSON: "We used to go down Jonathan's Creek a short distance to the mouth of Cove Creek. Then we followed the trail up Cove Creek to the high gap in the Cataloochee range... one of the highest gaps in the mountains... The trail used to follow the ridge down to the creek, the last part of it being quite steep... We followed Big Cataloochee (Creek) up to a point nearly opposite Fayette Palmer's, and then we climbed over a high ridge, and so came down to Little Cataloochee, not far from our camp near the 'Bunk.'"

When Allen Davidson died, his obituary of January 24, 1905, hearkened back to those old days.

ASHEVILLE GAZETTE-NEWS: "The announcement of the passing of this historic figure from the familiar scenes of life will awaken sorrow in many hearts from the Blue Ridge to the Unakas and the Great Smokies, for it was upon this elevated stage that his active life was spent. It was here he began, a strong-limbed herder of cattle upon the verdant slopes and ghostly balds of the Cataloochee Mountains, that career of activity that led him by successive stages to the bar, to the Confederate Congress, to the Chancel rail of the church, and to a warm place in the hearts of many of the best people in the State."

"Twelve years ago (1893), he stood on the Bunk Mountain (in Little Cataloochee) in Haywood County with a boyhood companion, Lafayette Palmer, and pointed out the place of the lick-logs where he had been wont to repair at intervals to tend the cattle pastured there; and, looking fondly around at the once familiar scene, said, as great tears streamed down the age-furrowed face, 'Goodbye, world!' That was his last visit to that sacred spot, and he said then that he would never look upon that scene again. Probably there was no tie that he had to break as age grew upon him that caused him a sharper pang than parting from his beloved mountains."

From the Bishop, saved from Hell, "Farewell, western world!" From the sorrowing cattle herder, at age seventy-four, a fervent "Goodbye, World!" and a Paradise lost.

CHAPTER 3

Dirt Captains and Land Pirates

(Surveyors, Speculators, and Settlers)

The picture, made about 1928, includes a party of men scouting with surveying equipment. In 1924, the legislature of North Carolina established the North Carolina Park Commission to set boundaries and purchase land for the new park. No doubt, this group was one of several who surveyed the area within the boundaries of the proposed Great Smoky Mountains National Park. Courtesy Great Smoky Mountains National Park Archives.

STILL CATALOOCHEE HELD itself, hooded and waiting, within its Great Wall of precipitous mountainsides. These high green flanks were the ramparts and watchtowers of this valley fortress which for so many years had protected the unseen land from speculation. So steep were its walls that a bear, pursued by a dog in the wild Caldwell Fork area, would crash like a juggernaut through thick-branched rhododendron hells, carried downward by his own momentum at an incredible rate of speed in his sharp descent to safety. Only the narrow valley floor remained serene. The headlong mountains to this day, are still awesome, vanquishing.

Though Indians had unleashed countless arrows in these borders, and white hunters, free ranging herders, and wayfaring strangers had dipped into its honey pot, the valley was not to be settled until well into the nineteenth century.

Ohio was settled; even Tennessee and Kentucky were settled; Virginia, South Carolina, and Georgia were not only settled, but thoroughly civilized and prospering long before Western North Carolina, with its thickly forested mountain coves, was penetrated to any extent.

Then, late in the eighteenth century, the Cherokees had to relinquish their land, which suddenly opened to white occupancy all of their ancient claims in North Carolina north and east of a line approximating the present western boundary of the Cataloochee watershed. Shortly before this, the state had begun to make land grants in this area, mostly small allotments, but some as large as 100,000 acres and over to each grantee. Revolutionary soldiers were often rewarded by such land grants. It's possible that William Mitchell Davidson may have inherited such a Revolutionary grant on the Cataloochee Divide from his soldier father, William, whose name is mentioned in an early deed.

Some of these grants were careless as to the actual boundaries of Indian territory (it was ever thus!) and had to be settled in court many years later. On November 29, 1796, prior to the treaties of Tellico, two of the largest land grants west of the Blue Ridge were made to John Gray Blount and David Allison. Together the grants comprised over 570,880 acres and included, it is thought, all of the Cataloochee acreage and much, much more, although that land was still supposedly part of the hunting grounds of the Cherokee. On September 19, 1798, John Strother, previously land agent for John Gray Blount, purchased at least 176,000 acres of these lands at Sheriff James Hughey's tax sale in newly incorporated Asheville. This parcel included Cataloochee. Later, Strother made a will which inexplicably gave the land back to John Gray Blount.

Blount was a famous name in these parts, for, in 1790, John Gray's brother, William A. Blount, was the first governor of the territory south of the River Ohio, and, as such, was involved in such a huge scandal that he was impeached in 1797. Later, he became one of the administrators of his brother's estate which included the Cataloochee lands. The Indians had long despised William as an avaricious landseeker. They bestowed upon him, therefore, the derisive title of "Dirt Captain". Similarly, compasses were known by the Cherokees as "Landstealers" because that was how speculators measured Indian lands.

Colonel Robert Love, who became land agent for the Blount lands, fared no better under the sharp tongue of his friend, Andrew Jackson. During an argument in 1788 over a horse race in which Love's horse, a famous champion of the western country, known as Victor of All, won against "Old Hickory's", Jackson, who himself later became quite a speculator in Cherokee lands, denounced Love and his family as

"Land Pirates" because they held nearly all the choice lands in that section. He was only twenty-one at the time. He received a sharp retort in return.

ROBERT LOVE: "(And you) are a damned long gangling, sorrel-topped soap stick!"

Friends were finally able to part these two. But, by 1837, Andrew Jackson had more than forgiven his friend, particularly as Robert Love had always given him political support, and wrote the following appraisal of Colonel Love when he made application for a pension.

ANDREW JACKSON: "There is no man in this Union who has sustained a higher reputation for integrity than Colonel Robert Love, with all men and all parties, although himself a uniform democratic Republican, and that no man stands deservedly higher as a man of great moral worth than Colonel Love has always stood in the estimation of all who knew him."

By December 10, 1834, what remained of the Blount lands was conveyed to Robert and his son, James R. Love, for $3,000. And so was added another parcel to the lands that became known as "The Love Speculation" which, by 1865, totaled over 375,000 acres. The final Love estate was not administered until 1920-25 by Capt. W. J. Hannah of Cataloochee.

It is interesting to note that, on the earliest survey, in 1799, of the Tennessee-North Carolina boundary which ended at a stone in the Cataloochee Turnpike (then only a track) at Davenport Gap, still several miles from Cataloochee itself, members of the party included John Strother, later a Cataloochee landowner, and Robert Love, later land agent for Cataloochee, and Colonel David Vance, whose son-in-law was Mitchell Davidson, a later Cataloochee land holder. No doubt their willingness to serve in such a survey was prompted by curiosity about land they owned or hoped to acquire!

John Strother kept an amusing diary about the arduous journey which was apparently made tolerable (despite rain, cold, and "rattlebugs") because of the miraculous powers of whiskey.

The survey was not resumed until 1821 with Colonel Love again as a member of this party. The starting point was the stone in the Cataloochee Turnpike.

Now that Cataloochee was open for business, however, it was still hard to induce permanent settlers to buy land in such an isolated place. As land entry records are available only from 1809 onwards (others may have been burnt), the earliest known land entry for Cataloochee was that of Henry Colwell in 1814, "... beginning in north side of said creek and running down the Creek so as to include a Punchin (puncheon) Camp of Thomas Colwell's." But this was only a hunting cabin and not part of a permanent settlement.

1818 found Mitchell Davidson, who had settled in Jonathan's Creek in 1806 (on 300 acres which included some Indian old fields and the Indian path leading into Cataloochee at Cove Creek), buying 150 acres on the Cataloochee Divide "at the head of Hemphill Creek on the dividing ridge between Hemphill and Cove Creeks on the old Solomon Messer foundation." However, this merely fringed on the Cataloochee watershed and was probably used only for grazing lands as it partly is today on the cleared balds on The Swag and The Purchase.

Then there was a long wait of fourteen years before a venturesome soul named Feldred Davis entered two tracts in Cataloochee in 1832.

On February 6 of the same year, John L. and Jacob Smith bravely joined that intrepid Indian fighter, Neddy McFalls, who had come in from Rabbit Skin. Together they entered 100 acres lying on Little Cataloochee. This was always Ned's favorite hunting spot, which accounts for his early willingness to herd cattle for Mitchell Davidson in Little Cataloochee.

Reuben Moody came forward in that banner year for speculation in 1832, and entered 640 acres in September, "beginning near where the road crosses said creek and running up both sides of creek", plus a second tract of 240 acres.

Again no permanent settlements were recorded in these entries, but, at least it is known from Reuben Moody's entry, that the free-ranging herders had begun a real cattle track by then.

The lure of hunting, and, no doubt, the persuasive qualities of Neddy McFalls, had begun to work upon his twenty-two year-old friend "Twitty", as he affectionately called Allen Davidson, son of Mitchell, for, in 1841, Allen felt bold enough and old enough to enter 300 acres "lying on Cataloocha Creek... middle prong of said creek including Barnes Old Camp..." He now owned prime hunting area, the site of the famous Hollow Log Camp, and was to remember this as the favorite spot of his entire lifetime. He was then about to marry Reuben Moody's grand-daughter, Elizabeth Adeline Howell of Cove Creek. But he kept the Cataloochee ground strictly as bachelor territory and never brought Adeline to settle there. Instead, he remained reading for the law with Michael Francis and Robert Henry on Jonathan's Creek. Henry was an old and valued friend of his family since the days he had fought at King's Mountain with Allen's grandfather, Colonel David Vance, and later accompanied him on the famous original Tennessee survey which ended at the stone in the Cataloochee track.

Still, there were no real settlers to please the Loves who, by 1834 had become the new owners of the huge Cataloochee tract. In order to hold title to the land, they had to maintain settlements on it. It must have been with true relief, therefore, in 1839 that they welcomed the arrival of the very first solid settlers, Evan and Elizabeth Noland Hannah, their sons, John Jackson and Benjamin, and Betsy's father, William Noland. Michael Frome, the writer, said Mark Hannah told him that his great-grandfather had come in as a wandering hunter and just stayed on.

MARK HANNAH: "They moved to Cataloochee about 1839 from Fines Creek... They settled in a cove (now called the Preacher Hall Place), just south of the old

Bennett house place about 1/10 miles from the intersection of old Cataloochee road and 284 N.C. Highway. In 1963 the chimney and house pillars could still be seen. This being the first settlers to make their home in Cataloochee. The Noland Branch and Noland Mountain were named in honor of William Noland, Evan Hannah's father-in-law."

"They settled down there and started to clearing the land around there. And I understand from what (was) told me that the first two-wheeled carts that they ever brought in there came across the mountains from Cove Creek. They just pulled it with two oxen. And they just wound around through the woods and going down the hill there. They had to cut a tree down when it got too steep to hold the cart back off of the oxen. They didn't have any road; they just wound around through the open area, and finally made it down to the house at the foot of the hill. That was the first cart comin' in there... No trail, unless it was the Indian trail. They just deadended right down at their house, what little trail they had."

Levi B. and his father, James Colwell, were the next permanent settlers, moving in from Spring Creek, Madison County, as of 1841, though some say a Colwell named Ellsworth came first. They settled on Big Cataloochee, though so far away from the Hannah family as to hardly be aware of their existence. They soon began to spell their name Caldwell, but to this day, it is pronounced "Ca'well" locally, or even more succinctly, "Quell", when in a hurry.

Eldridge Caldwell had promised to talk about his forebears. One brilliant sunny afternoon he was found at Campbell Creek where he and his wife, Pearl, had settled after they came out of Cataloochee. His pristine white clapboard farmhouse, backed by green meadows sloping gracefully up toward Waterrock Knob, was a fine place for such a meeting which had been engineered by his niece, Ernestine Upchurch.

Eldridge then was a man of about seventy-four with a closely shaven head, a jolly round face, with no teeth, and a thin thread of tobacco juice in the corner of his mischievous mouth.

He talked against a bewildering array of background noises such as a grandfather clock's chiming, cows moo-ing, dogs barking, roosters crowing, pots and pans clanging, telephones ringing, tobacco juice spattering a can.

Towards the end of the interview, Pearl's delectable amber rhubarb wine was proffered, which, together with the heat of the stove, made all so sleepy that justice could hardly be done to the sumptuous midday meal which was later put before them. Pearl Caldwell, originally from Cosby, Tennessee, just beyond the stone in the Cataloochee Turnpike, was a handsome, well-dressed, pert woman, and a fine hand in the kitchen.

He spoke again about his ancestors at the 1972 Cataloochee Reunion, as he listened to the Hannah boys make music. He had got his new teeth by then, but was having a little trouble with them. His rheumatism seemed to be getting the best of him, and, when he was not getting about with his cane, he was sitting in a fold-up deck chair by the little white church, wearing the ubiquitous long-billed baseball cap so often sported by the local people. He was in pain, but cheerful.

The last time Eldridge talked about the Caldwell family, he was again at his home on Campbell Creek, sitting outside on a white-washed bench under a cedar tree with his collie dog at his feet. In poor health, unable to use his new teeth, with blood pressure giving him fierce headaches, and the old rheumatism plaguing him, a hangover from when a horse and wagon ran away with him breaking nearly every bone in his body, he was still cheerful and mischievous. It was then that he finally talked about his ancestor, the early settler, Levi B. Caldwell.

Soon after, in May, 1973, Eldridge fell out of bed, breaking a hip. An infection set in, and he did not last long.

ELDRIDGE CALDWELL: "That was my grandfather's place up there which I was borned in. Levi. It was on the right hand side of the creek above my father's house about five hundred yards."

ERNESTINE UPCHURCH: "There's still a little mound and a few rocks of the fireplace left. It's right above the barn."

ELDRIDGE CALDWELL: "My grandfather, Levi Caldwell, and a Mr. Bennett, they moved into Cataloochee together. And they built a cabin each up there in that pine grove, and that's where they first settled down. When they came in there, they just brought their rifle and their axe and their pot to cook in. So they practically lived on wild meat and fish. Oh, there was an abundance of fish. Well, the first year they got their little crops cleared up, planted corn and beans and things like that. Well, the frost bit their corn. So they picked out the best of it, dried it, shelled it, carried it on their backs across Purchase Mountain, out across Caldwell Fork."

"Well, they crossed through there, and it took 'em a day to come over to where the Rock Hill schoolhouse is now. An old fellow they called Dr. Howell had a grist mill there. So... that land had been cleared longer, and his corn had got ripe. So he told my grandfather and Mr. Bennett: 'I can feed your frostbitten corn to my stock. I'm a-goin' to grind you some corn out of my corn what got ripe for your bread.' So he exchanged corn with 'em. Well, they'd have to be gone from home one night to make the trip because they's just a-goin' through the rugged area, no trail or anything."

"Now my grandmother, she'd stay in her cabin... I never understood that about those two women... and Mrs. Bennett would stay in hers. And they had a breezeway (dogtrot) between these two cabins... well, they cut 'em a hole in a log facin' each other. Well, before night fall, they had built 'em a roarin' big fire in the fireplace, filled the house pretty well with green wood. And about the time it began to get dusk, the pant'ers come down, hollerin' and screamin' around on the roofs of their house. And that's the reason they kept the fire—so them pant'ers wouldn't come down that hot chimney. See, they could smell that fresh meat cookin' in there, and that's what they were after."

"Well, when the sun come out of a mornin', they'd (the panthers) disappear and go back to the outside. And that's the way my grandmother and Mrs. Bennett carried on. But I never did understand why each one of 'em wanted to stay in their own house!"

Mrs. Bennett was probably Allie Mease Bennett who had moved in with her husband, Young Bennett from East Fork Township between 1845-50. Mary Dowdy (or Nailin or Nailon) Caldwell was wife to Levi. When he died, she married another of the first settlers, widower Jonathan Woody. Together their combined children numbered sixteen. Mary became known as "Granny Pop" to her many descendants, who seem to be nearly everybody who ever lived in Cataloochee!

Seven years after the Caldwells were settled and fighting off panthers, George Palmer arrived with a full fledged family at the age of fifty-four in 1848. He brought with him his wife, Polly Starrett, whom he married in 1821.

Why had George come in as a settler at such a mature age? Glenn Palmer, his great grandson, who unfortunately died before this book was finished, thought he knew why.

Glenn was a sweet courtly old man to whom tears came easily as he remembered scenes of his childhood. It was a hot day as he talked on the long gracious porch of Rush Fork Farm, which is a showplace for cattle against its fine background of Crabtree Bald. The breezes from Crabtree cooled the summer air. There was tremendous activity about the farm all afternoon—jeeps, trucks, sons, grandchildren coming and going, but always pausing long enough to greet the old man.

GLENN PALMER: "Old George Palmer came into Cataloochee because he drank liquor and lost his farm and holdings in Sandymush. He (was ashamed and) said he would go back in the woods as far as he could go."

Catalooch' was the "back of beyond" as far as he was concerned. His forebears from England were called Palmer because of the palms they carried to denote their pilgrimage to the Holy Land. But George's pilgrimage into the "back of beyond" was marked, not so much by crossed palms as by the small trees he had to tie on the back of his wagon as a brake as they half slid down the steep mountain side.

George, was born on January 15, 1794 in Sandymush, North Carolina, dying on his birthday in 1859 while working on the Cataloochee Turnpike one murderously cold day. It was a short life for him after he arrived in Cataloochee sad and dejected but he had already begun a dynasty which was to more than vindicate his earlier misfortunes.

As for the next permanent settler, Jonathan Woody, whom "Granny Pop" later married after both had lost their spouses, left Fines Creek about 1851 and came in with his wife, Malinda Plemmons and their family. Mark Hannah's father, Mack, said that he was reputedly the best hunter in the country, which may account wholly for his entry!

His bouncing grandson, Floyd Woody, a man of eighty-eight years, lived in Canton where he was once the mayor, and it is said that if he felt like having a holiday, he usually gave all the town employees a day off.

No one enjoyed telling a story as much as Floyd Woody. He laughed, chuckled, wheezed, and giggled so much that one feared he might have a touch of apoplexy before he finished the best part. He had a voice very similar to that of Hal Holbrook who toured the country in recent years giving his famous stage interpretation of Mark Twain... rather, Floyd's voice was that of Hal Holbrook's imitation of Mark Twain's imitation of his favorite character, Huckleberry Finn. If one can imagine a Huckleberry Finn eighty-eight years old, then that was Floyd Woody! He was a big man, white-haired and rotund, with the merriest eyes, as opposed to his wife, Folsom, who is fine-boned, chic, and has her own laconic brand of humor. Folsom, who came to Cataloochee as a schoolteacher and apparently lived at the Woody house, often joined him in pranks, to hear her tell. All of Cataloochee has said that the Woody boys were full of mischief. Floyd threw new life into a group of Senior Citizens who bowled regularly by doing a fantastic dance that he called "The Cataloochee Twist", whenever he made a strike or a spare.

FLOYD WOODY: "'Granny Pop' married my grandaddy after Levi Caldwell died. And when her husband died and my Grandpaw Woody's wife died, why they married. He come from Spring Creek and married her. She had eight children, and he had eight children. My Daddy, Steve Woody, was ten year old when he come there. And they raised up together. And they wasn't no kin, and they married... these two families married each other. Uncle Harrison Caldwell married Aunt Susie Woody. And Uncle Tine Woody married one of the girls (Matilda Caldwell Bennett after Creighton Bennett died). They just kept spreading out... Caldwells and Woodys, and they just kept growin'."

There is a rumor flying about that the whole of Appalachia was settled by the Scotch-Irish. Not so in Cataloochee! The Hannahs, originally called de Annethe, were of French Norman descent, while the Caldwells and Palmers came out from England. Aside from these, there was a regular distillation in Cataloochee of German, Irish, Welsh, and Scotch (both Scotch Irish and Scotch Canadian), making quite a heady brew.

They had plenty of room to grow in, for, in twelve years, between 1839 and 1851, only five families had settled in that wilderness. But they must have banded together closely, and interacted in a way that only pioneers do when they are placed in lonely situations, as Colonel Davidson much later commented on this interaction in 1891.

ALLEN DAVIDSON: "It is a striking fact... that they were entirely devoted to each other, clannish in the extreme; and when affliction, sorrow, trouble, vexation, or offense came to one, it came to all. It was like a bee-hive... always someone on guard, and all affected by the attack from without... Is it a fact that these men were better than those of the present day, or does it only exist in my imagination? When I look back to them, I think that they were the best men I ever knew; and the dear old mothers of these humble people are now strikingly engraved on my memory. The men rolled each others' logs in common; they gathered their harvests, built their cabins, and all work of a heavy character was done in common and without price..."

The grandsons and great grandsons of those early pioneers were often asked what had prompted their ancestors to come into Cataloochee in the first place. To be sure, the valley was beautiful and full of game: it was a paradise but with thorns, as the old Bishop Asbury knew. Perhaps Allen Davidson's words, "done in common and without price" would nowadays, seem a sufficient reason and reward for braving those considerable wilds.

CHAPTER 4

The Life Line
(The Road)

Jim Hannah's cabin sat a short distance up from Little Cataloochee Baptist Church. It is one of the two remaining cabins in Little Cataloochee, both of which are only accessible on foot. A hike into this part of the Park takes you past the W.G.B. Messer place, the Jim Hannah cabin, the church, and on up to the Dan Cook cabin and the remains of an old apple house.
Courtesy Great Smoky Mountains National Park Archives.

THE DREAM OF the road meant everything to the settlers. It would be an artery that would soon pulsate with drovers going from Tennessee to Augusta or Charleston. Cattle rangers could more easily herd their charges up into the grassy balds for the spring and summer. Traders could come through. Permanent settlers would be enticed. Preachers and doctors would be able to ride in to minister to the needs of the new settlers. No longer would they be enclosed by the formidable walls of the Cataloochee watershed. This road, only a tiny vein in the beginning, was a faint throb in the wilderness, begging for life's blood and communication.

The present country road into Cataloochee has undergone as many changes and taken as many forms as a creek bed that leaps its course at floodtime. First, it was an aboriginal Indian trail, then a track blasted and blazed out for early cattle-herders. After settlement began in earnest, it was a chartered turnpike with a toll gate.

Nowadays the ascent to Cataloochee is a leisurely, sensuous experience. The road begins outside the watershed at the junction of Jonathan and Cove Creeks, where a simple state historical sign marks the old Cataloochee Indian trail, now paved for a short way before becoming rather gravelly, always dusty, passing Turkey George's house, which was bought and bodily lifted out of the park by an admirer, Henry Allison. The road passes the graveyards of Lizzie Howell Caldwell's ancestors and the Suttontown Road up to even steeper grades... twisting, turning, everlastingly snaking past plain mountain shacks and more prosperous brick homes, past the ubiquitous trailers, old log barns, raddled apple houses or root cellars, and wrecks of abandoned cars riddled with gun shot, up to the overgrazed high meadows where cowpaths ream the earth like green-ribbed Ottoman and conical cornshocks hang onto the terraces, shadowing as long as tepees in the early light. A gaunt mule forages here and there. Around interminable curves, past the board and batten house in the bank above the turn, with its trim rows of flowers in tin cans set on the railings, and the old wash pot, no longer used, but hung and planted with flowers in the front yard past the Bennett Turn, the road finally reaches the morning-glory blue sky at Cove Creek Gap where a marker notes the Bishop Asbury trail of 1810 that follows the Cataloochee Divide in a northeasterly direction. In September one can find blue lobelias hiding in the shade of the evergreens. A boy once killed a rattler there, too.

Once past the Divide, the road begins its sinuous descent into Cataloochee Valley, both the road and the flora change radically once inside the park... no longer covered with a beige snowfall of dust, but green and shaded, pine needles carpeting much of the way, and trailing arbutus garlanding the ferny banks together with wintergreen.

Past Sal Patch Gap, named after Sally Hannah, one of the earliest pioneers, one begins to catch glimpses of the majestic ridges that make up the rim of the valley. The forest becomes thicker, taller. Finally when a section of new paved park road hurtles through Hell's Half Acre, one has diverged from the old country road and is in virgin timber that was once a moonshiner's haven of hemlock statesmen and rhododendrons as tall as trees. The immense hardwoods are fierce with color in the autumn.

Then from Mark's Overlook the north and west walls of this fine fortress of a valley are revealed. Mt. Sterling Ridge with the remains of the old Indian Fields and a prickly ridge silhouette of Canadian-type firs and spruces. The Balsam Mountains and the home of the Cherokee rise in the West. Now one plainly sees the spread of the valley below, with the massif of Noland Mountain dividing Little Cataloochee from Big Cataloochee, evoking again the pleasure of the slow, leisurely ascent and descent into the valley where the new section of paved Park road crosses broad Cataloochee Creek for the first time.

One always has to stop and lean over the bridge to look at the stream, clear and swift over the slippery moss-green rocks, with hardwoods and evergreens hanging from either side, touching overhead like a proscenium arch out of Orpheus. Here, the original gravel road turns off the new paved road to recross the creek past Fayt Palmer's old dogtrot log house, for long years the home of Mark Hannah while he was ranger there, now weather-boarded over neatly, on the way to pass Little Cataloochee and the Bishop's Crossing to Mt. Sterling and Big Creek, eventually to Tennessee.

As one traverses the intricate road, around the Candy Turn, the Bennett turn, and a hundred others, one cannot help but feel strong telepathic communication with the early roadbuilders who forged this track out by hand and pickaxe. There is blood and sweat enough on these old stones to freeze the marrow in one's bones. Here the rocks were heated to be exploded by the swift dashing of icy water on them; here trees were girdled and grubbed out. There was a deadening of workers, as well as trees. Here is where pioneer George Palmer died that cold January day in 1859 as he labored to finish the road in time, and here is where Ben Hannah fell, slain by the mattock. Here is where Creighton Bennett had to cut out ice steps for his horses one bitter winter.

How did it all begin? Perhaps with the buffalo as bulldozers! It is said that buffaloes instinctively sought the levelest and shortest ways between the best pastures, thus insuring passage through the lowest gaps and to the richest lands. That is probably how the first road into Cataloochee started, with the Cherokees following soon after, keeping the greenery down with soft mocassined feet. Then the hunters came, Neddy McFalls, Tom Barnes, and Tobe Phillips, and the Davidsons as cattle herders. Even the poor Bishop helped keep the trail alive.

By 1825, though settlement had not begun, a stockdriver's road had actually been authorized by the Haywood County court. It began below Cove Creek Mountain near Mitchell Davidson's house in Jonathan Creek Valley and tortuously meandered up, then down, into Cataloochee, to the fair valley and to the mountain meadows, those high summer pastures where men and cattle gathered for the best times of all. It dead-ended in Cataloochee, apart from the old Indian trail which carried on. Later it became known as the old Cataloochee Settlement Road, but the makers of it referred to it grandiosely as the Cataloochee Turnpike.

ALLEN DAVIDSON (in 1890): "That trail followed much the same course now followed by the wagon road; but, after reaching the gap, the road now follows down the side of the ridge which leads to the ford of Cataloochee, coming down to that creek about three miles south of the old ford, and near to where Fayette Palmer had lived for many years. The trail used to follow the ridge down to the creek, the last part of it being quite steep. The same ford is used now (1890) as was used then, for, after following the side of the ridge down to the creek, the well-graded wagon road takes down the right side of the creek and does not cross it till it comes to the mouth of Little Cataloochee Creek, which comes into Big Cataloochee from the West. There it crosses the big creek at the same place we used to cross it after following down the top of the ridge by the trail."

Reuben Moody, grandfather of Allen Davidson's wife, referred to the "road" in his deed for 640 acres in 1832. Because of their penchant for cattle ranging, the Moodys and Davidsons, along with others of Jonathan's Creek, were thought to be among the prime movers of the early turnpike company.

As early as 1821, the surveyor, W. Davenport, of the second trip to determine the North Carolina-Tennessee line, referred to what must have been the early beginnings of this cattle road, later to be the Cataloochee Turnpike, but emphasized as did Allen Davidson, that it was a mere track. The indefatigable Haywood County historian, the late W. Clark Medford, dug up all the salient facts of the corporation.

CLARK MEDFORD: "It seems they had organized a sort of little stock company amongst themselves after getting permission, and had done right much work on the road, extending from below Cove Creek Mountain about the Davis Place into the Cataloochee range. They chopped off, graded, widened in places, heated rock obstructions and battered them down with sledge hammers, built a few 'breastworks' for retaining walls."

"The organization had done so much work, it was now nothing but right that they try to make a little something off the road... or, at least, get back their expenses... It was done, it seems, by a few Jonathan's Creek citizens, Joshua Allison, being one of the leaders of the movement, and it was called 'The Catalooch Turnpike'... Allison was made 'Keeper of the Toll-Gate'; he was to have the gate fees as pay... for keeping said road in repair... Here are the stated fees that Allison was to collect:

'For man and single horse, 18 3/4 cents; for extra packhorse, 6 1/2 cents; for each head of hogs, 1 cent; for cattle, 2 cents per head'. No fees for vehicles were mentioned whatsoever, because, we suppose it was entirely impassable for such... except possibly a half-sled... It was discontinued as a toll road long before 1860 when the new road was finished."

Then came the fabulous era when the life line became a real wagon road, and extended for twenty-eight miles, now cutting through Mt. Sterling Gap into Tennessee, thus opening up Cataloochee for the onslaught of the vast cattle drives from East Tennessee to the markets of Charleston, South Carolina and Augusta, Georgia. At that time, there was only one other entrance to Tennessee from North Carolina through the Great Smokies, being the wagon road at the 101st mile post on the Hiwassee River.

At the North Carolina session of 1846-47, "an Act to incorporate the Jonathan Creek and Tennessee Mountain Turnpike Co." was passed, but unfortunately annulled by the Act of 1849, and not fully ratified until January 28, 1851. It stipulated that, as soon as the road was completed to a width of four feet, the company would have the right to collect toll and erect tollgates. The amount of the tolls were to be the same as in the case of the Ocona Lufty toll road, which were as follows:

Pleasure carriages, 50 cents; gigs or sulkies, 37 1/2 cents; a 6-horse wagon, 62 1/2 cents; a 5-horse wagon, 55 cents; a 4-horse wagon, 50 cents; a 2-horse, or peddler's wagon, 50 cents; 1-horse carts, 25 cents; each horse or mule without rider, 2 cents, with rider, 10 cents; each head of hogs or sheep, 1 cent; animals for public exhibition (lions, tigers?! what might they mean?), $1.00 evasion fine, $10.00 for each offense.

MITCHELL SUTTON (of Mt. Sterling): "Sage Sutton was a roadworker. He says that mudcaps were placed on rocks which had first been heated by building fires on them, and water was then poured on to crack the rocks. To make holes in the rocks for the purpose of blasting, (he) just had to peck and peck for days and sometimes weeks to get a hole."

"'Gillett's Defeat', just North of Mt. Sterling Gap was where Gillett, in building the road in that area, missed the survey. He had the contract from Mt. Sterling Gap to the Ball Place, which was two miles (on the other side of the Cataloochee watershed)."

HIRAM WILBURN: "Carrell (Correll) Branch of Little Cataloochee Creek was named by the old North Carolina Nomenclature Committee after J. Clark Carrell (Correll), who formerly owned and lived upon Tract 231... and was the road contractor (who) had constructed that section of Cataloochee road from the Kerr Place on Cataloochee Creek to Mt. Sterling Gap in the 1850s."

Others had contracts on that part of the road, too, in different years.

MARK HANNAH: "My grandfather (John Jackson Hannah) had the contract for grading the road, from the Carr Place to Mt. Sterling in 1859 before the Confederate War. Jack Vess had a laborer's camp beside Vess Camp Branch. This is the first road that crosses south of Mt. Sterling Gap. The camp was just below the road 1/2 mile from the gap. The remains of the Vess camp burnt when I was fourteen years old."

Until 1913, roads of this type were kept up by an arrangement which amounted to a type of taxation on every able-bodied man who could give six days' free labor.

Benjamin Hopkins sold his charter for the Turnpike to the famous old hunter, Tobe Phillips, but continued to collect tolls at Mt. Sterling Gap.

The new turnpike, with its high-sounding name, was to begin at a point near Mitchell Davidson's on Jonathan's Creek and continue over Mt. Sterling and the Cataloochee watershed down to Big Creek and the Tennessee line at Cosby. With few exceptions, the present Highway 32 follows this old survey, making what Clark Medford calls "a thousand turns" in its course.

Unfortunately, this glorious accomplishment was completed in 1860, thereby affording a triumphant entry for Union troops invading from Tennessee. No longer would history pass Cataloochee by. Now that the final drawbridge had been let down, the valley was to have its own share of horror and delight in the years to come.

CHAPTER 5

Mt. Sterling: The Last Bastion

(The Civil War)

Known as The Steve Woody House, this home has been preserved by the National Park Service and is an excellent example of the type of home that was built by the settlers in Cataloochee. Steve and Mary Palmer Woody built the home in the 1880s and raised 8 children here. The property included the home, a barn, a carriage house, a springhouse, 10 acres of corn, an apple orchard and was 150 acres in total. The Park offered the Woodys $5600 for the entire property - they sued and received $11,000. Steve Woody chose to live out his life here and remained on the property until it got too difficult under Park restrictions and moved to Waynesville in the early 1940s. Courtesy Great Smoky Mountains National Park Archives.

AFTER FORT SUMTER was fired on, North Carolina reluctantly joined the Confederacy at the Secession Convention on May 20, 1861, to which Allen Davidson was a hesitant delegate.

None were so unwilling to join as were the mountaineers of Western Carolina. The story of the Civil War in their region, such as Cataloochee, with its proximity to the Union sentiment of East Tennessee, is a particularly pathetic one. The mountaineers had no stomach for the reasons behind the war. Those that did join the Confederacy did so out of loyalty for the State rather than for the cause itself.

Many fought and acquitted themselves well, dying either for the Blue or the Grey. But a huge number, which grew as the war progressed, eventually joined that ghostly army called The Outliers, who shrank from joining either side in their "rebellion against rebellion", and by their actions became such pariahs that they lived in constant fear in the mountain fastnesses, finally forced by circumstances to forage and steal in order to survive. The nearness to the Virginia battlefields led non-mountain deserters to hide in the mountains... from both Union and Confederate sides. It soon became one of the most terrifying problems of war in the Cataloochee section.

MARK HANNAH: "Some of the old 1861 war veterans hid out, were 'sposed to have hid out in the Camp Rock between Cove Creek Gap and the ranger station there. I've been told that they hid in under there a few times, 'cause it was a good shelter out of the storms."

Allen Davidson's first cousin, Zeb Vance, had just become governor of the State and, being a mountain man himself from both Buncombe and Madison Counties, was not at all deeply committed to the Confederate cause. Indeed, no mountain man in his tiny self-sufficient kingdom could feel the pangs that some great Southern landowner in the Delta or Georgia or Virginia might feel.

Though Mitchell Davidson had once used a negro, "Old Smart", as a cattleherder long ago, slaves were practically unheard of in Cataloochee. Colonel Robert Love, the old land speculator, had first introduced slaves to Haywood County. The entire population of the County in 1850 consisted of 5,931 whites, 710 Indians, 418 slaves, and 15 free negroes. In Cataloochee, at his hunting lodge, only O. E. Kerr is supposed to have employed any slaves at all. There is still a place locally known as the Nigger Graveyard where there are a quantity of small unnamed headstones.

Speaking for the whole of Western Carolina on April 4, 1861, a few weeks before he attended the Secession Convention, Allen Davidson wrote to his Cove Creek-bred wife, Adeline Howell, from Atlanta en route to Florida on business. He wrote in the flowery prose of the period, indicating the righteous wrath that was boiling up not only in him, but also in many mountain folk who wanted no part of the bloody mess.

ALLEN DAVIDSON: "I will send you this in an envelope... with this flag of the Confederate States thereon... not that I bow the knee or even throw up my hat to it; but as a curiosity for you. I could have... fought or done anything else honorable this morning when I saw this contemptible rag floating where the Stars and Stripes ought to be."

However, he wrote a later letter on April 7, 1861, to his growing son, Theo, who, as a young major during the Civil War was to escape with his life through Cataloochee:

"If, however, Old Abe does make war on the south, our destiny must be with the south as a state. I would not encourage disloyalty to our section, but only to speak of things from a standpoint at which I am able to form a correct opinion..."

In Cataloochee, sentiment prevailed mostly for the Confederacy under Allen Davidson's later influence as a member of the Confederate Congress and possibly because Asheville, only fifty miles away, had become quite a center for Confederate activity with its railroad. On the other hand, just on the northern side of Cataloochee and Mt. Sterling Gap, members of the Big Creek community were throwing their support to their near Tennessee neighbors in Cosby, who had cast their lot with the Union. Elijah "Fiddlin' 'Lige" Messer, who came from Cove Creek to settle first on Sugar Fork (now called Messer Fork) then in the Caldwell Fork area of Cataloochee just after the war, had been pro-Union, too. Many surrounding districts were out of sympathy with Cataloochee. But the sentiment of Big Creek, almost a part of Cataloochee, meant the cruelest division of friends and relatives.

Later, out of bewilderment and disillusionment, both communities were to have the lion's share of outliers who refused to serve either army. And outliers from other districts came to hide here and prey on the settlers for food. The Smoky wilderness was so vast that it could swallow up many a deserter. Because of its almost total isolation, it became a fine breeding ground for bushwhackers, deserters, or "buffaloes", and escapees of all sorts. They penetrated the mountain fastnesses, living in hollow log shelters and lean-tos, surviving on wild game and berries.

Several killings were carried out in the deep virgin forests, witnessed only by the perpetrators and a few bears and howling wildcats who drowned out all other sounds of violence. Consequently, Cataloochee Valley, throughout the war, was disrupted by brutal searches by both armies for lost conscripts. And many a personal vendetta, unfortunately, was settled under the guise of war.

MARK HANNAH: "Some of those people that they killed, from my way of thinkin', knew that war was about over with, and they were just tripped out there, waitin' for it to get over with, and they slipped in and caught 'em and killed 'em. So they called them deserters. But they were just waitin' to keep from leavin' home, that's all. They had been fightin'."

The most infamous of the Confederate Scouts who searched for "buffaloes" was Captain Albert Teague. The name that struck real terror in the hearts of the outliers, however, was that of Colonel George Kirk, with his Union recruits out of both East Tennessee and North Carolina, a large proportion of them being from Haywood County. George Kirk, earlier a Confederate from Tennessee, had turned renegade and was made Colonel of a Union regiment composed chiefly of deserters and bushwhackers who no longer had any occupation, in short, some of the worst type of backcountry criminals. At least, this is how the Confederacy viewed him. His superiors in the Union army considered him without peer as far as guerilla warfare was concerned. Consequently, he was much hated in Cataloochee and the surrounding area for his reprisals. Both Teague and Kirk scouted the darker recesses of Cataloochee, and many a man was murdered without redress. These can scarcely have been called acts of war, for their brutality was often of a personal nature.

MITCHELL SUTTON (of Mt. Sterling): "Abraham Hopkins, the oldest son of Benjamin P. Hopkins was a Union sympathizer. He came on a visit to Big Creek and was killed. William Montgomery Hopkins then got mad and turned over to Kirk and helped locate and kill others in the Cataloochee and Big Creek area."

Bushwhacking became so bad in parts of Western North Carolina that Allen Davidson, during the middle of the war, feared for his family, and temporarily moved from the mountain region to Anderson, South Carolina, where his daughter, Addie, was born. A lot of refugees stayed there throughout the war as it was not a major army route. But not everyone could pull up roots as easily, and many stayed in the mountains and suffered through the mixed-up years.

The most notorious bushwhacking episode in Cataloochee was carried out by the Confederate Captain Albert Teague, and has been recounted in so many dramatic versions that it has taken on all the aspects of a true folktale. It will undoubtedly live forever in the imaginative minds of the mountainfolk.

Towards the end of the war, Teague, who specialized in raiding the Union sympathizers adjacent to Cataloochee in Big Creek, spent some time watching the homes of particular outliers of draft age in that section which boasted only ten or twelve families in all. Finally George and Henry Grooms, and a simple-minded man named Mitchell Caldwell, were captured, tied up, and marched on foot for seven or eight miles across Sterling Gap to the Little Cataloochee side of the mountain. They stopped on the Cataloochee Turnpike, near Indian Grave Branch, where the men were executed by shooting. For many years later the bullet-scarred tree remained as a grisly monument to these bewildered men. The story goes that before they were killed, Henry Grooms, a noted fiddler, was forced by his captors to play a last tune on his fiddle which, incongruously, he had clutched as he stumbled along. He chose, fittingly, the famous "Bonaparte's Retreat", which forever after throughout the mountains was recalled as "The Grooms Tune".

CLARK MEDFORD: "It is a sad one, running much to the minor key, musicians say. Dogs often howl whenever it is being played. But it evidently did not touch the hearts of the war-hardened scouts. For there in the shadows of "Ole' Starlin" Grooms held his cherished fiddle to his heart for the last time Its sweet plaintive strains were scarcely hushed in the deepwooded silence when the lives of Grooms and his two companions were hushed, too."

An interesting note, and one wonders who told it afterward, is that the simpleton, Mitchell Caldwell, continued to stand and grin at his captors as they were about to shoot him, which so unnerved these "war-hardened" scouts that they put his hat over his face.

Mitchell Sutton, in later years said that George Grooms had died cursing the scouts, while fiddler Henry asked to be allowed to pray. All three bodies were left lying by the roadside. Much later, Henry's wife, Eliza Grooms, a Sutton boy, and others came with an ox hitched to a sled and hauled the bodies back across the mountain to their homes where they were buried in the Sutton graveyard on Big Creek.

SAGE SUTTON: "The men killed at the Indian Grave Branch was named Henry and George Grooms, and one named Caldwell. My father took an ox-sled and hauled their bodies out, and they were buried in the graveyard near Kim Sutton's place, where my father lived at the time."

Kirk's men also operated in this area, killing Henry Barnes of Big Creek in March or April of 1865. And along the road near Mt. Sterling Gap at a place now called Wells Hollow, Manson Wells and another Wells of Buncombe County, were killed while Lewis Williams, who was with them, escaped.

Young Newton Francis, who had joined Thomas' Legion when he was sixteen, was captured at some unknown date during a skirmish in Cataloochee, and was taken to Camp Chace in Ohio, where he was held as a prisoner until his death on May 3, 1865, nearly a month after Lee surrendered at Appomattox.

Earlier, in 1863, Levi Shelton and Ellsworth (Elzie) Caldwell were killed on Caldwell Fork in Big Cataloochee between Jesse McGee's house and the gap of the mountain near Harrison Caldwell's place. It was thought that Kirk's men were responsible, but actually little is known of the killers. Billy Caldwell was then living at the McGee house. It was Billy's son, Elzie, who was killed, along with his son-in-law, Levi Shelton.

MRS. GEORGE IRA (IREY) McGEE: "During the war, soldiers whipped the women at the Caldwell place, trying to make them tell where Shelton and Caldwell were hiding. They would not tell, so they waited till night when the women went to see the men. And the soldiers followed them to the hiding place of the men, and took them out and killed them. This was Shelton and Caldwell who are buried in the small inclosure on the Caldwell Place nearby."

MARK HANNAH: "Caldwell and Shelton were killed at Rabbit Log Gap, buried at the Sinkhole between Rough Fork and Caldwell Creek. Their bodies were covered with chestnut bark. Their bodies were moved later by their wives and buried in one grave."

At the same time that Teague and Kirk were plaguing Cataloochee, Colonel Will Thomas was busily guarding the weak links of the Smokies. Mt. Sterling Gap in Cataloochee was one of these. The famous Cherokee Scouts became his mainstay.

Allen Davidson and his friends had agitated to form a Cherokee battalion, against the wishes of "Little Will" Thomas. Ever protective of his Cherokee brothers whom he considered his personal responsibility, "Little Will" refused to believe that Allen Davidson, now up for election to the Confederate Congress, was able to cherish them as much as he.

WILLIAM HOLLAND THOMAS (in a letter to Mercer Fain, October 17, 1861): "(Here is) a copy of (a) Bill authorizing the GN to raise a battalion of Cherokees which Squire Hayes has been (trying to do) with the aid of his friends and A. T. Davidson's... I presume, however, that A. T. Davidson gained much capital out of the Indian question for the reason that Congress has passed a law which makes all the Indians west who join the army citizens of the Confederate States... But Mr. Davidson and myself will, I presume, both be at Murphy before the election, and people will have an opportunity of deciding for themselves."

Allen Davidson did prevail at the elections in Murphy which Thomas had predicted would be their standoff, and was again elected to the Confederate Congress, while emphasizing his promise that the Cherokees would be full citizens in the Confederate States if they would serve three years in the Battalion.

Though a more ardent Confederate than Allen Davidson, Will Thomas, however, felt the war had nothing whatsoever to do with his cherished Indians and had discouraged their entry into it. When it looked as though others were going to organize them, in any event, he then took command of them himself, rather than risking them to another leader—who had not their best interests at heart. He kept them close to home as scouts and home guards in the mountain passes they knew so well. But not all fared well.

ADEN CARVER (of Oconaluftee): "I remember about Kirk. There were 1,000 Confederates and local people. Kirk had about 300 followers... foraging and stealing as they went. Only the old Indians were at home. The younger ones were with Colonel Thomas. These old Indians were carried off by Kirk, and some of them shot."

GRANDMOTHER ENLOE (of Tight Run near Ravensford): "Colonel Thomas was the richest man in this country. He was chief over all the Injuns. When my daddy was som'ers in the fifty (fifties), he went with Colonel Thomas to the top of Smoky to keep the Yankees back. But they come through here. I never saw the like of soldiers in my life. Every man had two hosses. Hit tuck from ten in the mornin' till late in the evenin' for 'em all to git through. They hit that river a-splungin'. During the war people had to go to Seviersville or Augusty to get their provisions. They'd be gone nearly a month."

Other companies joined, and soon Little Will was Colonel of a regiment of 2,083 men known as Thomas' Legion of Indians and Highlanders, or simply as Thomas' Legion. The first two companies of infantry were Cherokee and mixed bloods.

The Indian scouts flitted noiselessly in and out of the stronghold of Cataloochee with its steep fortress-like walls where only Mt. Sterling Gap was the chink in the armor. Famous Cherokee members of this Legion were Nimrod Jarrett Smith, one of the Cherokee chiefs; Climbing Bear; and Swimmer, the greatest of the Cherokee historians and medicine men or shamans, who was born in Big Cove next to Cataloochee about 1835. They undoubtedly knew by heart all the entrances and exits to this landlocked valley, for it was the hunting and grazing land of their childhood.

That little mention is made by Cataloochans of the presence of Indian scouts in their territory during the Civil War was probably due to the secrecy with which the Indians conducted their missions for other scouts and messengers are quite fully mentioned.

Thomas' Legion, with its Indian Scouts, may have accomplished a great deal in Cataloochee during the war, but alas, much is left unsung. The only recorded facts are of those members of the Legion who died in Cataloochee while fighting off Kirk's Marauders, and those who repulsed him after he had been through Cataloochee and was pushed back to Tennessee.

Outside the valley, too, Cataloochans were fighting for the Lost Cause, confusing the enemy by using the guerilla tactics of their mountain ancestors who had prevailed against the British at King's Mountain in the American Revolution.

MARK HANNAH: "My great-uncle was one of the soldiers in that war that they always comment about bein' so brave and doin' so many mean tricks in the war. Logan Hannah. He was brother to my grandfather. He was not in Cataloochee when Kirk came through because he was (off fighting) in the Confederate Army."

"You've heard of Logan runnin' the five hundred soldiers, didn't you? I've heard him tell it many a time. He said he was workin' in the lead, and they'us after 'im! (great laughter) Other people said he was aller time into something. He was a dispatcher, see. They sent an important paper through there, and they knew he had that paper. So they were chasin' him, tryin' to get that paper. And, he tells it, he ran five hundred soldiers. They were all after him, cuttin' his clothes up with bullets, and they're out to kill 'im! One of them came too far. And Logan picked him up and threw him astraddle of a sapling, jerked his boots off — and ran off with a fine pair of boots!"

Raymond Caldwell is a short, fast-talking, energetic man in his late forties, with a grey crewcut and piercing eyes. Though he had left Cataloochee, along with the general exodus, at age fifteen, he had a fantastic memory for things he had heard at the knee of his grandmother, Mag Mauney Caldwell, who was ten or eleven years old at the time of the Civil War.

RAYMOND CALDWELL: "She loved to talk, and as long as you would set with her and talk about olden things, things in the past, she had a wonderful memory. She could remember real well, and she loved to talk about her father's experiences in the Civil War."

He talked of the Civil War in Cataloochee, against the background of the small, incredibly tidy home of his parents, Jarvis and Bonnie Childers Caldwell, who settled on Allens Creek when they came out of Cataloochee. Raymond and his parents have a very close relationship, which is refreshingly common among clannish mountain families.

Sitting in a cheerful sunny kitchen, in stark contrast to the atmosphere of the bloody Civil War stories, Jarvis, his merry blue eyes twinkling in a ruddy round white-fringed face, whittled on a stick, and his small sturdy wife, with a white halo of hair and crinkly eyes, fixed coffee and doughnuts. The ubiquitous clock, found in all mountain homes of substance, boomed or chimed the hours and half hours away with the sounds of a wife bustling around, clanging saucepan lids.

RAYMOND CALDWELL: "Uncle Harrison (Caldwell) was old enough; he'd done volunteered and gone into the Confederate Army. See, my great granddaddy, Levi Caldwell (who went into the Confederate Army), was taken into East Tennessee by what they refer to as the Renegades. They got him, but he escaped over there, and when he got back, he didn't live but just a little while. He died in 1864; he was only forty-nine. He was done dead when Kirk came through."

"The story goes that my granddaddy, Hosey Mauney, and a brother was fightin' the Civil War together. The brother was an awful wicked man, and, of course, Granddaddy Hosey was an awful religious fellow. When the fightin' would get rough, and the wicked one would get to cussin' and cavortin' about and blessin' out the Yankees, Hosey would say, now, now, now, Brother Jim, just simmer down, simmer down, Brother Jim, says, everything'll come out all right. And that's just the way he looked upon everything."

Others escaped bad trouble, too, and made light of the war. Allen Davidson's young son, Captain Theo Davidson, was one of these.

His commander-in-chief, Brigadier General Robert Brank Vance, made a major tactical error by dividing his forces, sending Colonel Thomas and his Indians to Gatlinburg, Tennessee, while he went on with 300-500 men towards Sevierville. There he captured a large unguarded wagon train of eighty loaded wagons, and jubilantly started back to Cosby, but failed to post pickets as he stopped to eat dinner at Cosby Meeting House. He was captured in a Union surprise attack and taken to Camp Chace, Ohio, for the remainder of the war.

Fortunately, young Theo Davidson, who, at the tender age of twenty, was his acting adjutant general, escaped with Dr. I. A. Harris by going to Big Creek, through Mt. Sterling Gap and Cataloochee, over the very land where his father had once herded cattle. Young and adventurous, he evidently regarded much of this as a lark.

THEODORE DAVIDSON: "My reminiscences of the Civil War... are of mingled emotions... but too varied and often too sad to be more than generally recalled.

I served in the 'army of the west' under Johnston and Bragg in Tennessee, Kentucky, Georgia, Mississippi, and the Carolinas... at Lexington, Perryville, Chickamauga, and numbers of less well-known but as hotly contested engagements. I was a participant and spectator of most striking and inspiring exhibitions of soldierly valor and duty. We were not always fighting; the camp life was fruitful in social enjoyments, and around our campfires and Lucullan feasts of corn pone, sweet potatoes and rye coffee... humor, wit, anecdotes, and stories of battle and march prevailed. I admit, that, being young and perhaps thoughtless, and enamoured by the glory and adventure of war, I generally had rather a good time. I could fill volumes of incidents, tragic and comic, of that time."

Coming like Hannibal through the Alps, Kirk's triumphal entry through Mt. Sterling Gap in the earliest part of March, 1865, was the prelude to the very last engagement of the entire Civil War. Though it was suspected that something of the sort might happen, he apparently caught Will Thomas off his guard though he well knew his 49th N.C. Regiment could not be in all places at all times.

The story of this last slash of the Union Army five weeks before Appomattox is rather murky. Many war tales are. Apparently, Kirk, now aged only twenty-eight, came in by way of Newport, Tennessee to Big Creek, first killing Henry Barnes, a relative of Tom Barnes, the old hunter, on his way to Mt. Sterling Gap where he met a small Confederate company commanded by Capt. Robert Howell of the Home Guard who had swiftly come up from Bethel when couriers summoned him. Howell tried in vain to hold the Turnpike against Kirk, but Kirk, with six hundred men had a superior number of forces, with four hundred cavalry and two hundred foot soldiers.

MITCHELL SUTTON: "(William Montgomery Hopkins) went with Kirk's men to Big Cataloochee to the old Methodist church and caused a panic, and nine men got shot. Three men got away. Kirk and a company camped at the Kerr Place. Hopkins and another man slipped off up Cataloochee and killed the men at the church. "Climbing Bear" (was there with) Frank Hyatt who was brother to one of the men that was killed in the church, and he helped move the bodies of those killed. Three of the nine were killed outright, six others shot, but not killed."

"Climbing Bear" was the Cherokee scout, famous for his witchcraft, one of his spells being that he could make his enemies invisible!

Another small Confederate force retired when the courier, Will Hyatt, was wounded and left for dead while trying to get from East Tennessee through Cataloochee with a message for Colonel Thomas. Kirk continued to plunder his way through the valley, burning the Bennett place, intimidating the women, and finally capturing young Hiram and Andy Caldwell. It is uncertain whether this was the same time that young Newton Francis was captured, also. Then he cut a swath through Cove Creek on his way down Jonathan's Creek, meeting isolated Confederate cavalrymen, such as Wilburn Campbell and Raymond's great grandfather, Hosey Mauney, entering Waynesville on Saturday, March 3, 1865, where he liberated prisoners, burnt the jail, and also burnt Colonel Robert Love's fine mansion before the Cherokee Indians and a Confederate unit finally fell upon him and forced him back via Maggie Valley and Soco Gap into Tennessee after March 6, 1865.

It is more interesting, however disjointed, to hear the Cataloochans tell it in their own words. When Raymond and Jarvis Caldwell began to talk about Cataloochee and the Civil War, they got so excited and overlapped so much with antiphonal and choral responses, that one could scarcely tell where father and son began and left off.

RAYMOND CALDWELL: "They were all sympathetic with the Confederate move."

JARVIS CALDWELL: "Uncle Andy (Caldwell) was captured."

RAYMOND: "Uncle Hiram and Uncle Andy. They were just 15 or 16 year old boys."

JARVIS: "Down at the Bennett Place. Uncle Harrison was already in the Confederate Army. Daddy 'ist just a young boy. He was seven or eight years old. He stood and seen 'em throw 'em on behind horses, told the horses to git!"

RAYMOND: "That's when Granny Pop stood up and wouldn't tell 'em where her horses were at, y'know."

JARVIS: "They had a cave back in under the hill, and they was in that cave."

RAYMOND: "They knew they were comin'."

JARVIS: "Somehow or 'nother. I don't know how."

RAYMOND: "Well, messengers... (to his father). Now didn't you tell me that Booger Palmer was the one 'sposed to have taken in...?"

JARVIS: "Frank Palmer."

RAYMOND: "Frank Palmer took in this messenger... Hyatt, old man Hyatt. This Frank Palmer was not the one that took him in and..."

JARVIS: "Found him in the fence corner down there, shot, bushwhacked, you see. And he finally died, but he lived a long time."

RAYMOND: "He got back home. Frank Palmer is the one that took care of him. Frank Palmer is Uncle Jesse's boy. Uncle Turkey's brother."

JARVIS: "He lived right where you come to Cataloochee now, right there before you cross the bridge, where the CCC camp (was)..."

RAYMOND: "I don't think they burned anything but the Bennett House."

JARVIS: "They stole everything. They took everything. Meat. Everything they could take with 'em."

RAYMOND: "I think the reason they burnt the Bennett house was, they found some liquor."

JARVIS: "They all got drunk!"

RAYMOND: "Then Uncle Hiram and Uncle Andy..."

JARVIS (triumphantly): "Got away!"

Women as well as men were intimately involved in the war, and by no means did they spend their time cowering in the spring house or the barn, as the story of the two women who tried to protect their men, Elzie and Levi, told all too plainly.

A. M. (Andy) BENNETT: "Colonel Kirk, during the Confederate War, burned my father's house which stood not far from the Frank Palmer home at the bridge. Aunt 'Phronia carried out a valuable trunk. She whipped one of Kirk's soldiers. She later became the wife of Marion Rice."

MARK HANNAH: "They had to hide their cattle and everything to keep 'em from being killed. Take 'em out in the woods and hide 'em when those people came through there. They'us robbin' and just takin' everything they had come to... hogs, cattle, or anything they had to eat. Made hard times on the women and children."

Raymond Caldwell's grandmother, Mag Mauney Caldwell, was only about ten or eleven years old during the Civil War.

RAYMOND CALDWELL: "I've heard (my grandmother) tell about Granny Pop and her experiences during the Civil War with Kirk's men. I've heard tell about when she was a little girl on Jonathan's Creek when Kirk's men came through Cataloochee and on to Dellwood, had a skirmish there, and on to Waynesville. I've heard her tell about seein' those Federal soldiers comin' up Jonathan's Creek, Kirk's men, as they referred to. And I've heard her tell about what Granny Pop revealed (which was nothing) when they come by tryin' to find horses, and she stood up with 'em, and wouldn't let 'em take her meat and canned goods in old Cataloochee. Who hid all Levi Caldwell's possessions? The younger ones were still there. My granddaddy, for instance, was seven or eight years old."

"My great granddaddy, Hosey Mauney. He was in the Confederate Army, and he had come home. And his eldest son had taken him back with him on a horse where maybe he was goin' to get with some sort of transportation to get on back to wherever he was goin'. And, as he come back home, I heard my grandmother tell, that they just run right into Kirk's men a-comin' up Jonathan's Creek. They got on their horses and crossed the creek and run. They fired at 'em, but didn't hit 'em or anything."

When Kirk swept through Cataloochee, that was virtually the end of the war for that tattered community, though regiments continued to battle outside the valley for some weeks afterwards.

The very last shot of the entire Civil War was fired on May 6, 1865, twenty-five miles away in Waynesville near the White Sulphur Springs.

The next day, news of Lee's surrender at Appomattox was received through J. Perry Gaston of Hominy who had walked all the way from Appomattox and showed his parole to Colonel Stringfield. But the news was discounted.

Knoxville had been captured, and Asheville, fifty miles from Cataloochee, was in the hands of Union soldiers, but Colonel Will Thomas, slowly going mad from the ravages of war and his dwindling fortunes, still controlled the mountains of Haywood County and Cataloochee.

"That night the last Confederate stalwarts camped on the mountains surrounding Waynesville, while a N. Y. regiment of one thousand, commanded by Colonel Thomas Bartlett, occupied the town. Will Thomas showed he had no intention of surrendering by having his three hundred Indians build bonfires and war-whoop through the night. Next morning, Bartlett sent out a flag of truce and asked for a parley. Along with other officers, Thomas came to town, but he brought along twenty or twenty-five of his warriors painted, feathered in fighting style, and stripped to the waist, Colonel Thomas, according to Colonel Stringfield, demanding Bartlett's surrender and threatening to have him and his men scalped. Evidently this was a manifestation of his oncoming madness. But the powwow finally simmered into a discussion of peace terms."

"A truce was finally agreed upon between Colonel Thomas of the South and Colonel Bartlett of the North. Thomas agreed to surrender on May 8 and did so the following day. It was one of the most unusual surrenders of the war. The Confederates were allowed to keep their arms and the Yankees went back to Asheville."

News travelled very slowly in the mountains. Credibility was at its lowest. So that it was only after a very long time that people emerged from their hiding places in Cataloochee, truly believing that the conflict was at an end.

Or at an end for some. But not for the families who had been split by relatives fighting on both sides. These terrible hates were nurtured for many years. And not for Will Thomas who surrendered not only to Bartlett, but surrendered his mind and was incarcerated in an insane asylum at the end of the war. And not for the Indians, for whom the final irony was that their commissions expired exactly on April 9, 1865, the day that Lee surrendered at Appomattox. They were never to be full citizens of the Confederate States. Later they contracted smallpox from some soldiers, an event which nearly wiped out their entire nation.

And there was no end to strife for Colonel Kirk, either, who went on to greater infamy in the so-called Kirk-Holden War of 1870 until he was ousted from the state by former Union and Confederate sympathizers alike. He died in California in 1905, the same year that Allen Davidson died.

The forests of Cataloochee no longer heard the clanking of cavalry in the dead of night "a'splungin'" through the stream, but heard only the rushing of the water and the sighing of the wind. For a long time now, Cataloochee was to know a period of great peace and enjoyment.

CHAPTER 6

Blockade: Another Rebellion

(Moonshining)

The early settlers of Cataloochee had Scottish and Irish backgrounds and brought their distilling knowledge with them to the mountains. Corn was a staple crop in Cataloochee and the main ingredient in moonshine. Moonshining created a revenue stream for the farmers, even though it required a little more effort during the Prohibition years. *Courtesy Great Smoky Mountains National Park Archives.*

S CARCELY HAD KIRK'S men stopped "a-splungin'" through the waters of Cataloochee, then a new sort of warfare began. There were no soldiers, no uniforms, but there were all the trappings of an undeclared war continuing sporadically up until the 1930's when Cataloochans had to evacuate their valley to make room for the National Park.

Even now there is an occasional foray over there, with agent Colen Flack, and others, as a reminder of the old skirmishes. The continual battles waged between the time-honored independent mountain distiller and the revenue agent brought rise to a code of conduct as surely binding as the Geneva Convention.

CLARK MEDFORD: "Haywood County had been 'wet' in one form or another, for eighty years. First, citizens had the right to make their own spiritous liquors and sell it, by permits obtained from the old County Court; then, later, government-supervised distilleries were set up. So there was right much rejoicing here on the voting of it out. But immediately, moonshining sprung up more than ever. In the 1890s and 1900s this writer well remembers how the blockading stills were plentiful, and also the disturbances at religious services, school entertainments and box suppers. So, sentiment was building up again for the 'wets'. This continued until local option began again... when Haywood got the Waynesville Dispensary which lasted until January of 1909."

More interesting even than the actual facts of making "blockade" whiskey is the folklore which has risen from the exploits of the distiller, or the anti-hero, and the folk speech which evolved around the various namings of the corn liquor itself. "Anti-establishment" would be the term applied nowadays to those doughty Cataloochee warriors who guarded the castle keep... or, rather, posted lookouts on every little laurelly path for "The Revenue", now called ATF agents, after their official name of Alcohol Taxation and Firearms Division, located in Asheville.

It is just as useless to pretend that Cataloochee was exempt from the kind of violence that flaunts the law as it is to picture the valley peopled entirely with pious teetotal folk too virtuous either to touch the clear liquid, much less distill it, or sell it. The truth lies somewhere in between, though many an exquisite protestation was made that the latter was so.

RAYMOND CALDWELL: "They done a lot of making of liquor, which was a violation of the law... I don't think Cataloochee people are afraid of the law, but I think they're afraid to admit they had a part in it. I don't think (they should be). There certainly wasn't no liquor stores, like we have the ABC stores today to go get it. And they's gonna have it. There's one thing about it; it was the purest alcohol and the finest whiskey you could get. It wasn't goin' to make nobody poisoned. The people made what they needed for theirselves, very little of it sold... And I'm sure there was quite a bit of apple brandy."

Mark Hannah dryly added that Cataloochans made whiskey only for their own use until they found they could make whiskey more quickly out of sugar, at which time they began selling it.

ADEN CARVER (of Oconalufty, a nearby settlement): "Used to be every man had it (liquor) in his home. You never saw a drunk man."

The JARVIS CALDWELL FAMILY (all speaking together): "They made it for their own drinking. Robert said he helped... They never tried to... Back then it was... To later years when they were tryin' to make money out of it..."

The gist of this was that nobody was crazy enough to say that stills had never existed in Cataloochee. But everyone tried to justify what stilling had gone on, saying it had been made mostly for family consumption, out of pure water and pure copper stills, and that only a few daring people went even further beyond the law later to transport this illegal whiskey into Tennessee during Prohibition, though a scholar who did speech research in Cataloochee said otherwise.

PROFESSOR JOSEPH S. HALL: "The quiet, peaceful atmosphere which now pervades Cataloochee, certainly carries no suggestion of the once turbulent times. The illegal manufacture of liquor was quite extensive in this area, especially during Prohibition days. Naturally, every stranger was under suspicion of being an officer of some kind. I was told that several shots were fired at the car of a ranger when the National Park Service was first established there. In those days it was supposed that every government car was driven by a United States marshall."

Another scholar, a historian who grew up in Cataloochee, suggests that times were more tempered.

DR. ROBERT HILLIARD WOODY: "Well, once upon a time, the revenue agents left the people in Cataloochee alone. They had trouble finding them, and the people got off to themselves pretty well... I had a little hand in it myself... Uncle Jim (Hannah) was the justice of the peace. If he heard about anybody making moonshine, I'm sure he never considered it any of his part. Uncle Jim liked to refresh himself with it occasionally... Except when he was recovering from a weekend binge, he was an eloquent Sunday school teacher... The Saturday night frolic with plenty of mountain music and perchance a drop of 'that good old mountain dew' was a well-patronized institution."

"The idea of self-sufficiency... was sometimes carried to extremes, in the eyes of the law, if not the neighbors. By a certain process, which need not be described, the homegrown corn was converted into a potent beverage for local use. This was a sporadic enterprise and usually not continued long enough to attract any particular attention. A good spring in a handy cove was easy to find, and if one burned (dead) locust wood, no smoke would show above the trees. Officers of the law did not make themselves a nuisance..."

One fine summer's day, Mark Hannah drove over to Sylva to see doughty old 'Tine Bennett, named after his step-grandfather, Valentine Woody, also the same with whom Robert Hilliard Woody lived when he came back to visit Cataloochee. A rather short, solid man, square-faced, with a grey crew-cut sticking stiffly up like a fierce hedgerow, he has the look of a Maine lobsterman because of the independent jut of his jaw, the set of his mouth, and the crinkle of his eyes against the sun. He showed Mark around his considerable piece of land... a nice small cornfield on the inevitable slope, a lovely little orchard, a modest barn where a picture was taken of him standing sturdily, seriously, in the doorway with his pure white cat. But 'Tine was not as serious as the pose he struck when he confronted the camera. Later he and Mark chuckled mightily over many amusing memories of their past. He remembered some of the hot water he got into when he was young and came over from Little Cataloochee to play around with the rambunctious sons of Steve Woody who lived in Big Cataloochee.

JAMES HARDY YOUNG VALENTINE ('TINE) BENNETT: "Ossie, he's brother to Floyd, but he's older. Me and Ossie used to run around together all the time. Frank Palmer down there was sellin' whiskey. An' Aunt Lou, we called her. And me and Ossie we'd go down there and get us a bottle of whiskey. We always rode horses or mules, one. And we hid it, and Floyd found it, and Floyd got drunk on it!"

The gentleness and innate courtesy of the people who were interviewed often obscured more colorful details of their past. When one remarked on a charming old couple, a mountain friend said: "Why that old man was too lazy to make his own whiskey, but he used to set on a stump and watch (act as a sentinel) for me when I was 'stillin' and his woman, that 'sweet li'l ole lady' you talk about, why she used to <u>sell</u> it, and she was good at it, too!"

The fact that distilling could ever be legal was hardly ever taken into account. Nobody wanted to pay that extra tax which was put on during the Civil War in order to raise money for the troops, but was never repealed when the war ended. In fact, Mark Hannah could only recollect one licensed still in the whole of Cataloochee, and that didn't last long.

MARK HANNAH: "The Braz Whaley place up there a third of a mile north of the school-church where they used to make whiskey legally. Yep, there was a legal still in there one time. They had to have a government permit some way or other to make apple brandy and work up the apples where they was starvin'... I reckon he sold it to the Government... I don't know. Well, anyway, this went on for a little while. First thing we knew, the children got to slippin' off from school and goin' down there. Wasn't 'sposed to sell it to a school child. It wasn't long till people had that thing tore out and gone. It didn't last long! My Mother, I'm sure, had something to do with gettin' rid of (that). Yep, she wasn't goin' to put up with that deal!"

Irate citizens like Fannie Hannah still did not give as much trouble as the Federal law itself. A Canton car dealer who had once employed a Cataloochee mechanic said he was continually bailing him out of jail on moonshine charges. Others corroborated instances of revenue agents swarming through neighboring Cataloochee' on occasion.

FORMER HEMPHILL DISTILLER: "Liquor that came out of Cataloochee' was known as 'saddlebag' because that's how they transported it."

RAYMOND CALDWELL: "I remember, as a young fellow, bein' where there was quite a few furnaces where moonshine whiskey was bein' made, in the perimeter where we grew up. And I've seen the revenuers come in there and go up and down the valley and go by our house and come out in the afternoon and have two or three copper stills on their car that they'd captured that day. There was quite a bit made in (Big Cataloochee), and it was put on commercially (and taken over to Tennessee). I know there was one fellow, he was tracked with his horse. He had hauled this sugar, meal, whatever, mash to the (still). And the horse would just follow. All he had to do was start him, start the horse, and he'd come back home. This horse had a crooked foot, and the revenuers tracked him to the still and back to the man's barn and got a conviction out of it that way."

He reluctantly admitted: "Well, (the horse) belonged to a Caldwell." (Much laughter.)

With a thrill of excitement, Pearl Caldwell, herself a teetotaler, recalled an early experience.

PEARL VALENTINE CALDWELL: "Maude Caldwell and me rode horses. (Booger Man Palmer) lived on the hill, mountain, and so, Mrs. Palmer, she was a-- takin' care of her son ("Wild Bill"). He had been away and come back home, and he was real sick, and that's why we had went up there. And just before we got ready to go, here come the revenuers. And they come in the house, and they searched all around the house. Hah, hah! Excitin' to me! Cause I never seen revenuers! They was very nice, but they took some names, and they left later. Liquor-making was very common."

Liquor-making involved not only the distillers but the millers as well, for they had to grind the sprouted corn for stills. Vick Smith of Little Cataloochee told acting Park historian, Hiram Wilburn, that John A. Smith cut out the stones that Vick built into a mill for 'Tine Woody in the year 1909. Steve Waycaster had the mill built sometime prior to that time. Waycaster had it built to grind meal for moonshine liquor stills; he lived on 'Tine Woody's place. Other mills in the neighborhood would not grind for moonshiners.

RAYMOND CALDWELL: "I recall going to the (old Jesse Palmer) mill (run by my father up on Indian Creek) after I was thirteen or fourteen years old and pourin' up the corn for to grind meal and start up to find this here malt that had been ground during that week by somebody comin' in makin' their malt, and havin' to re-bed the rocks 'fore we could get goin' and grind the (other) man's cornmeal. (The corn would) swell up and they'd grind it, and it'd ferment much quicker. They'd slip into the mill at night-time and grind it under the nose of my father. And, of course, we wouldn't know it... and go on Saturday to start grindin' the regular corn meal, and there that malt was, and you'd have to re-bed your rocks, get rid of that (old malt corn) so you wouldn't have that fermented (stuff in your corn meal)..."

"I know there was a still that was broken up, cut down by revenuers. A few days after that still was taken out, my father was a-standin' by the hopper at the mill, grinding the meal, and he got a lick on the head. A man walked up behind him and knocked him in the head... thought he had turned him in for his still business. That fellow, that was quite a... I come in and found Dad all knocked out and the blood a-(pourin' out)" (Much laughter.)

MARK HANNAH: "The food chopper was used in probation (prohibition) days. It was easier to carry into a laurel-patch and hide while they ground the malt corn."

Aside from the distillers and the millers, the tin-smith's services were much in demand. One such talented artisan was crippled "Major" Woody, a famous Cataloochee character, known to all fishermen, hunters, and, apparently, distillers.

RAYMOND CALDWELL: "'Major' Woody was all the time tellin' about his experiences in moonshine days, makin' moonshine liquor. 'Major' was gifted with being able to do little odds and ends around for the ladyfolks. He used to solder washpots. He was pretty handy with a solderin' iron and that type of thing because he had that experience from puttin' the moonshine stills together."

Corn liquor and apple brandy were the main spirituous liquors distilled; but there was also a spirit of adventure which led some to experiment in other fields.

ELDRIDGE CALDWELL: "Some of them in later years got to making elderberry wine, but it wasn't much of a temptation to me! And cherry wine over there, too... some of the boys, in later years. But I didn't think much of it, either... wasn't very good. For that reason, I didn't drink much of that, and the boys that did said it hurt them awful bad, made them awful sick. I think they didn't age it long enough."

MARK HANNAH: "Maybe too much drink — its quantity, not quality!"

As every Cataloochan has sworn that only the best and purest ever came out of the valley, one would have to say that the dreaded "galvanize" was not used in there, unless in sublime ignorance of its ability to poison the system with the lead that came from a still made of this metal. The liquor from this type of still was sometimes known under the fanciful name of Grey Cloud or Silver Cloud because it was not as clear as the proverbial spring water which good corn whiskey made in a copper still was supposed to resemble.

BASCOM LAMAR LUNSFORD: "(The best of the doublings) is the first three gallons to come from the still. It's the color of bright straw and it's rich and mellow. You can bite it right off at the neck of the bottle."

Even careful supervision could not prevent certain distilling catastrophes. A common one was the exploding of a still from overheating.

JIM SUTTON: "One time away back when I was just a boy, me and my brother decided we'd make some liquor, 'way back in the Smoky Mountains in a place called Hell's Half Acre. We went in and put up a still. (My brother got drunk.) He was chunkin' the fire in that thing... blew the cap off it. I guess it went seventy-five or ninety feet in the air. A friend on Old Field Balsam, or Mt. Sterling, as it is otherwise called, happened to see the cap blown into the air and told my brother just where the still was 'settin'! The friend said: 'Well, it's right at the head of Sal Hannah Branch at the back of Ground Hog. He told him twenty feet of where it was settin'."

MARK HANNAH: "That was Sol Sutton's son, sometimes called 'Jim Twister' Sutton."

One might query the credibility of this story, as Mt. Sterling looms miles away from Hell's Half Acre. But a former mountain distiller insisted that it <u>was</u> possible to see such an event from a very great distance because of the amount of steam released when the cap blew, making a mushroom cloud rather like an atomic bomb in miniature. To prove the point, he recounted the story of his blowing the cap off his still long ago one December night in Cataloochee. He had chunked too much dry chestnut wood into the fire. The fire got too hot. Meanwhile he had wandered off down the trail because he heard a wildcat call. The cap blew off, and all the 'beer' boiled into the fire. The steam was so thick, said this informant, making fighting gestures with his arms at the remembrance of it, that he was lost in the thicket of forest and steamy sea for hours. His flashlight only made the steam seem even more like cotton batting!

Except for the tell-tale steam from an exploding cap, and perhaps the odor of spilt mash in a stream, a still in the Cataloochee wilds was as easily hidden as the proverbial needle in the haystack, unless some stool pigeon spilt the beans. It took a "heap o' lookin'" to find one, and then maybe one only chanced upon it while looking for something else, such as ginseng or a place to set a bear trap.

The late Glen Messer of Hemphill Valley was called to duty in Cataloochee one day by the Park Service. He had worked for the Park Service for a number of years, and also for Tom Alexander's ranch for nineteen years helping to guide pack trips in and out of Cataloochee. A plane had been lost over the Smokies, and the Service asked if he would help in searching the mountains which he knew intimately. Truckloads of soldiers were sent in to walk the trails. He said they were afraid to stray from the path, however.

He reluctantly agreed to fly in a helicopter all over the eastern slopes, although it scared him half to death. But he thought he had better do it. They covered every cove in Cataloochee, saw nothing and headed over the Tennessee border, the pilot radioing messages back now and again. They hovered over little hollows, almost shearing tops of trees off (Glen nervously spat tobacco juice at the memory of it). Finally coming back into the Cataloochee area, they spotted some metal shining and flew low, shimmying over the area in a most alarming way.

Glen saw at once that it was a still and even recognized some local people. He said to the pilot: "That's no plane... let's get back and say no more about it."

Unfortunately, the pilot got drunk that night in Waynesville and "spilt the beans". The next day, Mark Hannah, who was presently the ranger, and therefore responsible for miscreants in the Park, turned up with a truckload of men. He confronted Glen, affably but firmly, wanting to know what Cataloochee hollow the still was in.

Since the moonshiners were all well known to Glen, and it would have been a serious breach of honor for a mountain man to expose his friends, all he could say to Mark was, "That pilot was so drunk, he didn't even know the still was over in Tennessee. It'd take us three days... with dogs, to reach it by trail." The search was then abandoned.

Glen also told about going into the mountains when he first started working for the Park Service. He was met by two rough fellows in dirty slick-backed duck jackets, levelling two high-powered rifles at him. They said "you're the new feller, ain't ye?", and tried to bribe him by giving him a free jar of "white lightning". But he said he had seen too many cans of Red Devil lye lying around this still, and he never dared drink the stuff. Lye was sometimes used to give an artificial bead to bad whiskey made too quickly. He said no revenue agents would have gone in after them, anyway, as the whole place was mined with dynamite. And once an agent got on the property, he would most certainly have been blown up.

Mark Hannah, himself once a law man inasmuch as rangers had to go after offenders in the park, recounted a strange twist on the law routine.

MARK HANNAH: "Me and my brother-in-law, Willie Messer, were goin' down to Tennessee to a singin' convention. I'd bought a 1927 Model T from him. That was about 1929. And we were travellin' along through the Cosby area there. All of a sudden looked down the road and saw men, one car sittin' in the road, and men on the banks... everywhere. They were very busy, but we couldn't get by 'em. My brother-in-law had been through there before. He said, just sit right still, I'll stop right here. We were about a hundred feet away. And I walked down there to see what they were doin'. They were loadin' whiskey in these can cases, twelve half a gallon cans. And they were puttin' 'em in the car just as fast as they could, cases packed high to the top of the car, right in the middle of the road, that's what they were doin', see. The thing about it that I couldn't understand, when I looked up on the bank of the road, the sheriff was there with a badge on. What was he doin'? Well, said they made him drunk first thing so they could load (laughs heartily). The deputy sheriff was sittin' up on the bank drunker'n any of 'em! They loaded up. We had to wait about five minutes, and they pulled on out."

Not all was wine and roses and good sport. It was admitted that there were quite a few heavy drinkers in the area. In the parlance of the mountain man, "Frank, Booger Man, Tom (and others) were awful bad to drink." Drinking often led to violence, whereupon the good folk of Cataloochee would do well to scurry for cover.

"There used to be a mean bunch in Catalooch'" attested an informant of Ravensford to Professor Joseph Hall, "and 'Zeke' (not his real name) was the meanest of the lot. He burned 'Creek George's' barn down an' cut the years (ears) off a man named Miles (Milas)."

Mark added that "Zeke" felt he was justified in burning the barn because "Creek George" Palmer was a good religious fellow and had cut his still down. Similarly, the unfortunate Milas had his ears lopped off because he stole his partner's liquor in spite of "Zeke's" having warned him about it repeatedly... There was even a fanciful story that "Zeke" carried the little dried up ears with him for many years as an amusement and a grim warning to others not to tamper with what was not their business.

But, as Professor Hall quickly points out from happy experience, if there was a mean bunch in Cataloochee, there were also many honest and respectable people in that beautiful valley as well.

Views on Cataloochee's whiskey-making past changed according to who was interviewed. Some well known imbibers claimed that they never made nor touched a drop. Some said scarcely any liquor was made in the valley. Some say the revenuers never gave them any trouble. Others claim exactly the reverse. Little Cataloochans blame Big Cataloochans for drinking more than their share. Big Cataloochans say Little Cataloochans, not to mention the inhabitants of the Caldwell Fork settlement, were pretty cagey about making the stuff themselves. But all agree on one thing: it was much rougher over in Big Creek... out of Cataloochee! And Tennessee, of course, was beyond the pale, giving rise to a flock of Tennessee jokes that must have stemmed from age-old rivalries since the Civil War.

This is a typical jibe, told by an old mountain farmer.

Q. "Do you know how you kin tell a feller's from Tennessee?"
A. "No."
Q. "From the ring 'round his nose!"
A. "Oh!"
Q. "From liftin' the fruit jar, y'know!"
A. "Oh!"

CHAPTER 7

Lost!

(The Coming of the Park)

This photograph of President Franklin Delano Roosevelt speaking at
the park dedication is by National Park Service engineer, Robert P. White. The Great
Smoky Mountains National Park was dedicated on Labor Day, September 2, 1940.
A crowd of 10,000 came to Newfound Gap to hear President Franklin D. Roosevelt
speak with 500 members of the Civilian Conservation Corps on hand to direct and
manage the crowd. A podium was set up on the North Carolina and Tennessee
state lines, so that speakers stood with one foot in each state. The event was
presided over by the Secretary of the Interior, Harold Ickes.
Courtesy Great Smoky Mountains National Park Archives.

"IN SUCH A place, they were lost to time, but the earth was theirs." So said Michael Frome of Cataloochee.

Except for two cataclysmic dramas in its career, the times of Cataloochee Valley could be likened to the violet 'neath the mossy stone, or to a dappled fawn blending into the sunspecked leaves, so impervious were the people to the storms of the world which swirled round their battlements. Aside from that terrible moment of glory when they stood up to their intruders during the Civil War, a whole span of wars had left them practically untouched. Archdukes were assassinated, ships were blown up, volcanoes erupted, bathtub gin was invented, the Charleston was danced, fortunes were lost, and tycoons flung themselves to death while Cataloochee followed the slow round of the seasons, planting and harvesting, wedding, birthing, and burying, with a time to dance as well.

When the end came after one hundred years of settlement, there was no "terrible, swift sword". That might have been a more merciful way. Instead, rumors came in dribbles, long before the anguish began of parting nearly 700 people from their homes. The first inkling came in the late 1920's. In a special announcement in the church, the people were told that the United States Government wanted Cataloochee, along with the rest of the Great Smoky Mountains, as part of a national park for the American public who needed wilderness in their lives. The immediate effect among the ninety-five families was one of utter amazement, later combined with dumb despair, particularly among the older folk who were expecting to die peacefully in the valley where they had been born.

MARK HANNAH: "It seems to me that it was about nineteen hundred and twenty-seven or twenty-eight when they first heard about it. Somebody told them at the church house. We couldn't hardly believe it! The reaction was great among the people because Pat Davis, the preacher said, you will be scattered all over the United States, probably, and different parts won't be here anymore. We didn't think much of the idea. He said that we wouldn't live our life there too much longer. It was all we talked about for weeks. If that preacher had told them that one boy sitting in the back of the church would be put in charge of it, that boy would have been torn apart! I was that boy, of course."

JARVIS CALDWELL: "Most of 'em were upset. Some, Will Messer, three or four, started to fight it, y'know, to try to keep 'em from takin' it. 'Course, they didn't do too much good headway at it, but they just didn't want to sell."

MARK HANNAH: "Three men came in, estimated prices, came back and made the offers to the many families. If the family thought the price was unfair, they could contest it as did my father and others. For that time I guess the prices were fair, but nowadays, it would just be a drop in the bucket."

"The first direct thing we heard about was the surveyor. That was Mr. Wilburn comin' into Big Cataloochee. And he started surveyin' the different tracts of land. He came to Big Cataloochee first and worked that section out over there. Some of the boys worked with him, some of the resident people. And he tried to run out and get all the old lines straightened out fairly. That was quite a job. A very fine fellow to work with. Then he came over to Little Cataloochee. I ran into him down there on the road, and they told me they'd like for me to work with him. So I worked with the survey crew there."

"It was quite interesting finding the old marks that had been made on the trees fifty or a hundred years before. He kept a good diary of all the things that he did find out... even to the snows, and such things as that, that fell. The Park never actually developed to where they was buying until 1930 or 31."

At this point, Mark began to speak with a measure of controlled anger, saying slowly but emphatically: "George Bramlett was the purchasing agent of the North Car'lina Park Commission, worked out of Asheville, North Car'lina, and he was givin' prices on the land in Cataloochee (that) had been assessed by fair, or reasonably (fair means). He would offer only a percent of the amount that was allotted. He had the reputation of cheating the people... the local people... and was hated by almost all who had any dealings with him!"

"Woodbury (also) was hired to visit each farm in Cataloochee and to appraise the value of it, as to houses and buildings and so forth. He was unfair to everyone. He made a statement to me that he would not give his house and lot in Asheville for all of Cataloochee! Said the ground was shale. I returned him to Asheville once while he was in this deal in a Model T... 1927 Model T."

As Aden Carver, of neighboring Bradley Fork complained: "They just condemned and sold me out."

Some people did more than just get mad. Uncle Steve Woody up on Rough Fork in Cataloochee, contested the value of his land set by the Park Commission and exclaimed later: "I owned four hundred acres. We had the masterest law suit you ever seen!" Mack Hannah was another who hotly contested his land value in court.

MARK HANNAH: "Horizontal measurement reduced the acreage, caused the land owners to think they were taking our land."

JARVIS CALDWELL: "Once I thought they would have a shootout with some of the Park officials appraisin' their land and stuff. But they got 'em kind of settled down. Uncle Hiram Caldwell, my Daddy, and a few of them just out-talked the others not to have no murders... just to go on and do the best they could. They was some got up pretty high, and they was ready to fight or die, they was. At one time there they got Mr. Wilburn, or some other fellow, I forget his name. They was about to... I don't know. He was just a-tryin' to do a job, but the people just didn't want to have their homes taken away from 'em."

MARK HANNAH: "I think Jim Conard was the first fellow that sold on Little Cataloochee. I'm not for sure about Big Cataloochee, who sold first. Just a family go now and then. I believe most of 'em were gone by 1932. Some of 'em might have went in '29. I'm not positive when they started sellin' there, but some of them sold that very year. Caldwells and Palmers stayed, then we stayed. And some of the Messer folks at Little Cataloochee stayed for awhile, then they moved out... moved over into their own place. Irving Messer and 'Mericus Hall were last to move out of Little Cataloochee. Uncle Steve Woody stayed in Big Cataloochee until about 1942. Lush Caldwell was last to move from Big Cataloochee."

Moving out of the valley was a traumatic experience for the older folk, but not necessarily for the younger ones. They had heard enough of the excitement of the outside world to want to grasp it all for themselves. Raymond Caldwell tells of leaving the valley in the 1930s when the Park Service took over:

RAYMOND CALDWELL: "I was in Big Cataloochee my first fifteen years... well, up to that time, the old cow, mother's old milk cow, the family cow what had raised the family, she had to have her! She was gettin' up several years by then. 'Course, when leaving Cataloochee, we hauled part of (the cattle) and drove part of 'em. The last trip out of there I drove a wagon with a team and had some chicken coops on it. And Daddy had hired a fellow with a truck to haul the household plunder. We had to bring the wagon. Tied the cow to the wagon and let her walk."

"I think my father was terribly upset (to be leaving) but we kids were curious. Of course, goin' to a school over there and (having been) in a small one where there wouldn't be over fifteen or twenty people... I know the reaction when I went to a school where there was 400 people. I was scared to death!"

ROBERT HILLIARD WOODY: "I'm not aware of anyone I knew who was pleased with the prospect of selling out and leaving. I don't think they worried too much about money. But I heard any number of people... didn't want to leave... couldn't get good water, you know, out of these hills... would be unhealthy. And, just taking up roots and leaving..."

Horace Kephart knew an old man in another part of the Smokies who expressed it for all mountain people when he said: "I went down into the valley, wunst, and I declar I nigh sultered! 'Pears like there ain't breath enough to go round, with all them people. And the water don't do a body no good; an' you cain't eat hearty, nor sleep good o' nights. Course they pay big money down thar; but I'd a heap-sight ruther ketch me a big old 'coon fer his hide. Boys, I did hone fer my dog Fiddler, an' the times we'd have a-huntin', and the troutfishin', an' the smell o' the woods, and nobody bossin' and jowerin' at all. I'm a hillbilly, all right, and they needn't to glory their old flat lands to me!"

PROFESSOR JOSEPH S. HALL: "The elderly people had been given leases allowing them to spend the rest of their days on their old homeplaces. As one old woman (Docia Styles) in the Tennessee side of the park related, 'They told me I could stay as long as I lived. I told 'em that would be as long as I wanted to stay.'"

The thorn among the roses was that the remaining residents were not allowed to cut timber, hunt or raise cattle.

MARK HANNAH: "People moved out when the park began to apply their rules to them. They couldn't make a livin'. They kept cuttin' us down all the time, just have that field for a little while, then have this one... cuttin' down all the time and lettin' it go back to forest."

JARVIS CALDWELL: "They never did have a set rule that I know of, but... "

BONNIE CALDWELL (emphatically): "Made it so hard on us we couldn't live over there!"

JARVIS CALDWELL: "At our convenience, y'know."

BONNIE CALDWELL: "You couldn't have anything, no stock rangin'. And that's how people made their money over there."

JARVIS CALDWELL: "Well, you could farm a little, but you had to do it in places..."

BONNIE CALDWELL: "In places where they designated."

JARVIS CALDWELL: "You couldn't have no stock, no cattle outside. Had one horse. And a lot of time, you couldn't do much farmin' with one horse."

ELDRIDGE CALDWELL: "Major Woody, he'us a crippled man, bad crippled, had been all of his life. He was pretty high strung, if he got mad about something. He got mad with the Park Service about... Y'know, they promised us we could use all the timber we needed... these fellows that come and bought the land. Then they didn't! After the government got it, they didn't want to do nothin'. And 'Major' said he wished they'd come a herrycane and blow the cranberry bushes out of the ground! They'd let you take (blown-down timber) up now and then, y'know. And sure 'nough, there come one right up in above where he lived over there on Little Cataloochee. Just flattened out a strip. Must have been (a prophet)."

"Major" complained to Professor Hall about the new hunting rules imposed on him. "(The Park) has rernt this country. They have us hemmed in, 'n you cain't kill a thing. Over in Swain County a man named Calhoun was lawed fer killin' a bear that was breakin' into his chicken house. But Judge Webb told him to pertect what he had. (But, with us, in Cataloochee) the wust sorriest things they is, like bob-cats, you cain't kill."

With their activities so bitterly curtailed, they soon found out that they could not exist under the circumstances and quickly moved out. Only the ranger and his family and some maintenance men remained. At the end, the Cataloochee schoolhouse had dwindled down to six students.

In his book on the Smokies, *Strangers in High Places*, Michael Frome noted that "a few resent the National Park; they resent government regulations that deprived them of unrestricted hunting and fishing. They recall how they would burn the woods in order to 'green the grass' and to kill off snakes and ticks. In those days, when they managed the land, the woods were full of small game. Chestnuts were plentiful, which they could use at home or haul to market as a cash crop. Then came the park, with its rules and 'book learning'. What happened since? The mysterious chestnut blight struck. Small game isn't what it used to be. Neither is fishing. All of this, of course, they attribute to the way the Government runs the Smokies."

"Still, the game poaching continues, and the moonshine making, the occasional case of arson, either for spite against the government or for sport, and the illicit ginseng digging."

As recently as 1973, a local mountain man was heard to say darkly: "That new ranger in Cataloochee has already made some enemies. He'd better watch out in a dry season!"

This was at a time when feeling ran high over a news story that an assistant ranger in Cataloochee had been beaten up and his truck windshield smashed by a poacher who had no home and lived off the land. Though the poacher's act was distinctly illegal, it still held a certain charm for the independent mountain folk. For a time, this man's name was on everybody's lips and a folk ballad was even written about him.

But some acts against the rules had a certain pathos about them which held them above ordinary mischief. Once the families had left the Park, they were told they could not remove anything from their former homes. Lush Caldwell and Mary Lou Leatherwood Moody bravely stole in with a truck one day, defying the regulations, and removed the old hearthstones from Leona Caldwell's house and restored them to her new home in Jonathan's Creek. Hearthstones were, after all, the heart of the house, the heart of the family. Mary Lou was determined that her mother should not be denied her birthright.

Mark Hannah had early set a goal for himself... that he would eventually return to the place of his birth. With this in mind, he served as Haywood County fire warden, working for two years with the North Carolina Forest Service. In 1941, he got his first break; the County Fire Warden, George Burnette, appointed him to act as fire warden in Little Cataloochee. This appointment was unique in that it was only for fifteen days. At the end of that time, the Tennessee and North Carolina Parks Commissions were turning over the park land officially to the Federal Government. After this transaction, the government made him warden of the entire eastern section of the park, and in 1943, he became the ranger for Cataloochee and later for Big Creek, too.

Later in life, Mark was fond of saying: "I went there for fifteen days and stayed for thirty-one years!"

Before Mark, there was Chief Ranger John Needham, then Warden Smith in 1935, and Warden John Carroll from 1936-1943. Tom Porter, a former surveyor in the Park in the twenties, recalled the timber cruisers who could mimic any animal, and John Carroll who had been a great raconteur.

A prosperous world-travelled engineer, away from North Carolina for forty years, Tom has now 'retired' to become a major citizen of Franklin. His ancestors were old Smokies pioneers; Jesse Siler of Siler's Bald, for instance. Porter had been in

Cataloochee for three years, working with Hiram Wilburn when park lands were being bought in the late twenties and thirties. He helped build the log tower on Mt. Sterling in 1928 and mounted a theodolite for a triangulation tower, a geodetic survey marker, when they were mapping the Smoky Mountains.

Thirty-one years was long enough for Mark Hannah. It was lonesome there, especially in the winter, without all the friends and family he had grown up with. He could never pass an empty space or a grown-over thicket without remembering the life and vitality that had pervaded that spot where once a house had been.

It had been a terrible wrench to see all his friends leave. He alone had stayed behind as the new ranger of the Cataloochee section of the Great Smoky Mountains National Park. And it was his dreadful duty to blot out a community which he had known all his life. On orders from the Park Service, he was faced with the task of burning most of the old pioneer buildings. As he watched the flames envelop the hand-hewn logs, tears came to his eyes, and he recalled how the mill wheel had turned, how they had danced in a certain house, how they had merrily shucked corn in a certain barn, or piled the apples in the apple house, or smoked the meat in the meathouse... now nothing but ashes.

MARK HANNAH: "My children loved Cataloochee as I do. It makes them sick to think of its being all destroyed... our old home being destroyed..."

And yet he could not help feeling proud that his native Cataloochee would one day become known to millions. Although, strangely, the Park never consulted the one man who had been ranger in there for thirty-one years, he felt that the park should be kept aware of the right way to develop Cataloochee.

MARK HANNAH: "Most of the improved houses were sold. And the older style, log cabins... I had to go around and burn them. I don't know how many cabins I burned those first few years. We made a mistake by tearing down the old houses. They should have been left for development, creating another Cades Cove type area."

Cades Cove is a part of the Smokies in which the old pioneer settlement is totally preserved, down to the mill which still grinds corn, and the fields which still are dotted with cattle grazing peacefully under old Thunderhead Mountain. This and Cataloochee Valley were among the few areas of the Park which had large settlements of note.

Other people besides Mark thought it wrong for the park to burn interesting antique log structures when they might have been preserved as the pioneer way of life. Hiram Wilburn fought stubbornly to discontinue the destruction. But the Park Service at the time, was laboring under the mistaken idea that wilderness was the requisite for the Park. Therefore, the settlement would be allowed to revert to a wild state that only the Indians knew.

Hiram Wilburn singled out Chief Ranger John Needham as the 'big man' in getting buildings destroyed in the area. A good many people were afraid of John

Needham because of the power he wielded in the Park. The Caldwells corroborated this.

PEARL CALDWELL: "He was a man that people kinda dreaded and was afraid of, and he had the most alert mind of anyone that I've ever known. He could, oh, just observe ever'thing about ye. And they couldn't hide nothin' from 'im, y'know. He'd find out evey'thing!"

When someone commented that Hiram Wilburn couldn't stand the man, they both laughed.

ELDRIDGE CALDWELL: "Oh, I know... didn't like 'im at all!"

Out of its many champions, the great unsung hero of the struggle to give Cataloochee its rightful place was definitely Hiram Wilburn, this outsider from South Carolina.

He first came to Cataloochee in the twenties as a surveyor for the North Carolina Park Commission and came to love the place passionately. He appointed himself historian, later becoming known by the official title of Acting Historian of the Great Smoky Mountains National Park. Secretly, though, he had great contempt for the way the Park treated its new property.

He expressed not only concern for the people, but for the houses and civilization which were about to be destroyed by the Park, in the name of giving the land to the enjoyment of the country. He was a scrappy fighter but, in the end, was defeated and released from his job.

He was somewhat vindicated when the State of North Carolina made a resolution, November 10, 1952, to express appreciation of his distinguished services in research and historical writings in North Carolina.

Even after the local people were removed, they remained concerned about Cataloochee.

JARVIS CALDWELL: "... wish they'd never put in a big road in there. That was the worst thing they ever did. Just put that paved road in from the top of the mountain there, and it not connected up yet to the highway, you see, not to I-40 especially. And when it's all completed...(they just cut right through the big timber, interjected someone) Big timber! (working up to righteous indignation). Through what we call Hell's Half Acre! Of course, puttin' them roads through those fields... should have left 'em around where the old roads went. Not have any Expressway through Catalooch'. Have a good two-way road round the creek like it was. You'd see the beautifullest place in the world. Wouldn't have been no better to look at then that would have been. Now you don't see much of the creek. Just a few places, y'know."

But old Floyd Woody disagreed with the strict conservationists among his fellow Cataloochans. When it was pointed out that some of the prettiest timber... a virgin hemlock forest... was right above the Steve Woody place where he had grown up, he exclaimed joyfully:

"Oh, yeah! It'd be one of the grandest drives in the world. It's just four miles and a half to a hard surface road above the Uncle Steve house. They call it Poll's Gap. And that'd be the grandest drive in Ameriky for children to see this timber in there, four and five feet through it. I've seen, there's one big tree up there, it takes... I believe it takes sixteen men to reach around a big poplar tree! Well, I think a road graded to Poll's Gap would be the finest drive in the world. We need to develop. First thing, we need a nice highway in there. And we need then, a good horse camp... back up about Turkey George's. And there's a way of building a trail from Poll's Gap... I'd call it a ridin' road, too, and the Guv'mint would do that. Yeah, I was talkin' to some man, and they say they'd like to git that ridin' up there."

Meanwhile the Jarvis Caldwell family fondly proceeded to add their views in madrigal form.

RAYMOND CALDWELL: "Preserve! Keep some of the old footlogs that went across."

JARVIS CALDWELL: "Yeah! Yeah!"

BONNIE CALDWELL: "Well, they probably would have been washed away. We've had pretty bad wash-outs since we were in there."

JARVIS CALDWELL: "They'd stayed... been there a long time."

RAYMOND CALDWELL: "If they're throwin' Federal funds away, I can't think of no better place to throw 'em'"

JARVIS CALDWELL: "I helped put three or four footlogs back up so the school children could go across. Every time it would wash away, we'd raise it higher. We finally got one so it'd stay there, and they put the bridge there."

RAYMOND CALDWELL: "Is your Dead Man (i.e. anchor) not still under that bridge? Personally I'd like to see it all stay primitive. I wish the road would never be built."

The road to which he referred was a proposed major access road which might bring millions of visitors into what still seems a relatively quiet part of the Park. To this date, the road has not been built, perhaps partly due to the efforts of a conservation group headed by Raymond himself, perhaps partly because of the economy and cutbacks within the Department of the Interior.

MARK HANNAH: "If the access road opens... the pressure of the crowd will dictate what becomes of Cataloochee."

Things have already changed a lot since Mark Hannah took charge so many years ago. In 1978 there were two seasonal rangers besides the Chief Ranger. They ranged on foot, in jeeps, and on horseback through the forests, checking on fallen timber, trails, lost campers, backpackers, fishermen, horseback riders, flora and fauna, not to mention poachers, drug offenders, escaped criminals, and crashed planes.

In the summer, there are five men on the maintenance crew to repair washed-out roads and trails, to build guard rails and split rail fencing, to mow the old settlers' fields, and to maintain what few buildings remain. They are even now commencing the restoration of a few of these... as if to placate the ghost of Hiram Wilburn. In fact, they are doing a splendid job of maintaining what is one of the most beautiful and most often visited of our National Parks.

The FBI, is called in for major felonies, otherwise the ranger and his men deal with petty offenders. They can call army helicopters in emergencies, and the Forest Service, with its aircraft patrol out of Andrews during the fire season. They no longer use the old fire tower on Mt. Sterling.

There is electricity in the valley now... wonder of wonders, But still no telephone as the last estimate had put the cost at $30,000.00! Instead, the ranger communicates with the outside world by radio via the Oconaluftee Ranger Station, and they can relay his message by telephone.

Life goes on, muses Mark Hannah as he goes over there to fish and dream, but at a different pace, it seems to him.

PART II

The People

The last letter sent from the Cataloochee Post Office postmarked June 15, 1932. The letter is addressed to Mr. J. H. Woody in Atlanta, Georgia. In the top right corner of the envelope Maria L. Palmer, postmistress, wrote, "Everything in life has an end, they say: for this post office this is the last day." Courtesy of the Steve Woody family.

Cataloochee, N.C.
June 14, 1932
Mr. J. H. Woody
Atlanta, Ga.
Dear Jonathan:

Your letter received serval days ago. Was sure glad to hear from you, but sorry to hear times are so hard with you. We are all well and doing fine.

I am running my camps this summer but I'm not doing so well as this depression has hurt my business this year.

If things get too hard come up and we will go to the Lodge camp and try to forget our troubles.

I saw uncle Steve yesterday. He is doing fine, and seems to be happy.

This is the last day of the Cataloochee post office as it is being discontinued today. You might keep this letter for a souvenir as it will be the last one you will ever receive post marked at Cataloochee. From now on my address with be Cove Creek, N.C.

Come to see us when you can.

Yours truly,
Jarvis

CHAPTER 8

A Rose, a Snake, and a Dove

(Religion)

Little Cataloochee Baptist Church still stands up on the hill as a reminder that the church was a central part of the mountain community. Children would walk to Little Cataloochee church in the morning and Big Cataloochee church in the evening (uphill both directions in the snow being chased by a panther as some tell it.) Friends of the Smokies is raising an $8 million endowment to restore and preserve the historic structures (cabins, churches, school, mills and barns) within Great Smoky Mountains National Park. Courtesy David Huff Creative.

LITTLE CATALOOCHEE WAS almost totally deserted on a beautiful late autumn afternoon when Jim Waldroop's pick-up truck brought a writer in there. As temporary chief ranger after Mark retired, Jim had all the keys to the locked gates of the service roads, thereby saving the journalist a 5-mile walk over Noland Mountain from Big Catalooch'.

The woods were shimmering bronze and gold... a rich vermeil background for the starched white wooden Gothic church which stood above the road on the hill. It had a modest Baptist lace frill of Victorian gingerbread on its eaves, but was not too ornate for a little mountain church.

A mountain man who had just ridden his horse in from Tennessee squinted at him as he gave his lathery mount a chance to recoup. The horse's foamy sides, heaving in and out like bellows indicated that its rider had ridden across Sterling Gap at breakneck speed as though he were evading the law. Here, in Little Cataloochee, Jim was the law. Consequently there was a distinct air of quietness and respect.

In a voice as dry as an old stream bed, the rider warned him not to enter the church, saying, "I just been in thar. Seen a black snake—killed 'im."

But black snakes are rat-catchers. The journalist was not to be deterred.

At first it seemed an ordinary country church. The little benches were slightly askew, as though the congregation had recently pushed them aside on departure. But the floor was filmed over with dirt and cobwebs, indicating that a long time had passed since Decoration Day in the Little Cataloochee graveyards. The writer started to leave when something on the altar caught his eye.

It was a basket of red roses made of eternal plastic. Perched on it was an artificial white feathered dove, trembling, it seemed, in the strange half-light of the old whitewashed interior. He took it from the altar so that he might photograph it by the light of the window and there, at his feet lay the snake! It gave him a start, despite his fine regard for ratcatchers.

One could find symbols in this emotion-charged atmosphere without consciously looking... the rose of Eden's garden, the dove of the peaceful valley, the signs of a vanished people in the hastily vacated benches, and now, incredibly, the serpent himself as a déja vu of what had happened in Paradise.

When Methodist Bishop Asbury rode through Cataloochee on that bitter December day in 1810, he saw neither garden of Eden nor settlers. Nor was his influence felt in the valley until long after his lingering death from tuberculosis. But it was felt, all right. That stern old man! There was once a story about his indignation on discovering a party of "jolly flatboat men" who were carousing in a tavern on the French Broad River. His comment in his diary that night was: "I soon put a stop to their merriment!"

It is estimated that this remarkable man covered over 270,000 miles in his American ministry, preaching 16,500 sermons and ordaining more than 4,000 preachers.

The first minister both to cross the wilderness of Cataloochee and actually preach the gospel there was a pioneer preacher by the name of Doctor Collins Howell, half-brother to Nelson Howell, Allen Davidson's father-in-law. Like Asbury, he was a resilient Methodist. He organized the first Methodist church in Cataloochee, riding on Sundays ten and fifteen miles from his Jonathan's Creek house to preach to his people. Yet he would never take anything in the way of compensation. Like most of the Howells, he lived to a very old age, ninety-three years. He was born in 1812, just two years after the Bishop rode through Cataloochee, and died in 1905, the same year that Colonel George Kirk and Allen Davidson passed on.

Doctor Collins Howell must have preached in the fields, barns or in the private homes, for the present Palmer Methodist chapel in Big Cataloochee was not built until nearly 1899. It is a stark white clapboard church with a traditional steeple and bell, unlike the Baptist church on Little Cataloochee with its flourishes of Victorian gingerbread. It now stands rather diffidently alongside Cataloochee Creek, near the mouth of Palmer Creek, with its back to the National Park's paved road, for the simple reason that the old settlement road used to go in front of the church. The settlers' old fields of the bottoms, contained by split rail fences, surround the chapel, providing an aura of space and light that is lacking in the Baptist church, but the mountains rise with an amazing steepness on the other side of the stream.

Though the "Cataloochee" Baptist Church was first chartered in 1855, the little Baptist church on the other side of Noland mountain was not built in 1890. Another settlement church, the Caldwell Fork Baptist Church, did not become active until 1928.

Dr. Robert Woody described the nature of Baptist religion in Little Cataloochee when he was a boy.

ROBERT HILLIARD WOODY: "Men sat on one side, women on the other side. This was characteristic, I think, of such churches in the country. The men were apt to get up and go out and sit out, really, in the front on a log and tell tales. I remember one revival in the church. I don't remember much about it. I was pretty small. Only one I ever heard of there, may have been quite unusual. It was a very emotional thing."

This was the feeling of Kephart who first brought Appalachia to the attention of the public in books such as *Our Southern Highlanders*.

HORACE KEPHART: "When he (the preacher) warms up, he throws in a gasping <u>ah</u> or <u>uh</u> at short intervals, which constitute the 'holy tone'. Dr. MacClintock gives this example: 'Oh, brethren, repent ye, and repent ye of your sins, <u>ah</u>; fer if ye don't, <u>ah</u>, the Lord, ah, he will grab yer by the seat of yer pants, <u>ah</u>, and hold yer over hell fire till ye holler like a coon!'"

ROBERT HILLIARD WOODY: "Community gatherings, Sunday school and 'singing' once a week and preaching once a month brought a psychological lift over and above the strictly spiritual. Theological dogma was not a matter for concern; it was Fundamentalist in so far as it was consciously expressed, but its practical application in human relations was generous. A single community church, denominational though it was, could scarcely afford emphasis on creed. Nor did the democracy of the meeting house exclude those who might step outside the bounds of conventional rules of conduct. There was nothing of the pharasaical attitude, no aristocracy of those who communed with God to the exclusion of their fellow men."

Over on Big Cataloochee there were occasional reprimands for naughty ways!

FLOYD WOODY: "They like to ha' churched me (i.e. run me out of church for good) there when I was a young man. I taught Sunday school there to young folks. Back then you'd go out and get a lady come (to get on a horse). You'd have one box so high, and the next one (higher). They'd walk up on that box, without (i.e. until) they were even with the saddle, then set down in the saddle. Then you took 'em by the shoe-heel and put their foot in the stirrup. Well, there was a certain lady there decided that I wouldn't take her by the shoe-heel. I let my hand go a little too high. And she reported me to the deacons of the church. And they tried me for it! I had to quit teachin' fer six months."

Big Cataloochee had a religious event which was, in a way, kin to the old-time revival. There was plenty of good food and socializing as well. It was called Quarterly Meeting and brought in droves of people.

JARVIS CALDWELL: "We had a regular preacher at Palmer Chapel, the Methodist church in Big Cataloochee, who was appointed by the Conference for years and years. T. A. Groce served four years. 'Course, in between times, there'd be a preacher come in, want to hold a meetin' or something, y' know, other than the pastor. That happened on Little Cataloooch' a lot of times."

"Oh, yes, we had those camp meetings every summer.... July or August, for three or four days..."

FLOYD WOODY: "Why, we had what we called Quarterly meetings over there. And that's a big thing. We'd take our dinner back then, and we didn't think about havin' a table, put it on the ground."

"The preachers would come in two or three days ahead of time; they'd come in on Friday or Saturday. Uncle Andy Caldwell was our clostest neighbor down there where the gate is. You know where the gate is goes up to the Woody house? There was a big house sit out there, and it was Uncle Andy's house. There's a sag in there. And they'us a-stayin' up at Uncle Andy's. And they got up to go to church Sunday mornin'."

"Well, that night Folsom and m' sister, we went down and built a fence, a stud horse fence, across this road, across this lane until they couldn't get to church! (wheezes and chuckles fondly at the memory) And they'us late a-gettin' started and then got down there... had horses and buggies and all that. And they had to break, knock down, tear down this fence. We'd nailed it up!"

"They never knew who done it (laughs delightedly). We just went on back home and played ignorant all our lives!"

MARK HANNAH: "(Floyd Woody told me that) Uncle Andy said to the preacher, if I knew who in the Hell did this, I'd law Hell outern them! Preacher said, hold your temper, Brother Andy. If we're a little late, why we'll get through some way or 'nother."

T. A. Groce, the Methodist preacher to whom Floyd referred, came from South Carolina to a parish at Jonathan's Creek in October, 1909, which required him to preach at all the neighboring congregations of Maggie Valley, Cove Creek, Hemphill Valley, and Cataloochee, as well as Shady Grove on Jonathan's Creek. He was supposed to preach once a month in Cataloochee, going over on Saturday and often not returning until Monday morning.

Though Preacher Groce was a man noted for his humor, a very scratchy phonograph record of his first trip into Cataloochee in the cold November of 1909 echoed some of the bitter sentiments of Methodist Bishop Asbury, who had ridden through Cataloochee nearly a century before in November, 1810.

T. A. GROCE: "Uncle Erastus Howell walked out to me, said, better light a candle and put it down there at the foot (of your surrey), said, you're goin' to need it. It's blowin' blue snow! That's the first time I ever heard that. Blowin' blue snow! And it kept blowin'! I left out. I don't know just what time it was. But I know one thing: I was a little over four hours goin' cross that Cove Creek Mountain in that horse and buggy—and got it over there! Now, if you had went over there then—rocks, rocks, rocks, rocks all the way—and rough rocks!"

He was advised before he set off on his trip: "Don't you stop until you get to Hiram Caldwell's. You'll find the barn on the right hand side of the road after you get on the Cataloochee side. You'll find the home on the left hand side. Walk a foot log across the creek. You'll have to spend the night with him. If you don't, he won't come to church the whole time you're over here!"

Hiram was a little gruff on meeting Preacher Groce for the first time, and his own peculiar sense of humor evidenced itself when he replied, in effect, well, if some man in Haywood County said that, why, then, I'll have to keep you! But he was a good old soul, as was his wife, Lizzie Howell Caldwell, who, by eight o'clock had managed to put all manner of foods on the table. Preacher and his boy fell to so ravenously that they evoked another of Hiram's sarcastic remarks.

HIRAM CALDWELL: "Preacher, you needn't to mind about hurtin' yourself, we expect to have somethin' here in the mornin'!"

T. A. GROCE: "I may not be here in the mornin'! I'm going' to satisfy myself tonight."

By the morning, Hiram had accepted him, for he told him in a burst of generosity that "the latch-string's on the outside."... a mountain man's way of saying that he was always welcome to come back. But being notoriously tight with his money, he tactfully suggested that Preacher should go and visit all the others too. T. A. Groce obediently followed Uncle Hiram's advice.

T. A. GROCE: "The late Tom Jamieson, he was one of our members. Tom was helping in a meeting. (And we went) three miles to Uncle George Caldwell's (i.e. 'Big George', not 'Creek George'). And Uncle George Caldwell's wife was ole Uncle Hosey (Hosea) Mauney's daughter. Uncle Hosey Mauney was one of the best ole religious men that there was in Haywood County. When he died, they wrote up his obituary in the North Carolina Christian Advocate—'The Bishop of Haywood County'! And we went up (to) Uncle George Caldwell's and Aunt Mag's. And, of course, we were hungry. I guess we were hungry all the time. But, anyway, we got up there and sat down and went to eating our dinner. Tom drank up his coffee, handed it back, ate on awhile, handed his cup again, ate awhile, handed it back, another cup, handed it back. Aunt Mag said to him, 'Well, Mr. Jamieson, I believe you like coffee.' Tom had a way of pullin' his chin down: 'Well, yes'um, I do, but I have to drink so much just to get a little bit!'"

RAYMOND CALDWELL: "A couple of the older people stand out in my mind. And one of 'em, of course, is Uncle Hiram Caldwell's wife, Aunt Lizzie Howell. I can remember her comin' to church. Especially I remember her at church. She wore a big black skirt, and a black bonnet and a cape. She always led prayer in church, and how she'd kneel down, that big black skirt just out and over the floor, a great big thing."

"Did anyone ever tell you about my cousin, Brown Caldwell, preachin' in Cataloochee, and his grand-daddy, Uncle Sol Sutton? Well, Brown started preachin', and he was up (in the pulpit.) Uncle Sol, his grandaddy, was gettin' old, had a great big beard down to here. Brown was a-tellin' all these fellers now if they didn't do better what was goin' to happen to 'em... gonna end up in Hell! And Uncle Sol, back in the Amen Corner, he heard it, he said, 'Yesirree, brother, and from there on into the penitentiary!' He thought he said <u>jail</u> instead of <u>Hell</u>! And they say that actually happened..."

JARVIS CALDWELL (enthusiastically): "Oh, that happened, that happened! Yeah, yesirree, brother... into the pinitintiaree... !!"

Such is human nature that all people are fascinated by the redemption of sinners. One of the great catharses of all religions is to hear sinners repent. Someone has said that "the reformed sinner is always present in esteemed circumstances in the mountains." So it has been in Cataloochee where at least one or two of their finest preachers had pasts which bespoke of violence and law evasion. One might say that it was almost an advantage for a preacher to have once reached that human level where his flawed flock could identify with him.

Brown Caldwell, who became a respected preacher with a radio network following of considerable size, is a prime example.

FLOYD WOODY: "Brown Caldwell, the preacher, and some boys were mean as striped snakes (when they were little). They'd steal their neighbors' horses and ride them all night and put 'em back in the barn all lathered with sweat."

Brown went on to later exploits as a moonshiner and, then, much later, reformed and became the now-esteemed preacher.

RAYMOND CALDWELL: "That Tom King deal. That was quite a story in itself. (Brown Caldwell) over there had become a Baptist preacher and was holdin' a revival over there in Big Cataloch' at Palmer Chapel — even though it was Methodist. He had been pretty rough in his early days. This fellow, Tom King, was an outsider, had married, though, one of the Cataloch' girls. And he was tryin' to make this preacher take pay for some liquor he'd bought from him several years before that. And he wasn't goin' to let him preach unless he took this money. They had quite a night of that. Broke up the meetin'. Tom King shot straight up a time or two, scared some people. Not in the church, no, outside."

"Oh, yes, he's still preachin'. He's a well known preacher, went on and became well educated, around Greenville, South Carolina. That was Brown Caldwell, a third cousin of mine."

"But, anyhow, my grandmother, Mag Mauney Caldwell, she was real old at that time. She got ahold of this feller, Tom King, led him off, talked to him. He come up to the car where we were at, and I'us just a little feller."

"John Palmer's with us, and he had trouble with Tom King. My grandmother, real stooped and real little, got out and told Tom, said, Tom, you just gonna have to get away from here, not cause no trouble. Aw, he says, Aunt Mag, I wouldn't bother you. And she just tuck ahold of him and led him off. My grandmother was a person who didn't fear anything. He went on his way. But he broke the meetin' up. He told 'em wadn't nobody gonna preach that night, so they left. They didn't start the revival."

MARK HANNAH: "Tom King wasn't a bad fellow unless somebody broke on him."

ROBERT HILLIARD WOODY: "Noah Conard, over across Indian Knob, and married to one of my distant cousins, had been killed by his cousin who later became, so I was told, quite an evangelist."

The story goes that this killing was in self defense and this evangelist is still preaching from time to time.

A tiny, sprightly, handsome woman in her seventies and still proud of her good looks, the eldest daughter of wealthy landowner, Will Messer, of Little Cataloochee, said her father was adamant that they go to church in good style. She was ever a strong Southern Baptist and once even made a trip to the Holy Land.

FLORA MESSER MORROW: "He always wanted Mama to have the best-dressed children in the community. And I remember hearin' him say, Rachel, get all those children a pretty new white dress for church this Sunday. And she'd say, well,

well, how on earth can you have white dresses for all these children?! There were eleven! Ten girls and one boy! Daddy always put the horses and mules to the wagon on Sunday morning, and in winter, in bad weather, and when we were real little and couldn't walk all the way. We always had to go about a mile to church. And that's the way he took us. Mama'd dress us up, and I thought I, I... I'us always proud of my looks. I just thought I had the prettiest reddish-blonde hair of anybody, and Mama'd tie it up with ribbons and everything."

MARK HANNAH (her brother-in-law): "Your cheeks were the same color!"

FLORA MESSER MORROW: "Well, I've been told that. But that makes me think of one time... There was a funeral. After I got eleven or twelve years old and began to want to primp more and do up. We were goin' to somebody's funeral. And I slipped off in the room... didn't have no rouge or anything... but I got some red flowers off Mama's black straw hat, and wet 'em and painted my cheeks... to go to a funeral! And she made me wash that off."

That spurred her on to tell of the eerie death of her grandfather, Daniel J. Cook, in Little Cataloochee... He was living in her father's house, slowly dying of cancer in his old age when, one night at supper, he felt very ill and said to his son-in-law, "Will, it looks like I ain't a-gonna make it. Here's my pocketbook. Bury me as near Harriet as you can." Wherewith, he tumbled over.

RACHEL COOK MESSER (Flora's Mama): "Flora, run tell 'em your grandfather's dead!"

They put him on a cooling board, put nickels on his eyes to hold his eyelids down, put a sheet over him, and sent for an undertaker in Waynesville twenty-eight miles away. It was not usual to have an undertaker in the mountains, but D. J. Cook had a bit of money, and that's how he wanted it.

The undertaker found, to his surprise, that the "corpse's heart was still beating, and they got a doctor, presumably having to go back all the way, twenty-eight miles, to Waynesville again!

Daniel Cook had gone into something like a coma. Meanwhile, Will Messer's house was full of maybe as many as one hundred people, waiting on Daniel Cook's pulse to fade away so they could get on with their mourning. Suddenly he came up like a flash! And lived six months more!

MARK HANNAH: "In Little Cataloochee, they tolled the death bell. They'd ring it, ring it a little bit to get everybody's attention... would be listenin'. They'd hesitate for a minute, and then soon they'd knock one time for each year old."

ROBERT HILLIARD WOODY: "A death in the family meant that the best curly maple and walnut wood ... saved for such an event... was put into the hands of a good carpenter, who fashioned a simple coffin. The unostentatious funeral service, always held at the graveside and usually without a minister, was graced by such flowers and shrubs as were in season and was attended by the entire community. The subsequent bills were confined to the cost of the headstone. People tended to live long. One of the first funerals I remember was that of Grandpap Hannah, who died at the age of ninety after being confined to his bed for years with a broken back... Will Messer usually made the caskets in Little Cataloochee."

MARK HANNAH: "(My father), Mack Hannah, furnished cherry lumber for most of these caskets. Some chestnut lumber was also used."

RAYMOND CALDWELL: "Everybody most always had a coolin' board. This was a big wide oak board, about ten foot in length. And this is what they laid them out on until somebody could get into town to buy the clothing or the box. In many cases, they'd make it."

JARVIS CALDWELL: "Well, I've helped make most of 'em (in Big Catalooch')... me and Jim Caldwell, who, in his time, was the casket-maker. Made out of walnut or cherry."

RAYMOND CALDWELL: "I know the one you made for Blye Caldwell's little girl. You made it out of poplar, remember? That's the only one that I can remember being seen made. And you had this big pot of water so you could put it in and soak it..."

MARK HANNAH: "This hot water made the lumber pliable to bend in shape for the sides of the coffin."

BONNIE CALDWELL: "I put the lining in."

JARVIS CALDWELL: "It was wide at the top, narrow at the bottom."

'Turkey George' Palmer's daughter, the late Flora Palmer Medford, a frail little woman with a whispery voice, told us that, contrary to the usual custom, her father's coffin had been a steel casket bought in Waynesville. Evidently, 'Turkey George', a famous hunter, wanted to make sure that the bear population did not dig him up after death in revenge for the huge numbers he had killed.

When Homer Lockman died on Big Cataloochee, Mark said he had asked to be buried on Little Cataloochee. It was fortunate that his body was put into a home-made wooden coffin and not into a steel casket, for he had to be carried five miles up Nelson Branch (formerly Hall Branch) and over Noland Mountain. The coffin was carried by Floyd Burgess, Bartley Bennett, and two others. When they got to the narrow pass, two had to go in front, and two behind. After this tortuous journey, Lockman rested peacefully in the Little Cataloochee graveyard, behind a stout wire fence which was partly designed to keep out marauding bears and other wild animals.

There are fifteen separate burial grounds in Cataloochee, including one for negro slaves.

ROBERT HILLIARD WOODY: "Weddings customarily came before births; in any case, the marriage tie was seldom broken except by death."

It was said that blind Jess McGee, who lived on Caldwell Fork both before and after the Civil War, cried his eyes out weeping after his wife died. He would cry for days at a time.

One event in Little Cataloochee nearly made up for all of poor Jesse McGee's tears. That was Flora Messer Morrow's wedding, the only one ever held in Little Cataloochee church. Most were simple affairs at home by the hearthside; or couples like Flora Palmer and Manson Medford simply slipped away to be married quickly in a South Carolina parsonage.

But Flora Messer, nearly eighty years old, excitedly recounted her marriage to Charles Morrow as though it happened only last week.

FLORA MESSER MORROW: "Captain William Hannah's wife planned this wedding for us. My wedding dress was white satin, the veil and the orange blossoms and all of that. I never would do it again... the wedding we planned, because the wedding cost my father and mother a lot of hard work and a lot of money. They had two preachers there. The same preacher that married Charles and I married my father and mother... Preacher Frank Arrington."

"Here come... they used to call them, surreys, two-seated... from Waynesville, with four big horses, with all the bronze decoration and everything... Charles' cousin, Frank Williams, come driving the wedding party. I was already there, and Charles was staying up with his friend, Bartley Bennett. Anyway, he carried Bonnie and Nora and Fannie Burr."

"That church was a mass of flowers. Fifth of November, nineteen and sixteen. So it was chrysanthemums. And I think every chrysanthemum in the whole area of the two Cataloochees was brought. And when we came out of the church, you couldn't even see the surrey for the flowers... they were tied and pinned and stapled all over that (surrey)."

"The church was just filled with people as far back as you could see. All the Morrows were up for the wedding. I reckon everybody was happy except for a boyfriend or two stood back and shed a few tears."

"Preacher Will Hall, of Cataloochee, was the other preacher. And we had Rube Renfro out of Knoxville for the chef. And women had been cookin'. The table in Mama's dining room was just about as long as here to there... about a ten foot table. And it was loaded with food."

Her eyes glistened, and she clasped her hands for joy.

MARK HANNAH: "Little Cataloochee children were not christened by a preacher. Very few children were baptised or joined the church before they were twelve years of age. In Big Cataloochee the Methodist minister would sprinkle the children - not many - but a few did it. I never witnessed this. I've been told that they did it."

"The Baptist children would attend Sunday school. The very smallest ones were in the 'card class' — we received a badge for attendance, etc."

"One Sunday, I was sitting in the Baptist Church near the window on the north side and the Preacher Arrington was praying. A thunder storm was on. Lightning struck a chestnut tree about 20 feet from the church, and the concussion broke the windowpane by my side and knocked my straw hat from my hand onto the floor. One of my cousins had just left the tree and entered the church as the storm arrived. That was a close call for him."

"Another Sunday, Preacher Frank Arrington was praying for rain. And a storm came and almost washed some of the cornfields away! He believed in Prayer and Dreams."

Some other religious folks may have believed in prayer and dreams, but bolstered their religious feelings with spirits of another sort, as attested by Hobert Franklin who was the fire lookout on Mt. Sterling fire tower for twelve years.

HOBERT FRANKLIN: "Grandaddy Sutton, Uncle John Sutton, they always called 'im. Had a long beard. Right good ole fellow. Always b'lieved in the right thing in life, teach his children right. Taught 'em right, but they (all) loved to drink their liquor. 'Most people does... There were some folks were makin' a little whiskey up on the branch a little way from (Uncle Mack Hannah's) home. And he (Uncle John) decided he'd run up there on a Sunday morning and get him a little drink of this liquor. They had Sunday school of an evenin', and he'd get him a little drink of that liquor and bring it off, and get lined up for Sunday school. He already had a big nice bunch of children out there."

"He hadn't been up there but a few minutes by the stillyard till the still cap blowed off. Left the old feller's face and beard full of hot still slop. He just put his head down in an empty barrel there. It wasn't hurtin' him so much when he got that slop and stuff raked out of his face and out of his eyes. He didn't even wait to get him airy a little drink from the bottle. But he took down off of there, selling out! Come down at the house, complained to the old lady how he took a rash in his face some way or 'nother, and it was a-burnin' him up. And he got kindly cleaned up."

"Sunday school come right after twelve. And he went down to the schoolhouse where he taught Sunday school. And he made a plea that he had a rash or something that broke out on his face... not a thing in the world on him, just that hot still slop had burnt him. But he got by with that pretty good."

"But a few years after that, (he decided) that he'd organize a spring Sunday school... Jerry Franklin, my brother, and June Sutton, that's old man Mitch Sutton's boy, they'd been over in the Sugar Cove country, gatherin' some blockade liquor. And they'd come out there by the Big Laurel Section and down by the schoolhouse. When they got inside of the schoolhouse, the yard was all covered with children a-playin' around. And Jerry Franklin, he was pretty drunk, and June was, too. And Jerry hollered: "Hey, hurrah for Grandpap! Hurrah for Grandpap! Organizin' Sunday School!"

"He just kept going on up to the little house. Grandad Sutton ran out and said, 'Now, boys, I'm not a-holdin' with your cuttin' up, drinkin' and cavortin' around here. You'uns get away from here! I'm organizin' a Sunday school!'

"Jerry Franklin says: 'Well, Grandpap, I was goin' to give you a drink of liquor if you wanted it. But, you know, the way you'us turned about it, we don't give a doggone.' June Sutton expressed some of the same language out. And they were headed on down by the schoolhouse and headed on down towards a li'l bunch of la'rl."

"Granddaddy hollered, 'Don't go, boys, wait a minute! Wait a minute, boys. Don't go off. Wait! Said, take that (jar of liquor) right down there and lay it right in behind that log and hide it, and come on back up here till I can get this Sunday school organized. I want a drink or two of it!'"

When 550 people gathered for a recent Cataloochee Homecoming at Palmer Chapel in Big Cataloochee, it was decided to revive the ancient custom of tolling for the dead.

All the names were read of those who had died during the past year — among them old Floyd Burgess who had once helped carry Lockman's coffin over Noland Mountain, and Flora Palmer Medford, who had just quietly faded away.

Jonathan Woody read the names as Herschel Caldwell pulled the bell rope. The chapel bell echoed solemnly, over a long period, through the settler's old meadows and the wildwood, hitting against the steep mountain faces — only one toll this time for each person, as nineteen had died that year.

CHAPTER 9

As Cataloochee Goes...
(Politics)

Pearl Valentine Caldwell (before she married) rode a mule to carry the mail from Ola post office in Little Cataloochee, through Bald Gap to Nellie post office in Big Cataloochee, a distance of about 5 miles. While it wasn't unusual to transport the mail by horse or mule, it was unusual to have it transported by a woman in those days. Courtesy Great Smoky Mountains National Park Archives.

PRIOR TO THE settlement of the valley, the major land speculators had already set the political tone. Colonel Robert Love, who owned most of Cataloochee and was an elector for the president and vice-president when Jefferson was elected down to the last term of Andrew Jackson, often had to travel five hundred miles from western N.C. on political business at the State House in Raleigh. He wrote from Raleigh to William Welch on December 4, 1828.

COLONEL ROBERT LOVE: "All the electors were present on the 3rd and gave their votes in a very dignified manner and before a very large concourse of people, the State House being crowded. Fifteen cannons were fired for the number of electoral votes and one for the county of Haywood and the zeal she appeared to have had from the number of votes for the Old Hero's ticket. It was submitted to me to bring forward a motion to proceed to ballot for a president of the United States, and, of course, you may be well assured that I cheerfully nominated Andrew Jackson. I was much gratified to have that honor and respect paid me. From the most authentic accounts, Adams will not get a vote south of the Potomac or west of the mountains. Wonderful, what majority! For Jackson 178 and Adams only 83, leaving Jackson a majority of 95 votes. So much for bargain and intrigue."

In this last sentence he was referring to the staunch Whig of Haywood County, Cataloochee cattleman, William Mitchell Davidson of Jonathan's Creek, who had somehow been induced to refrain from voting for Colonel Thomas as an elector out of regard for his Democratic friend and neighbor, Robert Love. As a consequence, Love was elected and Jackson carried every vote in the valley.

Though, truly, politics played no large part in Cataloochee Valley after its settlement these citizens, whose ancestors had fought in the American Revolution, felt it was their right to be able to vote. In 1849, Cataloochee was made a voting precinct, with headquarters at the house of William Noland, one of the earliest settlers.

Mark's father, Mack Hannah, had told Hiram Wilburn, that terrier who dug out the history, that there had once been a Muster Ground located on Cataloochee Mountain beside the old trail not far west of the Hogland place. It was a comparatively broad, flat area. Here soldiers were mustered. Political campaigns were held, with attendant big picnics. Even the elections were held here sometimes, not to mention shooting matches and other social events. Mark thought that it had been a general meeting place, not only for Cataloochans, but also for residents of White Oak and Cove Creek, as well as those of Fines Creek, Jonathan's Creek, and other outlying neighborhoods. These gatherings were in the days before Mack Hannah, in fact, in Mark's grandfather's time. There was a spring there, near Cove Creek Ridge, to the left, as one comes up Cove Creek, where visitors refreshed themselves.

JARVIS CALDWELL: "At one time they (were all) Democrats over there, but later there got to be a few Republicans. On Little Catalooch' now there were some."

RAYMOND CALDWELL: "Basically, the politics was Democrat except for Uncle Jim Hannah. Uncle Jim Hannah was Mack Hannah's brother, but Uncle Mack always stayed Democrat, that's Mark's Daddy. Uncle Jim went Republican after the change-over. Lots of families split there."

JARVIS CALDWELL: "Well, (that was) not too long after the Civil War, back when they had the dispensers and made the whiskey. Those fellers split about that time, and stayed that way all their lives. During the Probation (i.e., Prohibition) Days is when it happened."

Old time politicians evidently had very little influence on the valley folk, though they did stump in there from time to time.

ROBERT HILLIARD WOODY: "These fellows who were up for Congress... Mr. Monroe Redden... would go in there and hobnob with the people on some occasion. But I think politics did not interest many people. Except... what Uncle 'Tine Woody used to talk about was somebody like Woodrow Wilson being president of the United States. Well, he'd been president long enough. He'd had enough of the great... y'know, a big job like that and lots of money."

"Now there was a fellow over on Big Cataloochee, one of the Palmers. His wife ran the post office on Big Cataloochee for many years, and I used to know his daughter, (Hattie). Well, he was elected, as they say in those days, High Sheriff."

That was the late Glenn Palmer's father, William A., whom Glenn remembered as an extraordinarily kind man. This is not difficult to believe as Glen himself was a very gentle person. He called his father a "one-legged politician" who met people through keeping fishermen in his house. One took this to mean that he had other callings, but always had one foot in the field of politics. He was widely known as a popular and good-hearted man. When William A. was elected High Sheriff of Haywood County, he had to leave his store and the Nellie Post office in Cataloochee Valley and move to Waynesville in 1910 or 1911. Young Glenn moved with him, later becoming his chief deputy during the six year term of his father's office.

Glen's younger brother, Gudger, repeated the sentiments that his father was a good-hearted man and the leader of Cataloochee of his time. He said that William A. Palmer had been a little better off than the average person in Cataloochee, but had given away most of his money to people who needed it.

William made a bet that, if he didn't get elected High Sheriff, he would sell Mac, his beloved horse. When his wife saw him come riding into Cataloochee on Mac, she knew he was elected!

When President Warren G. Harding died, the school children of Cataloochee planted an oak tree in his memory. Doubtless the oak will survive longer than the memory of the hapless Harding who was remembered best for the Teapot Dome Scandal during his term.

An outsider's experience with politics in Cataloochee was related by Tom Porter, a retired engineer from Franklin, who was once a surveyor in the valley. He made a bet among the other surveyors and timber cruisers in the twenties that Al Smith would win the presidency. Two weeks after Hoover was elected, Tom saw a fellow worker from a great distance up on Mt. Sterling and shouted down: "Who won?" The answer came back very indistinctly, and Tom mistakenly collected the money on Al Smith. Then he went down to Waynesville to have a luxurious shave, after many wilderness weeks, at Princess Massey's barbershop and got an irate retort: "You didn't bet on Hoover! Time you Yankee s.o.b's are paying!"

Small as Cataloochee was, however, it became nationally famous during its last years as a community because of its voting record. Big Catalooch' school was where the township voted.

Historian W. Clark Medford wrote at the time: "Cataloochee has attracted national attention in the past few years, particularly at election time. The community itself, just a few years ago embracing a land area as large as some whole townships, has a total population of three families and only seven registered voters. When the polls open at 6:00 a.m., all seven voters, including the Republican Justice of the Peace, who, incidentally votes a Democrat ticket, are at their posts. By 8:00 or 8:30, even though the community is twenty-three miles from the courthouse in Waynesville and has no telephone service, the returns go on the wires. The radio station in Waynesville usually broadcasts the returns as soon as they are in, and the wire service picks it up for other stations throughout the nation. By the time afternoon daily papers are on the street, every person in the county who is interested in the returns sees that they have voted seven straight tickets. For the past several general elections, Cataloochee has been the first precinct in the county to announce the results of the election."

It was the first to get its vote out in the nation... and so became justifiably famous.

MARK HANNAH: "It was then a little voting precinct but was the first in the nation. This remained true until New Hampshire changed their time to begin voting after midnight or A.M."

Colonel Robert Love's ghost undoubtedly itched to shoot off an extra cannon at the State House in Raleigh over this great Democratic achievement.

Unfortunately, there was never a slogan... "As Cataloochee goes, so goes the nation!" And now there is no one left there to vote except one lone Ranger. Nowadays, he has to leave Cataloochee and go over to Mt. Sterling village on Big Creek and vote at the Waterville Power Company's community building.

CHAPTER 10

The Long Arm

(The Law)

In the mountains, springhouses provided a way to keep food cool from the earliest times. A small house was built near the creek or spring, and the cold clear water was diverted through "troughs" in the springhouse. Stoneware crocks with perishable food could be kept cool in the springhouse while also being protected from critters. This photo shows Burrell McGaha's springhouse on Davidson Branch in Cataloochee. Cataloochee children carried their dinner to school in a metal pail which was lodged among the rocks in the creek until time for the noonday meal. Courtesy Great Smoky Mountains National Park Archives.

"THEY SWORE THEY'D law ever who done it!" said old Floyd Woody about a youthful prank. But he and his cohorts were never caught. Unable to catch up with miscreants in that wide-open country, the law did not lay a very firm hand on the shoulder of Cataloochans.

After Neddy McFalls enticed the unwitting Sam McGaha into shooting an Indian, the earliest recorded criminal in Cataloochee was Zack Clark who, in 1838, shot Rayburn, a sheriff's deputy, and hid out there. Long ago a Western North Carolina historian recounted the incident as told him by Allen Davidson.

JOHN PRESTON ARTHUR: "Owing to the fact that the late Colonel Allen T. Davidson spent much of his young manhood (ranging cattle on the balds and) hunting and fishing in Cataloochee Valley, much of its early history has been preserved. From him it was learned that years ago Zack White (Clark) shot a deputy sheriff named Rayburn when Colonel Davidson was a boy, and hid near a big rock in a little flat one half mile above the late Lafayette Palmer's home, where for years Neddy McFalls and Dick Clark (his brother) fed him. He also stayed on Shanty Branch near where Harrison Caldwell now lives. This branch got its name from a shanty or shed that Old Smart, a slave of Mitchell Davidson, built there while he tended cattle for his master years before any white people ever lived in that valley."

Found among family papers were other details.

ALLEN DAVIDSON: "He (Ned McFalls) told me that he had killed the biggest kind of buck there (at the ford of Cataloochee). He showed me the exact spot and went into all the details. He had come over there to fetch rations to a man of the name of Zack Clark who had shot and wounded another man by the name of Rayburn, both neighbors of ours. Clark was 'lying out' to keep the sheriff from catching him, and Ned, who had a tender heart for all who were in distress, was fetching him some rations."

This same Zack Clark had cleared a field on White Oak Mountain which is still known as "Zack's Tobacco Patch".

Later on there were terrible Civil War crimes in Cataloochee. They were committed under the guise of war, but were often personal vendettas and, in peacetime, would have come to court trials.

Who were the law men then? Who brought people to justice? Revenue officers came out of Asheville. Lawyers such as Allen Davidson and John Queen came out of Jonathan's Creek and Waynesville. John Queen, having taught in the valley for many years, was well acquainted with the local people.

ALLEN DAVIDSON: "I entered the profession of law on January 1, 1845, with General R. M. Henry and J. A. B. Fitzgerald as my classmates. We were the students of Michael Francis of Waynesville... (Francis), a Scotchman, educated in Edinburgh, a thorough scholar... weighed 330 lbs."

He became an old-time circuit riding lawyer, going from court to court, finding clients along the way. Ten or twelve lawyers might all travel together and stay at the same place, at James Patton's beyond the Pigeon River, at Daniel Bryson's on Scott's Creek, or William Walker's at Valleytown, or at Nimrod Jarrett's on the Nantahala.

The columnist who writes "Roaming the Mountains" for the *Asheville Citizen-Times*, said anybody back then could have spotted a lawyer in a crowd.

JOHN PARRIS: "In those days lawyers wore the same kind of costume. Dress set them apart. (The lawyer's) coat was of the finest French broadcloth, either a swallow-tail or a cutaway. His pants were of fine doeskin. He wore a silk or satin vest, 'nine-biler' silk hat, ruffled and fluted bosom shirt, a handsome necktie, and French calf-skin boots."

Quite a departure for a former Cataloochee herder!

Allen Davidson recalled the mountain circuit of 1845 to 1861 as a happy time for him, with his cheerful travelling companions, a body which impressed him with their sincerity, force and logic.

'Fayt Palmer, Jesse's younger brother, born in 1836, perhaps emulating his older friend, Allen, was a self-appointed lawyer and helped settle disputes. He certainly looked the part of Solomon with his long white beard and patrician features. Though he was untutored, he was brighter than average. Glenn Palmer called him a "secret" lawyer.

MARK HANNAH: "And he was just that, too!"

Aside from a spate of revenue officers which periodically swarmed through the valley, few law enforcement officers seem to have come into Cataloochee. There were only George Bennett, who was much respected on Little Cataloochee as a deputy sheriff, Uncle Jim Hannah who was a Justice of the Peace, and "Squire" Mitchell Sutton, who was called a "magistrate back of the law" and occasionally performed a wedding ceremony. Joshua Allison was the truant officer. In the 1920's, he was shot at by an irate parent when Allison came up to see why the children would not go to school.

Murders and moonshining seemed to be the major crimes that required the intervention of the law in Cataloochee.

DR. ROBERT HILLIARD WOODY: "Death by violence did occur, infrequently, but feuds in the Kentucky style were unknown. Somebody gets killed, you just bury him."

To be sent to the penitentiary was rather unusual, he thought.

"I suppose they just got away, left the country, stayed away awhile. Now they would occasionally arrest somebody for moonshining. Uncle Jim Hannah was the justice of the peace. If he heard about anybody making moonshine, I'm sure he never considered it any of his part. Uncle Jim like to refresh himself with it occasionally."

There is still a prevalent belief among mountain men that distillers are punished more cruelly than murderers. One said recently about a man in White Oak who had been accused of killing his cousin: "Get caught with a still, you're in for life. Kill a man, you're out the next day!"

MARK HANNAH: "Maybe he might be charged with temporary manslaughter."

Former Cataloochans were naturally reluctant to talk about past crimes, especially murders, as many innocent family members are still alive. However, Raymond Caldwell and his father, Jarvis, did relate with gusto the adventure of Sheriff Palmer in Cataloochee on Christmas Day.

JARVIS CALDWELL: "Rudolph Caldwell got shot right there where you turn up Shanty Branch... one Christmas morning."

RAYMOND CALDWELL: "They'd been arguin' over some dogs. Dogs and liquor, wasn't it?"

JARVIS CALDWELL: "Well, they claim that Rudolph had been goin' to see this man's wife."

ELIZABETH POWERS: "Well, those are three good motives right there!"

JARVIS CALDWELL: "He just walked up. Here's Rudolph and Jim on their horses. And he just rupt (reached) up, took a shotgun and shot (Rudolph) right in the eye. It was Smiley. John Smiley. He went to the penitentiary for thirty years, but he got out after twelve or fifteen years."

"William Palmer was the Sheriff. He was the Sheriff of Haywood County, but he was a native of Cataloochee. He lived at the Courthouse at that time. Uncle William came in and helped hunt for Smiley. In fact, he's the man that walked up on him when he was hidin' behind the logs."

"Smiley said, 'Don't shoot me! Don't shoot me, Sheriff!'" (Jarvis acts it out beautifully, with a tremor in his voice.) "Smiley run up the Indian Creek until you come to the Davidson Branch Road, until you come to the first little branch. He run right up in the branch in the logs. 'Course, they's just trackin' 'im, and he just suspicious. He ran in there. Uncle William just went in that la'rl patch, and there he laid."

RAYMOND CALDWELL: "Mark Hannah has the shotgun that did the murder. He told me he did. He got the shotgun (an old 20 gauge)."

JARVIS CALDWELL: "Somebody was about to break into jail and take Smiley away from 'em. The Sheriff tuk him out of jail. And Glenn Palmer was a-drivin' the car. Glenn was his son, and he was a deputy sheriff. And, as they went, jumped in the car, Uncle William, the Sheriff, lost his hat. He had a word: Tom-Walker-Nation-on-the-Devil! Don't stop here, he said, we ain't got time to get that hat!"

RAYMOND CALDWELL: "Fraid somebody would see him with this prisoner. Took him out of jail in Waynesville, goin' to Asheville."

JARVIS CALDWELL: "There's a crowd threatened to come and take him, you see."

RAYMOND CALDWELL: "Lynch him."

JARVIS CALDWELL: "Yeah, yeah! Lynch him!"

A comic sequence, straight out of a Marx Brothers comedy, was once enacted in court by two indefatigable Cataloochee cut-ups, "Dude" and 'Ras Hannah.

"Dude", whose real name was Ivan, or Evan, after the first Hannah pioneer, was the second son of Ben Hannah, who had been struck dead with a mattock by a man named Ward while doing roadwork. "Dude" and his brother, Erastus, were "like Amos 'n Andy", claims Mark Hannah, their cousin.

DR. ROBERT HILLIARD WOODY: "They were distantly related to me. These brothers both lived way up the mountain in various remote cabins and (Dude) lived with some red-headed woman who produced a red-headed son named Jethro. Once

I met one of them on Mt. Sterling... just roaming around. I think they were law-abiding and did not make moonshine, as Uncle Blaine did on occasion. I think they were not enterprising enough."

HIRAM WILBURN: "Dude Branch, off of Little Cataloochee Creek, was named by the old North Carolina Nomenclature Committee after 'Dude' Hannah, a colorful and characteristic old mountaineer who lived a good many years on this creek. 'Dude' was witty, curt, and full of practical jokes."

ELDRIDGE CALDWELL: "Dude was always sayin' and doin' things that we laughed at every day. But I now can't remember what. If I'd known you were goin' to write a book, I'd a-put it all down!"

PEARL VALENTINE CALDWELL: "To look at Dude and 'Ras, you wouldn't think they had enough sense to know which side of the house the door was on!"

Yet, when they were in legal trouble, they would not "har a lawyer", but would often defend their own cases... and would win, too.

Mark Hannah chortled as he related their most memorable court case which involved an accusation against 'Ras for making illegal whiskey, whatever opinion Dr. Woody might have had of him for not being enterprising.

A spy was sent to buy a quart of moonshine in order to entrap Cataloochee people. He got a quart from Erastus Hannah, Dude's brother and look-a-like. When 'Ras was brought to trial, Dude came to court, too, presented himself to the public, then went outside the courtroom and changed clothes with his brother, 'Ras. They were shaved, and their hair was cut in a similar fashion.

The spy pointed at Dude during the case, saying this was 'Ras Hannah, from whom he had bought the liquor.

"Stand up, 'Rastus", said the lawyer, John Queen.

In the back of the courtroom, 'Ras stood up, in Dude's clothing. The Judge said then that the spy was a liar or a fool and did not know the man he had bought the liquor from. He then threw out, not only Dude's case, but twenty-six other cases to which this man had witnessed!

Mark Hannah spoke truly when he said that Dude and 'Ras had been a pair of real comedians.

ELDRIDGE CALDWELL: "Well, they were that. They sure was!"

Other Cataloochans were not so lighthearted and playful. There was a man so mean that writer Joe Hall gave him the fictitious name of Zeke. He burnt "Creek George's" barn down when "Creek George" cut down his still. Worse, Zeke cut the ears off his partner who had run off with Zeke's liquor. Those little dried-up ears may still be around in a box somewhere to remind Cataloochans of those grisly times! Zeke would show them occasionally to anyone who might consider tampering with him. He died fairly early in life, leaving a long-suffering wife who had the misfortune to take a second husband as violent as her former.

But the second husband, Tom King, was not such a bad fellow, said Mark, unless somebody "broke on him". He was the subject of a most curious case which has never been completely resolved to anyone's satisfaction. The law kept out of this one!

Tom had come into the valley originally from West Virginia on a timber operation. He was a loner and had no relatives or friends to back him up in a fight.

One day he disappeared, perhaps not long after he had threatened to shoot up the church gathering where Mag Mauney Caldwell had to calm him down. The story got about that he had been murdered in Cataloochee by a bunch who had got tired of his rough ways.

Later some human rags and bones were found, and Widow Lou claimed them, gave them a decent funeral and mourned over them.

Three years later, John Queen, the former Cataloochee schoolteacher who had by then become a solicitor and district attorney in Waynesville, received a strange message. Raymond Caldwell now owns the original letter, having received it from lawyer Frank Ferguson who thought it of interest to Cataloochans.

> RAYMOND CALDWELL: "It was on regular little tablet paper, written by pencil, a nice legible hand."

Legerwood, N. C.
Aug. 30, 1933

To the State Attorney at Law
Waynesville, N. C.

Dear Sir:

On or about the 4th of July, 1930 Tom King was murdered by Burl Caldwell and Arlo Palmer and a mob at Catalooch, N.C. near the Nellie post office they killed him and buried him in the corn field when later the dogs dug him out and Burl Caldwell took him to the woods and buried him. Jim Sutton that lives at Cataloochee is a witness you can get also Brown Caldwell at Waynesville, N. C. Please don't expose these men for their Lives has been threatened. Arlo Palmer lives at Yadkin Valley, N. C., 12 miles from Lenoir, N. C. Burl Caldwell lives at Cataloochee, N. C. Please arrest these men and then get Jim Sutton and Brown Caldwell for witness. Please bring these murders to justice and punish hard.

I will not sign my name!

"It is not known whether John Queen took any action toward the accused men or not. It is just as well if he did not for they were not guilty. And Tom King turned up again in Cataloochee one fine day, hale and hearty! And no one knows, or perhaps only a few know, whose bones were mourned over by the 'widow'".

Tom did come to a predictably violent end a few years later, and Burl Caldwell died in an automobile accident in 1936. But that was another time and another place and has no relevance to Cataloochee.

Some incidents did not necessarily reflect upon the killer, as friends and relatives carefully explained. Noah Conard (a corruption of Conrad), for instance, was killed by his cousin, but in self-defense. Noah's father, who ganged up on him was shot but not killed. The cousin did a little time, said Mark, for shooting Noah's father, but not for killing Noah. The cousin, a respected evangelist, still preaches occasionally today.

When the Park Service went into operation, however, in 1929, buying up land for the Great Smoky Mountain National Park, all hell broke loose. The local folk were for taking up arms and shooting the government officials until cooler heads prevailed.

A more recent development in July and August of 1973 had echoes of the old rankling sentiment against the government's taking away land that, it was thought, rightfully belonged to the people who lived on it, used it. What transpired became quite a cause célèbre.

That July, a local bulldozer man got onto the subject of the new rangers in the park. Tom Kloos was an admirable ranger, well-liked by Mark and others. But the "doser" man said darkly: "The new ranger's already made some enemies. He'll be sorry in a dry season!" The inference being that someone might start a forest fire out of spite.

His remarks were based on an event caused by what the *Asheville Citizen-Times* called "The Cataloochee Wild Man". For several days the papers carried the story, and thousands followed its denouement with bated breath.

Young Ranger Charles Hughes, a temporary summer ranger, sturdily built, was informed by some National Pony Club members in the Park that an unusually large catch of trout had been found on the banks of a creek in Cataloochee, with the fisherman nowhere in sight. Ranger Hughes sped to the spot and found a strange, ragged, bearded creature in an old canvasback jacket blackened with wear. He asked the man for his fishing license, his name and address, and got the reply:

"I ain't got no name. I just live in these woods."

TOM KLOOS: "The man had a little dog with him. A white dog with red and black spots. About the size of a fox terrier."

"About that time, Hughes saw the barrel of a pistol sticking out of the left-hand pocket of the man's coat. And almost in the same moment the fellow started to reach across with his right hand for the gun."

Young Hughes and the man scuffled for possession of the gun which fell to the ground when the ranger managed to rip off the man's jacket. Not knowing where the gun was, Hughes ran to his jeep to get help. The desperate fellow busted Hughes' windshield with a rock as the ranger drove past him.

Later Chief Ranger Tom Kloos came back with Hughes to search for the man. But he had thoroughly disappeared by then. They did discover his gun hiding in the grass... an old Smith and Wesson .38, unloaded.

They immediately sent for Hugh Smith, a Deputy Sheriff down in Waynesville, and his bloodhound. But the dog lost the trail up Rough Fork about 1:15 A.M. near Paul's Gap, and they had to come in.

The Asheville paper picked up the story in John Parris' column on The Wild Man of Cataloochee. To his surprise, this caused quite a furor. The paper was inundated with letters. It seems everybody in the mountains knew who this man was and wanted to protect him. He was, they said, a harmless man who lived in fear of being sent to an institution, as had happened to his two brothers. So he lived off the land, constantly on the move, with only a little feist dog for a companion.

The charm of being free and "on the loose" was well understood by these descendants of pioneer mountain men. Soon it was the only topic of conversation at all mountain gatherings.

The refrain was taken up by Sam Parsons, a young guitar player from Texas, who was spending a year or two exploring the mountains and its people. For a time he lived in a small one-room cabin near the Cataloochee Divide. He and a friend, Ruffin Shackelford, had seen and talked with whom they took to be "the wild man" while they were hiking in the rugged Raven Fork and Three Forks area of the Smokies. The description fitted him; he had a little feist dog who would not leave his side.

Sam wrote "Cataloochee Wild Man", a modern ballad about this loner's predicament in a world where he could no longer legally live off the land in a government-owned wilderness such as the Great Smokies. It was an instant success. Soon it was sung and played in every cove and hollow a week or so after it was first heard. Later Sam and Ruffin were even flown to Nashville to present this song on a television show, for it was a song which echoed the sentiments of every yearning mountain man.

A bulldozer man met Sam on the Pinch Gut road a little later on and told him: "They caught him. My mother told me. They just got him over at Sugar Cove."

The news came later that law men had been up along the Cataloochee Divide in the Hemphill section and had mistaken another long-bearded mountaineer, Hubert Burgess, for the wild man. He had eluded them again.

CHAPTER 11

The Hickory Stick

(Education)

Class picture of Beech Grove School students standing in rows in front of building, Cataloochee, North Carolina, 1918. Courtesy Great Smoky Mountains National Park Archives. Beech Grove School Students - 1918 Row 1 (seated) Fred Rogers, Wilma Caldwell, Odell Lockman, Julia Burress, Pauline Palmer, Arvil Caldwell, Mattie Caldwell, Reuben Palmer. Row 2 (standing) Carl Palmer, Maggie Caldwell, Arlo Palmer, Wayne Lockman, Gudger Palmer, Paul Lockman, Blye Caldwell, Boone Caldwell, Kimsey Palmer, Maggie Palmer. Row 3 (standing) Nellie Rogers, Goldy Rogers, Laura Noland, Vernon Palmer, Lavada Palmer (teacher), Flora Palmer (teacher), Eulala Palmer, Jessie Lockman, Callie Burress, Rachel Ewart. Row 4 (by window) Guy Caldwell, Robert Palmer.

SO WIDELY APART did these fiercely independent inhabitants live from each other that, like Caesar's Gaul, they were divided into three parts: Big Catalooch', Little Catalooch', and the tiny Caldwell Fork Settlement.

That gave them plenty of breathing space. But this decentralization caused anguish to those who wanted to gather the children together for education.

No yellow school buses ever traversed this valley! Shank's mare was their favorite mode of transportation. Thus the problem was solved by following the line of least resistance; there was a schoolhouse for each settlement. In the 1920s and 30s, three of the old schoolhouses were still standing, though they had been moved or replaced many times since the days of the earliest settlers. Of these three, now only the one between Shanty Branch and Indian (or Palmer) Creek in Big Catalooch' remains.

Many years before that, the Beech Grove Schoolhouse of Big Catalooch' had gone up in flames, accidentally... so the county school board was given to believe. Some of the oldest living Cataloochans recollected that stirring night.

JARVIS CALDWELL: "(The Shanty Branch schoolhouse) was the only one I ever had except I got one year when I was six years old at the old Beech Grove schoolhouse that got burnt up. That's right down below where this one is. It was burnt up on purpose because they wanted a new schoolhouse. Got too many children for that one. It was too small."

JONATHAN WOODY: "My father, everybody called him 'Uncle Steve' and I did, too - and Uncle George Caldwell came to Waynesville to get some money from the county commissioners. All they needed was enough to pay the carpenters and get some paint. But the commissioners said, 'Sorry we can't do that... we don't have any money and you don't pay enough taxes over there... no chance of getting a new schoolhouse.'"

"Well, my father and the others had told the folks at Cataloochee that they were going to Waynesville to get a schoolhouse and they were mighty disappointed. There was a dispensary across from the courthouse at that time and they went over and got a pint of whiskey. They had brought their lunch with them so, going back, they stopped to eat and drink the whiskey. They dreaded telling the people that they couldn't have a new school."

So they rode on back to Cataloochee and it was dark when they got there. They rode by the old school and stopped to look at it. One of them said, 'I'll tell you what we'll do, we'll burn'er down.'"

"Then they went in the school and took out all the tables and little sweaters and some dinner buckets the children had left and they got the books and the blackboard. They covered the other things up with the blackboard in case it rained."

"Then they struck a match and set fire to the building and when it was burning pretty good, they got on their horses and rode off. By the time they got to Uncle Andy Caldwell's lane they looked back and it looked like the whole world was on fire."

"They shook hands and agreed never to tell what they had done until only one was left alive."

"But they soon got the money for the new schoolhouse."

"My father was the last one alive and he told me this story shortly before he died when he was 90."

JARVIS CALDWELL: "And we had the rest of the year up where Eldridge Caldwell lived... up in the old house where he was born, an old log house."

MARK HANNAH: "These modern parents who complain about transporting their children, they don't know the half of it! I can't help but think how (some) children in Cataloochee had to hike to school ten miles round trip. The family I am referring to lived one mile north of Mt. Sterling Gap—Mr. and Mrs. David B. Nelson. Their sons and daughters would hike to Little Cataloochee school by a near way trail and in the woods, sometimes getting there by 10 A.M. In the P.M. if the weather was gloomy or cold, they'd leave for home about 3:30. I personally knew this to be true as I was there in school, too. Another family (who) lived on Big Cataloochee, namely, Charlie Hall and his sons and daughters, would hike around the side of Noland Mountain and into the road near the Baptist Church and another mile to school. Others walked at least four miles round trip. I made it in two, by following an old skidding road part of the way.

What kind of life did a Cataloochee child lead during a school year which was usually only five months long in the old days because the children had to help with the harvesting?

'TINE BENNETT: "Well, we had to quit school, stop and pick apples, pull fodder, and cut tops and cut rye. I'd go about three months out of a five month school."

MARK HANNAH: "Some couldn't go long enough to graduate. Yeah, sometimes they'd shut the whole school down for a couple of weeks, and everybody got behind. Otherwise, why the children would just drop out back then. Sometimes they would have to close down for a couple of weeks to pull fodder and make molasses."

Turkey George Palmer's daughter, the gentle Flora, compiled a wonderfully graphic account of her childhood school days. She, like Jarvis Caldwell, went to the Beech Grove School for one or two years before it was burnt down.

After getting up before daylight in order to get her chores done, she would walk one and a half miles to school where they gathered around the big wood stove on winter days. She remembered the home-made shingles or shakes of the old schoolhouse. Eight-thirty was when school began. Ten-fifteen was recess with time out for Tap Hand, Base, Town Ball, Drop the Hankerchief, or any of the other childhood games. Lunch was at twelve o'clock. Most children carried an Indian basket which often held a glass of molasses and butter, sometimes biscuits, sometimes green beans, cukes, tomatoes, or corn, an apple, or blackberry pie, ham, though meat was not always included, and sweet potatoes. Heavier fare than the skimpy peanut butter and jelly sandwiches of today's schoolchildren!

The children used slates and rags and chalk for writing in Flora's day. Spelling, reading, 'rithmetic, geography, and history were the only subjects that were taught, of which history was Flora's favorite because she could remember dates.

Verlin Campbell was Flora's first school teacher. He once hit her head with a pencil... the only punishment she could ever remember receiving. Actually, Flora, to her great embarrassment, was teacher's pet. Verlin was a big rough, gruff fellow, and used to carry her around on his shoulder while she would beat him and pull his hair.

Some of the other teachers she remembered were John Queen, of the old schoolhouse which burnt down, Mattie Henry, and Jarvis Allison, who later became a truant officer in the 1920's. John Queen was destined to become District Attorney in Waynesville.

Aside from a fifteen minute recess in the afternoon, school stopped at four o'clock, at which time all the children would scramble back up into the coves and valleys to begin their chores at home. It was a long day for a Cataloochee child who had risen before daylight.

Coming to school was sometimes a traumatic experience for the smaller children, who had lingered long with their mothers in the familiar surroundings of the cabin. Young Robert Palmer was so frightened on his very first day of school when asked his name that he put his head down on his desk and said the first thing that came to mind: "Booger Man!" The name stuck for life, and the Booger Man Trail up near Caldwell Fork has been named for him.

The Woody boys, as usual, added zest to otherwise dull days of recitation.

FLOYD WOODY: "We was a-settin' at the Beech Grove school. It was the winter-time, and we had slates. Erastus, brother to Hub Caldwell, he was bent over (writing on his slate). Jim Caldwell and I got some corn and put on the stove, shelled corn... you know grains o' corn? We got that corn red hot."

Floyd began wheezing with laughter.

"He (Jim) dropped it down back o' his (Hub's) neck, and it went down and burnt a... (Floyd can't finish the sentence, he is so breathless with laughter)... He jumped! He hollered and screamed! I think they whupped me and Jim for a week! Daddy and Mother at home'ud whup us and..."

When asked if he had learned anything at school, he replied, still wheezing.

FLOYD WOODY: "No, you can tell't I didn't! Verlin Campbell, he taught over there four years. He married a Catalooch' girl, Hattie, Uncle Hiram's daughter. He'us a good teacher. Yeah, law, oh, he did, yeah, he'd make us mind. He shore... Yeah, he had to whup me nearly every day. And he put a ring on the blackboard and made me stand there with my nose in it."

"He'd teach. And he'us talkin', sayin' he hated to leave, that he's gonna not come back next year. That was the last year he taught there. And no-one wouldn't cry. We hared (hired) Leony Caldwell and Nory Woody. They could cry. Just say a little sad word to 'em. And we gave them some candy, striped, to cry. They were professional criers, both of 'em, and ever'body knowed that. They'd cry... you go to a gatherin' there, happy gatherin' round the church. Why, they'd act to cry by the time you got ready to leave."

FOLSOM DAVIS WOODY (Floyd's wife): "Why, they could turn them tears on and off just like you could a water spigot!"

FLODY WOODY: "Yeah, and you never heerd sech a bawlin' in yer life they done!"

Folsom herself, had once taught school in Cataloch' in 1913.

Mark Hannah's late brother, Fred, provided the teacher's point of view. He and another brother, Mont, both taught in Little Cataloochee. Fred was there about 1922 for two or three years after he got his teaching certificate at Berea College, Kentucky. At first, he said, he had sixty-seven pupils in the Little Cataloch' school at the maple tree, although May Barton was finally brought in as a second teacher to help alleviate the crush the next year.

The school only went through the seventh grade. Pupils were usually punished by being switched, or by being made to sweep the floor, or, like Floyd, by being forced to stand against the blackboard with their noses in a chalk ring. Another punishment, more educational, was being made to stay in and memorize the Twenty-third Psalm.

The school bell at Little Cataloch' was made of pure silver from Nevada, and is now owned by Mark's older sister, Iva Hannah Bennett, who married Bartley Bennett, and today lives in the beautiful Iotla Valley near Franklin. She taught school in the neighboring lumber settlement of Crestmont behind Mt. Sterling when she was in her early teens, and was often a substitute in Cataloochee schools.

At graduation, the school usually sent off for a dialogue to fit the occasion. There was also a valedictory address, but not the usual sort about going out into the world. The address dwelt on the forest and nature, as befitted children who grew up in a natural paradise.

Cataloochee's present to Duke University, history professor emeritus Dr. Robert Woody, was the first to admit that the valley was not noted for the higher pursuits of the mind.

ROBERT HILLIARD WOODY: "It was certainly not a breeding ground for intellectuals... Most families subscribed to a newspaper; all studied the mail-order catalogues...; some sent their children off to school... to Berea College in Kentucky or to Cullowhee nearer home."

He himself had had to leave Cataloochee at a very early age when his father died, and his mother went to Berea to study nursing. There he was subjected to more intellectual stimulation than those who remained in the valley although he still blissfully spent most of his summers with Uncle 'Tine Woody.

Others seemed to have come by an education merely because of their curiosity. Tom Porter, who came into Cataloochee as a surveyor, said that he had met old

"Fiddlin' 'Lige" Messer, up on Sugar Fork, of the Caldwell Fork Community, and had taken him for an educated man. But Mark's wife, Verda Messer Hannah, said that her grandfather, Elijah, was not formally educated. He just read a lot, as did Mag Mauney Caldwell. Mag Mauney claimed that her shoulder, always hunched up in later life, got that way from leaning toward the faint lamplight in order to read the papers. Robert Woody said that Uncle Jim Hannah of Little Catalooch', subscribed to the Tri-Weekly Constitution, and was considered to be the best-read man in the vicinity. Flora Palmer remembered, as a young girl, that after she finished her studies in the evening, if there was any time left, she might curl up with the Comfort Papers, which had little stories in them. But none had access to libraries of any size until they left the valley. Unfortunately, the Bookmobile, which often wheels along the mountain valleys today, was not available then. Mark Hannah owns a sizeable library, with emphasis on mountain material, because of his natural curiosity about his own habitat. His long stint as the ranger of Cataloochee brought him into contact with many of the great ecologists, writers, and park planners of the time.

Elizabeth Bennett, Andy's daughter, just "walked out of Cataloochee" and went to Brevard College. Old Glenn Palmer, a schoolteacher before he became deputy sheriff, went to Weaver College. Flora Messer Morrow went to Brevard College, also. Brevard College was only a two-year school when Flora Messer and Iva Hannah went there. Afterwards, Flora taught in Cataloochee. But Berea College in Kentucky was, and is, the most popular place in the mountains for getting a free education while working one's way through college.

FLORA MESSER MORROW: "I taught for fifty dollars a month. One year I had seventy-two pupils! And now they grumble if they have over twenty-five in a class. And salaries are eight hundred dollars now, I guess."

Once Will Messer moved his family to Newport, Tennessee, where he owned a building, in order to put a large part of his children in high school. But they only stayed one school term because Rachel Messer, his wife, did not like it in the city. It was probably because "the water was no good"... the excuse that one still hears today from mountaineers returning from New Jersey, or Norfolk, where they have worked and made good money.

FLORA MESSER MORROW: "Back then I had good children. Back then children were nearly all good. And now it seems they're nearly all the other way."

Others recall differently.

RAYMOND CALDWELL: "School was fun. It was a lot of fun. Too much fun, I guess. I can recall one time our teacher, Mary Davis, was standing in the door. Some of us kids throwin' rocks, and somebody hit her in the head with a rock and like to killed her. We thought we'd killed her! Knocked her out!"

"And I can remember Mr. Chambers, an old man who was substituting for his daughter. Some of the larger older boys undertook to lock him out of school... out of comin' in one mornin'"

"I must have been in the second or third grade. Little mean boys will do things, y'know. We'uns piled us up a bunch of rocks and broke all the glasses out of the schoolhouse! Throwed rocks through the glasses! When we got through with that thing, there wasn't no windows left in it so we went inside and turned over the stove. They say kids are mean today. They're no meaner than they was then."

"But the thing about it, of course, Dad had to put 'em all back in... cost the school about one hundred dollars to fix the thing back up. And he got Mr. Jake Lowe... he was sheriff about that time... to 'arrest' me and my brother, and he was goin' to take us to jail."

"Now if that wasn't the worst hurt boys you ever saw... goin' to have to take us out to jail in Waynesville, goin' to have to leave over there. We'us a-cryin'... of course, it was a put-up deal, but we didn't know it. But I never will forgit it!"

Gudger Palmer, now a retired accountant for Champion International Paper Co. in Canton, had a light-hearted view of school, too. One fine day he tossed his black hat out the schoolhouse window. The teacher asked him to fetch it. He went outside, something stirred within him, and he never went back into the schoolhouse ever again, though he did go on elsewhere to finish school later, moving up to Weaver College, and finally graduating from the University of North Carolina.

He met his wife, Mary Davis, from Iron Duff, when she lived with the Palmer family and taught at the Big Cataloochee school about 1930 when she was twenty-one years old. By then there were two teachers for fifty or sixty pupils. But she did teach all grades for one year, going back and forth between the two rooms.

The late Glenn Palmer, Gudger's older brother, had attended the old Beech Grove School, then Waynesville High School. After an education at Weaver College in Weaverville, he came back to Cataloochee and taught at the new school that was built after Beech Grove burnt. In his first year, he had fifty-six pupils, of which all were related to him except a Conard brother and sister from Little Catalooch'.

Little Cataloochee was the only place where 'Tine Bennett ever went to school. That was when the Baptist Church was still used as a school. One of his teachers was W. Clark Medford, the late Haywood historian, who 'Tine and Mark remember as so slow to turn around that a pupil could sneak up the aisle behind him and back again without being noticed.

Craggy old 'Tine said his teachers were not 'too much' strict and that he had had a pretty good time growing up.

MARK HANNAH: "Pick up a hickory about four feet long and make you be quiet! Glen Bennett was my first school teacher and the only one to whip me, for fighting. It was a good one, too!"

'TINE BENNETT: "Yeah, they sure would! The first school I ever went to there was an old log cabin. Andy Hall taught that school. He got twenty-five dollars a month, or thirty-five I won't say which, and he boarded at our house."

"Well, I'us a-settin' between my brother, Eldridge, and Floyd Burgess. We didn't have no backs to the seats, just a board across to sit on. And I got to talkin' to Eldridge and Floyd just like we're talkin' now. Andy came around and hit me in the head a few times with a big long pencil. I looked up; it scared me. I just a li'l ole tot. I said, 'If you don't quit that, I'll go home and tell my mother on you!' He turned his head to keep from laughing, and as long as I lived, he'd tell that one on me and laugh about it!"

A relation of Andy Hall's did not fare as well.

FLORA MESSER MORROW: "I can't remember whipping but one boy. And he was as big as you, Mark... Charlie Hall's boy... for stealing a French harp from another little boy. We found out that evening. And I whipped him. He said, 'I'll go home.' And next morning his daddy came bringing him back. And he said, 'Miss Messer, I don't 'low him to steal. I gave him a good one and brought him back. If he doesn't do the right thing, lay it on to him! Great big tall, lanky-looking boy. My children were good, seem to me like. Blaine Conard says I took out my spite on him! He made a country preacher."

When the settlement days were over, and Mark was the park ranger, the school bus only came part-way up the Cove Creek Road towards Cataloochee, and the Park employees had to get their children miles up there in heavy winter snows, by hook or crook, or else board them out, as some did, in Waynesville, for their high school years.

All of Mark Hannah's children finished high school in Waynesville.

MARK HANNAH: "We had to transport 'em out of there in a jeep to catch the bus. The bus... the closest place... was Bennett Turn, this side of Cove Creek Gap over there, about a mile this side of Cove Creek Gap. We got up about five o'clock. I've even got up at four o'clock in the winter time. We've transported them, and the mail boys carried them part of the time, just anyway we could."

In the early 1950s, the National Geographic published an article by Val Hart on Cataloochee Valley, and recorded something of the very last days that classes were held in the little old Shanty Branch schoolhouse.

VAL HART: "Mildred Deal, who teaches first, second, fourth and fifth grades in one room, invited us in. The children, seven healthy, happy youngsters, were shy but pleased at this invasion of their schoolyard. We admired their old fashioned double desks and their crayon drawings above the blackboard. A potbellied stove in a corner provided heat. A second room in the back, with no panes in the windows, served as a recreation room on unpleasant days."

The last class was composed of Ranger Mark Hannah's youngest son, Don, and the children of Lush Caldwell, Cole Sutton, and Fowler Pilkington, who had remained in Cataloochee as maintenance men. A picture was taken to commemorate the occasion. Soon after, it was disbanded completely, and the hickory stick would no longer serve as a symbol of discipline in Cataloochee schools, but only as the walking staff of hikers who would come in droves to explore the beauties of the valley.

CHAPTER 12

The Best Days of All
(Social Life)

The Jarvis Palmer house, used by Mark Hannah as the ranger station and family home for thirty years is the oldest standing structure in Cataloochee, and one of the oldest in the entire park. The park is working to turn the kitchen building of the house into an interpretive museum. Courtesy Great Smoky Mountains National Park Archives.

"WELL, 'TWARN'T ALL hard work in Cataloochee," said Eldridge Caldwell with a twinkle in his eye.

Even the Musters, which began purely as military meetings at the local Muster Ground near Cove Creek Gap, changed character over the years, becoming rousing social events in which the rollicking inhabitants of Cataloochee and neighboring Cove Creek, Fines Creek, and White Oak were participants. If they could get to town in the fall, The Big Muster at the courthouse was a downright lively occasion, so claimed an eminent historian of Western North Carolina.

PRESTON ARTHUR: "On the second Saturday of October each year, there was a general muster at each county seat, when the various companies drilled in battalion or regimental formation; and each separate company met on its local muster grounds quarterly, and on the Fourth of July the commanding officers met at the court house to drill. The Big Musters called most of the people together, and there was much fun and many rough games to beguile the time. Cider and ginger cakes were sold, and many men got drunk. There was also some fighting, but seldom with stones or weapons. There were shooting matches at which a young steer was divided and shot for, foot races, wrestling bouts..."

FLORA PALMER MEDFORD: "I remember I heard 'em talkin' about goin' up to Cove Creek Gap (to the Muster Ground). That was 'fore I was big enough to go."

Before Flora's time, the meetings at the Muster Ground had ceased altogether, except in the memories of the elderly. What was true of these Quarterly Musters was true of the church Quarterly Meetings, also. Originally begun with another purpose in mind, as a religious event, the Quarterly Meeting seems to live in the minds of its participants as The Big Picnic, enlivened by rousing rhetoric from visiting preachers.

Even community work was turned into work-play parties, with the sting taken out of hard labor by general hilarity. Corn huskings, quiltings, barn-raisings, bean-stringings, hog killings... all had their joyful sides.

ROBERT HILLIARD WOODY: "Cooperation was both a matter of practical necessity and an avenue for social activity. A house-raising or a log-rolling, physically speaking, required more hands than two. The convivial nature of these occasions was appreciated by the men; the bean stringing and quilting parties of the women combined pleasure and work to advantage."

IVA HANNAH BENNETT (Mark's sister and wife of Bartley Bennett): "Once we were having a great time in a bean-breaking. Everyone was working hard and getting a large pile of those green beans ready for pickling in a 25-gallon barrel. Some of the girls would be stringing (i.e., pulling the strings from the beans). Others would be breaking the green beans into pieces about 3/4 inches in length. When the job was about finished, some games were played. 'Thimble' was a favorite. While the fun was going, some mischievous boy put some liquor in the water pail. This happened at one of the deacon's homes, and my! did he get hot about 'that stinkin' stuff a-smellin' his water bucket!' Maybe last a week."

Of all these homely working affairs, cornshuckings seem to have been the most fun. With shining eyes, an old man recalled those times.

JARVIS CALDWELL: "... Cornshuckin's, we called 'em, huskin's, and all 'at. Big time! They would generally have a big gallon jug of whiskey in the middle of the corn pile. Yeah!"

When Mark Hannah was a boy of fifteen, he had gone over to Big Cataloochee on a bear hunt with his father. But first he got conned into doing some work for canny old Hiram Caldwell.

MARK HANNAH: "The weather was rough; it was pouring rain. Dad and I decided to go over to see Uncle Hiram Caldwell and Eldridge and see when they predicted the rain would stop so we could try the dogs on this big bear we had heard of up on Purty Land Mountain.

"Uncle Hiram suggested that we all go over to the Dillard Cove and shuck corn, for a pastime 'while we rested'. When the group rounded up, there were Hiram, Dillard, Eldridge and Boone Caldwell, Floyd Harrell, Mack and Mark Hannah. Four were riding horses, Dad and Uncle Hiram, Dillard and myself (I had a sprained ankle). It was less than a mile to the Dillard Cove farm. The corn was stored in an old log cabin. Looked to be fifty bushels or more in the pile. The shucks started flying and the old fellows started lying and stretching the truth. My Country! what a good evening we spent there... working for fun. Since I was only fifteen, I done most of the listening. If I had only had a tape recorder in those days, it would have been something great. One fellow would tell a good one... maybe a coon hunting story. Then another man would butt in before he hardly finished with another story of some strange incident that had occurred."

"After the corn was all shucked and piled in the crib and a big lock placed on it, we returned to the woodpile and cut Aunt Lizzie Howell, as Uncle Hiram would call his wife, some wood. More jokes were being spread, as the sun went over Spruce Mountain, than I had ever heard in one day."...

Traditional holidays were rarely celebrated in conventional ways, nor with as much fanfare as is associated with them today. Flora, daughter of "Turkey George" Palmer, presented a rather sober picture of Christmas up on Pretty Hollow Creek. Yes, they did talk about Santa Claus, however, and did manage to hang up a little stocking.

FLORA PALMER MEDFORD: "Oh, we'd find an orange and a pretty apple, and some stick candy. That's about all. Well, anyhow, Pop and Mom, they'd get it and slip it in the house, y'know. Then, after we went to bed, they'd distribute it around. It was a long time we didn't know that there was (no) Santa Claus. And I was kinda disappointed when I found out it wasn't."

MARK HANNAH: "I remember that somebody stole a chicken once on Christmas Eve from their best neighbor so they'd have chicken and dumplin's on Christmas Day! (hearty laughter from him) It was the way some people celebrated! Stolen chickens made better dumplin's!"

"Someone pulled a dirty trick over at Little Cataloochee on Christmas Eve. They stole a neighbor's horse, to cover up their identity, and rode to the house of a very likeable and highly respected citizen in our community. They called at his door at night. Hello, Hello! And the good man came to the door, in his underwear. The door was opened. Here came a bucket of ice water into his face. Oooch! And the rider mounted and galloped away. Next day, the man had dry clothes on, and he followed the horse tracks about 1/2 mile to a neighbor's barn. But the owner said he had not ridden his horse during the night. Who was the rider? That's the 64 dollar question!"

ELDRIDGE CALDWELL: "We didn't have no big celebration for Christmas. They rabbit-hunted quite a bit on Christmas Day, just for the fun of the thing. Yeah, rabbit-huntin' and Christmas trees, and maybe a few little parties round... little dances, wasn't too big."

Jonathan Woody, a descendent of the original settler by the same name, is now a retired banker living in Waynesville. It's hard to find a touch of the country boy when one sees him at the local country club in his fine sports jacket. But he wrote fervently of the remembered joys of a simple Christmas in Catalooch'.

JONATHAN WOODY: "Christmas was observed at Cataloochee sixty-five years ago somewhat differently from our present celebrations. Our father would haul a wagon load of farm products to Waynesville in the middle of December and exchange them for clothes, shoes, a box of stick candy and one orange for each member of the family. He would never show the purchases but would lock them in a closet and later they would be put under the Christmas tree. The trip to Waynesville required three days."

"Never had we seen a tree that impressed us so much. It evidently was the personal touch, as it was decorated with popcorn that was grown in the garden, with galax leaves, holly. Also, candles our mother made by using an old mold. Each child was helped in making a present for every member of the family. Our mother and sisters would bake a batch of pies, sweet bread and apply layer fruit cake. It was all mighty good eating."

"There were three families of renters that lived on our father's place, and our parents would give each family a ham, some fresh pork ribs and a part of a beef we had fattened and slaughtered. Everyone shared. There were no telephones, radio or TV to interrupt. We enjoyed each other... it was a good life and we will always remember those days with a lot of pleasure."

Thanksgiving in Cataloochee was not noted, as it is today, as the festival of the turkey and the Pilgrim, but rather as the day of the traditional Bear Hunt. Strangely, even the family of Turkey George Palmer, famous as the greatest turkey hunter of all Cataloochee, failed to have turkey on that day, plentiful though the wildbirds were in the area.

FLORA PALMER MEDFORD: "We always had an extra dinner. And sometimes some of the friends in. We'd have a baked hen. Not because there were no wild turkeys around, but we never happened to have them on those occasions."

When Mark Hannah and Eldridge Caldwell related that Thanksgiving was the time for the traditional bear hunt and also the wild hog race, an outsider mistakenly conjured up a picture of racing hogs, as at a dog track, for sport and betting, but was later told, with muffled laughs, that a 'race' was the same as a hunt. They would race the small hogs or 'ridgerooters', four or five year olds, each weighing two or three hundred pounds, way back in the mountains, sometimes to Hell's Half Acre or Piney Butt Mountain.

Easter seems to have had no great religious significance in Cataloochee... no massed lilies on the altars of the two little churches, if there were any flowers at all.

But the custom of Easter eggs prevailed, at least for the children. Mark remembered Easter egg hunts at Will Messer's, Bartley Bennett's, 'Mericus Hall's, Mack Hannah's, and also at the Little Cataloochee School.

FLORA PALMER MEDFORD: "We celebrated by having scrambled eggs for breakfast. Then they'd let us color some and dye (them)... then crack'em. Y'know how people (hit them together)? It's who cracks the egg wins. Yeah, we'd do that some. Yeah, we did a little... on a small scale."

The very mention of Halloween brought a scornful retort from her.

FLORA PALMER MEDFORD: "I never <u>heard</u> of Halloween until I was grown. And I think the least of Halloween of anything that's a-goin'!"

Conversely, the Fourth of July seemed to have been the memorable holiday in everyone's life, perhaps because freedom and independence were always the true religion of every mountaineer! Boys and girls celebrated and courted and played games at the big Fourth of July picnic held sometimes at the Kerr Place, as Flora recalled, where they'd often meet up with Little Cataloochee folk. The Kerr Place had been built as a hunting lodge, and was popular as a picnic place because of the great banjo player, "Squire" Mitch Sutton who lived there for several years. "We always like to go down there because he'd pick the banjer and sing."

MARK HANNAH: "In 1916 a group of Little Cataloochee people went to the Kerr Place. We ate a picnic lunch on the grass field just north of the bridge. Some in the group were Mae McCullough (Hannah), Agnes, Iva, and Maggie Messer, Laura, Roy Albert, Fred and Mont Hannah and others. (They) were making pictures with a small box camera and waiting for the Palmers and Caldwells from Big Cataloochee. They came on horses about three P.M. I recall one girl's name, Ida Palmer. She was rated the most beautiful girl in Turkey George's family. There were about six or eight girls and boys. I believe Mag Ola Caldwell and Faye were there. We enjoyed a good day and then returned home late in the P.M. on foot."

Little Cataloochans travelled more often in a different direction, however.

MARK HANNAH: "We had a picnic, hiking to the top of the Balsam... having a picnic was a big day every Fourth of July. Up top of Mt. Sterling. We'd play Tap-Hand up there in the old field. Tap-Hand, one of those old games. Hold hands around this way in a big circle, and one fellow'd tap and went around the ring, and the other'n see if he could catch him. The old Tap Hand Ring. Boys would tap the girls. And the girls would tap the boys. Foot race. Ha, ha!".

Before Mark's time, Fourth of July had been celebrated with shooting matches out at the Muster Ground, so his grandfather and his Uncle Logan told him.

The late Fred Hannah, Mark's older brother, a former Cataloochee schoolteacher of striking dignity, served iced tea one hot summer's day on the verandah of his beautiful home in the Patton Community of Franklin where he was head of Macon County Areo, Inc. and told of the celebrations of old Catalooch'.

FRED HANNAH: "After almost any celebration in Big Cataloochee, such as a graduation, you could see your way home by the light of pistol fire. Everyone had pistols, and they were shot off like firecrackers... straight up in the air. "

Box suppers, too, were high social events for the young people. Once the lamps were stolen from Little Cataloochee church. Even this was a reason to celebrate! Money had to be raised to buy new lamps.

MARK HANNAH: "This was a great bunch of fun for the young folks when the parents got together and decided they needed to raise some money for a good cause, as they always said it. You see we had to advertise for about two weeks prior to the box supper. All the boys would write to any girls in Big Cataloochee or Big Creek, sometimes White Oak boys and girls would come to help out with the worthy cause."

"This box supper was on or about 1914. There were persons from all the creeks and valleys. Some of the loggers from Swallow Fork in the Big Creek area, came over Mt. Sterling Ridge. They were moneyed men, we thought, because all those 'guys' were making two dollars a day and their board. They could well afford to throw some 'long green' and pay for the girl's box of their choice, eat supper with her and walk home with her if she o.k.'d the deal. If she didn't, you walked with the menfolks or by yourself. When the boxes were all in and about ready for sale, the banjo and the fiddle were tuned up..."

Dancing was the great outlet for nearly all members of the community who were not lame. Everyone had something to say on the subject, whereas they might have been hesitant or shy or 'disremembering' on other things.

'TINE BENNETT: "We used to have them old-time dances. We call 'em squar' dances now. We'd just crowd up, gangs of us. We just jumped around all over the floor. Some of us could dance, and some couldn't. Now, <u>Milas</u> could dance. He was a real dancer. We always had a special caller. Floyd Burgess used to call them dances for us."

MARK HANNAH: "Sometimes we'd have an old-time square dance at someone's home. Everybody that wanted to would gather up at that house. We didn't require so much space. Usually dance in the dinin' room or someplace like that where there's a little more room. We'd go up some of those creeks, went up to Carl Woody's and had a few good plays up there. Sometimes up to Willie Messer's up near the Davidson Gap. The stringband was Willie and Myrtle Messer, guitars, Cal Messer, fiddle, and myself on the autoharp."

Jarvis Caldwell discussed the differences in square dancing technique, then and now. Mountain folk several years ago didn't go in for the more violent buckdancing, but did a sort of shuffle, hardly picking their feet off the ground, merely slipping and sliding comfortably along to the music. Bonnie and Jarvis Caldwell both agreed that nowadays "folks did a lot of kickin' up their heels. Clog, mostly."

ELDRIDGE CALDWELL: "Yeah, we more or less did smooth dancin'. We didn't do that cloggin' and all that. We didn't do that at all. That come out later... since my dancin' days."

It's been said that the Texas cowboy invented buck dancing as an exercise after a long day in the saddle. He would squat and kick his legs rapidly, rather like a Cossack, in order to keep his circulation going. They called it "Weaving the Buckskin." Someone exercised to music one day, in a standing position, and buckdancing was born.

Jarvis claimed that no one frowned on dancing, but another Caldwell told an amusing story about Jarvis' own mother, Mag Mauney Caldwell.

ELDRIDGE CALDWELL: "Bunch of us boys decided to go up there one night for a li'l party, have a li'l dance. And we knew Aunt Mag would object to it, but we went on, anyway. I believe I was the one, I said, let's have a li'l dance. Aunt Mag said, Lord, no, child, Lord, no, can't have no dance. Somebody else said, well, we'd wanted to play something, said we might just play Virginia Reel. Well, she said, that suits me just fine. I ain't played that since I'us a girl, said we used to play that a lot. But it wasn't no dance! So we started and went ahead and had our dance, and she joined in!"

PEARL VALENTINE CALDWELL: "At the third ramp convention, they had it up here at Black Camp Gap, and she was up there. Someone had a movie camera, and they got her. They'us playin' the ole Virginia Reel, and she was a-pattin'. And, oh, that hurt her awful bad when she found she was on the picture! A-pattin' for that dance!"

Patting and aiding, abetting, and encouraging someone else to dance. Some Western Carolina history mentioned that, in the old days, a man was actually fined for "patting" for some young boys to dance. It may have been a Sunday fine in this case.

MARK HANNAH: "The first Ramp (wild onion) Convention was five men at or near Black Camp Gap (out of Cataloochee). Three of those men were plum full of ramps and booze. Dewey was a heavy drinker. Floyd (Woody) was so full of talk or something that he was hauled home later in the P.M. Floyd says, Fellows, let's not come here next year like we are today. Let's invite all our friends and make it sorter like a convention. Yes, yes, let everybody have a good time with us. This was the beginning of the Ramp Conventions."

Mark smiled as he recalled that, as a young boy, he had been enticed up the mountain by other boys saying the school girls would pat for Rachel Ewart to dance. She pulled up her skirts above her knees and danced on the foot bridge in the light of the moon, apparently unaware that she was being observed.

Mark said: "I never saw such dancing!"

But as soon as she caught sight of him, hidden in the bushes, she abruptly dropped her skirts and fled toward Mitchell Top Mountain.

Mark good-humouredly reminded her of this after she became an old lady living out her days in a nursing home in Clyde. She could still sing snatches of ballads on cue, with only shreds of memory from her childhood, which Mark says, was a very hard one. Her bright sparkling eyes, still had a hint of that child who danced with such abandon in the moonlight by herself in 1919 in wild Cataloochee.

ROBERT HILLIARD WOODY: "The first money I ever earned was by dancing at a Cataloochee wedding, while someone, probably Mitch Sutton, picked the banjo."

When the Champion Lumber Company had their operation behind Mt. Sterling, or The Balsam, as Cataloochans were fond of calling it, Dr. Woody recalled: "They brought in a lot of Italians. These Italians would set up their own logging camp, and they were quite sociable and friendly. Some of them used to come over to Uncle 'Tine's. They would bring their accordion, and all men... danced to the accordion. Whether the dancing was authentic, no one ever knew. It seemed a little strange to us."

It is characteristic of Carolina mountain men often to dance solo or with each other, as the Greek men do, improvising intricate steps, and competing in dancing. Roy Smith, a famous bearhunter of Maggie Valley, said that Mark himself, after a hunt at The Big Cut, had danced all night against Rufe Sutton, a well known dancer, in competition for the bear liver, a great prize. But Mark scoffed at this, saying the story was a fable.

MARK HANNAH: "Some of the boys called it buckdancing. The best of them were (Big Creek) Mitchel Sutton, Tilson Griffith, John Hicks, and Ben Sutton. The first one mentioned danced at age eighty to our string band in Cataloochee. He used more steps to the tunes than any other person I've seen."

A special kind of entertainment, ever since pioneer days and the Muster Ground, has been the beef or turkey shoot, according to Jarvis Caldwell. Usually home-made muzzle loaders or hog rifles were used in these competitions, with the winner carrying off a side of beef or a turkey as a prize. Tom Alexander's Cataloochee Dude Ranch, now removed from the Park, carried on the old muzzle-loader's beef shoot tradition up on Fie Top until Tom died a few years ago. Now the city of Waynesville retains the tradition during their Folk Festival week in July.

A more barbaric kind of entertainment was the animal fight, a small variation of the old Roman arena baitings. When Mark Hannah and the author were sitting with 'Tine Bennett in Sylva on his verandah, the two men laughed about events of their childhood.

MARK HANNAH: "Did you ever tie a 'possum's tail to a cat's tail and throw it over a clothes line war (wire) and see 'em fight?"

'TINE BENNETT: "I've done that, too."

MARK HANNAH: "Hair was flyin', wadn't it?"

ELIZABETH POWERS: "Well, I would think the cat would win."

MARK HANNAH: "It's hard to tell... that 'possum, if he can't get away, he <u>does fight</u>!"

Children seem to have had an enormous amount of fun in old Cataloochee, although most of their toys were spare and entirely home-made. Mark remembers the simple pleasure of a whistle. Dr. Woody told me, as he sat in his book-lined study near Duke University:

"I was thinking about the toys we had back in the hills. The biggest thing that ever happened to me was that I got a little red wagon for Christmas. Now you know, something like that you did't get very often. We had a thing, I'm not sure what it was called, I'll call it a ratchet. It was made of wood about so long, and at one end was a kind of sprocket arrangement with a handle. And you could make that thing go around and make a lot of noise. A thing like that would be very hard to find nowadays, but we had one."

MARK HANNAH: "I've seen this one, too. I could also make one. I called it a Rattle Trap. Robert Hilliard (Woody) and I made hickory bark whips, willow whistles, crossbows, and searched the fields for Indian arrowheads. We also used homemade paddles or bats on the incoming bumble bees to our north side chimney that was mud and rock. We could pop 'em real good, too!"

ROBERT HILLIARD WOODY: "And we made other playthings. Uncle 'Tine made this thing for me: it was a little, well, hard to describe, well a stick of wood with a head on the end of it, and you could shoot it out through this reed with a string and a bow. You see, the bow was attached to the... and I used to slip around out to the porch and try to kill flies with it. Hard to describe, but sort of like a bow and arrow except that it had a tunnel for this rod to shoot out through."

These were cross-bows, explained Mark.

'TINE BENNETT: "We made a little wagon. Cut down a black gum and cut off the wheels, about two inches thick. Tilman Early, well, he helped me and Eldridge and Bartley make one of them wagons. He had a big ole auger, worked by hand. He bored the holes through the center. Everything was wood about it. It wasn't a piece of iron about it."

MARK HANNAH: "Use a piece of hickory wood for the axle, that'll do it."

'TINE BENNETT: "Yeah, yeah. And putt a tongue, split the white oaks up, and putt a tongue to the front wheels, yeah. He fixed it so we could work little steers to it. I don't know the little steers we broke. George and Reuben had a big drove of cattle, and we'd hook up some of 'em steers."

MARK HANNAH: "We had a small yoke to fit the calves and a large one for the big steers. Then when a boy would jump astride a steer back, you would see some fun. The steer would run a spell and stop real quick. The rider would usually go over the steer's head. Once a boy had one steer named Old Buck. He had a double yoke. A runaway took place and almost killed the boy. A neighbor came to get them loose and began on the boy's side first. (The boy shouted) 'Stop that! Unhook Ole Buck first. I'll stand (but) he may not."

On Little Cataloochee, Fred Hannah remembered that rope had been too scarce and precious to use for their jump ropes, so the pliant ginger vine was used instead. His brother, Mark, retorted that those ginger vine ropes were really rough on your ankles if you failed to jump quickly enough!

Though the children's games that were played at home and school were similar to those played by children today, there were slight variations. "Town Ball", for instance, was not quite the same as baseball. Flora Palmer Medford said that girls, also, played Town Ball...

'TINE BENNETT: "We never had a baseball. We didn't know what a baseball was. But we made a ball about the same size as a baseball to play Town Ball with."

MARK HANNAH:" Take a yam stocking and ravel it out, make a ball of it. Everybody on Sunday would gang up at some boy's house. And we'd have a ball game. Played... we called it, Town Ball. It's a little bit on the style of baseball."

His companion, 'Tine Bennett, relived a game of the past, his craggy face alive with excitement.

'TINE BENNETT: "Yeah, that's one we'd play out in the field if it was pretty Sunday afternoon. Gonna make the whole round. If you made a home run, you got another chance at it, then and go down here and th'ow the ball up here to 'im, and he knock it down in the woods whar it couldn't be found easy. And he'd round them bases agin'!"

That was on Little Cataloochee. On Big Cataloochee Eldridge Caldwell claimed they played Indian Ball, a game similar to the lacrosse-type ball game played by their Cherokee neighbors, but without the same kind of sticks with the little woven leather catch pouch on the end.

It was quite natural for Cataloochans to adopt this rather rough game, as the Big Cove Indians lived just beyond the western ridge of the Cataloochee watershed, where both Indians and whites grazed their cattle on the natural balds... Perhaps they even played ball together to while away those long dreamy periods when the men all went to the mountains in a group, herded the cattle, and ate those little speckled trout.

The more simple school games, besides Tap Hand and jump rope were the familiar Crack-the-Whip, Base, like Prisoner's Base, marbles, Mumblety-Peg, and Ant'ny-Over (Anthony-Over). This last we scarcely hear of today, but it was then very common.

FLOYD WOODY (chortling): "And then we'd get around the barn and play... we'd call it cobbin' each other. We'd break corn cobs and th'ow them at each other. We'd peep around and catch one, why, we'd th'ow and try to hit 'im. The barn would be... the spring of the year after it's empty. And we'd get all over the barn."

VERDA MESSER HANNAH (Mark's wife, daughter of Will Messer): "Another game we played in the barn that was filled with hay was 'I Spy' or 'Whoopie Hide'.

Very often the Little Cataloochee girls and sometimes visiting girls would gang up at our house for fun. We would start this game by selecting one to hide her eyes, or blind them with a handkerchief, (or) maybe (with) her hands, while all the others hid themselves in the hay loft. The blinded person would count to a hundred, then say, 'Bushel of wheat and bushel of rye! All a'nt hid, holler I!' If no one hollered 'I', then the hunt was on. If anyone could get to the spot or base of the caller before they were seen, they scored. If the caller saw anyone hiding, he would holler 'I spy' and call their name, such as Ola, Eula, Vera, Valerie, Cora, Bea, Myrtle, Zala, Milia, Maggie, Ressie, or Ella. Those that were spied would come to the base and wait until the entire group won or lost. Then another one would do the counting."

In order to appreciate these simple games, one has to understand the boundless energy and natural resources of Cataloochans. There were no sophisticated toys of rich children to envy. Often, there was no need for any kind of toy, merely the imagination and delight of the participants, as in 'Tine Bennett's joyful description of a game of Blind Man's Buff, a game known in 18th Century France by the painter, Boucher, but played, doubtless, with more verve in Little Cataloochee than the French children played it.

'TINE BENNETT: "We'd play Blindfold. We'd all us young, kinda my age, a little older or a little younger than me. We'd meet at some neighbor's house and play Blindfold till midnight. Take a ole red hankerchief or a towel or somethin'. And the feller's blindfold, whether it's a boy or a girl. Well, he was tryin' to catch ever'body. And we just got around him. All had big houses then. I mean a big room. That was the best days of all of it, to tell the truth."

Mischievous boys could always create a rousing diversion out of the material at hand.

ELDRIDGE CALDWELL: "For a little extry excitement, we'd herd up all the cattle we could in the wintertime and break 'em to ride, seein' who was the best rider! Had a bunch herded up there at the Mull meadow one time in the barn. We'us 'bout to get lawed on that. Man came along and caught us down there."

"We'd tell our parents we were goin' 'possum huntin'. We'd get our lanterns and our ole 'possum dogs and take off like we're goin' 'possum huntin'. We'us goin' down there to ride those steers. Harley Palmer had about forty, I believe it was."

"Hard to ride? Oh, yes! Buck? Yes! You ain't never been th'owed from anything like that!"

"Harley did't do anything. He wasn't the one who caught us. But they 'bout to get us in court for it. We weren't hurtin' the cattle at all. We had to go out to Waynesville. But they just threw it out (of court). There was nothin' to it, y'know... Put *us* to a little bother, though."

Widowed Flora, gamely living by herself in Iron Duff just before she died, shyly talked about her father Turkey George Palmer. She spoke in a small fragile voice.

Turkey, she told me, delighted in playing games with his dogs. He would run in the front door, his dogs after him, and race out the back, the whole pack after him. Then he would run in the front again, in an endless circle. One could imagine her Mother's looks as that tribe came whirling exuberantly through her newly cleaned house like a twister.

Peck's Bad Boy of Big Cataloochee and Rough Fork seems to have been, according to his own accounts, Floyd Woody, that mastermind of practical jokes and other escapades. Everyone agreed with Floyd; the Woody boys in general were said to have pulled more than their share of the pranks.

A typical remark was: "The Woodys, they's bad to git into chickens! They'd git their tail full of buck shot. Least that's what we heard."

The butt of many of the Woody brothers' pranks was Uncle Andy Caldwell, who was their closest neighbor, living only a mile from the Steve Woody place on Rough Fork. They could always 'get a rise' out of him, and usually got away with the joke, too.

FOLSOM WOODY: "We always liked Uncle Andy. But I had a idea that if he'd a-found out who did those tricks, we wouldn't have a-liked him when he got through!"

FLOYD WOODY: "Uncle Andy had a big field there. And we got cow bells way in the night, y'know. Well, Folsom, and m' sister went to one end of the field, and we went to the other'n, right below his house. Well, we commenced ringin' these cowbells in his cornfield, and he thought the cows had broken in and was eatin' up his corn… y'know what I mean, corn growin' up. And he got out, hollerin' for his dogs, and come down through the field a-hollerin' and screamin' 'way in the night, y'know. We could hear him hollerin' Hey! here… and so, when he come close to me, I'd quit ringin' my bell. Well, they'd be at the other end, they'd ring their bells. Well, he'd go yon way. He got nearly to them, I'd commence back a-ringin' my bell (Floyd can't finish, he is so breathless from laughing) Hee, Hee…"

Pranks with animals, like Eldridge's riding the steers, were commonplace in Cataloochee.

FLOYD WOODY: "We had a fish pond above the Uncle Steve house, and sometimes we boys would baig (beg) not to go to church. We had a buck sheep, and we went up there. We'd stick a stick down here at the fish pond. And then put a coat on that there stick and get behind it. And that buck would run to hit us, to butt us, y'know. They'd fight; they'd butt; they'd fight, y'know. Well, we'd just jump aside, and he'd go into the hole of water!"

Humans got the water treatment, as well.

FLOYD WOODY: 'Tine Bennett, he's a visitin' us from Little Cataloochee… we'd go and see each other on Saturday night. So he come over there to spend Saturday night with us… in the winter time. It's pretty cold. Ossie, m' brother, and 'Tine went to bed. And when they got asleep, why we got a big tub of water and filled it up. 'Tine had rode a horse over there, mule. And then I run upstairs in the loft and told 'Tine to git up, that his mule was hung down in the barn. He jumped out of bed and jumped in this big tub of ice water, and he went: 'Hoo! Hoo! Hold on, Ossie, hold on!"

Their cousin tricked his Uncle, too, in the same Woody spirit.

ROBERT HILLIARD WOODY: "I fooled my uncle ('Tine) once. I found a horse-shoe-shaped piece of metal that people used to wear on their heels (called a heel iron). So I took that and pressed it down in the dirt along this path from the barn toward the smoke-house. And I called out and showed him... somebody... oh, he got quite excited. He was afraid somebody had stolen the meat out of the smokehouse. In the meantime, I had thrown this thing away in the branch..."

The classic Cataloochee practical joke of all time, as told by Mark's elderly parents, Mack and Fannie Hannah, was recorded for the Library of Congress by Professor Joseph Hall. The local copy of this record is so worn and unintelligible from loving use that Mark offered his private account.

MARK HANNAH: "Robert V. Hannah had returned to Little Cataloochee to visit his brothers and his parents, Mr. and Mrs. Mack Hannah. One beautiful afternoon, he decided to go for a walk via the old orchard to see if the 'Mountain Boomer' apple tree was ready to gather some ripe apples. When he found the apple tree and ripe apples, there was a swarm of honeybees hanging on the limbs among the apples. Also, he discovered bear-tracks and apples partly eaten by bears... two bears, a large one and a cub. He decided to leave the beartracks, honeybees, apples and all, where he found them and go home to tell the news. It was sundown when he arrived at Dad's house. He spread the news that night."

"Next day my nephew, Johnny Hannah, was staying there and working in the tobacco field with me. Just after lunch that day Johnny decided to borrow a bee veil and nail keg to carry the bees in, and the smoker from me. He would go get those bees! Johnny asked all or anyone to go with him. We suspicioned that he was scared of bears. No one would offer to go along."

"Robert and I watched him leave the house, going to the orchard about two and one-half miles away. I went to Dad's house and found him taking an afternoon nap. I awoke him and told him that Johnny had gone to get the honey bees, and we could see he was scared to death, almost, by himself. Dad said, you boys, check here closely and see if he has taken a gun with him. The check was, all guns are here. Dad said, I'll give either one of you a dollar if you will take this bearskin that has the feet and toes on it, go out there and scare him."

"Robert answered, I'll go. I okayed the deal and he was on his way, rather fast, because he wanted to go a near way to beat Johnny there, so as to hide himself in a briar-patch. Robert hid near the apple tree and soon."

"He saw that Johnny did not find any honey bees. Then Johnny started to roll himself a cigarette of Prince Albert. A noise caused Johnny to look, and Robert reared up with the bearskin over him! Johnny whirled around and jumped a ten rail fence and ran to a tree to climb away from the huge bear, and he decided it was too far to the first limb. Johnny then barked woof-woof, like a dog, trying to scare the big mother bear away, but this didn't work. Robert had the bearskin over him and reared up, making a noise."

(From Mack Hannah's original record: "Johnny jumped a fence and never knocked a rail off. He wan't just a-runnin' a little, they said he was tryin' to fly! They said he was a-steppin' on the ground so hard that he went in shoe-mouth deep!").

"Johnny left there making leaps over ten feet apart down a steep hill and never slowed any until he arrived at the neighbor house 3/4 miles away. Almost exhausted, he told his cousin that 'the biggest damn bear' he had ever seen had been trying to catch him. 'I ran as fast as I could and the bear didn't follow me. It must be that old she-bear because I saw its' foot one time.'"

"Robert ran out of the briars into open field to see the race, but it was over - Johnny was at the house of the neighbor. Johnny rested a few minutes and went home to see me in the tobacco field. When he arrived, I was by far the busiest man, too busy to look up! The sweat was still running from his neck onto his chest. Johnny says, 'Uncle, where is Robert?' I answered that he must be out at Dad's house 'cause a city slicker can't stand tobacco cutting. 'Well, then, I saw the damnest biggest bear out yonder at the Orr Place and it almost got me. I believe it was that old She Bear. I saw one of its paws one time. I tried to climb a tree but it was too far up the tree to the first limb!' I said, 'Did you run fast down that steep slope?' 'Yes, I did everything that was in me to outrun him. I left your bee veil, nail keg, and smoker there at the spring. You can go back and get them, for I'm not facing that bear anymore.'"

"He began to get suspicious because I laughed so much. Then he decided it must be a joke pulled on him by Robert. Later when he saw Robert looking so innocent, but showing guilt every other way, Johnny told Robert, 'I'll get even with you if I live!'"

That kind of practical joke was child's play according to the daring Woodys, however.

"The most dangerous one we ever done," breathed Floyd Woody excitedly, "... Indian come over there... Jess Swayney was the Indian's name. He'd come and pick the banjer and spend the night."

"He come in there one evenin', and he says, 'Do you boys like heap fun?' We told him, yes! He said, 'Floyd, you go up yonder and get some poke berries, and me and Ossie go down here and get an elderberry stem for a blowpipe.' So, we went ahead and made the juice, some red juice out of them pokeberries."

"And they loaded this gun up. This Indian had what we call an owlhead pistol. I don't know why they called them that. But anyhow he had an owlhead pistol."

"Yeah. And we waited till ten o'clock, went down just 'fore bedtime, knocked on Uncle Andy Caldwell's door. Yeah, we knocked on his door."

"Ossie and the Indian, Jess Swayney, stood back out in the yard, y'know, with this old owlhead pistol to shoot straight up in the air."

"When he opened the door, why I squirted this hyere red berries in his face, and he gave a swipe... thought it's blood, and he said: 'Lord ha' mercy! I'm killed!' And here he had a lamp in his hand (Floyd can hardly continue the story, he is wheezing so with laughter), dropped hit, and here come two women, his wife, Aunt Charlie (Charlotte), and Annie Caldwell, his daughter-in-law."

"And we run, y'see, down in the field and hid. You never heerd the like in your life! He screamed murder. When Uncle Hiram heerd this a-screamin' and a-hollerin', they run to 'im. And come a ha'r (hair) a-runnin' over us in the field hid. We never thought about anyone a-comin' to them. They come as clost as that television... yeah... in ten feet of, nearly. And they went on and tuck on and screamed so that when their Mother come and seen that blood, that red stuff on the floor, why, they thought he's really shot, y'know. They's all a-screamin' and a-hollerin'."

"We got in a (fight), Indian and my brother. I jumped on 'em, claimed that they really shot him, that they must have made a mis-take and shot Uncle Andy. And we got into an argument over that. Yeah, I got scared, it went on so long."

"So we went on back. And we seen that we'd done such a turrible crime. About four o'clock in the mornin', we got that Indian up and give 'im his breakfast and said now you git back in Swain County! They never would tell nothin'."

"And so they rode up and down and got people everywhere, tryin' to locate evidence. And said they'd law or prosecute ever who did that. But they never did find no one that done it!"

CHAPTER 13

Two by Two

(Men and Women)

When Charles Morrow and Flora Messer were married in 1916 at the Little Cataloochee Baptist Church, W.G.B. Messer offered his daughter Flora her choice of some land or $1,000.00. Flora chose the cash. After their marriage, the couple left on their honeymoon in a surrey with fringe on top. W.G.B. Messer hired a Knoxville caterer to cater the affair. This was the largest such celebration ever held in Little Cataloochee.
Courtesy Great Smoky Mountains National Park Archives.

Every spring, in answer to the pull of the vernal tides, the boys and girls of Cataloochee would come prancing out, breathing the fecund smell of the earth, feeling the strange surge of spirits after a long winter spent close to the hearth studying, mending, weaving, sewing, carving, repairing, quilting, and minding their elders.

Even though the ancient rituals of spring were repeated every year, the world would present itself as a washed slate with a brand new message for them to write upon it. And most of the young people would pair off, as if to dance a Virginia Reel in honor of the season.

Early boy and girl games resulted in young Mark Hannah's being crippled on his very first bear kill as a result of two girls chasing him at school.

MARK HANNAH: "Two school girls, Ressie Valentine and Milia Brown, were chasing me in a game of 'Base' at Little Cataloochee School. I fell down and sprained my ankle. That is why I had to ride to the cornpile and to the bear hunt the next day. But I killed the bear anyway. The latter girl mentioned was my sweetheart at school."

RAYMOND CALDWELL: "Little as you'd think, most of the courtin' was done ridin' horses and things like that. Ada Palmer, that's Uncle Will's granddaughter, and her sister Ruth... we used to ride horses about every Sunday and date those girls, just ridin' horses. I know we'd ride plumb up to Spruce Tower and back to Trail Ridge. And, of course, with Cataloochee Ranch, we'd have big square dances down there in the summertime. So everybody'd go down there."

"I've heard my Daddy tell this one. They used to slip the horses out and ride 'em. He had taken his Daddy's horse out and was goin' courtin' at night. Of course, his Daddy didn't want him ridin' the horse, 'cause they had to work. On a moonlight night goin' down the road, the horse seen the (his) shadow in the mud puddle. It spooked the horse, and he stopped. Dad went over the horse. It had a saddle horn, and Dad had on his Sunday best, and he ripped his pants. When he got back, he made some excuses to tell Grandmaw what had happened. She mended his pants. And his Daddy never did know the horse had ever been taken out."

"And I've heard my Dad tell about goin' courtin' and havin' to pass a man's house that had a bitin' dog. And the dog tore his suit of clothes off him once."

"They'd maybe stay all night with the family, maybe a whole weekend back then when they'd go a-courtin'."

"Granny Pop", or Mary Douty (Nailon, some say), the Mother of Them All, was married to Levi Caldwell, one of the earliest settlers of Cataloochee. Raymond described their whirlwind courtship.

"My great-granddaddy's bride was a girl of fourteen. The way he met her, she was with a group of people a-drivin' their cattle from the East Tennessee market to Charleston, South Carolina and come through there. Their route was across Mt. Sterling, across Cataloochee and down Jonathan Creek - stopping along the way to spend the night. He met her, just captured her. And she never did go back on one of them trips. He married her and built a house and raised a family of twelve children."

When Levi Caldwell died during the Civil War in 1864, the pioneer Jonathan Woody courted his widow. When they married out of great mutual need, widower Jonathan brought all his children along, too, totalling sixteen between them. They all lived together in one cabin. To further complicate the genealogy, some of the stepbrothers and sisters married each other. At one time, the cabin held twenty or more people!

Eldridge Caldwell met outsider Pearl Valentine at a beanstringing. She had come in from Cosby, Tennessee, to look after her brother Claude's wife who was ill in the great flu epidemic of 1918 or thereabouts.

PEARL VALENTINE CALDWELL: "Eldridge and me was a-datin' then. And he'd always come down to the post office (where I worked sometimes), y'know. He'd make it convenient to come down... the cows 'ud get out or somethin'."

The earliest Cataloochee settler, Mark's great grandfather, Evan Hannah, according to historical records, was hard pressed when he was courting his future mate, Miss Elizabeth Noland. He had to make bond for one thousand dollars on April 30, 1829, in order to guarantee that he would support his wife. One wonders about the circumstances. Was it because he was taking his wife into the wilds of Cataloochee... an unknown territory? Her father must have been very concerned over his daughter's fate, for, in the end, William Noland came into Cataloochee with his son-in-law, Evan, settling there at the same time.

Expense, to some, was apparently no object in courting, at least, not to the Italians who had come into the nearby area on a timber project.

DR. ROBERT HILLIARD WOODY: "At least one of those Italians wanted to marry one of the women whose husband had been killed and offered her, I think, five thousand dollars, which seemed like a lot in those days."

But logger Charlie Bogus only gave Leona Caldwell a pair of scissors as a "sweetheart present". Lush Leatherwood of Jonathan Creek won her later. As to whether all Cataloochee girls were so sought after and desirable became debatable. The local Civilian Conservation Corps boys in the '30s, for instance, referred to some of the women as "wildcats".

A way to bypass all the trouble and fuss of courtship was the method used by old Jesse Palmer's boys, William A. and Turkey George. When Andy Caldwell's wife gave birth to a daughter, William and George turned up to admire the new baby. William, aged fifteen, pointed to tiny red, wrinkled Milia, and said: "I'll take that one, George. You take the next one..." And Turkey George did take the next, Alice Cumi Caldwell. They say that William built a house for his promised bride when Milia was only ten years old, then waited till she was sixteen, married her, and "raised her to suit himself".

Flora Messer and Charles Morrow had a more traditional courtship. She remembers it romantically to this day and says she could "write a book about it".

FLORA MESSER MORROW: "Bartley Bennett said, I got a friend comin' from Cove Creek tomorrow, I want you to meet him. Lloyd Teague was coming with Charles. Lloyd was a terrible ugly-looking boy. And I'd never seen either one of 'em. They came to the church, though. I was singing in the choir when Bartley came in and brought his two friends, sat in the back of the church. Well, I said to myself, I don't know which of those boys I'm supposed to entertain today, but, if it's that ugly one, I'm sure today will be the first and last. I saw Bartley give kind of a grin and nod his head toward Charles. So I sang louder."

"Then that evenin', oh, say two dozen boys and girls gathered up at my mother's house under the apple trees out at the big spring. We'd sing, play games. I enjoyed bein' with him... well, had a good time. A large bunch was gatherin' flowers, y'know, just playin' along and talkin' and having fun. Might have been watermelon time, I guess. And two or three days after that, got a letter, asking if he could come back the next Sunday... and from that the courtship began. We went together about five years. I always said I would never get married until I was twenty-two."

Flora, who was the oldest of Will Messer's ten daughters, played a coquettish trick on Charles when she accepted a date one Sunday with Gentry Hall, who later became a state senator.

"I sort of acted ugly... in the first days of our courtship. That week I thought he wasn't comin' back and he hadn't asked for a date that weekend. I wrote a letter and got it to Charles that I'us goin' to Crestmont Lumber Co. on a picnic that day. Well, instead of comin' to Cataloochee, he just gets on the train, come around by Newport and came up to Mt. Sterling, (on the T&NC railroad) and I didn't show up. I was back home sittin' in the parlor with Gentry Hall. Oh... he caught up with me! Somebody sorta suspicioned. It was a long time, a long time, maybe two or three months before he.... I had to do a lot of apologizin', and Bartley had to do a lot of beggin'. Bartley Bennett acted as the go between."

Aside from Flora Messer's spectacular wedding in the Little Cataloochee Baptist Church, a wedding was rarely held in any Cataloochee church until 1972 when a Palmer descendent, Margaret Lynne Palmer, asked the Park Service if she could be married to a Noland in Palmer Chapel, on land which had been donated by her great-great-grandfather.

Most couples merely went away to "South Car'liny" and got a license, the quickest way, said Flora Palmer, who was married to Manson Medford in a parsonage down there.

FLORA PALMER MEDFORD: "I went to South Carolina and got married in a parsonage. Went to Greenville. Here they had to wait three days after you applied for a license. So we just went down there and got married, stayed two or three days and came back home. When I think of all the money they spend on that nowadays that they could go to keepin' house with!"

Leona Caldwell married Lucious Leatherwood in the parlor of her own Cataloochee house, on the hearthstones that later her sentimental daughter, Mary Lou Leatherwood Moody, sneaked out from under the nose of the Park.

When Jesse Palmer married Miss Rogers, from Fines Creek, in the old days, he came to get her on a horse, nearly drowned while crossing the Pigeon River and was rescued by Uncle Hardy Noland. After he had dried out, he married her in a cow-pasture and took her on horseback to Cataloochee where he hewed a house out of logs and spawned sixteen children... so old Glenn Palmer recounted in his sweet, quavering voice as he sat on the broad front porch of Rush Fork Farm, looking out over large fields of corn, huge barns full of Holsteins, with Crabtree Bald in the distance.

It was not hard for Mark Hannah to meet his future wife, Verda Messer, although it is doubtful if the shy young Verda ever resorted to chasing him, as did his other sweetheart.

MARK HANNAH: "Yeah, she grew up there at the same school I did. I had to ask her father when I married her. Oh yeah! Do all those things! But it was no surprise to him. Everybody suspected it. I lived with my father and mother there for awhile after the marriage."

As with Mark, it was traditional to ask the father for permission to marry his daughter. Mark had to ask Verda's father, Will Messer. At an earlier date, Charles Morrow, who married Verda's older sister, Flora, had quite a time getting through to his future father-in-law.

FLORA MESSER MORROW: "After five years' courtship, he finally said to everyone, 'Now I'm goin' to ask Mr. Messer next Sunday. If I have to do it, I'm goin' to.' Daddy wasn't surprised, but that was just one of my demands or commands. I said that was one time when I didn't get to speak a dozen words to Charles 'cause just after we ate dinner, Daddy went out around the field and around the barn, and all over the place, and Charles followed him. They walked nearly the whole afternoon. Charles said that just about everytime he'd come to the point that Mr. Messer was he going to be willing for our wedding, that he'd change the subject to something else. And he said that he like to never in the world... I suppose my father was only teasing Charles. Daddy liked fun. He wasn't no sour somebody. He liked good clean fun, and I guess he grinned a lot of times..."

But one of Uncle Turkey George Palmer's daughters married without permission because Uncle Turkey did not care for the match with a Caldwell boy. The marriage was an unlucky one, and the girl died soon after. Flora Palmer suspected later that it might have been a case of undiagnosed appendicitis rather than a curse upon the unblessed union, however.

"Squire" Mitchell Sutton sometimes performed marriages in Cataloochee in his capacity as a magistrate "back of the law". Pearl Caldwell pictured him as exceedingly nervous at these events, "shaking in his boots". After the wedding, the bridegroom might well be nervous, also, for it was the joyful custom in Cataloochee to torment the poor fellow on his wedding night.

DR. ROBERT HILLIARD WOODY: "A bride and groom were apt to be greeted with a charivari which might include riding the groom on a rail... in his night clothes, and dumping him into a cold creek."

MARK HANNAH: "Gene Sutton, son of Mitchell Sutton, was also a magistrate. He was so nervous that he had to go through (the marriage) ceremony twice. He was performing this at Mack Hannah's house when Clyde McCullough married one of my schoolgirl friends, Ressie Valentine, Pearl's sister. He was shaking like a leaf. We rode them (the couple) on a rail and wheelbarrow during the night. Those who joined me were Bud Messer, Fred Hannah, Claude Valentine and others."

Most didn't have honeymoons and just moved in with their parents until they could afford a place of their own.

But Charles Morrow took Flora Messer off for an eleven-day honeymoon to Greensboro, Asheville, "and around". A strange juxtaposition: the children of Allen Davidson, living in Asheville, had happily ridden into Cataloochee for their honeymoons! After the honeymoon, however, men and women did separate themselves in everyday life a good bit of the time. According to the old-fashioned pattern evident in Dr. Woody's description, the two sexes behaved differently, the women sitting sedately on the benches at church while the menfolk often went out in the middle of the service and swapped tales on a log in front. If a woman had done this, she would most likely have been severely censured.

Nowadays, sociologists and feminists, in particular, are very fond of saying that there is very little difference between the sexes. In the Cataloochee known by Mark and his father and his grandfather, however, there were marked distinctions. These women were no less important than they are today... they were vitally important to this isolated wilderness life. Only then, of course, the roles of men and women were more clearly defined and separated. Generally, women were nurses, midwives, housewives, bearers of children and farmworkers.

Men were supposed to be talked about and celebrated as heroes and breadwinners. And so they were. They did not necessarily work less hard than women, for many of them possessed great physical endurance and strength. But they did not, as women did, toil in the fields prior to childbirth. And, in those days, husbands often survived their worn-out women by many years and sometimes took two, or in the case of Mack Hannah, even three wives in a lifetime.

Women's work was cut out for them at birth. Even the youngest girls had a tremendous load upon them. Witness a typical day in the life of little Flora Palmer in the early part of this century:

There were eleven children in Turkey George Palmer's family. Flora was the third child. She lived on the north side of Shanty Mountain, at the end of Big Butt

Mountain about 400 or 500 feet from Pretty Hollow Creek near Indian Creek. There her father had built a comfortable two-story, six-room framed poplar house which had two porches and two chimneys of hand-made brick.

This little girl's chores included milking, hoeing corn, and going with a couple of her brothers and sisters to find the free-ranging lead cow with the bell in the evening. She also cooked, carried spring water, chopped stove wood, pulled fodder, cut tops, tied fodder, made hay stacks, helped with molasses-making, and got saw briers out of the cradled oats.

Not an unusual day when she was a school girl was one during which she got up before daylight, helped make breakfast, washed the dishes, milked the cows, strained the milk, churned, and washed clothes in the wash pot before going off to school in her calico dress.

FLORA PALMER MEDFORD: "Boil 'em with lye soap! Would eat your hands!"

If Flora went on horseback, she wouldn't ride sidesaddle, but went astride, as did most practical Cataloochee girls. But usually she walked, by eight o'clock, one and a half miles to the school with its rived shake roof. On cold winter days they would gather round the big wood stove when they first arrived. School ended at four o'clock. And Flora headed home to pick beans, dig 'taters, get the cows in, gather stove wood, dig ramps, or pick blackberries in season. There was always a pot of cornfield beans with bacon cooking on the stove when the children came in, and big pitchers of sweet milk on the table from the spring house. After supper, when she had washed the dishes and done her lessons, she was allowed to read the "Comfort" papers, or Turkey George would tell bear tales to his children. Sometimes her mother would sing hymns while they quilted for the beds, later pulling up the quilting frame to the ceiling at the end of the evening. Some evenings Flora carded and spun wool, but did no weaving, as they sold the wool and bought linsey cloth with the money. There were no idle hands for the Devil's work in Turkey George's family, especially for little girls like Flora.

One of two females who diverged from the usual pattern of femininity, though she was then and is today, an uncommonly handsome woman, was Pearl Valentine Caldwell. Before she married Eldridge Caldwell, she rode a mule to carry the mail from Ola post office in Little Cataloochee, through Bald Gap to Nellie post office in Big Cataloochee... a distance of about five miles over rugged mountains via Mossy Branch, without a road most of the way.

PEARL VALENTINE CALDWELL: "Americus Hall had the star route. And when he'd go to the mountains to see about his cattle, why, he had me sworn in. I'd just ride anything there was to ride. Sometimes it'd be a mule, sometimes it'd be a horse. They'd always leave <u>something</u>, though. Most of the men would go all at one time to see about the cattle. They'd use (graze) their cattle in on the head of Big Creek, and they'd stay all night..."

MARK HANNAH: "He decided he should buy a good riding horse for Ella and Pearl to ride with the mail. He sent over to Tennessee, maybe to John Louis Moore's and purchased a safe good old horse. The girls were pleased with the deal, called the horse 'Ole Fat.'"

"In a few days, 'Mericus Hall decided to try the new riding horse in the 'gears' (harness) to see if he would pull a plow. He asked his tenant, Bob Brown, a good church worker, to come and assist him. They harnessed 'Ole Fat' and Bob was behind the plow. When they gave the go signal - 'get up here' - 'Ole Fat' came backwards and almost ran over Bob who said, 'Get up here, ole Hell, have I put the harness on the wrong end?!'"

The menfolks' chores usually included herding cattle in the high mountains, hunting for meat to salt away for the winter months, doing the heavier farm work and repairing, though women, too, were required to help in the fields, even through their pregnancies. It was the men who went to town in the wagons and traded their marketable goods, or left for the far markets of Augusta for weeks at a time.

One suspects that "getting away" from the womenfolk was one of the great male diversions, from the stories that are told about cattle herding on the natural balds. They might go away for days to see about their cattle among the beautiful meadows in good spring and summer weather, swapping tales around the campfire.

MARK HANNAH: "(The men would stay away) sometimes two or more nights and eat those little speckle trouts about four inches in length. Oh, boy! How sweet they were... bones and all!"

RAYMOND CALDWELL: "It was our delight in the spring of the year to get to go and take the cattle out there!"

DR. NICK MEDFORD: "'Creek George' Palmer used to take a poke of rations and a poke of salt to the salt lick near The Ledge. He said he would lie down in the shade and listen to the sound of cattle pulling the grass between their teeth... the sweetest music this side of heaven, according to him."

A story often related with much amusement, fortunately by the family involved, is that of what happened to Uncle Hiram Caldwell on one of his cattle herding diversions.

RAYMOND CALDWELL: "'Course these old timers had their land around different places. Uncle Hiram owned a piece of property down around Mt. Sterling, High Top. He'd go out down there and see about his cattle."

"He was probably a man about the community pretty well, and he come in one afternoon about dark. Aunt Lizzie's the best ole soul. She died thinking every son she had never did anything wrong at all. But, anyhow, Uncle Hiram come in. He'd been gone three or four days, lookin' 'bout his cattle."

"He was helpin' her 'round the barn with the chores and he picked up a pitch fork and was just a-workin' on some of those cattle (with an) awful yellin' and just a-fussin' and a-growlin'."

"Aunt Lizzie says, 'H'arm, what in the world is wrong with you? 'Says, 'You never act like that much. What in the world is wrong with you?'"

(Hiram had a slight speech defect and, like the Chinese, substituted "r" for "l".)

"Says he, 'Hey-o, now, here, Rizzie!' Says, 'You know that (an) ole gal goin' to swear a young'un to us?'"

"She says, 'Us? What do you mean, H'arm? I had nothin' to do with it and, if I don't care, you shouldn't care!'"

"Says, 'Hey-o, now, Rizzie, that's the way to talk to old fellowster!'"

The greatest symbol of machismo in Cataloochee, however, was not the siring of children, although Jarvis Caldwell once said that was the largest crop raised in the valley. It was the hunting of the bear... an exclusively male affair fraught with violence, danger, bloodshed, the chase, with its accompanying exultant cries of victory. Turkey George used to choke the dead bear, stand on the carcass, and shout for joy, yelling at the top of his voice.

The maleness of the hunt persists today. And the protagonists of those bearhunting tales will live longer in memory than the number of stitches women took in their intricate quilting patterns, or the number of times women chopped weeds with their hoes, or carried water from the spring, or cried out in childbirth.

Women seemed to have become memorable only when they departed from the norm... with the possible exception of the grannywomen who brought everybody into the world, male and female, and were therefore regarded with some awe.

Miss Maria Palmer, for instance, became memorable for not getting married at all. In a society where a single independent woman past marriageable age might be regarded with some suspicion, Miss Maria chose to remain free.

In a playful photograph of the period she reclines on the grass with her beau, Zack, and another couple, settled in studied postures arranged by the photographer.

Few people would recognize her here as the firm-mouthed spinster, Aunt Maria Palmer, daughter of 'Fayt, who, in later years, sat on her porch, to snare everybody who came by and to find out their business.

Once she badgered "Dude" Hannah, the feckless wit from Dude Creek up in Little Cataloochee, until he struck deep, shrivelling her heart with his retort.

ELDRIDGE CALDWELL: "Dude had just spent the night with Loge (Logan) Hannah that lived up there above the Booger Man Place. And he'd come down by what's the ranger station now... s'whar Aunt Maria and Jarvis and that bunch lived. She'us pretty bad to ask people questions about whar they'us a-goin'. And when he got aside the house, he knew how she was goin' to see ever'body passin' and ask questions. He started runnin' just as hard as he could down the road. 'Hey, Dude! (Eldridge used a marvelous falsetto to imitate Aunt Maria), said, 'What's the matter? What's wrong?'"

"He wanted to get her off his back and said, 'Well, if you want another Dude, you'd better raise one, 'cause this ole Dude's gonna pass out some of these days! And you will be Dude-less as Hell!' She'us an ole maid, y'know, and never raised any children. He'us hittin' her pretty hard!"

A different view of the rather grim-visaged spinster with her apron was presented by Mrs. Tom Alexander who, with her late husband, ran the Cataloochee Guest Ranch in the valley for a few years during the Depression.

JUDITH BARKSDALE ALEXANDER: "Aunt Maria and I were great friends. She told me she didn't get married but, she said, she had a good time. She said, 'I did a lot of things they didn't know I did... I'd slip out when I was a girl. I had some beaux, and I'd slip out the window, saddle up my horse, and they didn't know I was gone!'"

Miss Maria was not as adventurous in other aspects as her night-time escapades might suggest. She was afraid of water and couldn't swim, in true mountain tradition, saying that the only safe place to go in Cataloochee Creek was by the Sycamore Pond, in front of her house, where the water was only "shoe-mouth" deep.

Other notable Cataloochee women had a high degree of independence and spirit. Aunt 'Phronia Bennett was fighting mad when she whipped one of Kirk's men who burnt her house down during the Civil War. She then dragged out a family trunk of valuables, doubtless with a strength born of ferocity. She must have caused some consternation in this war where, as in the case of the Caldwell wives who would not tell where their men were hid, it was usually the women who were whipped by the soldiers.

"Granny Pop" Caldwell, her Levi off to war, was another who was far from subservient to men. She stood up to the Union troops when they swarmed through the valley and would not tell where the horses and meat were hid.

To see her stern, compressed features in a photograph of her later years, is to understand her obstinacy. The prune-mouthed old lady with a tiny black bonnet and a white frill around her neck still conveys a little of the undaunted wife of earlier days. Yet there is still the perplexed expression of the 14-year old girl who was 'stolen' from the Charleston cattle drive and made to leave her free-ranging life to stay within the walls of the mountain fortress.

Tiny old Mag Mauney Caldwell was not afraid of anything on earth except the thought of her sons' getting killed in World War I. She was a great peacemaker, and was able to gentle rowdy Tom King at a time when he was ready to shoot up the community. Beloved grandmother of Raymond, she was a catch-all of Cataloochee oral history. Fortunately he sat at her knee and remembered every detail she ever told him.

She was both gentle and firm. She thought dancing a "device of the Devil", yet considered the Virginia Reel a "game"! Raymond best remembers her as absentmindedly rocking an empty cradle with her foot as she read a newspaper, with one shoulder hunched up toward the light. The children and grandchildren were all grown, but her maternal instincts kept her foot busy.

Mag Mauney smoked a pipe, as did the two grandmothers of Mark Hannah, who both lived peaceably together in his father's house. Mark has a rare genre photograph of the two old ladies smoking on the porch. One has her hands folded in her lap. But Rebecca Hoyle, Fannie Mack's mother, has her hands outstretched. At the very instant of the photograph, some one called out to Granny Hoyle: "Here's your can of Prince Albert! Catch it!"

Mark's grandmothers quite properly smoked the old clay pipes, as pipe smoking was considered fitting for elderly women back then. Grandmaw Palmer, mother of Steve Woody's wife, also smoked a graceful long-stemmed clay pipe with equanimity, long into the twentieth century. But Mag Mauney Caldwell's photograph shows her holding a man's regular briar pipe in her mouth.

Mark's mother, Fannie Hannah, sometimes known as Fannie Mack, to distinguish her from another Fannie Hannah, was, in her own way, a formidable woman in the community. She not only was instrumental in getting rid of Braz Whaley's still which was leading school children to ruin, but she was a selftaught doctor-woman, who actually read medical books to further her knowledge, and helped with the birthing of nearly every child on Little Cataloochee, without some of the preconceived superstitions of many another self-appointed grannywoman.

Unknowingly Mark displayed a good deal of male chauvinism while describing his admirable mother when he said proudly, "She was a good reader and speller, and could pronounce anything good, and could write good — for a woman." And later, when describing a very rough trip she had to make as a midwife, "That was about three miles, I'd say — just straight up trail in places — just all she could do to stay on a horse — for a man, much less a woman. She made it anyway."

Eleanor Noland Palmer was another local midwife with a mind of her own, as was Jonathan's daughter, Aunt Susie Woody Caldwell.

RAYMOND CALDWELL: "She was raised over on Jonathan's Creek, married Uncle Will Palmer. And she was quite an industrious worker. She was the leader in her family. I've heard my grandmother tell about Aunt Ellender had to lay all of the first rails of the crooked fence (called the 'worm' of the fence). She didn't trust Uncle Will. She did that."

Her niece, Lillian Hannah Stokes, says Flora Messer Morrow was the most beautiful woman to come out of Cataloochee and, therefore, might have been remembered for this alone. Always contradictory, Flora took up a trade later in life which, as the eldest in a family of eleven children, may have been prompted by her father's treating her as the son he did not have for so long. She often had to do a boy's chores when she was young. And she continued in this vein in Newport, Tennessee, where she built a total of fourteen houses. She was known there as The Little Carpenter, though one could scarcely ever remember so feminine a person. By coincidence, this was also the nickname of a famous Cherokee Indian Chief, Attakullakulla.

MARK HANNAH: "Mattie Bennett was a good horse rider. She would saddle 'Old Doll' and ride to (the) top of Mt. Sterling and hunt the sheep and cattle and give them salt — just as a man would. Never afraid of anything because 'Old Doll' could outrun any animal of her kind. Once we were racing horses on Sterling, and she entered and won easily over Willie and Troy. They were on mules, of course — they were young. She also was an expert on baking light-bread. Rachel Messer and Verna Woody were her assistants in this deal. They could roll the dough! Boys!"

Certainly it was hard, if not impossible for a woman to take up much of a competitive profession in Cataloochee Valley where the men tended to be as assertive as Hiram Caldwell and Uncle Steve Woody.

Hiram, in a snapshot, leans toward the viewer with rather an aggressive air under his long mustachios. Lizzie looks a little apprehensive, as do most of the wives in the old photographs. Hiram did tend to dominate the scene. He was very methodical, a hard worker, and expected the same of everyone around him.

Strength played a large part in the testing of Cataloochee men. Steve's nephew, "Major" Woody, though crippled from birth, compensated for his lameness by the tremendous power of his arms. Mark Hannah told me that his brother, Fred Hannah, a football player, was once challenged by "Major" who said, "Fred, I can lift you and all you can lift." He thereby lifted Fred and also a two hundred pound pole which Fred was holding.

But an air of authority was as important as physical strength. Steve Woody made folks sit up and take notice whenever he arrived on the scene. He came on just as strong as Hiram, in his own way. No one can recollect a time that he was bested in a business deal or a legal battle.

ELDRIDGE CALDWELL: "I guess he was probably around six feet tall, rode a black horse all the time. Before he got her, she wouldn't walk a lick with anybody ridin' her. He got her to walkin' faster'n anything in that country. How he done it I never did know."

RAYMOND CALDWELL: "He loved to ride his big black horse. And he was very active, for his age (ninety). He could stand flat-footed and get on any horse."

PEARL VALENTINE CALDWELL: "He always carried a switch with him. Our little girls was wadin' the creek... it was cold, but they just decided they'd go in the creek. And Uncle Steve came long with his hickory (switch). He stopped and said that'd make them sick! He hit his hickory, y'know. on the saddle! My daughter said she never _would_ forget that..."

The rollicking Woody boys obviously inherited their sense of fun from their father. As Mrs. Tom Alexander said, "He had a _beautiful_ sense of humor." At the time she knew him, he was an old man in his eighties. But she thought he had been pretty much of a ladies man.

RAYMOND CALDWELL: "Oh, yes, he was fun. He loved a big time, and he loved to pull jokes and pranks on people. He was a fellow that was very joyful... happy-go-lucky type of fellow."

A photograph of Steve Woody and his wife against an appropriate backdrop of a handwoven coverlet indicates a tough, goodlooking mountain man, son of the original settler, Jonathan Woody... sure of himself and confident of his future. His checked suit is casual and tieless, though he does carry the impressive weight of a watch and chain. His wife fits squarely, doggedly beside him in a sensible wool dress with a white jabot collar which barely relieves the severity. She is just as determined as Steve himself as she stares fixedly at the photographer. Together they seem to be of the very stuff that bound wilderness folk together.

Another picture outside Palmer Chapel on a sunny Sunday morning reveals many of the women dressed elaborately in the extreme fashions of the '90's. The men, also, are standing uncomfortably in unaccustomed hard collars and ties. Uncle Steve Woody, alone, remains simply dressed, with plain collar buttoned at the neck and no tie, seemingly a man of stature, with no need for pretense or special clothes for the Lord's Day. His air of authority conveys all that has to be known.

Though Steve Woody apparently preferred simply cut clothes and looked good in them, these isolated mountain people, as a rule, succumbed to the tides of fashion much more than one might have supposed.

By the 1890s, the mail order catalogues had already made obsolete a great deal of the carding, weaving and sewing, forever diminishing women's burden and freeing them for other pursuits.

Miss Maria Palmer, in her exquisite clothes, together with other pictures of wide-eyed Fannie Hannah, posing gravely for an early portrait in a large hat of the period piled high with both bows and flowers, quite change the layman's misconception of the simple mountain gal who milked the cows and chopped the weeds in a calico dress. She wore that, too, but she could also rise to an occasion.

Some girls managed to reach pure pinnacles of fashion while looking miserable in pinching corsets and layers of material and elaborate decoration.

Others carried it off with aplomb. Misses Maria Palmer and Effie Woody, one of Uncle Steve's daughters, were captured by a photographer with a Victorian imagination. He portrayed them with books held languidly by long slender fingers as the girls gazed off into space in the best romantic tradition.

They are wearing again, dresses with pinched willowy waists which may account for their faint expressions. The dresses, heavy with leg o'mutton sleeves, are bravely decorated with embroidered frogs, braid, brooches, flounces, pleats, and ruffles. Their heads are coiffed with curled fringes.

As Miss Maria grew older, she did her hair in severe, no-nonsense arrangements, and she began to wear a pince-nez in the manner of a typical disciplinary schoolmarm. Finally, in shapeless dresses, voluminous aprons and sunbonnets, she left all her earlier dreams and foolishness aside.

Verda and Flora Messer's mother, with ten girls to dress, could scarcely afford to order everything from the catalogue. As her father liked for all the girls to be dressed in clean starched white dresses on Sunday, Flora told me, in a masterpiece of understatement, that, as the eldest of the brood, she "did a lot of sewing".

Mrs. Will Palmer, looking desperate in her frizzled topknot, (no doubt the strain of staying still for the photographer was very great) sat, also, with leg o'mutton, braid and brooch next to her husband, Will, who self-consciously combed his tonsure over his forehead in an effort to keep up with the times.

But Uncle Steve Woody's son, Floyd, remembers that the Woody boys only wore new "overhauls" on Sunday, as opposed to workaday "overhauls", echoing the brash simplicity of their father. Yet some of the class pictures show little boys squirming in a variety of fancy outfits, one resembling a rustic Little Lord Fauntleroy, others in wide-brimmed hats, jackets, large ruffled collars, ties, sailor middies and special boots. Some of the boys are dressed in the height of fashion, but are without shoes! One small boy had evidently been made to stick his legs behind a boulder by either the photographer or the teacher because he had arrived unshod.

One imagines with what relief the individuals in these photographs must have rushed to get back into their comfortable everyday clothes when the ordeal was over.

As a young man of eighteen, the famous bear hunter, Turkey George Palmer, sat for a ferocious mustachioed portrait, his rifle clasped in a menacing manner across his breast. But his clothes are not those of the huntsman. He wears a jacket piped with braid, a double-breasted waistcoat, a plaid bowtie, and an ostentatious watch fob.

In later years, he sensibly eschewed this "fotched-on" garb, and went about comfortably in red suspenders, baggy trousers darned at the knee, a wool shirt buttoned at the throat with no tie, a coat fastened with a safety pin, an everpresent knapsack hung on his chest instead of his back, and an old soft felt hat which seemed to have been made for him to sleep in. Around this hat his white hair curled crisply like a duck's tail.

Fred Caldwell, too, posed with his weapon, a pistol held dramatically across his breast as he sported a wing collar, a bowtie, coat, waistcoat, and a political campaign button on his lapel.

Old Man 'Fayt Palmer, fine-boned and patriarchal, closely resembling the aged photographs of his friend, Allen Davidson, didn't have to wear either tie or collar with his best suit as his long white beard covered all!

Certainly by the twenties and the thirties, the tide of fashion had washed over the valley and left only a sensible residue. Most older women still wore long-sleeved calico or gingham dresses with skirts down to their ankles, and voluminous checked, bibbed aprons covering their capacious middles. No self-respecting older woman would work outside in the heat without a large sunbonnet which hid nearly all her features from both strangers and the elements. Younger girls wore bobby-sox and saddle shoes with short neat cotton dresses.

At the end of Cataloochee's days as a community, overalls and battered soft felt hats amounted to what was a uniform among the mountain men, with an occasional 'duck-back' cap worn by Eldridge Caldwell and others. In recent years, the plain felt hat or Fedora seems to have been replaced by the ubiquitous duck-billed baseball cap. This uniform seems rather colorless as a substitute for our ancestors' more rustic garb.

Joe Sutton of Allen's Creek, a descendent of settlers from Cataloochee and Mt. Sterling, appeared at the Bicentennial of the founding of Waynesville, North Carolina, in a hunting costume which he had made to fit the descriptions of 18th century settler's dress. His clothes looked extraordinarily legitimate, even dashing — the full-sleeved linen shirt, a deer leather jerkin and deerskin trews, with fur shoulderpieces on which to hoist his ancient muzzle loader. He wore a wide-brimmed felt (or beaver?) hat in the manner of most pioneers, including Daniel Boone, who actually preferred this to his much vaunted coonskin cap. Crossed upon his chest were rawhide straps holding his powder horn, bullets, patching and so forth. He was a formidable sight with his full beard and mustachioes. One could imagine the legendary Scots hunter, Ned McFalls, going forth to Cataloochee in such an outfit in the very earliest romantic days before the valley was settled.

But clothes do not make the man, nor do they really emphasize the important differences between men and women.

Most of the stories handed down from Cataloochee tell of the exploits of great hunters because that is how men measured each other. And that is how their womenfolk wanted to remember them! A man could dress up in a wing collar for a photograph and, in an instant, be preserved for all posterity as a fashion model. But he lived longer in the minds of his descendants if a bear had nearly disemboweled him as the hunter tried to breach his den! Brave, or foolhardy, his memory would stay.

On the other hand, for a woman, only to be supremely beautiful or to be supremely contrary, was a sure ticket to immortality.

CHAPTER 14

Running with the Pack

(Bear Hunting Stories)

Bear hunting in Cataloochee was not just a means of "sport" but a way to
provide meat for their families. None of the bear was wasted and many homes
had bear skin rugs or comforters to help keep warm in the winter.
Courtesy Great Smoky Mountains National Park Archives.

THE MYTHICAL STORY of *Shardik*, a compelling novel by Richard Adams, told of a great bear who was revered as a god by peasants. A powerful cult was built up in his name, with much resultant bloodshed and superstition.
Part of the authentic Cherokee tradition, too, elevated the bear as a god. In the eyes of Cataloochee white men, the bear, if not actually a god, was almost as feared and respected as one.
Men's reputations were made or lost over how they conducted themselves in bear fights. They fed on the idea of hunting the bear much as they might eat its meat afterward. The fixation alone was a life-giving sustenance.

More hunting stories revolved around the bear than all the animals of the Smokies. If one listened for a lifetime, he'd never hear the end of the eager recounting of the famous bearhunts of old Catalooch'.

Much of Mark Hannah's life has been bound up with the romance of the hunt because his childhood home was in the very heart of bear country. Later, as a ranger for thirty-odd years, he had to vow to protect the wild life that he had chased during his early years.

MARK HANNAH: "Adjoining the Flats of the Bunk (where I lived) on the north side of Bunk Mountain was a tract of land owned by Jarvis L. Palmer (earlier by Allen Davidson). It was a long strip of land, went to a high peak above Hollow Maple Gap, then towards Mt. Sterling Gap almost a mile. In the center of the tract was a stream, known as Dude Creek... and a lot of land along its banks was nearly level. There were chestnut trees everywhere anyone went. These trees bore nuts every year when I was a boy. The wildlife gathered in the area for food. Bears, coons, turkeys, squirrels, grouse, groundhogs, oppossums were plentiful. This wildlife would feed in the Pig Pen Flats at night then go high on the mountains into the rough 'yellow patches' or 'slicks', as they are sometimes called, to sleep in the daylight hours. Bears were pushed out of the area by dogs and made to go into the head of Big Creek, deep in the forests."

On December 3, 1921, when he was fifteen and had a badly sprained ankle, Mark killed his first bear. Ironically, it was old Hiram Caldwell's last hunt before he died of lingering aftereffects of the Great Influenza Epidemic. Mark modestly entitled the account of his moment of glory as "Uncle Hiram's Last Bear Hunt".

MARK HANNAH: "My father and I were notified by messenger to come to Big Cataloochee and bring my dogs, Moove and Fly... Dad and I rode horses up Shanty Branch trail to the top of the mountain via Little Indian Creek and up Trail Ridge to the Ledge Mountain. We were to stay at the Tate Rock bear stand for at least two hours. Big George Caldwell had rode his horse and joined us. He was carrying a 32 rimfire single shot rifle to kill the bear. Buddy, that was too small for me! After we rested and listened until about noontime, we decided to climb up the ridge to the top of Spruce Mountain. This was a steep cattle or bear trail but we rode those horses anyway."

"We arrived at the top of the mountain and soon heard the dogs fighting the bear about one half mile down on Horse Creek. Later a gun was heard but the dogs only yelped louder and louder. We soon knew that the shot someone had fired had either missed the bear or the gun was too small to kill the bear."

"Later in the day the bear came near where Dad and I were and started fighting the dogs something terrible to listen to. I then gave my horse to Dad and Big George and joined John Burress, who did not have a gun, and we went to the dogs. About two hundred yards of the bear and dogs, we found Floyd Harrell coming out of the rough of rhododendron or laurel slick and asked him to go back with us. (He said) 'No siree... I'm not going in there. Can't you hear him growling and crippling those dogs?!' Yes, we heard that, but we had to go into that place to get a shot. And away we went. About fifteen minutes we were within fifteen feet of a large hemlock tree that we guessed the bear to be sitting under."

"Just then the bear came around the tree right in our face almost. The dogs, Moove, Fly, Track, Blue, Big Moove, and two airdales of John Burress', were hanging onto his legs and rear end. My! How that bear was growling and crashing his big teeth together. He looked us square in the eye and reared up on his hindlegs, then grabbed hold of this big hemlock and climbed it. The dogs turned loose of him and they fell back to the ground. The bear climbed out 15 or 20 feet and stopped with his head on the other side of the tree from me, his rear end toward me. And John says, 'Shoot in the rear end! It will kill it anyway.' I shot it with a 45-90 single-shot. Seemed the pressure of the gun just carried the bear away, it fell so hard. The dogs covered it up and were on its back part of the time. It went about 200 yards off the steep hill into a branch and was dying. Mr. Floyd Harrell then ran to it and shot it. The party gave him credit for 'killing' a dead bear!"

"Soon there were men coming to us from every direction. The drivers that turned the dogs loose were soon there. Among others was Old Turkey George Palmer. Guess what his reaction was? He threw his gun on the ground and jumped on the dead bear as if he was wrestling it. Then he got his fingers on its throat and said he was choking it to death. Says he, 'I shet his wind off, didn't I?'"

"They dragged and pulled at the bear until it was near the 'Slideoff'. Uncle Hiram had listened to all the race and heard the big gun fire, so he saddled, his horse and 'put the gears on it', too, then hooked to a small sled and rode about two miles up the creek to meet us above Steve Woody's place".

"The crew sure were glad to load the bear on the sled and haul it out over logs. It was taken to Uncle Hiram's to be skinned and divided with hunters. The names of all eligible hunters were placed on a sheet of paper and the same number of piles of meat, equalized as nearly as possible. A man, with back to the piles of meat, says, whose pile is this? The man using a pointer has his pointer already on one. Then the man with the list calls a name off, and the man comes forward and takes the pile from the pointer."

There were very special rules of etiquette for the bearhunt, and woe betide him who tried to buck the system, said Nick Medford.

DR. NICK MEDFORD: "Steve Woody told me of a bear on Prettyland Mountain, so I took a half dozen dogs and went over there to spend the night. We saw signs: old logs had been torn up by bears digging for grubs. 'Old Smoky' slow-tracked it... the scent was slowed down by the dry warm side... then tracked the bear on down to rich soil where, with the shade and the damp leaves, the dogs could smell over there on the north side. This bear was about 400 pounds. An old coonhunter, not in our party, killed the bear in a laurel patch. The bear had climbed into a dead hemlock. I found Uncle Steve and the fellow sitting on top of the bear in a rhododendron patch. It was the prettiest sight I ever saw."

"One of the party was helping to skin the bear when the outsider, the coon hunter, said to take one ham and he would take the skin and the rest. The skinner, getting madder by the minute, said, 'Where is the skin now?' The coonhunter said, 'In my car. You take a ham, and I'll take the rest.' Exasperated, the skinner told the coon hunter the rules of sportsmanship, saying, 'You bring that skin back here and leave it! That bear will be divided evenly among twenty men who got the dogs together, tracked the bear all day until the bear just happened to come your way!'"

MARK HANNAH: "The hunters used to take their places in special stands. They were called drivers and standers, in bearhunting, beaters in deerhunting. A bearhunt usually doesn't last over twenty-six hours because that's about the longest a dog could stay."

"Blueticks, sometimes crossed with Plott bearhounds (first crossed about 100 years ago) were good beardogs. Vaughn Plott gave me the first Plott hound in the Valley. I called him 'Lead'."

One dog was usually the lead dog, and another was the strike dog. Before the fighters came in, the other dogs would bark about ten or fifteen feet away from the bear. The fighters didn't bark; they just fought, according to Roy Smith.

Dogs were horribly expendable. Mark could remember a bear who, hunted down by eleven vicious airedales, killed all but three of them.

DR. NICK MEDFORD: "I was bearhunting up Butt Mountain with Uncle Turkey once. Uncle Joe Hargrove and Uncle Turkey were near the bearfight. Joe's dog, 'Alabam' was killed. He found where the dog was lying and put him between some logs. Uncle Joe buried the dog the following Sunday and planted a balsam tree on the grave. People were very sentimental about their dogs."

Mark Hannah may have killed his first bear at age fifteen, but Raymond Caldwell, who grew up a little later, had to wait longer for his gun.

RAYMOND CALDWELL: "I imagine that most of them got guns a lot earlier than we did. Dad wasn't bad to have a gun. But I can remember goin' bear huntin' when I was thirteen... or fourteen, along there. And I can't remember ever havin' a shot gun or anything like that. I'd go along on the hunts without guns. And we'd help lead the dogs. We'us a man, see, when we could lead a dog."

"My father never did keep any beardogs, but the bear hunters always came and stayed there. He took care of all the dogs. He kept a farm dog, a shepherd or something like that... a sheep dog. I can remember we had sheep when I was a little fellow, but had too much trouble with the bear and the dogs a-killin' 'em, so we didn't have sheep very much."

MARK HANNAH: "Bear dogs were usually Renfros, Blueticks, Plotts. Squirrel dogs were often feists. We had a dog, 'Old Moove', part Bluetick, who would sometimes go and hunt people. Most Cataloochee beardogs were Blueticks. They would chase a bear twenty-four to thirty-six hours. Bob Caldwell bred them, and they were fast and good in the fight. In the late '20s and '30s, I bred the Plott and Bluetick, and they were good as any man's dog."

It is now illegal to bring a dog inside the Park limits, even on a leash, though many's the unsuspecting dog that still gets lost in the Cataloochee wilderness. Knowing no boundaries, a hunting dog may track some animal past the park fence and down into the wild Caldwell Fork area. One often sees mountain men there in pick-up trucks, searching anxiously for members of their pack for days at a time.

There may yet be a spirit throng of beloved hound dogs still bugling soundlessly up and down the steep coves and valleys of Cataloochee. For this was the happy hunting ground of "Little Fly", "Moove", "Jug", "Blue", "Alabam", "Smoky", "Lead", "Rock", — now long dead, but still trailing the famous bears of old, now ghosts themselves. "Old Pink", "Honest John", "Old Kettlefoot", "Old Villa" — those are the names of huge wily bears that still bring a chill to those who remember the excitement of those hunts.

"Old Villa", a monster bear who escaped and was never more seen again, was the killer of "Alabam". But "Old Pink", another huge bruin, did not fare as well. This was a fight that really separated the men from the boys.

MARK HANNAH: "Big George Caldwell, Hiram Caldwell, and Turkey George Palmer learned of a hog's being killed in the Shanty Mountain area. They contacted some other men and dogs and all went out to chase the old hog killer. Standers, as opposed to drivers, were placed in the gaps best known for bear to escape from the area and get away from the dogs. Two men, Clyde Capps and Mr. _____ , were standing on a ridge south of the home of Big George Caldwell near a laurel patch, because bears travel in the roughest places they can find. Capps and his partner were listening for the dogs when they suddenly seen the largest bear they had ever heard of, Old Pink, heading for the log they were sitting on. It reared up on its hind legs and made for them."

"Capps fired on it with his .32 rifle. The bear fell to the ground. By the time Capps reloaded his rifle, the bear was up on its feet again and still walking towards Capps. Another bullet was placed in the bear's side near the heart. The huge bear again went down on the ground."

"At this time Capps looked around to see why his partner was not helping to shoot and keep the bear down. Lo and behold, Mr. _____ had run away, scared to death. Capps reloaded and placed another bullet very near the same place in Old Pink's side... down again and up again, and this time the bear was within ten feet of Capps. He fired one more and was expecting to run if the bear came to his feet. But Old Pink could not go any further and died in seconds. Clyde Capps admitted later that he had never been scared so bad in his whole life and that he would never go bearhunting again. He never did, as I know of, go hunting."

RAYMOND CALDWELL: "You've heard of 'Honest John', of course? Well, you see, he'd got caught in a trap and had a toe pulled off is the reason they could tell it was 'Honest John'."

He was written up in a book called *Hunting and Fishing in the Great Smokies:* "... for almost two decades, he made the headlines... This bear, reputed to weigh in the neighborhood of six hundred pounds, conspicuous for his huge tracks, and the absence of a foretoe that was once left in a steel trap, never killed just for the sake of killing, but only to satisfy his appetite. Instead of making a fresh kill he returned to the scene of his slaughter and finished up a yearling killed a night or two before. By killing for food only, he came by his prefix 'Honest'... Honest John wasn't just another big bear; his fame had indeed spread afar — so far as to attract the attention in 1935 of John Halzworth, Chairman of the Alaskan Bear Society of the N. Y. Zoological Society, who came to Western North Carolina to obtain information regarding his habitat."

As time wore on, so did the tales of "Honest John" enlarge, as legends so often do!

LEE ALLEN (in 1943): "('Honest John' was said to be) the biggest brute in all North Carolina, and his weight is estimated at upwards of 700 pounds. A good sized hat will scarcely cover the huge bear's footprints. Some are of the opinion that Honest John is part grizzly and predict that when he is finally bagged he will tip the scales at close to 1000 pounds."

Another bear called "Old Kettlefoot", unlike "Honest John", apparently killed purely for the love of killing and was much feared by all hunters.

Bears are extremely unpredictable animals, though they sometimes give a warning sigh a blowing grunt like hogs, especially when cubs are around. In the days of Cataloochee past, the old-timers used hog rifles with flint and powder when hunting bear. Nowadays, a 25-35 Winchester or 30-30 is considered a likely weapon. Mark emphasized that one should never aim at the head of a bear... its skull is very thick, as Turkey George was to learn the hard way... but at the heart in the left side, right behind the foreleg.

TURKEY GEORGE PALMER (as told to Mark Hannah a month prior to his death): "We were chasin' the bear in Hell's Half Acre and the dogs brought it into the head of or near the falls of Winding Stair Branch, about 1/2 mile west of Sal Patch Gap, and treed it up a large white pine. I happen to beat the other men to it, and I shot it in the side with a 38-40 pistol. The bear fell out of the tree and the dogs started fighting it, for it was not dead, only wounded and dangerous. I crawled in through the thick mountain laurel and found it was biting my dogs very badly. I got close enough to the bear to put my pistol against its head, and fired. The concussion almost blew my arm off. I learned a lesson there... Never put a gun to a bear's skull; it's too hard to bust!"

Turkey George's cousin, Will Palmer, and Steve Woody were famous bearhunters, too. In 1936, when they were old men, they told Joe Hall about some of their adventures. He made records of their stories for the Library of Congress.

WILL PALMER: "Well, about nineteen years ago, me and William Stafford from Tennessee took a notion we'd go out and look for some bear sign. We located a big bear and found where he was usin', and decided we'd come back and get some men and dogs... So we started early next mornin'. We got our dogs, guns, men, and me and Mr. Steve Woody went on the stand."

"Dogs jumped the bear, and the bear come through the stand where we was at. And I give him two good shots, and the bear ran off down under the mountain a little, and started down by Big Balsam. Old Uncle Steve Woody says, 'I'll go down this way to below 'im, and you go down on 'im and give 'im another shot.'"

"Bear done just rolled right down on Uncle Steve Woody, without touchin' him. Uncle Steve hollered, 'Oh, Lord, shoot, Will, shoot!' Pretty soon, then, one of the little dogs hammed (i.e. got him in the hams) the bear and turned him away from Uncle Steve Woody, turned the bear right off up toward me, come off and up the hill... I'us still a-shootin' 'im. I shot him ten times... before I killed him and he went down on his face dead."

"Mr. Woody come up to me and said, 'Give me that gun. I want to blow his brains out!' Heh. Heh. I give him the gun, and he stepped up and put the gun right agin his head and fired, says, 'I kill you!'... William Stafford said old Uncle Steve Woody wouldn't be any happier than he would to enter the gates of heaven."

MARK HANNAH: "That was... a good hunt up on Prettyland Mountain. And the dogs they were using were owned by Eldridge Caldwell, and Charlie C'well, and Boone Ca'well, (he pronounced Caldwell three different ways!), and Mack Hannah, and Bartley Bennett. I b'lieve they had six dogs. They were real good. And the little Bluetick that Boone owned was the one that caught the bear, (the one) that saved Uncle Steve's life. When (the bear) turned around and fought the dog, Uncle Steve got away."

Uncle Steve told Joe Hall about another remarkable bear hunt compromised by lost guns and many an anxious moment.

STEVE WOODY: "There'us some fellers come in there, was a-comin' through from Swain, heard, what they call, on the Trail Ridge there'd been five bear had passed and went on to Shanty Mountain. Well, there may have been little skifts of snow how come they to see their signs... I got up some fellers and we started out next mornin'. Some of 'em didn't have no gun. We got to the top of Shanty Mountain. We be wantin' to send some fellers to the stand. Me and another feller, Jack Williamson, was a-goin' in there, didn' think (the bears) would go in the den. I had a Winchester, .38, and I let a feller have it and that th'owed me without my gun, a-sendin' him to the stand. We had some dogs, some bear dogs... and... cold-trailed 'em right onto side of Shanty Mountain. They'd gone to den. They (the bears) dug 'em out a den right in under where an ole big balsam tree had turned up. Hit made only one li'l place a-goin' in. Well, the dogs broke when we got pretty close. Why, we couldn' do nothin' with our dogs."

"Well, when me and Jack we was off twenty steps, I guess, from 'em or more, the bear, the old 'un, two ole she's and three yearlings... they commenced snappin' at the dogs, and the dogs just a-grabbin' at them. While atter while, an old 'un run out. And the next 'un come out... one of the yearlings. We was there in the lar'l thicket, and Jack, he had a gun. He had one of these here hog rifles. It was a good 'un, too. And if he'd a-shot, he'd a-shot the old 'un as she come out. Why, she'd just a-blockaded the hole, and we'd a-got all of 'em. But he never done it. And here come that little mouth yearnin' out to 'im, where we'us a-standin' in the lar'l. He just laid his gun down. Little skifts of snow here and there. And it just went and scooted off down the hill about thirty steps."

"He reached down and took it (the cub) right by the side of the head, by each ear. I'us up above the den. And he says, 'Come here, Steve! Come here and let's cut it's damned heart out of it!'"

"Well, I started to 'im and, as I went, there's a green brier caught me round the foot, right in the instep, and pulled me right into the mouth of the den. Thinks, meself, I'm gone this time, sure! Here they came, just kep' a-comin' out. Here come the next old 'un. Just kep' a-comin' out. Well, out come five."

"Well, 'fore I could get to 'im, I just got scared... couldn't hardly do anything. And Jack, he had to turn that (cub) loose. He didn't have a thing on his shirt, only his shirt collar. It tore everything off of him, and the blood just a-flyin' out of him! He had to turn hit loose... and away went the bear... Then it took us about thirty minutes to hunt up his gun, where it run to..."

"And, as we got nuthin' to do, we just put our dogs in there with one of the yearlings, and they run hit and treed hit... Well, when we got there, why, Jack... we'd got Jack's gun... got right in with the dogs, just laid his gun down again, never offered to give it to me, just laid his gun down and went right in with the dogs. And here comes the bear down the tree, just jumpin' down thataway. And (Jack) just went right in with 'em, him and them dogs. I just stood back and watched 'em. And him and them dogs killed that bear..."

Besides Steve Woody and Will Palmer, there were several quite unorthodox hunters who came into Cataloochee, brave, stubborn, and often fanatical.

JAMES A. HANNAH: "Bill Barnes (who came over from Tennessee) was a great bear hunter. 'Still hunted' mostly. He would dig a pit in the ground in the winter time during the day and built a big fire in it to warm it up, and then stand in it to shoot the bear when they would come by in the dark. He killed several bear with his knife. In order to accomplish this, he would wait till the dogs had the bear bayed against a log or bank, then rush in and make the fatal stab."

His father, Tom Barnes, was among the first of the renowned Cataloochee hunters.

MAJOR WOODY: "He was once hunting in a river bottom when he saw a panther crossing the river on a fallen tree trunk. At the moment when he raised his gun to shoot it, he saw a bear following the panther. He killed both."

Tom Barnes was born in 1818, only a year before Allen Davidson, and, like Allen, died when a very old man. As Allen eventually acquired that prized piece of land where Barnes' old camp lay, they undoubtedly hunted together.

Much later on, another relentless bear hunter, who for the purposes of this story shall be called "Josh", once illegally tracked a bear into the wilds of the Park and shot it when it had climbed way up a giant tree, only to have the bear become irretrievably lodged in the crotch of one of the huge limbs. Chagrined, he sat there thinking how to get his prize down. His fellow hunters left. Finally he got an axe and... it must have taken days... chopped down this gigantic virgin tree that had stood for so many centuries. He was, and still is, one of the most indefatigable hunters of the area. And the fallen log is still referred to by the natives as "Josh's" Tree. The mind boggles to think of the sonic boom as the tree toppled over, crushing other trees in its wake. As for what remained of the bear after that crash, one can only surmise.

But of all the hunters, the name that crops up time and again whenever tales are told of old Cataloochee is that of Turkey George Palmer.

Uncle Turkey was evidently a very special sort of man, though he was not flamboyant in habit, nor was he tall in stature or even particularly handsome.

There are two or three fine photographs of him. In the earliest one, when he was a young man of eighteen, already with a splendid dark moustache, he faces the photographer with a fierce, menacing expression that was not at all typical of him. However, as he is holding an old hog rifle close to his chest, he evidently felt he ought to project the bravado called for by this weapon. Later, in the 1930's, he was photographed as an old man with an impish smile. Here one sees the Uncle Turkey whose favorite game was racing in and out of his two-door house with the hounds in hot pursuit. In extreme old age, he was apparently as gentle and mild as an Indian summer.

Everybody talked about him all the time. They talked of his peculiar habit of walking beside but never riding his old horse "Sank", of carrying his knapsack on his chest instead of his back. They talked of his hunting strategy. He often hunted alone with traps and with no dogs. They talked of his victory shout when he had finished off his prey. It could be heard for miles. They spoke of the fantastic numbers of animals he had killed — often by himself — and of his unbelievable daring.

ELDRIDGE CALDWELL: "He was a great bearhunter, and he was also a hard worker, stayed at home pretty well all the time without he wasn't in the mountains. He was no hand at loaferin' at all. He had quite a bit of a sense of humor. He'd get some good ones off... He'us about five feet eight. I guess, wasn't too tall a man. And he'us all muscly, not a big old heavy man, but what there was, was muscle. He loved to bearhunt and catch wild turkeys; that's where he got his name, from that turkey pen.

JOHN PARRIS: "Turkey George was a small man in size, weighed about 140 pounds. He was wiry and tough and had the reputation of being able to outwalk anybody in the mountains."

RAYMOND CALDWELL: "Uncle Turkey was a-gettin' up in years when I was a young chap. I remember him as a witty type fellow that loved, enjoyed tellin' his stories of his past years and his experience of huntin' and catchin' the wild turkeys, and his experience in the many bears that he had killed. And I remember Old Turkey George with his horse 'Old Sank', that he led up and down the road and back to my father's mill... and his goin' to the post office and leadin' the horse, never ridin' it."

It's true that he always walked, and never rode his horse. He had a little homemade denim knapsack round his neck, and would often walk to Waynesville and back, leading tired "Old Sank". It was a distance of nearly fifty miles.

MARK HANNAH: "Most all of Turkey George's bears were trapped. Very few he had killed except in bearpens, steel traps, He didn't own bear dogs. Most likely he set his traps on Big Butt Mountain between Beech Creek and Pretty Hollow Creek... that was Turkey George's favorite trappin' ground. He had one trap that he called his 'Grizzly Trap'. It weighed about eighty pounds. And he had others that weighed about fifty pounds each. But he was a great hunter. And he trapped bears in the fall of the year when they were fat... and then after they would go to den and come out, he would trap them again. So he had two trappin' seasons... and bear meat 'bout all the time, I guess. He was a great hunter and trapper."

DR. NICK MEDFORD: "Uncle Turkey told me that if bears have plenty to eat all fall, they'll hibernate real early. Once he went up Beech Ridge and scared a bear out of hibernation. It had made a tepee out of branches, with leaves over it. This was in May. They don't hibernate long any more because there's not enough food or mast."

John Parris talked to Turkey George's son one Sunday afternoon when the newspaperman was in the Cataloochee mountains gathering material for his column, "Roamin'the Mountains".

ROBERT PALMER: "My father had a reputation for being a mighty hunter. He hunted all the time. He knew every foot of these mountains. And he sure gave the wild turkeys and the bear a fit. That is, until the Government came in and took our land and run us out."

"Why, before he had to hang up his rifle, he had killed off 106 bear one way or another. Some of them he trapped. And one he killed with a pistol."

"... my Mother always could tell before my father ever got to the house whether he had got a bear. When my father got to Butt Mountain — that was just off above the home place between here and Pretty Hollow Creek — he would let out a powerful yell. When he done that, my mother knew to get the water boiling. She knew he had a bear and would fetch it along directly."

"... Back then a fellow had to be mighty saving with his shot and powder. It was hard to come by, and hunters like my father didn't squander it. They made every shot count. He run his own bullets and he could still chew his own lead right up to the end of his hunting days."

"... Most of his hunting was done with a hog-rifle, a muzzle-loader. But when he was getting along in years, he bought himself a 38 Winchester. Got it down in Waynesville. It was after dark when he got back home and he was so proud of that rifle he thought he would have himself some fun."

"When he got close to the house, he hauled off and fired his rifle into the air and let out a big whoop. As it happened, his father-in-law, Andy Caldwell, was there at the house, and he was sitting close to the front window."

"Well, when that rifle went off, the window pane fell out and broke all over the place. Don't know what caused it to fall out just at that minute. Anyway, Andy thought for sure he was shot. He jumped up and yelled that he was shot."

"My father heard the commotion and come on into the house. They looked Andy over and couldn't find a drop of blood. They finally convinced him he hadn't been shot and then my father told him about firing his rifle into the air. He told them he had fired it into the air. But I don't think Andy ever believed it. I think he always thought my father put a bullet right through that window."

Poor old gun-shy Uncle Andy — often the victim, but never shot!

Joe Hall recorded Uncle Turkey's Cousin Will one September day in 1939, who told, in typical cousinly fashion of one time when Turkey's gun failed him.

WILL PALMER: "Me and him (Turkey) decided to go down to the traps one day. Got a big bear in the trap. And we come off down to the open woods and we had to step across a little swampy dreen. So we just go on to the trap... Beartrap was hung over a laurel stump by the grabs. George raised up with his Winchester to fire, and he never touched a hair on that bear. I said, George, help yourself again to a shot with mine and kill him. So George steadied hisself agin a saplin' and just busted that bear's head open. So we dressed the bear and carried him in home."

MARK HANNAH: "Somebody asked Uncle Steve what he thought about a shotgun... he had an ole shotgun... And he said, "Lord ha' mercy, I wouldn't have a shotgun in a bearfight. They're just nuthin', just as leave had a walkin' cane. They'll git ye killed. Sie!, yes, they'll git ye killed!""

Even the fabulous Turkey George couldn't live forever. He began to go downhill. His friends worried about him. What would he do when he could no longer hunt?

DR. NICK MEDFORD: "Turkey was getting feeble. His back hurt, but the inspiration was still there. His friends said they would carry his gun up Butt Mountain. But when Turkey heard the dogs start the bear, he got his gun and went ahead and got to the bear before anyone!"

That's how he began to grow into a legend even in his own time. People boasted about him to outsiders. They told of him as not only the greatest hunter but also the greatest storyteller. But sometimes he was surprisingly modest and taciturn.

ELDRIDGE CALDWELL: "Bunch of surveyors over there, surveying out that land for the park. And they had one feller that was awful bad. These surveyors! They tell big windy tales. A sight to hear 'em! The rest of 'em got sorta burnt up with it. He'd always done more bigger things than anybody else. So Harley Palmer saw Uncle Turkey comin' down the road one mornin'. Harley's along with these surveyors. 'Come on down, Uncle George,' said Harley, 'tell us one this mornin',' said, 'I wanta know how many bears that you killed in your lifetime'. He said, 'A hundred and four...' (Eldridge drily imitated the coolness and matter-of-factness of old Turkey). Jist on down the road he went, said he never cracked a smile!" (Eldridge cackled happily).

He killed two more bears after that. Then his life just quietly ebbed away when he could no longer join in the hunt. He was eighty-seven years old when he died in 1944.

This is a True Poetic Story by Mark E. Hannah, 1989

We lived in the mountains and backwoods hills,
Where the winters were rough and you got many chills,
Built fires in the chimneys and by them sat,
Waiting for Dad's return from the Pig Pen Flats.

Dad fed the pigs a poke full of corn,
Then headed down the trail in a bad snowstorm,
In the Waycaster laurel, he lost his hat,
But he kept on trudging from the Pig Pen Flat.

The wind was blowing the snow through the trees,
Mother got uneasy that Dad was going to freeze,
About that moment we saw him limping in,
With snow on his leggings and ice on his chin.

The boys chunked up the fire to thaw out his feet,
Mother made some coffee and Iva fried some meat.
They both agreed that he needed something hot,
So they made him a run of that Betsy sop.

Granny and Grandma, in the chimney corner sat,
Smoking clay pipes and having a little chat,
They were waiting to hear what Mack had to say,
For being caught out, such a terrible day.

He related a story, to keep down a quarrel,
For they didn't know much 'bout the Waycaster laurel,
He told them a story 'bout him and his dog,
Ole Watch had bayed a bear, Dad thought was a hog.

Ole Watch started yelping in a furious fight,
Dad had a .38 and a pine knot light.
He crawled out a log in the middle of the patch,
Then waited for the dog to make a good catch.

Hours passed slowly through the rest of the night,
He could see something faintly, for the moon wasn't bright,
With his pistol in his hand, he sat on the log,
And saw it was a bear and not a wild hog.

Just before daybreak, the bear began to tramp,
Going through brush towards the Tom Barnes' camp,
It went up the trail to the Hollow Maple Gap,
There it stopped long enough to give the dog a slap.

The chase was going at a very fast rate,
Dad trying to get close enough to use his .38.
When the bear caught the dog, it gave him a slap,
That sent him backwards toward the Hollow Maple Gap.

At the top of the balsam near the Bear Wallow Gap,
Ole Watch caught the bear and got several slaps,
This ended the chase early in the day,
Soon Dad and ole Watch were on the homeward way.

As they returned home down the Long Bunk Trail,
Each one was thinking the other had failed,
Ole Watch though Dad should have come off that log,
And have shot that thing that wasn't a hog.

– From *Smoky Mountain Reflections: A Collection of Poems*, p. 4

CHAPTER 15

The Blooming of the Beezlebubs
(Medicine)

Eldridge Caldwell's mother used Calycanthus floridus (eastern sweetshrub, Carolina all spice, or Beelzebub) much like the Cherokee, who used the resin from the bark for sores and wounds, and used an infusion to treat hives. Courtesy Bettina Darveaux.

RECENTLY, DEEP IN the wilds of Cataloochee on a pack trip, a young girl was catapulted over the head of her horse. He had suddenly tripped and fallen on his knees, rolling on the hapless girl. This was just a stone's throw from Uncle Steve Woody's quiet, deserted farmhouse. She seemed distressingly near death as she lay there, momentarily stunned, in the old stony roadbed near the stream. A few autumn leaves fluttered down on her. The yellow jackets buzzed ominously.

As it happened, the riders were only a few miles from the ranger station, and had it been required, someone could easily have spurred a horse quickly to put in a radio message for an emergency ambulance to meet them in less than an hour.

This could not have been done in old Cataloochee. Not only were distances great, but roads were mere rocky tracks. Transportation was practically nil. Also, licensed doctors were non-existent in the valley.

In the early days, "Dock" Bennett was the so-called doctor of the valley, so Mark was told. Then a real doctor, Dr. George David Allen Simpson, who was born in 1824, came to Haywood County in 1858 and located at Pigeon River where he practiced medicine for a number of years. During this period of the 1860s and 70s, he answered calls from a wide territory both East and West forks of Pigeon River, from Crabtree, Fines Creek, Cataloochee, and Jonathan's Creek.

Then there was Dr. Winton.

W. CLARK MEDFORD: "Although he did not live directly in the Great Smokies, he nonetheless spent half his time with the Cataloochee-Big Creek people as their doctor. It was the hardest riding he had to do... to travel horseback to reach them from his home, an average of some forty miles round trip over the worst of roads, mere bridle paths. He travelled on 'Old Baldy', his trusted saddle horse. At times, in epidemics of fever, this old mountain doctor would ride for ten days and nights maybe, but with very little sleep. He would 'catch a nap', as he put it, in some patient's home at the bedside, or lie down for an hour or so. Covered in winter with a big buffalo-hide overcoat, Dr. Winton would sometimes 'nod off' in his deep McClelland saddle. If he did so, his travel-wise old 'blaze-faced' horse would seldom ever take the wrong road or path."

He died about 1927, unfortunately for the people of Cataloochee.

When Flora Messer's grandfather, Daniel J. Cook, got cancer of the mouth, he first sent away to Chicago for mail order medicine, not trusting the herbal concoctions of the region. Then he decided that a doctor from 'furrin parts' was the only hope for this strange disease that was destroying him. Desperate, he brought a doctor out of Chicago who burnt his mouth, took plenty of money, and then left Daniel to die miserably. The brief respite after his sensational 'resurrection' on the cooling board, in which he seemingly came to life after having passed away, was only six months long. City doctors were no good after all!

A better doctor was Dr. Will Kirkpatrick, remembered Mark.

MARK HANNAH: "I remember goin' after him one time on a horse. And I got in that little Model T Ford he had, and he drove me across Cove Creek Mountain about as fast as I had ever been! We rode into Little Cataloochee, and then we had to get on a mule, and rode about another mile and a half to where a woman was sick, and he gave her a shot of medicine. She got all right. She 'us havin' convulsions. She was Mrs. Nelson, who lived in the last house under Indian Knob."

Dr. Kirkpatrick came in from Waynesville to attend the birth of Raymond Caldwell's brother, Joe, which was unusual, as local midwives usually looked after such things.

RAYMOND CALDWELL: "By then, the mail had a star route, and they could come out and call a doctor from Cove Creek."

As a nephew of both Andy Bennett's wife and "Creek George" Palmer's wife, Dr. Nick Medford, the oldest practicing dentist in Waynesville today, came into Cataloochee often, mainly because of the lure of bear-hunting.

He remembers practicing dentistry there only once, when he pulled the teeth of Harley Palmer in Harley's front yard. The event was duly recorded by someone who had a camera on hand. The scene: Jarvis Palmer's house, a chair in the front yard, a group of curious, amused onlookers on the porch, a blurred Harley flailing his arms while Nick pulled. The caption below the picture: "Poor Harley!"

Dr. Medford talked fondly of his much older half-brother, Dr. Bob Medford, who lived at the junction of Cove Creek and Jonathan Creek, just outside Cataloochee, where he was much loved and revered. He often went into Cataloochee on medical missions, riding a horse named "John." In winter his feet sometimes froze to the stirrups. He began going in about 1890 and practiced there for thirty years.

MARK HANNAH: "We didn't have a doctor in Cataloochee. I used to tell people that that was because all that hard work, clean water and fresh air keep us so healthy, we didn't need a doctor."

"I do remember the first time I saw a doctor, though. It was Dr. McMahan, from Crestmont over where the CCC Camp was at Big Creek. He was the nearest and the one who was usually brought in when someone was really sick. Of course, you didn't just call a doctor then."

"The doctor would just come when you'd go after him on a horse. Get on horseback and ride out across the mountain at Cove Creek, and catch a way to Waynesville, if you had to go to Waynesville after him. A lot of lives were lost from waiting too long. That's why there're so many little graves over there, too."

"But, anyway, I was only about three years old at the time. And grandfather was real sick. I remember the doctor pulling out that thing, and it stuck out of his ears, and he put it on grandfather's chest. Grandfather Hannah died about 1910. That's about as far back as I can remember. I was just a little thing and there I stood, just looking and looking between the boards at all that equipment. Grandfather's cabin is still there."

His eyes crinkled up in the corners of his pink, cheerful face as he told me of Dr. Bob Medford's being called in to examine a little girl named Doanie. (Doanie, or Doney is the mountain man's corruption of the word, Donna, which was first used by American sailors in South American ports. "Doney-gal" is another name for sweetheart in the mountains.) This little girl had been struck dumb, and had not spoken for weeks, much to the distress of her parents. Dr. Bob commenced to examine her, beginning with her head, ears, throat, neck, and, as he went lower into the chest region, Doanie was instantly cured. She spoke up indignantly: "Mama, tell this old man to git his hands off me!"

VERDA HANNAH (from the next room): "Oh, Mark!"

Even by the time that Tom Alexander came into Cataloochee in the 1930's and opened his dude ranch, there was still no immediate doctor. His wife, "Miss Judy", was often called on by the local people for doctoring, on the sole evidence of her owning a first-aid kit.

JUDITH BARKSDALE ALEXANDER: "My father was a doctor so he thought our pioneering back into Cataloochee was marvelous. Said, my child, you must have a complete medical kit. I hadn't even had first aid at that time. When I went there, it was, and almost still is, back country..."

"There were very high class mountain people who lived in Cataloochee Valley. We went in as strangers. They didn't know what we were going to do (when we first established the ranch). As far as they were concerned, we were some foreigners who had come down and taken the Preacher Hall Place. And they weren't sure how we were going to operate it. Then they found out that I did have some medication. And it got to be a sort of a common practice that everybody's problems (were brought to me)... did what I could. I wasn't any kind of a professional."

"I wish time and time again I had had real (medical knowledge)! But you absorb a lot and your father tells you a lot. We didn't have any miracle drugs then, just had good old standbys. Always put in something for diarrhea, fever, things you could diagnose fairly easily. That was the hardest thing to do was try to diagnose."

"We had lots of hard times understanding the terms that (Cataloochans) would use. For instance they woke me up one night. 'Please come on up, Aunt Maria's bad off!' I said, 'What's the trouble, Jarvis?' 'Well, she got the bloody flux and we can't do anything about it.' Well, it was a man I was talking to, and I was trying to decide what was the bloody flux. It was diarrhea or dysentery. I had a little puddlejumper, a little Model T or Model A, and I went over there. But we didn't have any mode of taking care of diarrhea in those days. We had to get some bismuth or paregoric... especially bismuth if you had any dysentery involved. And correct the diet. Not let them eat anything but... not eat any fruit or vegetables. Boil all the milk."

"I didn't see any tuberculosis. There were just fairly simple ailments... pain, extreme constipation maybe. I'd have to give enemas. Larry Caldwell's mother was visiting because Larry was living with us. She had a terrible seizure during the night, with vomiting and intense pain. It could be other things, but to me it looked like appendicitis. I said, Tom, we better just send her in... it's a long trip to Waynesville... I'm afraid it might rupture. There was nobody to telephone the hospital so we just put her in the car and drove on over the mountain. It was appendicitis. The serious things, well, I wouldn't try to do anything. Now, if somebody had cut himself with an axe, I had suture material."

"It disturbed us greatly that no public health nurses ever came in, that there was no kind of medical instruction. Even after we came up here to Fie Top, there still was no nursing service. But of course they can get out of there now that they have roads. Tom and I made this special trip to Kentucky to the Frontier Nursing Service... Mrs.

Breckinridge... and had a very interesting talk with her. We were talking about people on Hemphill and Cataloochee when they had no way out. I almost started a frontier nursing service here, because we had several doctors staying with us who didn't mind getting on a horse and taking care of any situation."

"When I went with the grannywoman to Bly Caldwell's, (whose husband, George, worked for us) the only thing we had to have was plenty of boiling water, which everybody knows. Everything was washed. She didn't have any instruments that I recall. But more or less just lots of pads, lots of newspaper, and sterilized all the cloths that you used after the birth of the baby. They had real knowledge of what they were doing. Had, of course, scissors to cut the umbilical cord and cleaned up the baby. I didn't do much. I was just helping."

Fannie Hannah (Mark Hannah's mother) was one of four famous midwives in Cataloochee, all of whom were very much respected because they brought nearly everyone into the world. Such women were greeted with awe, as well they might, for they were willing to make extraordinary sacrifices, to lay down their work, and forego their sleep at all times of night and in any kind of weather in order to traipse or ride the most difficult mountain trails to attend birthings, many of which were false alarms, so that they often had to do the same tortuous journey over again. Grannywoman, a term often used in the mountains, was not used by Fannie Hannah, who preferred to be known as a doctor-woman.

The earliest known midwife was Elizabeth Noland Hannah, the first settled housewife.

Then Aunt Easter Sutton, Sol Sutton's wife, was one of the early midwives in Big Catalooch'. There was also Susie Woody, Steve's sister, married to Harrison Caldwell.

Floyd Woody, her nephew, was sitting around telling tales on his front porch one hot day in late June. His wife, Folsom, wanted him to tell a story about his old pranks, in which she had often participated.

FLOYD WOODY: "You keep that till I get this one! I got another little short one. We'us settin', eatin' supper one night. My Daddy had a renter, helped my Daddy farm. And this man couldn't talk plain, sorta tongue-tied. It's dark, and we'us a-eatin' supper, and he come at the winder. There's a big winder where the dinin' room table's at, in the kitchen. Just sorta stuck his head there and says, Woody, bring your maul and come up to my house right quick!"

"Well, I jumped out, and we got what we call old mauls around here, that you drive stakes in the ground, or drive arn (iron) wedges to split timber with. Well, I grabbed that ole maul and started. And when I got up there, why, I went carryin' this maul in the house, and they'us in the bedroom."

"And he says, 'Where's yer Maw, m'wife's havin' a baby!?'"

"Yeah, and I had to throw that maul down and run back and git my Maw! He called her Maw. We'd say Mommy, and we never heered the word Maw. It sounded like he said maul; he's tongue-tied."

"Yep, I got my Mother there on time. Yeah, and she pinch hit for them till the next mornin'. We got Aunt Susie to come then and finish the job. Aunt Susie Caldwell, married Harrison Caldwell, Aunt Susie did. The best midwives in the valley were Aunt Susie Caldwell and Aunt Easter Sutton. Now Aunt Easter'us the one what brought me to this country. She'us a great, was an awful good woman, yeah, and ever'body loved 'er. She was Sol Sutton's wife."

FLORA PALMER MEDFORD: "Grannywoman? (laughs) I don't remember but one livin' over there, and she lived till everybody had their babies. That was Aunt Susie, Uncle Harrison Caldwell's wife. And she lived right over here, across the creek from my grandfather, Andy Caldwell. I guess you've been told where his house was. Uncle Harrison lived over there, and she was Jonathan Woody's aunt, Uncle Steve's sister. And so everybody that had a baby there sent for her."

When asked if she was brought into the world by Aunt Susie, she dispensed the usual dose of laconic mountain humor.

FLORA PALMER MEDFORD: "Yeah, I don't remember it. (laughs) They'd take a horse for her to ride, when I remember. She'd ride a-straddle, y'know, usually had on pants or a big skirt like they had, and she'd get up on that ole horse and ride. And she'd go anywhere. And always it'ud be bad weather when the baby'ud be born... a night. Well, Aunt Susan's a good ole woman, and I think she'us real successful. I don't know that she ever lost any of 'em. Well, Aunt Susie, I reckon she didn't turn nobody down. She went every place in any kind of weather."

MARK HANNAH: "One time she (my mother) was supposed to go out to Bob Ewart's... Bob 'Canadian', we called him. And he came after her on the gray horse."

"As they were riding down by the big hill through Little Cataloochee, why, they crossed Dude Creek. It'us very rough and dark there, of a night, especially... this was in the night sometime. And, riding along, my Mother was riding, and he was walking in front, she heard something she thought was a panther walking along in the leaves above the road. And she kept hearin' it, but didn't say anything about it."

"After they got through into a light place, into more or less the highway, she asked Bob, did you hear anything down there?"

"And Bob said, 'Yes, I ess hear sumpin', but when I hear sumpin', I say nuthin'. I was afraid I would skeer you.'" (Bob was one of the Ewarts who had speech difficulties.)

"Mother said (to us), 'I believe that was a panther. It was on the upper side of the road walking along by us, and then it would get below the road. And I was very scared.'"

"They went on up to the Grooms Boys Branch (where the Grooms boys were killed during the Civil War) and then up what they call the Mack Trail and out to High Top... My father built a near way from the old Indian trail that's on that map now... a near way coming off to the Grooms Boys Branch from the Asbury Trail. And they went on out by the Indian Grave to High Top."

"She was goin' to be the doctor, but nothing happened. False alarm. So she came back the next day. That was about three miles, I'd say... just straight up trail in places... just all she could do to stay on the horse... for a man, much less a woman. She made it anyway, and came back in the next day... nothing doing on the case."

"Bob told her the next time anything like that happened, he was goin' to holler and scream just like a panther as he came down the ridge over there. Said she could be ready to start with him."

"So one night, about nine o'clock, Mother was in bed. But I hadn't went to bed yet. I heard some screamin' over on Indian Grave Ridge, just like a panther. 'And I said, well, that's Bob now... he said he was goin' to holler.' And in a very short time I saw a glimpse of him walkin' up the near way. He didn't ride up the road. He just hooked his horse up and walked right up a little near way that was there... it's only 'bout half a mile... to cut off some of the distance."

"And he just came through the gate... threw it open and on up the steps and knocked on the door, then opened it and came right on in. He said, 'Whur's Fannah? Whur Fannah?'"

"I said, 'she's in there in the bed.'"

"And he just went in there and said: 'Ess jump outer there, Fannah! Ess a sho' Pop this time!'"

"And she got up, and they went down the branch there. She got ready and got on this horse again, rode up by the Grooms Boys Branch and up the steep trail again!"

"Naw, no doctor today would do that. There never been a doctor would do that way. But that time she got the baby. There were several out there, and I think she was doctor to every one of them, as far as I know. She made many trips."

"Bob Brown. That was another case. Bob lived over on the Will Messer farm in the old Braz Whaley house. Mother was supposed to go. He'd talked to her. And one day while we were restin'... I believe we'd been mowin' hay. Came in for lunch, looked and saw Bob comin'. He was kindy a bashful man. He came in and sat down, and fifteen minutes 'fore he ever did tell his business. Finally he asked where my Mother was. We told him in the house. And he went in and told her, and she got ready for equipment. she just went walkin'. It's only about a mile, so she could walk that far."

"And then, after they'd been gone a little while... Dad had some hounds there that you could set on anybody's track and they'd run just like it was a fox a-racin'. He let 'em get about a half mile away and said, Boys, let's have a little fun out of the old man Bob. He's so dry and won't talk hardly. Let's put these dogs after him."

"So he started the dogs. And it's just like a fox race, barkin' every breath, those two hounds. And they caught up with them down about the Hannah cemetary half a mile away."

"Mother said, 'Now them boys is havin' fun out of us. They put them dogs on our tracks. They ran up there.'"

"He laughed a little bit about it. And they went on home then. But Dad <u>reeeely</u> laughed about that dogs chasin' Bob Brown!"

"She always did doctoring as long as I can remember, farther back than that. And I don't know how many... I counted up... I wrote down in a book here somewhere... of families I just about know she was there for every one of their children... six and eight in a family... all over Cataloochee, some on Big Cataloochee. A few times in Big Creek, even. A few times she would say, I can't handle the case, you'll have to call a doctor. But it seldom happened. And she saved many lives in there by being a midwife, I'm sure of that. She was a fine person to know and a good doctor. She seldom ever had anybody to help her... the neighbor women would come in, naturally. But she didn't have any special one, and she didn't have any special instruments that I know of."

Most often Cataloochans doctored themselves. Faith healing was not particularly prevalent in the valley, though today it is still said that Fred Hannah's widow can "take fire out of burns" and effect other cures, also.

MRS. FRED HANNAH: "One time when my husband was away from home, teaching, my daughter Maxine was playing and stepped on an old rusty nail that had been driven into a piece of lumber. The nail almost penetrated the foot. I called for help and my brother-in-law, Mont Hannah, came to me. We had to stand on the lumber and lift my daughter off to pull the nail from the foot. I knew this was dangerous to blood-poison and no one to take her to a Doctor. A man told us of a remedy: get woolen rags, socks or anything just woolen — place them in a washpan or pot, then set the woolen rags on fire and hold the child's foot over the smoke for several minutes, maybe hours. This they did, and the child slept good that night and was soon well again. She never seem to hurt any time."

Eldridge Caldwell once presented a puzzling bit of information which was quite difficult to unravel as he died soon afterwards.

Earlier in May, at his beautiful white clapboard farmhouse seventy-four year old Eldridge was still getting about, though in fairly poor health, unable to use his new set of false teeth, and blood pressure giving him a headache, plus the added woes of rheumatism. But he was cheerful and mischievous as he sat on the bench outdoors, a thin golden thread of 'baccy spilling out of the corner of his mouth. He spoke of health and medicine since both were much on his mind.

ELDRIDGE CALDWELL: "My mother's little brother passed away when he'us young, with what they called yellow fever back then. They had that turrible high fever, and they had no doctor. My mother's grandfather'us a Ferguson. He'd come over there. They lived on Laurel Branch down below Cove Creek. And he'd come across the mountain there from the other side, and he'd cross the river on the ice. Winters used to be turribly cold here, much colder. He'd cross the river on the ice and come up there. He doctored with herbs, just things he made himself, the only doctor they had."

When asked if he knew of any doctors that used to come into Cataloochee, he gave the mountain man's ambiguous reply:

"The only ones I remember are since I was big enough to remember."

He continued: "There was a salve made out of Beezlebubs and olive. There're two other ingredients. There were four things. And, with home-made lard, she made this up into a mixture out of stuff, my mother did. Good for any kind of infection, boil, or whatever you might have on you."

This was intriguing, this mention of Beelzebub who was, in Milton's epic poem, the fallen angel ranking just below Satan, a Devil, in fact, a Leading Devil, also called Prince of Demons, and Lord of the Flies. What was this medicine made of in Cataloochee... this Paradise Lost?

ELDRIDGE CALDWELL: "Well, in the spring of the year, it blooms, comes out in a great big bulb as big as the end of my finger... all over the branches of it. And it doesn't get too high... maybe thirty feet (his niece, Ernestine, knows what it is... can't remember the name). I don't know if it's all gone yet over at the Kerr Place in Cataloochee or not, used to be a big grove of them there (Mark says there are plenty of them left). Kerr buried some of his slaves over on the other side. The spring of the year, I believe in May, is when the odor was on for those Beezlebubs. Oh, you could smell 'em from here to the barn. Pretty good smell."

The name mystified Mark, too. Of course, remedies vary from family to family in the mountains... and he and Eldridge lived in two widely separated sections of Catalooch'.

MARK HANNAH: "Maybe Bamagilia? They used to have a salve they'd make out of that Bamagilia. Now it used to break some people out. I know some people it wouldn't even help. There're very few places you can find it... some on Little Cataloochee Bridge near the Kerr Place. It smelled good in May! I believe the slaves used these trees for their medicine."

Suddenly the realization came that Mark was saying "Balm-of-Gilead". Further investigation in Arthur Stupka's invaluable book on trees of the Smokies explained that this tree was introduced by early settlers in East Tennessee and that Randolph Shields actually recalled having seen the Balm-of-Gilead in Cataloochee!

Another source reported that the terminal buds of this tree, sometimes called the balsam poplar, an introduced tree from the north, "are about one inch long, and the lateral buds smaller...: they are taper-pointed and are covered by five scales and saturated with a pungently fragrant, amber-colored balsam which is called Balm-of-Gilead in the drug trade and is used medicinally as a constituent of cough medicine."

Pursuing this strangely-named remedy, one felt by now as dogged a detective as Hiram Wilburn on the scent. In the *Waynesville Mountaineer* of 1973, an article was published about Miss Janie of Cedar Mountain who used to live near Caesar's Head where her husband, Solomon, was known as the community doctor, while Miss Janie was its druggist, nurse, and midwife. What was really thrilling was the discovery that Miss Janie used to make a burn salve out of 'Balm-of-Gideon' buds, heart leaves, hoglard, and hog hair ammonia!

Turkey George's daughter, Flora, talked about some of the medicinal teas used. The uses of these teas varied from community to community.

FLORA PALMER MEDFORD: "In the medicine line, we had catnip and pennyroyal (sometimes pronounced 'pennyrile'). That pennyroyal, we used to pull it up; it grows 'bout this high. You see it? Smells <u>good</u>. And we used to dry it, y'know, hang it up and tie it and dry it so we'd have it in the wintertime to take when we had colds. We'd make it into a tea. And then we had catnip. I think they gave that to babies mostly. Now we didn't drink those at the table. Now, catnip, pennyroyal, what else did we have? Mullein! Yeah. Now that's something not good at all... it was something about colds. I don't know what. I'd rather be sick than try to drink that. Well, there's more than that, but now that pennyroyal and catnip was really good, especially that pennyroyal, put a little sugar in it."

She carefully wrote the recipes out in a cramped pencil hand on lined paper:

"Brew catnip teas in water and drink for colds (I think this was for babies)."

"Penneroyal tea. Good for adults to drink for colds."

"Mullen tea. Plants grow tall and have large fuzzy leaves. Make tea for tonic in spring of year."

"Boneset tea. A spring tonic. It grew in and around swamps."

There were other recipes for salves and medicines, written painstakingly in her careful old lady's hand:

"Groundhog grease: render groundhog fat. Strain and put in jar. Its used on chest for colds. Grease chest with grease and cover chest with wool flannel cloth that has been greased on one side and a few drops of turpentine dropped on it spread on chest and cover patient up to keep warm. Also rub some grease on throat and give one half teaspoon grease to swallow."

"Bear grease was used for same thing. Groundhog grease more plentiful. Therefore was used more."

"Spring tonic: one teacup of molasses, three tablespoons sulphur. Stir and take some for spring tonic."

"Make poltice of wheat bran by cooking bran in water few minutes, cool, and spread a layer on cloth and apply to sores. boils, etc. to draw out the inflammation and pus."

"Horse oats boiled in water. Drain off water and bathe affected parts for poison oak."

"Moisten tobacco leaf in water and place over boil and tie cloth on to draw out pus. If fever causes tobacco leaf to dry moisten it again and keep on sore for longer time."

"Worm medicine: Get seeds off Jerusely-moke (Jerusalem Oak) plant in fall put handful of seeds in pint of molasses on stove and bring to boil, when cool let child eat several spoonfull once or twice and the worms will be gotten rid of."

"Preventive of diseases: tie small ball or wad of assidifidy (asafoetida) in rag: tie with string around neck and wear constantly through the winter months."

Later, when she died after a bad fall which resulted in a broken hip, one thought of Flora, with the big clock ticking away in her lonely, musty house, carefully preserving these formulas for this book... magic formulas that could do nothing to save her.

Bloodroot was a good spring medicine, Mark remembered hearing. However, Ross Hutchins, in *Hidden Valley of the Smokies*, claimed that bloodroot was extremely poisonous, the roots containing morphine! Spignet, like Indian turnips, said Mark, was good for the back.

His mother had gathered these herbs in the days when she was a well known midwife and doctor in Little Cataloochee.

MARK HANNAH: "She'd go on cases of fever. A lot of times they'd come for her. She read a doctor book she had and studied up on it, and was pretty good on such things. I'd say good for her time. Seems like it was called *Pierce's Medical Discovery Book* or something of that name. She kept well read on such cases as fever, measles..."

"She would use teas, like boneset, to sweat anybody and things like that. No, boneset doesn't really have anything to do with setting bones, not at all. Take boneset and it'll sweat you. It's a bitter, bitter thing. But she used a lot of quinine, laxatives. I don't know where that quinine come from, but she used that to give to patients to sweat 'em, too."

"I didn't go out and gather things for her. She did that herself. They had one baby tea they called catnip tea. I think colic is about what it was for. They had a disease then of babies. I never hear of it anymore. It was called hives... break out and so forth. She talked about the hives. I remember some of her recipes for those things."

"There was a vine she called 'ground ivy', maybe house leak (leek?). She boiled it to make a tea to give small babies to break them out with the hives."

Passion flower was sometimes called "ground ivy" in the mountains.

"She just got interested in medicine, got these books and started studying. She was a good reader and speller, and could pronounce anything good, and could write good... for a woman."

An old photograph shows that in her old age, Fannie Hannah had a goiter, which was fairly common in the mountains. It stemmed from a lack of natural iodine in the diet as mountain water is so pure that it is extraordinarily free of minerals. Nowadays, of course, most salt is iodized, and the difficulty rarely occurs.

The usual medical cases were for births, the fever (whatever that meant... typhoid, scarlet or otherwise), broken bones, and death from complications of old age.

MARK HANNAH: "For a broken leg, the local treatment was just splinter 'em up with splints made out of bark or something. Put that leg back together and let it grow back. Just cut you some the size of the arm or leg or whatever it was. If it was birch, just peel the bark off of it, shave it just right. It was smooth, and put that round your leg... to make your leg grow back straight."

A more unusual illness, but confined to mountain areas, it would seem, was that of "milk-sick"... a serious disease which sometimes claimed lives.

W. CLARK MEDFORD: "Jim Price was found dead of milk sick in the early days west of The Purchase, formerly the home of John L. Ferguson on top of Cataloochee Mountain, on a branch, known as the Long Branch (new name, McGee Branch). A little dog stayed with the body and attracted searchers to it by getting on a foot log and howling."

Though the U. S. Department of Agriculture could not account for the disease as late as 1912, we now know that the white snakeroot plant is poisonous to cattle because of the tremetol in its leaves and stems. Yet few of the local people seem to accept the fact that white snakeroot is really the cause. They are inclined to think it is the fault of minerals in the soil, and often will not drink out of a fine bold spring because it is in "milk-sick" territory.

Worse than World War I itself, for Cataloochee, was the great influenza epidemic which swept the country in 1918, coming to the valley about 1920. This virus eventually killed 20 million people around the world. Verda and Flora Messer's sister, Loretta, who married Claude Valentine, became very ill during this siege. Claude's sister, Pearl, was called in from Cosby, Tennessee, to look after his children and help with the housework and nursing. Loretta did not live through the cruel illness, and did not live to witness the courtship and marriage of her sister-in-law, Pearl, to Eldridge Caldwell. The whole of the epidemic was indelibly imprinted in Eldridge's mind.

ELDRIDGE CALDWELL: "Back in 1918 that flu broke out. I'us at loggin' camp at Round Bottom (beyond the western boundary of Cataloochee) when Aunt Mag Mauney and her husband, 'Big George' Caldwell tuck it. Uncle George came in after me. I came back home. My father and mother both down with it, and that's why he come."

"So, when they got a little better till when I could leave 'em, we hadn't heard a thing from the other Caldwells. We knew they're just up on the mountain by theyselves. Father said, I want you to go up and see about Uncle George and the family. Said, they may ever' one of 'em be down up there. I got on a horse and rode up there, went to the door."

"Aunt Mag met me at the door, she'us sweepin' and cleanin' up the floor. I said, how are you'uns, Aunt Mag? She said, I reckon we'll make it, said, this ole flu just about killed us all, said, hit's the nastiest ole disease's ever been in this world. Yeah, you know, been vomitin' all over the place. My father was never well a day after it. Lived two years, but..."

Many of the small, unmarked graves in the cemetary in Little Cataloochee are the result of a diphtheria epidemic many years ago that took the lives of many children. There were overtones of the Black Death, or the Bubonic Plague in Europe.

MARK HANNAH: "Diptheria hit there, killed three in one family in a couple of days. These little graves aren't marked... just old stones there, is all there is there. Yeah, just buried people in a hurry to stop the epidemic, and put up a rock there. Just a stone, field stone is all there is. They didn't put any names or anything. The ones that we know about... the old folks gone, that's it. I been tryin' to make a record, try to keep some of those names."

Not too many years ago, a rare blood disease stemming from an enzyme deficiency was discovered... among others, in a Cataloochee-based family whose forebears had originally brought this hereditary disease from their native Wales. A carrier intermarrying with another carrier could conceivably produce a child who would inherit the disease.

A Dutch-born doctor from Vanderbilt University became fascinated by this rare occurrence which he had heretofore seen only in pockets of Northern Europe. He decided to test every related person he could find. Now at the University of Houston, he confessed he was astounded at the size of the mountain-born families he had to investigate — many of them stemming from Cataloochee. Their clannishness was extreme. Most of them, hundreds, in fact, still remained in and around their original territory. Their names covered a whole wall in the lab at Vanderbilt University. He remarked, also, on the honesty with which the clan admitted to some bastardy, realizing the dangers of perpetuating such a disease.

Cataloochee was no worse than any other inbred settlement isolated from the world, as far as genetic defects, unwanted pregnancies and bastards. These were all absorbed into the community where there was no special secret made of the facts. Often bastards or 'woods colts' were given the names of their fathers to soften the impact later in life. There were few opportunities to marry anyone who wasn't some kind of a blood relative. Speech defects, retardation, and simpletons were treated kindly in the valley, unlike the city where these things were more likely hidden away in a closet. Kephart wrote that "home ties are so powerful that mountaineers never sent their 'fitified' folks or half-wits, or other unfortunates to any institution in the lowlands, as long as it is bearable to have them around."

The few known simpletons were apparently harmless rather happy individuals who liked to dance in the light of the moon or who, when disturbed by the outside world, went "all shackelty" and lay down in the corn rows until the disturbed feeling passed.

Senility in old age was a medical problem once in a while. Nowadays, these old folks are relegated to nursing homes.

Fortunately, the large families of Cataloochee were able to absorb these old people into their households, as we do not seem to be able to do today. Grannies sitting on the front porch with their little clay pipes were an accepted part of valley life.

"Granny Pop", wife of the early Cataloochee pioneer, Levi Caldwell, lived to an advanced age and with it came approaching senility. Finally, in order to protect her, the family fenced or caged her in the front yard when they could not watch her. Mary Lou Leatherwood Moody said that her mother, Leona Caldwell, as a young girl, passing by her Uncle Hiram Caldwell's house, perhaps on a Sunday when the family had gone to church, would listen to the pleas of "Granny Pop" to let her out. The softhearted Leona would open the gate, "Granny Pop" would be off in the wildwood immediately, and the rest of the day would be spent in the community search parties which often went looking for the old lady.

Heart attacks and cancer were common causes of death, said Mark, as they are now. George Palmer, the original Palmer settler, died one cold January 19, 1859, of a heart attack while completing the construction of the Cataloochee Turnpike. Tuberculosis was not particularly prevalent. Flora Palmer's sister, Evvie, died six months after she married the man that Turkey George objected to. She died, Flora now thinks, from a ruptured appendix, though at the time, Dr. Bob Medford was unable to do much for her except to look on helplessly. Then Daniel Cook was taken away by cancer, despite his fancy doctor from Chicago. But these are universal diseases of man.

Fatal accidents were something else. How ingeniously the people of Cataloochee injured themselves! How dramatically they died! Consider how a visitor, the Reverend Camel was killed, not by falling off of a cliff, but by having the cliff fall on him.

MARK HANNAH: "On or about the year of 1922 a man came over to Turkey George Palmer's to spend a few days in the mountains. This was Mr. Camel, a veteran of World War I, who went over the Top in four battles. He and another man from Cosby, Tennessee, decided they would go up Indian Creek to the mouth of Lost Bottom Creek and locate a camping spot. They walked about two miles and came to a place they thought would be a nice spot by a huge rock cliff."

"They hung their pack sacks up and gathered fire wood enough to last through the night. It was cool weather, spring time. And they built a huge bonfire against the rock cliff. I believe that the fire heated this rock which was at least eight to ten feet in length and about ten inches thick, to a degree that caused this slab to fall down on its edges by the side of Reverend Wilson Camel, who was sleeping on the ground. The rock then turned over and covered Camel's body except one foot was out visible. The lone companion tried in vain to get the rock off of the Preacher. He worked all night in the dark, but failed to release the body of Camel. It was a lonesome night to spend with your friend buried under a rock."

"When daybreak came next day, the companion started hiking out, wading the creek, as there was no trail at this date. He came to Turkey George's house and told the sad story. The news was carried by horse riders to the people in Cataloochee Valley. Palmers, Caldwells, were quickly found. Mont Hannah was teaching school at Beech Grove, and he gave the children the day off, while he and the larger boys went up the creek to assist in carrying the body out. The big job was prying the large rock off of him. A large maple sapling about sixteen feet long was cut and a bait rock, as it was called, was used, and they pried from every angle with other poles before they released the body. This rock had to be picked up and wedges placed under it to hold the weight, perhaps ten tons, until the men could pull the dead body of Preacher Wilson Camel from under it."

"The group of volunteers then made a stretcher out of two poles and tied the body to them. And they took turns about, four men at each turn carried, then four more would relieve them, etc. until they arrived at the Turkey George Place. There Turkey George's wife gave them a sheet to wrap him in. A wagon was made available and the body was hauled over Mt. Sterling and into Cosby, Tennessee for burial. Any one wishing to see this rock may do so by hiking up Palmer Creek Trail to Lost Bottom Creek then follow Indian Creek about one eighth mile on left hand side of creek."

Or consider the fate of poor Marion Caldwell who set fire to a tree he wanted to be rid of, and went about his plowing. Halfway through a row, he failed to notice that the tree had burned through and was falling. That was the end of Marion.

Even a night's drinking party could be dangerous to one's health as Mark graphically wrote in a piece he entitled: "A Man Froze to Death in the Snow Covered Area on Pretty Hollow Creek... Cataloochee".

MARK HANNAH: "Robert (Bobby) Caldwell and a Mr. Bob Forester left Caldwell Fork Community one cold day. It was snowing. Bobby volunteered to take Mr. Forester, horse-back, as far up on Pretty Hollow Creek as he could, due to the rugged little trail that existed at this time... about 1915, I guess. They rode the horse over Fork Mountain, into Big Cataloochee, then down creek to Palmer Creek (then called Indian Creek), and rode up to Turkey George Palmer's. Talked to them and rode on towards Pretty Hollow Gap. Both men seemed to be drinking but able to ride horses. After a few hours, Bobby came back and went on home on Caldwell Fork Creek, the old Jess McGee home. Nothing was heard of the Mr. Forester for several days, (everyone) believing that he had gone on over the mountain to his home and work. A man was up in the woods trapping or fishing and found the body whom they believed to be Forester. It is believed that he froze to death in the snow during the night that Bobby Caldwell left him."

"The body was carried out on homemade stretchers, wrapped in a sheet that Mrs. Alice Palmer gave them, placed in a wagon and hauled twenty-two miles to Mt. Sterling Depot of the T. and N. C. Railroad. They taken him home to Tennessee."

By this time Turkey George and Alice Cumi Palmer must have become very fatalistic about life. Their mission seemed to be to provide winding sheets.

Some barely lived to tell the tale. Eldridge Caldwell nearly died of the immense number of yellow jacket stings he received when we went to look for his father's lost hogs. Interestingly enough, a recent Park ranger in Cataloochee, Tom Kloos, said that the most serious injuries he had to contend with among visitors were insect stings; some had terrible allergies to bees and wasps, and could die if not treated in time. Eldridge had suffered massive stings, and barely got home on Uncle Steve's borrowed horse.

ELDRIDGE CALDWELL: "I rode up to the porch, and they had to help me off that horse into that bed. Then father sent after a doctor, Bob Medford. But before he ever got there, I had vomited. And he said that's all saved me. Yeah, and he said I wouldn't have lasted till he got there. See, he had to ride a horse, man did, after him, and then ride back...'bout fourteen miles, y'know. Yeah, we didn't have no communication at all. I was too sick to get out of the house. That's about the worst thing that ever happened to me in there."

Another time, his horse, "Old Frank", slipped, threw Eldridge down and fell on him, much as had happened to the young girl many years later in an abandoned Cataloochee. This time, however, a foot was broken.

"I had that big cowboy saddle a man brought from Washington. It had a steel tree. That steel tree was all that protected me if any at all. It had oxbow stirrups on, copperbound... busted that stirrup all to pieces with my foot."

"That dog, he stayed with me awhile, and then he went on home and started scratchin' and whinin' at the front door. It was after my father got sick, wasn't long before he died. One of my brothers, Dillard, slept in the room with 'im, without I was there, and we'd set the night about. So he called Dillard and told him to git up, wanted to see what had happened, said that dog wouldna come home... so Dillard he just rolled out of bed and run over to the barn and caught another horse."

"And here he come, met me, right above the church. I'us crawlin'. It was rainin'. I could have lost that foot crawlin'. And the dog, his name was Ted, beat 'im back."

Old Jarvis Caldwell nearly drowned in Cataloochee Creek recently in a freak accident, though he lived to grin over it and tell it as a great joke on himself.

Wearing his big hip boots while fishing, he slipped on the creek's notoriously green and treacherous stones, breaking his ankle. He sat down in icy waters up to his chin, filling up his waders in the process. Desperately, he tried to unhook the leaden water-filled waders, but was unable to do so. He hallooed, without much success, as he was fishing alone. There he had to sit, icy-cold, wondering how to get out of his predicament. Above his head, he saw a thunderous black storm-cloud, and thought to himself:

"Jarvis, if it rains, and the river rises, you're done for!"

So he began to call out again mightily. After an hour had passed, a head appeared above the river bank, startled to see Jarvis sitting there, resting his chin on the water.

The man, a slight fellow, tried to pull Jarvis out without success, and said, to Jarvis' consternation, "Wait here (as though Jarvis could move!). I'll get my wife."

The wife was a stout woman, and with the help of Jarvis' son who had suddenly arrived, they pulled him out of what might well have been his grave.

There were not only wasp stings to mar this garden of Eden, but also the fangs of rattlesnakes and copperheads, the teeth of raccoons, and the long curved claws of the black bear. But none of these caused any human fatalities, as far as Mark could recall. He said snake bites were not nearly as dangerous as most people thought. Tom Kloos corroborated this. Mark's leisurely occupation while he was alone in Cataloochee for so many years as ranger, was killing rattlers, much as some people collect stamps or matchbook covers. During his last year in the valley, he killed twenty-five of them, though these days the Park Service does not condone killing of any animal, dangerous or otherwise. No doubt he did this in memory of a tough battle his brother Robert had had with a rattlesnake. Robert lost a finger, as a result.

MARK HANNAH: "The more poison you can remove from the snakebite, the better off you are. If you can get half a drop of it, well, it'll be that much done. If Robert'd known to do that then, he'd probably have saved that finger. He'd a-put it out of there, even with his mouth, sucked it out."

"But the best thing to do is to put cold packs on it if you know how to do it. That's what they taught us in the Park Service. Yep, put ice on. That keeps the blood from flowin', and that stops that long enough to freeze it (actually one shouldn't completely freeze the flesh as this might lead to gangrene). A tourniquet, too. Tie that and just split that place to get all of that blood runnin' out of there that you can, sling it out of there. I always carried just a little suction cup, and a rubber band and a razor blade."

JARVIS CALDWELL: "My oldest brother, Roscoe, was tying oats that had been cradled about two days. He picked up the bundle of oats and a copperhead snake. As he tied the bundle the snake bit him on the hand, lightly; it almost missed his hand but drew blood. Our mother had a small chicken caught and she quickly split the chicken open and placed Roscoe's hand inside then tied it with a bandage. This remedy was to draw the poison out of the blood stream."

"Another remedy for snake bites or bee stings was to hold a small bottle filled with turpentine (old timers carried this frequently) to the snake bite and you could even see the poison coming into the bottle. Ira McGee did this once in the back woods."

Though raccoons were apt to bite when cornered and bears to claw, domestic animals actually caused the fatal accidents.

LLOYD B. CALDWELL: "My grandfather, Dock Caldwell, son of Levi and Granny Pop, was herding some large hogs and getting them ready to turn onto the outside range. One very large hog ran against his legs tripping him and caused him to fall solidly against the ground. He was hurt badly and the home folks carried him inside the house. A few hours later they decided to send for Dr. Bob Medford. The doctor arrived during the night but could not save the patient. He passed in the next twenty-four hours."

Even snakes never got the better of a human being, said Mark, although he had once backtracked a cow to the old Jim Caldwell Place. She had been snake-bit, ran down there and died. More often dogs were bitten by snakes.

MARK HANNAH: "Yeah, but I never did lose one. They'd always get well. This dog here (patting his collie, Foxy, on the head) was bitten by a rattlesnake and a copperhead. Went to town and got a shot for him... in thirty-five minutes, I was. That's comin' out of there!!"

Times have changed radically. A few years ago, 'Tine Bennett's son-in-law, Jay Ensley, was up on Little Cataloochee Mountain where his father-in-law had been born. They were holding a homecoming celebration at the little church there when Jay became violently ill. His wife, Mildred, wrote a letter to the *Waynesville Mountaineer* to tell of the medical help he got.

MILDRED BENNETT ENSLEY: "... I found him bent double with pain, with a Forest (Park) Ranger attending. Immediately he placed Jay in the back of our station wagon on a pillow. With one ranger in front with siren blowing and another following, we began our nightmare ride down the mountain... those of you who know Little Cataloochee will agree that the road in some places is most frightening."

"The rangers were meanwhile broadcasting for help and when we reached the Bennett Turn the Rescue Squad met us. With efficiency and care they transferred Jay to the ambulance and right there, in the road, they performed an EKG. The results of this test were taped directly into the Haywood County Hospital where we found them fully prepared for our arrival. I later learned this direct transmission from ambulance to hospital is only done in one place in the United States, and that's Haywood County..."

Jay Ensley survived because of this prompt attention. But in the old days in Cataloochee many died because there was no car, no road, no shots... and no communication. At least Mark had a radio and a ranger truck in the end. Still, many lives were lost needlessly... and many ghosts remain... many tiny bodies in the churchyard, relics of times before modern immunization techniques were widespread.

CHAPTER 16

Hiram's Fixation

(Farm Work)

This 1936 photograph of a team of oxen pulling a sled was made by H. M. Jennison.
This oxen team was used at the Paul Messer place on Upper Hemphill Creek
in the Cataloochee section of the Great Smoky Mountains.
Courtesy Great Smoky Mountains National Park Archives.

HIRAM CALDWELL COULD never stand to see someone idle. It riled his restless soul to the point that he would actually snare hapless school boys on their way to play, just as the British used to impress American seamen during the War of 1812!

RAYMOND CALDWELL: "The days was never long enough (for Hiram). Couldn't no one do enough work to suit him. He could never get enough done himself. I've heard Dad tell, they'd be aimin' from where Granddaddy lived, up to Uncle Harrison's. They had to go right by Uncle Hiram. And, he see them a-comin', he'd meet them right by the foot log where it is now. He'd want them to help come do something. Says the old fellowster, 'come on, come on, and help us saw a little wood while you rest!'"

"He would have people help him in the fall of the year, take in the crop, cut the corn, you know. And he would run the clock ahead two or three hours, unbeknownst to Aunt Lizzie or any of 'em, to get 'em up early... so he'd be havin' 'em cook breakfast at two o'clock in the morning so at three o'clock he could get into the field... payin' 'em by the day, you know. He wasn't payin' 'em by the hour."

"Uncle Andy (Caldwell) was like that, too. The Caldwells were tight. Couldn't ever get enough done. Nobody could please 'em!"

"They tell the story on Uncle Turkey George. He married Uncle Andy Caldwell's daughter, Aunt Alice. At this corn shuckin', they'd come to a good ear of corn that would make good seed corn — well, Uncle Turkey would just lay it out. He had enough seed corn picked out for his crop of corn the next year. Of course, after they had the corn all shucked and cleaned and everything, my Uncle Andy, he's a pretty tight old fellow, he didn't want his son-in-law to even have that corn. And when he come to it, he just throwed it right back into the crib with the other. Said Uncle Turkey didn't speak to his father-in-law for over a year!"

Sometimes harvest help was paid in kind.

"I can remember Bob Canadian comin' in there, worked for my father during the harvest time, a-pickin' the crops, and 'specially in haytime. My father would pay him, not in cash, but maybe in ham or meat, or a bushel of corn."

At harvest-time, the children got out of school, which made the educational year very short. There were various times of year when a child might be taken out of school to help his family, but the fall of the year was the most likely time.

HELEN HANNAH TRANTHAM (Mark's daughter): "I recall many things about Cataloochee before dad became a ranger. I remember so vividly how the folks used to farm and the 'chores' I dreaded so badly. Dad usually hired some of the neighbors to help with the farm work, especially when there was a lot of hoeing to do. So that called for a 'water-boy'. And, being the oldest child, and not quite old enough to keep up my row through the field, I was water-boy. I carried water in an 8-lb. lard bucket, which was plenty for a child my age. Somehow those fellows always seemed to consume any amount of water I took them. By the time I'd get to the house, I'd hear that 'water-boy' call ringing out again. I never remember minding a chore as much as that one. Soon, however, I graduated to hoeing, helping plant, milking, stacking hay, or whatever was on the day's schedule, but, believe me, none of it was as bad as that 'water-boy' bit!"

If a man didn't care for farming in Cataloochee, he was likely to starve to death, even if he had another trade or avocation, such as Vick Smith, the millwright. If a man's wealth could be measured in the valley, it was likely to be by what he had stored away in his larder. By these standards, the big landowners, such as the Palmers, Hannahs, Caldwells, Woodys, and Messers lived what seemed to them an exceedingly comfortable life.

If a fellow lived way up on the mountain where ploughing was difficult, he was more likely to live in a small cabin, than if he lived down where there were a few good level fields and rich bottomland to till. There was not really enough fertile soil to go around in this wild, steep-sided, landlocked valley. So some of the hillier land-owners often lived as tenants on the larger farms and helped with the chores, although there were very few walls between landowner and tenant in this community where everybody depended on one another for help.

ROBERT HILLIARD WOODY: "Class distinctions, in fact, did not exist. Every man was a capitalist, every man a laborer."

Actually it was not good enough to have only bottom land. Cattle had to be pastured somewhere in the summer. The ideal combination was that of cove and highland bald. Consequently, most big landowners had land in more than one place.

Cataloochans got a great deal of pleasure out of salting and ranging the cattle on the balds from May until November. It was the natural diversion of all the men who used it as an excuse to get away from their more irksome chores around the farm and family. And they sometimes got into mischief, as attested by Uncle Hiram.

One late spring when the buckeye trees were in leaf, but few others were — the oaks just faintly pink with buds and others a pale green, an old mountain man commented that it was an ancient rule of thumb: "Never put your cattle on the mountain pasture until the sugars (maples) are blooming."

A family story came down through the Davidsons about Ned McFalls, that redoubtable Indian-hater, who herded cattle for that family in the very earliest days of Cataloochee grazing. Davidson, who was called "Twitty" by the much older McFalls, wrote a reminiscence of his early happy days.

ALLEN DAVIDSON: "My recollections of Ned McFalls are quite vivid, as he was the companion of much of my boyhood. He was my father's factotum. He was herder, farmer, and man of all work, and a most valuable man he was, too. I used to go with him to the range in the Cataloochee mountains to salt stock. Nothing gave me so much pleasure."

"We were on the Bunk looking for the cattle which we had failed to find anywhere in their usual haunts. Ned went on top of the mountain and, making a trumpet of his hands, he called, 'Low, Dudley, low!'"

"Dudley was a bull, and Ned knew that wherever he was, the other cattle were apt to be. We waited some time, and, as if in answer to his call, we heard far away the low of the bull. He was over in the direction of Mt. Starling (Sterling), one of the highest of the Smokies, and about three miles away, yet in that still air we had heard him; for when we reached Mt. Starling, there he and all the stray cattle were."

Western Carolina historian John Preston Arthur explained: "Those who had bought up the wild lands at low figures encouraged cattle herders to pasture or 'range' their stock there. In the first place it gained their good will, and in the second it enabled landowners to become aware of the presence of any squatters who might seek to hold by adverse possession. Two other reasons were that landowners could not have prevented the ranging of cattle except by fencing in their lands, an impossible task at that time, and the suppression of fires in their incipiency."

W. CLARK MEDFORD (historian of Haywood County): "The Cataloochee country was one of our most noted ranging grounds... wild, rugged, vast, and distant from most points, the ranging grounds of the Davidsons of Jonathan's Creek, Reuben Moody, some of the Howells or Allisons, Bill Boyd, and others, who were maybe proving up on claims or owned range-land in fee simple."

"Haywood, as a county, beginning March 1809 and as part of Buncombe County for seventeen years prior thereto, had the stock-range law for about 125 years. In many sections of our county it was voted out... in favor of the Stock Law in the early 1890s. But in certain sections like Cataloochee and Big Creek, Hurricane and White Oak, it was kept until well into the present century."

"Farmers generally brought in most of their stock in October. Hogs certainly would not be brought in before they got the full benefit of the mast. Often a ranger would make two or three drives from his herds, taking out just what he needed to market each time."

"Cattle had to bear the owner's registered mark on the ears before turning on... marks being registered with the Range Master at the courthouse."

When Mark was asked about lead animals, in cattle ranging, he said there were no special lead bulls, such as old Dudley of yore, but that maybe a half dozen out of thirty or forty animals had bells on them, not only cattle, but other livestock were belled as well.

He mentioned that his family had special "crap" (crop) marks... the Mack Hannah signature being "a smooth crap in the right ear, a half crap in the left".

Some raised sheep and tried to graze them on the balds. But they were very susceptible to raids from the bears. The life of a lamb in Cataloochee was apt to be very short, indeed, if ranged outside — hence they were usually kept quite close to home.

RAYMOND CALDWELL: "Mt. Sterling has some natural balds on it. We had some problems out there with rangin' animals. The bears killed young calves, and we had to quit rangin' sheep... couldn't range any sheep out there. Yep, there's quite a few bear in there."

"My family ranged livestock in The Ledge, out near Pin Oak Gap, Heintoogy, the Bald, the Big Swag, what we call Balsam Corner. Good plumb down toward the head of Round Bottom. We'd go off down there. Those were natural range in there. There was a lot of good grass... the Big Swag, and all that in there".

"The last trip I was out there was in 1936 and the last time we ranged any cattle. And we had some young horses out there. And Mr. Burl Caldwell... we were out there in... no, it was in '35, and rounded those up and brought them in, and he got killed in June of '36, in an automobile accident. That was the last time I was in the Big Swag."

HIRAM WILBURN: "Ledge Bald, so named by the N. C. Nomenclature Committee (height 5,175 feet), Balsam Mountain, formerly called The Ledge by settlers and cattle rangers. It was the main grazing lands for Cataloochee. A well beaten path leads up Indian Creek (now Palmer Creek) and along Trail Ridge into Pin Oak Gap and thence along Balsam Mountain to The Ledge. A flat or tablelike area gave rise to the name."

"Poll's Gap, not Paul's Gap, as is commonly thought, was named after old Polly Moody's milch cow that sickened and died there. The bones bleached and were frequently seen and remarked about by passersby. Aunt Polly raised cain with her menfolk for carrying her 'springing' milk cow along with the others to the mountains. As a result, at the time of her calving, without attention, she died."

Aside from the famous bull, Dudley, no other Cataloochee cattle were particularly singled out for prominence until the handsome, redoubtable Flora Messer Morrow gave her entrancing imitations of her cow, "Old Red". She was an unmistakable presence as she slapped her neighbor on the leg for emphasis as she talked, calling her "Honey".

FLORA MESSER MORROW: "I was about fourteen. We milked at that time about fourteen cows. We had to go out a little ways from the house to the barn. And we had this one big old red cow. I always claimed it was mine, and Daddy did give it to me, I think."

"She always stood like I see a lot of women stand in church. She's lazy, y'know (imitates how the cow stands, shifting her weight all to one hip). I don't know whatever made me be mean... and it wasn't mean. Mama like to whip me over it. We always set out milk buckets along the big rock fence. I had this big yellow cat. He'd come and steal into the milk buckets if we didn't just watch him. So, when the fourteen cows was milked and started on to get on back to the fields, Old Red stood first on one side and then the other... wouldn't move. Finally I just got big old yellow tomcat and just gave him a pitch like that way, and he just landed all four paws in Red's back!"

"Honey, she took up through that Long Mile Bottom of land (Mark guffaws), and I guess she's runnin' yet! It's been about sixty years ago. Honey, she just stretched out, and the faster she's run, the claws would stick into her back, tryin' to stay on, y'know. She was already milked, y'know, when we started 'em back. And she went out of sight. And Mama said, 'Flora, I've a notion to whip you,' says, 'that cow may have a heart attack, be dead up there!'"

"This same lazy red cow. Well, it was comin' a storm, and the cattle were up there on the hillside there cross to Jim Hannah's... Sunny Point. Mama sent me after the cows. She couldn't get the dog to go up after them. And it was a-fixin' to come a storm. Well, smarty me, I thought I'd walk around the road and go up this hollow with my umbrella on. I got up in the hollow and was comin' over the top of the hill where the cattle were... with my umbrella. And Old Red was there; she <u>was</u> as lazy as can be. And she happened to look up and spied me with the first umbrella she ever seen in her life. And, I <u>mean</u>, she took down that mountain making ninety! That umbrella excited her to death. Old Red never stopped till she got to the milkin' place. She just loped off that mountain. It was really something to see how scarey she was."

Psychologists now say that pigs are among the smartest of animals. Certainly they were among the most dangerous in Cataloochee. When hogs went wild, they were known as ridgerooters. And it was quite a chase to round them up. Everybody raised a few hogs. Ham was a staple part of the Cataloochee diet, and still is a major part of the mountain diet. Hog killing time was a major event in the usual mountain family.

When Preacher T. A. Groce made his first preaching trip into Cataloochee with his little son, he was so exhausted he couldn't believe what he saw.

T. A. GROCE: "(It was) gettin' late. (We were) 'way down this side, goin' along, windin' around up the creek. And after awhile, out of the laurel, and out of the thicket of bushes there, a bunch of hogs ran out. And they had red ribbons tied on their tails and red bandanas around their necks. T. A. (Jr.) said, 'what in the world is that?!' I said, 'son, it's about time to light because you think you're watchin' the wheel turn and go up the mountain and down the mountain. He just got real sick. I said, are you comin' to life?' He said, 'well, what was that come out of the bushes?! I said they were hogs, they're just old razorback mountain hogs, that's all, that (we nearly got) run over with. That's a fact. They put this red ribbon with some kind of grease or oil around them, y'know, to keep the lice or... things off of the hogs. And consequently that's what we got to see.'"

Mark wrote about the vagaries of raising hogs in the mountains along the chestnut trees of Dude Creek where land along the banks was nearly level. That was an area known as the Pig Pen Flats. When bears were pushed out of the area by dogs and made to go into the head of Big Creek, deep in the forests, then Mark's father, Mack Hannah, began raising hogs and cattle in this forest.

MARK HANNAH: "We built a pig pen out of logs about 10 x 20 feet in size and covered it with slabs and bark to shelter the pigs from rain and snow. The side of the pen had a 'slip-gap'... two logs could be slid over and let hogs come outside. It was sometimes left open for months."

"Then, when a new litter of pigs were born in the forest nearby, we would give the old sow some corn and soon we could get her into this pen and shut the slip gap and prop it real good (to secure her), and we would open small holes in the pen and leave them for pigs to get to their mother. Later we would return to the pen and find pigs in there with their mother. We would close the holes in pen and have them caught ready to mark in ears. Our old mark was make a smooth crop in right ear and half crop in left ear. All our cattle and stock were marked in ear this way."

"The hogs would stay in the mountains until about 15th December. Then we would go out and try to gentle them with some corn, to bring them in and 'corn fatten' them for killing. Sometimes, after they were fat on mast, they went wild, and we had to catch them with a dog. This was fun, but dangerous!"

"The wild hogs that used to roam the mountains were more frequently mentioned by the Caldwells... as they had many of them in different sections of the woods: like the Brushy Mountain sow, or the old belled sow on Little Fork Ridge. Maybe the sow with pigs that Uncle Hiram called 'Old Chiltose' because she stayed in the mountains between Poll's Gap and Chiltose or Cataloochee Balsam. He also had hogs on Early Creek and Piney Butt Mountain on Little Cataloochee, and, too, they were scattered from there to the Nancy Hicks farm in the Big Bend of the river."

'Tater Hill Knob — the name recalled, more than anything, a wild hog fight to Mark. His brother Robert had hit a four year old hog with a pistol but didn't kill it. This one was six inches around the teeth and chattered its teeth, as hogs will do, in a very scary way. No one liked to fool with an aggressive hog very much.

There is an old mountain "ballad" taken from an English folk song that issues a dire warning:

> "There is a wild boar lives in these woods,
> Eats men and women, drinks their blood!"

Turkey George Palmer certainly had grim memories from his hog-rasing days, according to a well-known columnist from the *Asheville Citizen-Times* who had interviewed Uncle Turkey's son.

JOHN PARRIS: "Back then (in March of 1919), Turkey George raised his hogs out in the mountains. Let them run loose to fleshen up on acorns and chestnuts. Once he was out in the hills looking after his hogs when he ran upon a sight that fairly set him boiling. He could read signs and knew what had happened right away. There before him were the bloody remains of eight pigs. A bloody trail led off through the woods. Turkey George read the sign and knew a bear had killed the pigs and the sow and carried off the sow to feast on later. So he hurried home, got his bear trap, and came back. He took up the trail and found where the bear had dragged the sow to a sunken place in the ground and pulled brush over the carcass. Turkey George set his trap right there. And when he came back a couple of days later, there was the bear in the trap... a whopping big one of 526 pounds."

Ernestine Upchurch, whose great grandfather was Hiram Caldwell, remembered, "Grandmaw used to tell us stories about havin' to climb trees to get away from the wild boars that were feedin' on acorns."

ELDRIDGE CALDWELL: "Oh... acorns and chestnuts. There used to be an abundance of chestnuts there."

It was traditional to go wild hog racing on Cataloochee at Thanksgiving. A mention of this made old Eldridge's eyes turn keen. He spit tobacco into a handy can, adjusted his red billed cap, readying for a long heartfelt story.

ELDRIDGE CALDWELL: "Oh, well, yeah, I'us just about as afraid of a wild hog as I was of a bear. After you learn 'em though, there's one way you can protect yourself pretty well."

"How's that?" an outlander queried.

"Just stand still."

"And they go right past you?" the tenderfoot asked, in consternation.

He grinned impishly, "<u>Then</u> you move... if you didn' they'd cut you down. 'Fore they'd start, they'd just take a dead aim at you... it'us like somebody shootin' a rifle. And you'd wait till they got almost to you, step aside, and they'd just run on by. And they'd go on a little way (with the sheer momentum) and then turn back again but you'd have time to get to a tree, or you'd do something to dodge 'em!"

"My father had a sow that'd raised a bunch of shoats in the mountains, and he sent me in there to see if I could find them in them berries. But these shoats'r just as wild as they can be. Weigh two hundred pound. So he wanted me to go next day and catch 'em, bring 'em home."

"I got up a bunch o' boys there to go wi' me; there's four of us. And we had a bunch o' bear dogs we tuck over there and putt on the sign. Them things had come nearly into Poll's Gap. After I'd been there they (the shoats) got scared, y'see, left there. (My father) tole us to foiler 'em along and beat 'em. We went in there and caught three of 'em. And this one got away from us, and crossed Big Ridge and went into George Irey (Ira) Creek. I give them other boys a hog each to drive out."

"I went in there after dogs. And, oh, it'us hot. I had my shirt open, and my hat in my pocket to get through the brush. Had a duck-back hat, and I just rolled it up and stuck it in my hip pocket. Got in there to 'im. They (the dogs) had this hog laid there in a sink hole. And I thought I'd just ease around above and throw a rope on that hog.

And I did. But there's two dogs right in a line, and they'd been in a fight with that hog we first met, stirred up them (yellow) jackets… the most jackets I've ever seen in my life. Might have been the first of October."

"So first thing I knowed I was yellow with jackets all over me. Never stung so bad in my life… I walked out, went out on that big la'rl, dropped a rope down around this hog, pulled him up as tight as I could, had him up there, sorta choked. That rascal wouldn't drive, but he'd-foller me… trying to catch me. I'd let him get set fer me, and I'd step aside, and he'd run on by me. He follered me. And I had no lunch. We eat breakfast about four o'clock that mornin'."

"I got that hog down to about within a mile of Uncle Steve Woody's, and I seed I was gettin' sick. I couldn't stand it no longer. I tied 'im up there and went on down to Uncle Steve's. He'us out in the yard, and I told 'im I'us awful sick, and I wanted a horse to ride home. Yessir, yessir, said, I'll get you a horse right quick. And he run down to the barn there, said, you <u>look</u> awful sick. I said, well, I am, sho-nuff sick. And he saddled up his horse, and I got home…"

"The other boys… they never got theirs all the way in. They went to fightin' on them, too. But they got 'em down there on the Caldwell Fork to Bobby Caldwell's barn, and putt 'em up. Come in on home. They were all starved to death, too. Next day they ran 'em up."

Yellow jackets may have been bad news, but bees weren't. As honey was a valuable sweetening, the art of bee-keeping was much practiced on the farm. Most people had bee-gums around. Though Raymond Caldwell was of a fairly late generation, he said he knew how a log bee gum worked; he had taken honey out of one, robbing it down to the cross-sticks.

ROBERT HILLIARD WOODY: "(Uncle Jim Hannah's) great aim in life was to find and cut bee trees. In this avocation, he was positively expert. He could 'course' a bee with an unerring eye, and he seldom got a sting."

The Park historian who interviewed Mitchell Sutton in 1937 got a report on other forms of sweetening.

HIRAM WILBURN: "Neil Sutton had a camp at the 'Ras Hannah place on Little Cataloochee where he made maple sugar. He also made 'piggins' (wooden buckets) and other containers. In boiling the sugar sap, he would put a meat skin near the top of the pot, and when it would boil onto it, it would not boil any higher."

MARK HANNAH: "I recently talked to Hobert Franklin about the many sugar maple trees that he saw from Mt. Sterling (fire) tower during the twelve years he had spent as lookout for the Great Smoky Mountains National Park. He assured me that there were more sugar maple trees in this Ras' Hannah Cove than he had seen in the Park elsewhere. This makes me think the story of the location of the Neil Sutton sugar mill to be correct. Mr. Sutton was one of the first settlers in the Mt. Sterling settlement. He was also the great-great-grandfather of Hobert Franklin."

Because of the difficulty of obtaining sugar, however, molasses was used in many of the Cataloochee recipes. Once an ordinary but exacting chore in Cataloochee, the home processes of the cane mill, turned by a horse, and the boiling of extracted juice for the correct amount of time were very tedious and have long since gone out of fashion except as an illustration of pioneer effort in some reconstructed homestead scene, such as they now have in Cades Cove in the Western boundaries of the Park, or at Oconaluftee where there is a simulated pioneer farm.

MARK HANNAH: "Little Cataloochee people usually had lots of chickens, and sometimes the menfolks would gather the eggs each day. Well, my Uncle Rhode (Rhodeman) Hannah had his old hens named — he knew them that way. Sometimes when a hen cackled he would go immediately and get her egg. Fresh egg, eh?"

"One time the neighbors decided to play a trick on him. They slipped into the hen-house and got every one of his laying hens and the rooster, too. Great day! Uncle Rhode went to the post office, store and church telling the bad news. He was worried to death, nearly — chickens all gone. Several days passed and the chickens were all returned one night to their old home. Uncle said: 'Maybe — nobody stole them — I believe they've been on vacation!'"

"Once upon a time Aunt Emma Valentine heard her chickens squalling and cackling. Claude was not at home so she just got her lantern and went to the barn to check on the 'varmint'. Lo and behold! It was two men climbing down the wall with two of her chickens. — 'Wait there, fellows,' she said — 'You climb right back up there and get two more.' They were scared not to obey her command, so they did as she said. And she told them to go and not come back anymore at night. If they had to have another one — to ask for it — and she would give them one. She was a wonderful old lady — always joking and jolly. She had five daughters: Mae, Lillie, Stella, Pearl, and Ressie and a son, Claude."

Burley tobacco was a fairly small crop in Cataloochee, but widely utilized by the local folk, as attested by Eldridge Caldwell, a frequent user of snuff or chewing tobacco. His mouth always had a thin golden line oozing out of its corner.

ROBERT HILLIARD WOODY: "Uncle Rhode Hannah's wife liked her snuff and tobacco and so did the daughter. And they made their own sweet tobacco by putting it in some sort of press sort of like you would make a big cheese in. And they would use molasses and possibly sugar and I don't know what else. They would press this and soak it with the stuff. And it was pretty good chewing tobacco and sweet. Almost everybody used snuff, the women particularly. And they dipped it with a stick, about so long, that was made of (yellow) birch... just a birch stick that you would cut, and chew the end so and get it sort of bushy and dip it in the snuff. And you put it in your jaw, and you see, you can keep it there a long time. The men didn't dip snuff that way. I suppose this was not manly. But they would cut it in their lip or jaw. And I'm sure this is still done in a place like Waynesville... take, in a garage, where a fellow's not allowed to smoke."

Flora and Verda Messer's father, Will, would spit tobacco juice into the fire, and her mother, Rachel, would spit snuff into the fire, with all the children watching them One day he said, "Rachel, these children are just watching us." And they made a pact to give it up. Will did, but Rachel sometimes got the children to slip snuff to her.

This made a strong impression on susceptible Flora who was once persuaded by some older school girls, named Burdine and Emmaline, to take snuff. She took some with the stem of a maple leaf, she remembers, and passed out, never again to repeat the traumatic performance!

Cattle, burley tobacco, and apples were the principal marketable produce, though sheep and hogs were raised, moonshine was often exported to Tennessee, and grain was sometimes sold or bartered for salt, sugar and coffee. Molasses was usually for home consumption, as were maple sugar and honey. Apple brandy and peach brandy were small-time items, as were vegetables, which Uncle 'Tine sometimes peddled to the adjacent loggers. Ginseng-digging had a following because the price of the root was absurdly inflated. The famous botanist, Andre Michaux, first taught the mountain people its value and how to prepare it for the market of China as early as August, 1794.

It's hard today to keep 'sang' diggers from poaching in the confines of the National Park. It was just as hard to protect one's crop back in the old days. Gudger Palmer told us with amusement of his mother's being swindled by Mollie Runningwolf, an ancient Indian from Big Cove who is still alive today. She sold ginseng roots to the Palmer store and post office which Mrs. Palmer later discovered were withered poke roots or some other masquerader. The medicine men of Indian Big Cove had certainly treated ginseng with great respect, which may account for Mollie's unwillingness to part with the true article.

Professor Hall who went into Cataloochee primarily to study speech and record for the Library of Congress, also got valuable information on the ginseng market of the time.

PROFESSOR JOSEPH S. HALL: "Questioned about the activities of his youth, he (Turkey George) said that he had made some money gathering and selling ginseng, commonly known as 'seng' or 'sang'..."

TURKEY GEORGE PALMER: "Ther' used to be a good big scope of seng on the mountain. I could fill a tow-sack in half a day and sell it fer fifteen cents a pound green, or twenty-five dry. I raised seng, too... had a patch of it measurin' six by eighteen feet... an' made fifty or sixty dollars a season. Reagan had a store over in Caton's Grove across the mountains in Tennessee. He bought our seng every fall."

Mark Hannah once had a patch of domestic ginseng growing near his place... labor of love, as it was a seven-year wait until maturity. The larger wild roots were therefore more valuable. Mark had left an old lady to tend his patch and water it when he had to leave the valley for some reason or other, and returned to find that some one had 'rustled' every single root.

Cultivated ginseng was half the price of wild ginseng. People were apt to slip in and steal it. When the old woman stole Mark's and sold it to Mack Caldwell of Mt. Sterling, Mack said he was cheated, thought it was wild. There used to be good 'sang' digging back in Uncle Logan Hannah's place. And Verda Messer Hannah's father, Will Messer, cultivated a 'sang' garden 100 feet by 40 feet. The best time to dig 'sang' is in October when it's yellow.

Where land was at all tillable, rye, wheat, oats, and corn were raised. 'Tine Bennett and Mark Hannah enjoyed reminiscing about it one fine July day on 'Tine's screened porch in Sylva.

'TINE BENNETT: "We done a lot of work by hand then more. Machinery's took all that place now. But we didn't do much in the winter-time, maybe ploughin' new ground, tear up a hillside and look around and about."

MARK HANNAH: "And haul poles (logs) from the new cleared ground for firewood. What was one of the hardest things we did on the farm back in those days? How about cradlin' rye, was that about it?"

'TINE BENNETT: "Yes, I guess it was! (Both laugh)... The older boys used to sow a lot of oats, and they'd make us briar them oats. Had something like a top-knife with a handle 'bout that long. You'd just have to go through the field, and reach down and cut that briar off... blackberry briars, saw briars."

MARK HANNAH: "And bull nettles! That was before you went to cradlin' it, to keep it from stickin' your hand when you pull 'em up off the cradle-fingers."

'TINE BENNETT: "That piece of ground right above our big barn there. It was about three acres of it. Me and Eldridge, and 'Mericus Hall, we jumped in there, the prettiest field of oats you ever looked at in your life. We'us all good with the cradle, and we could spread 'em off the cradle like that. (Never touch them with our hands.) We cut that three acres of oats down in less than a day."

MARK: "Did you ever see anybody who could tie oats up any faster than your brother Eldridge?"

'TINE: "He could do 'em all right."

MARK: "He was the best hand I ever saw."

'TINE: "He was good. He would just get a bundle, th'ow it around like that, pitch it up."

MARK: "That's right. I've heard him tell that he and someone else could nearly keep a bundle in the air. They'd throw it up that way and pick another'n up, and tie it very quickly."

'TINE: "We used to raise a lot of rye and wheat and have to take it to Crabtree to get it ground."

MARK: "Get it bolted, made into really flour or meal."

'TINE: "At the mouth of Cove Creek they had a mill there. They could grind rye, but they couldn't bolt it. (In order to bolt it, they had) just a big seive, well, it's about ten feet long. Water wheel had a chain on it and turned it over."

MARK: "In other words, it just sifted around through there, and the little fine would fall out through that thing, called 'bolter.'"

One cool night as Mark sat talking to a bunch of horsemen around a campfire in Cataloochee outside the old schoolhouse, he repeated a soothing litany of apple tree names. They rolled sonorously off his tongue: Milams, Sour Johns, Ben Davis, Wolf Rivers, Golden Pippens, Junes, Mealies, Royal Limbertwigs, Red Limbertwigs, Cortlands, Mountain Boomers, Preachers, Bellflowers, California Sweets... on and on he sang into the darkness.

His section of Little Cataloochee was famous for its apples.

MARK HANNAH: "Pick 'em off, put 'em in three-bushel basket apple barrels and haul 'em fifteen miles to Mt. Sterling Depot and then put them on the T. and N.C. Railroad, ship 'em into Knoxville, Tennessee, and then foiler 'em up, sell 'em on the market."

"Mostly apples, that was the big market. And, of course, cattle and sheep. We'd raise 'em for market. But these here apples had to go out of there. We raised several hundred bushels on Little Cataloochee. Four big orchards down there. Once in awhile a fellow would drive in with a mule team from Cosby or somewhere, like Sim McMahan or Dan Mathis, and get thirty or forty bushel on a wagon. And he'd haul them all the way back to Knoxville. I don't know how they ever made anything out of it, hauling them seventy-five miles on a wagon on a narrow dirt road via Cosby-Jones Cove to Knoxville. They would pad the wagon bed with fodder and use it to feed the mules. We'd get about $1.25, $1.50 a bushel, and he'd sell 'em at three or four dollars a bushel in Knoxville."

A recent Park publication on the historic structures of Little Cataloochee reported: "Apples were the real source of Will Messer's prosperity."

"Apples had become the major cash crop by 1914, and Will Messer did more to develop that industry than any other man. He designed his apple house for commercial purposes, to store and ship the 2500 or more bushels of apples produced annually in his extensive orchards. Those apples were shipped to markets as far away as Charlotte and Gastonia, North Carolina, Greenville, South Carolina, and Knoxville, Tennessee."

"Indeed, the introduction of apple growing into the area around the turn of the century transformed the economic and social framework of Little Cataloochee. After the development of the orchards, the area ceased to be an isolated backwoods subsistence farming community with few ties to the outside world. The income derived from apples permitted the growers to purchase manufactured goods in Newport and Cosby, Tennessee, in Waynesville on the North Carolina side, and from mail order houses such as Sears and Roebuck... thus at the time of the establishment of the Park, Little Cataloochee was <u>not</u> the stereotypical stagnant mountaineer settlement, but a vital and growing community."

"Apple growing for commercial purposes was introduced into Coggins Branch — Little Cataloochee Creek near by Will Messer and his neighbors, John Burgess and Mack Hannah. Messer and Burgess were brothers-in-law, and Hannah, of course, was a close friend and father of Messer's son-in-law, Mark Hannah..."

"During the harvest season, running from about September 15 through early November, apples were gathered and graded in bins and barrels inside the storage houses. The entire community participated. The wives and small children were kept busy cooking food and feeding the extra hands that were brought in to help collect the crop. In addition, meals had to be prepared for the buyers and teamsters who came into the area to load apples. During the winter and spring, Messer and the other growers sold apples for 50¢ to $1.50 per bushel in markets in Tennessee and to the lumbering camps at Crestmont, Sunburst, and Mt. Sterling..."

"At the time of the establishment of the Park, Messer stated that his apple crop brought in between $500 and $3000 per year, with $2000 being the average. The Burgess orchard produced about 1800 bushels per year."

There was some competition for selling apples over on Big Cataloch', too, it was reported.

RAYMOND CALDWELL: "Steve Woody... well, he was for Steve Woody. Uncle Steve was anxious to sell his crop of apples, and it didn't really make much difference whether anyone else sold theirs or not. But Uncle Steve was anxious to get the buyer to his place... the buyer come in to buy the apples from the orchards... Uncle Hiram Caldwell had several apples, and this man was looking for Uncle Hiram. And Uncle Steve said, well, now, Hiram sold his apples last week, says, come on up. I'll load you up so you won't have to go out of here empty with a wagon. And, of course, Uncle Hiram still a-waitin' on him to come up to his place. Uncle Steve was a very shrewd, good business man, in that respect..."

ELDRIDGE CALDWELL: "There was a storm tore my father's apple trees down when I was just a kid... it just twisted them apple trees up by the roots, all of 'em's any account. I think there was just three left we let stand. Yeah, they was pretty good apples. We had the Pippin, and all of our Milam trees blew down. The Pippins were great big white apples, pretty well white, and they were a fall apple. Them trees would bear 'most every year."

In Big Cataloochee a few springs ago, only one lone, contorted apple tree could still be found standing... unclaimed by the wilderness that had grown up around it... in Uncle Hiram Caldwell's field, an old, old tree, perhaps one that had withstood the hurricane of 1898.

CHAPTER 17

The Compleat Cataloochan

(Trades, Occupations, and Crafts)

Doc Medford pulls Uncle Harley Palmer's tooth at the Palmer House in Big Cataloochee. There were no "specialists" in Cataloochee — a doctor had to be a "jack-of-all-trades" from pulling teeth to sewing up a cut from an axe. They sometimes "mis-diagnosed" as well, mistaking a living soul for a dead body — but that usually worked itself out.
Courtesy Great Smoky Mountains National Park Archives.

NO WONDER HIRAM Caldwell lay in wait to corral young men to help him. For a man, in order to make ends meet as a farmer in this valley, must need be a regular Renaissance man, with a huge wealth of certain kinds of learning, trades and crafts behind him, such as only those who live in completely self-contained communities possess.

He had to be a wagon-maker, wheelwright, veterinarian, bee-keeper, orchardist, cattleman, herder, poultryman, butcher, cooper, distiller, blacksmith, farrier, stone-cutter, yokemaker, mason, miller, millwright and toolmaker, as well as a painter, ploughman, and harvester.

To get things to market, he had to be a drover, teamster, peddler, and small business man.

To keep his community in order, he had to be a justice-of-the peace, a magistrate, lawyer, self-imposed or other, sheriff, home guard, and soldier in time of war, fire warden, wildlife protector, ranger, and, in the early days of the turnpike, a gate-keeper, or toll-taker.

To get that needed protein for his family, he had to be a good trapper, hunter, fisherman, and gunsmith.

To administer to the spiritual needs of the populace, there had to be some homegrown preachers of the hellfire variety, preferably a redeemed sinner.

To look after the inquiring minds of children there had to be teachers and truant officers.

To look after their health, there had to be self appointed doctors and dentists when the real thing couldn't make it in time. There had to be "yarbwomen" in lieu of pharmacists. And, from the beginning, of course, there had to be the indispensable grannywomen, or midwives.

To communicate with others in far places, there had to be postmasters and mail carriers.

To administer to the small needs of the community, there had to be part-time storekeepers, who were usually the postmasters, too.

To put shelter together, there had to be loggers, sawyers, carpenters, and also bridge and road builders, in order to get there, or to leave there.

Somebody had to be the barber, too. Often, it was Mark on Sunday mornings, getting people tidied up for the week ahead.

To keep their families warm and comfortable, the women had to be spinners, weavers, quilters, knitters, seamstresses, tailors, dyers, while the men were often tanners, hatters, and shoemakers.

One sat and ate on furniture made by the cabinetmakers and chairmakers.

Women provided the meals by being gardeners, cooks, and preservers.

There were also basketmakers, when the Indians did not wander through often enough to provide these. And there were leatherworkers and candlemakers, though this was scarcely a little Williamsburg with quaint shops along the High Street!

In later times, they had to become machinists and electricians to cope with the generator that was hooked up to the water mill, and mechanics to understand Henry Ford's Model T.

For fun, they were musicians, dancers and balladeers, distillers, and clowns like 'Ras and Dude Hannah.

In the end, they were coffin-makers and undertakers.

Now most people in Cataloochee knew a little bit about all of these things. A few were complete specialists, perhaps, such as Frank Stines, the chairmaker, but this was rare in the valley. Will Messer was a good example of the Compleat Cataloochan, to use the archaic phrase, what with running his gristmill, sawmill, post office, store, farm, and coping with eleven children, as well, keeping them housed and fed. How he found time, also, to market apples, make the pulpit and the steeple for the Little Cataloochee church, and make coffins is nothing short of incredible.

JARVIS CALDWELL: "Some of the Messers were the craftsmen, the millwrights. Will Messer made a mill. He kept the lumber. Well, he made all of 'em back in there."

RAYMOND CALDWELL: "He made the pulpit that's in that church now, that's some of his work."

JARVIS CALDWELL: "He was just about the Daddy Man of all of it. He made everything he had. He made the saw mill, he sawed the lumber, cut the special trees, and dried lumber. He made furniture, too, for homes."

A National Park publication corroborates this.

"At the time of the establishment of the Great Smoky Mountains National Park, William G. B. Messer was by far the most prominent member of the Little Cataloochee community. He owned the most property, operated several service businesses, and was a leader in educational and church affairs… As a man of considerable native talent and curiosity, he brought many innovations to the community. His remarkable energy and leadership qualities seem to have infused the entire community. After his passing, Will Messer was remembered as a man who was constantly in motion tending his crops, building something, or tinkering to find a solution to 'some problem that was on his mind.'"

"But before that his father Elijah 'had been an expert axman, cornerman, and stonemason, and had a reputation as one of the best fiddle players in the region.' Will certainly inherited his father's alertness and curiosity."

"The construction of (Will) Messer's 'big house' on Little Cataloochee Creek marked his arrival as the most prosperous and industrious citizen in the community. Between 1894 and 1915 he acquired several houses and some 340 acres of the best land in the area. He farmed, raising subsistence crops, corn and perhaps some tobacco, as well as cattle, hogs, sheep and horses. With the aid of his family and tenant labor, he developed three highly productive apple orchards, established a furnishing store and post office for the community and installed a sawmill, a canemill and a gristmill. Messer operated his gristmill on Saturdays. He charged one gallon of meal out of eight ground as his toll. The toll corn was then frequently sold to renters and tenants in the area."

"Messer eventually became something of a businessman and banker. He acquired a store and other property in Newport, Tennessee; and he frequently loaned money-at-interest and made deed-of-trust arrangements with his neighbors. He established a cattlescale and a small stockyard near the old Cook homeplace. He charged 5 cents to 10 cents per head to weigh cattle and he purchased stock which he marketed in Tennessee and at various lumbering camps in the area. Finally, Messer was an undertaker (of sorts), since he made and sold most of the coffins used in the area. He saved the finest lumber that he collected for coffins, and Rachel sewed the linings. A coffin normally sold for seven dollars but was provided without charge to impoverished neighbors."

"Will Messer was a true jack-of-all-trades who could 'make anything he wanted out of iron or wood' (so said Carl Woody). A niece (Beatrice Sisk) recalls that he was a 'wellread, very intelligent, money-making man' and that 'everything he touched turned to money'. Messer's inventiveness was constantly challenged by the rugged mountain environment, but he worked incessantly to improve his surroundings... he owned the first touring car and pickup truck to appear in Little Cataloochee..."

"Even though he was a shrewd businessman, Messer's drive to make money was tempered by the needs of his community. He is said to have been 'helpful, generous, and honest'. He extended credit in his store, carrying a neighbor's account for as long as twelve months. He accepted eggs and honey in trade for coffee, sugar, salt, and other needed 'store-bought' supplies. Children frequently earned money by bringing in harvests of nuts and berries."

This is what Will Messer's wagon master had to contend with in his job.

FLOYD BURGESS: "One morning, bright and early at daybreak, Crawford Messer, another mule driver, and I loaded our wagons with 18 barrels of apples, headed towards Crestmont (a former lumber operation, on the other side of Cataloochee, now it's Big Creek campground). Just after reaching the old 284 highway, one of the front wheels of my wagon broke down. Crawford said, 'Now what will we do?' I examined the wheel and told him to get a pole or small tree to jack the load up so we could take the wheel off. I told him we would tie two mules up and put the brake on, and then we could each ride a mule and hang one side of the broken wheel on his mule's harness and the other side of the wheel on my mule's harness and carry it to Uncle Will's, only about two miles."

"I knew he could make any part of that wagon because he had made both of these wagons in his blacksmith shop. We returned to Uncle Will's, and he immediately began repairing the wheel. It only took about two hours, and we loaded it on the mules' harnesses, and, riding side by side, we went to our wagons, placed the wheel on and were soon on our way to Crestmont."

"There we sold our apples to Mr. Fryemayer at the commissary, loaded the wagons with the articles that Uncle Will needed and returned home in the dark hours over that narrow turn-pike road. Some places we could not see the mules, it was so dark. We always dreaded passing the Williams Rock at night because the road was only 12 inches wider than a wagon or a buggy. There was no upper ditch to drive in — just pulled on the upper line a little and braked the wagon enough to hold it off of the mules and hope you didn't meet another wagoneer!"

Will Messer was not the only one to keep a store. Will Palmer and Verlin Campbell had little stores, from time to time. Lou Palmer, daughter of Harrison Caldwell, bought the old Jarrett mill and store, the first store in the valley.

MARK HANNAH: "Things that were sold in (those) little country stores were cloth to make dresses, by the yard; gloves, hats and caps; tobacco, chewing by plug; snuff, Bruton, Scotch and Sweet; matches, pipes and cigarettes; smoking tobacco in bags and tins; a few toys around Christmas-time; oranges and bananas; stick candy, chocolate bars, silver bells and gum candies; chewing gum, by the stick or pack; coffee, green or in buckets or bags; salt, soda, meal and flour by the 25 lb. bag; sugar by the lb.; side meat by the lb.; nails and staples, any size; gate hinges and locks; horse shoes and mule shoes; ammunition, shotgun or .22; black powder and lead."

These little stores were very apt to be the post offices of their small communities, too. There were actually three separate post offices in the valley: Ola, in Little Cataloochee, named after one of Will Messer's daughters, Viola; Cataloochee Post Office; and Nellie Post Office, named after Neller Palmer Wright, Turkey's daughter, in Big Cataloochee, also. William and Miley (Milia) Palmer ran the Nellie Post Office in their own store, one quarter of a mile on the old road, before Palmer Chapel. The roving Indian who painted their sign drew the N backward. But Miley thought it amusing and preserved the sign.

The post offices often changed location. The Cataloochee one was variously at Young Bennett's place, then at Frank Palmer's, and was last heard of at Jarvis Palmer's in the little room on the back porch. Ola Post Office was first in Will Messer's house, then he moved it into his store, which used to be an apple house.

W. CLARK MEDFORD: "Ben Nelson was (one) of the old mail boys of this county. He had perhaps the longest route of all... from Waynesville to Big Creek, to Cataloochee. The round trip, of about seventy miles, was made twice a week."

Later on some of the local mail carriers were 'Mericus Hall, and Pearl Valentine on her mule, when 'Mericus went up into the mountain balds to tend his cattle..... then 'Tine Bennett, Vernon Palmer, and Kimsey Palmer, who are all alive today to tell the tale. Kimsey rode in 1936 on horseback from Nellie to Cove Creek, and 'Tine Bennett by mule from Nellie to Ola, via Mossy Branch and Bald Gap. Old Mr. Bobby Howell, who died recently, used to carry the mail from Waynesville to Cataloochee on a horse. He lived in Jonathan Creek, outside of Catalooch'. The last mailman for Catalooch' was Enos Boyd. He came to the job in the automobile age.

Enos said that the mail route used to be a star route, not actually a Civil service job, and was turned in on a bid from Newport, Tennessee. Orville Caldwell had the star route in Cataloochee to Nellie in the 1920's. And Bill Boyd did, too, later. Enos first began carrying the mail into the ranger in May, 1969, and didn't stop until February, 1974. It took him 8 1/2 or 9 hours to make his total rounds. There was almost nobody in Cataloochee at that time.

Enos said he loved his job, especially in the wintertime, the quiet snow, when his vehicle made virgin tracks into the valley. He was able to observe the wild animals, deer every day in fall and winter, grouse in the fall of the year, rattlesnakes and bobcats. He was not allowed to carry passengers, but once picked up a lost couple, and often relayed messages to campers. Sometimes the snow was eight to ten inches deep, and the temperatures below zero, but still Enos Boyd got rather a dreamy look when he thought about his quiet time silently skimming the rugged roads of Catalooch'.

Robert Woody was nostalgic about other things, watermills, for instance. Mills, millers, and millwrights were unusually prolific in this little community.

ROBERT HILLIARD WOODY: "Up the creek a short distance, and not far from the sheep-house, was a water-powered mill for grinding corn... A mill race diverted the water to the wheel which turned the stones. If the water got low, we could use a public mill further down the creek by paying the toll... The noise and vibration of the mill, the smell of freshly ground meal as we ran it through our fingers to test for fineness are not easily forgotten."

Mills and millwrights held a fatal fascination for Hiram Wilburn, too. In 1937, that astute detective traced down all the old millstones as inexorably as Javet tracked the luckless Jean-Valjean in "Les Miserables". His minute notes on the subject makes one admire the man for his singlemindedness, the mark of a true genius. In his pursuit of the elusive millstones, he was as busy as a beagle on the track of a rabbit, scurrying from one warren hole to another.

The mill that Hilliard Woody remembered was a little water trough mill built for 'Tine Woody in 1909 by Vick Smith up on 'Tine Woody Branch of Little Cataloochee. Vick was the masterbuilder of mills and cutter of millstones as had been his grandfather, John A. Smith.

John A., the cutter of these original stones, had had a mill of his own at Lucky Bottom, near the Lucky Button Hole below Palmer Chapel. John's father, Marion Caldwell, was the one who lost his life across from Lucky Bottom when a blackgum tree he was burning fell sooner than he expected as he ploughed his field below.

'TINE BENNETT: "I use to stay lots with Uncle 'Tine Woody. McKinley Sutton came up there and made a little mill above the house near the creek. He cut his hand on a saw that he had running by the power of the water wheel. We had to take him to a Waynesville doctor to get the wound dressed. I remember pulling old nails from some old house lumber, getting the mill-race built. McKinley Sutton also sawed shingles for the 'Tine Woody house on the little mill."

These stones were later sold by Sherman Woody to Sage Sutton for a mill on Mt. Sterling Creek in 1929, after the Park began to come in. They were cut out at the mouth of Fines Creek and were new at the time the first mill was built.

Vick Smith said he had helped his grandfather hew out the timbers of the old undershot mill at Lucky Bottom west of the Schoolhouse Patch. He said the stones in that mill had been cut out by Elijah Messer and were later installed in a mill for Charles Jarrett which Vick built at the Frank Palmer place, where the old settler, Evan Hannah, had first lived.

Although there is a place name called the John Mull Meadow, no one in Cataloochee seems to recall exactly why it was named this. But the Haywood County historian, W. Clark Medford, stated that when the first small settlement of Cataloochee was formed the settlers had only a hand-operated corncracker which took twelve hours to grind a bushel of corn.

Allen Davidson's brother, John, took one on his journey from Jonathan's Creek to Texas. He called it an Armstrong mill and said he and Brother Robert worked it together by the strength of their arms.

The land speculator, Colonel Love, who was trying to sell land in Cataloochee, offered free land on Indian Creek to a German named John Mull (originally Möll?) if he would build a mill in there. The exact site or type of mill is not known, but presumably it was near the John Mull Meadow and may have been the Tom Palmer mill. Harrison Caldwell named one of his sons, John Mull Caldwell, so the memory of the early millwright must have been green at that time. Hiram Wilburn believed it to be the forerunner of the Jesse Palmer mill which was maintained up through a large part of the twentieth century.

It seems astonishing that so few items of clothing remain from pioneer days. Recently the Viking comrades of Eric the Red were dug up in a graveyard in Greenland, with their ancient clothing perfectly preserved by the cold, as it was with the famous Danish peat bog man, called the Tollund man, found by peat cutters in May, 1950. The Tollund man had been hanged and buried about two thousand years before. He wore the braided leather rope that killed him, a cap, and a belt, all in a perfect state of preservation. Yet, what clothing remained from the so-called bones of Tom King that were dug up in Catalooch'? Not even enough to make a positive identification!

The Smokies escaped the worst ravages of the Ice Age, and has few true peat bogs. The weather quickly takes its toll... humidity and rot go hand in hand, and this area has the second highest amount of rainfall in the country, surpassed only by the Pacific Northwest. This has played havoc with many of the items that might have come down through the descendents in the way of cloth, leather or wooden items.

When material for clothes was woven, it was often linsey-woolsey, which was a wool weft of a linen (cotton?) warp, an almost indestructible cloth unless left outdoors to rot in the extraordinary damp of the Smokies climate. Linsey alone was used for underwear. There was a world of spinning wheels and looms in old Cataloochee, said Mark, but scarcely a one is now preserved.

There is a fine woven coverlet used as a decorative background in an old photo of Steve Woody and his wife, but where is it now? Some coverlets or "coverlids" have been kept, and a few old quilts are known to exist, but not many because of the potential feasts that exist there for the field mice.

Uncle Hiram's sister, Harriet Caldwell, who married Daniel J. Cook, was known as weaver of coverlets, and quilter of quilts, such as the Texas Star. She was a low, fat woman, remembered her grand-daughter, Flora Messer Morrow, wobbling but pleasant and happy, who picked up a big apronful of chestnuts in the rain, dying later of pneumonia contracted from this damp excursion. None of her "coverlids" remain as memorials to this cheerful woman.

Mark Hannah volunteered that Aunt 'Tildy (Matilda) Woody, Uncle 'Tine Woody's wife, could weave beautiful "coverlids", but he couldn't remember the names of the drafts, such as an existing pattern known as "Road to Soco", although Soco Gap is within hailing distance of him. Flora Palmer's mother was another who quilted for the beds. Of an evening, she would pull the quilting frame up to the ceiling to get it out of the way for the night.

The late Tom Alexander owned Miss Maria's quilts after her death, and some may still be in use at his Cataloochee Ranch and ski resort which has since been moved to Fie Top out of the Park.

JUDITH BARKSDALE ALEXANDER: "She (Miss Maria) wanted me to come in and see her quilts (after she had moved out of the valley to Howell Mill Road in Waynesville). That's where I'm sure I lost face. I know I did. You know, if you're a good trader... you're supposed to do a little trading. She'd bring out these quilts: well, this one is more, four dollars 'cause it's got a lot of work in it. She expected me to bargain with her. Then she'd say, here's another one, that's three."

"Finally, I said, now listen,... you're livin' way back in the past. You've worked awful hard. And here you're pretty close to town. Now one thing you've got to realize is that what you've done with your hands is valuable and very pretty, and you just stop giving them away. I said, the one you want four dollars for is worth double that. And I got quite a few... still have some of her old ones..."

Ducks and geese furnished feathers for bed "ticks" and pillows in Cataloochee. Sheepskins were used as throws, rugs or small bed blankets. Brooms were made, not unnaturally, of broom corn. Candles were often made in molds, according to the best pioneer tradition, said Hilliard Woody, speaking of his own day.

Mark's grandmother, Rebecca Hoyle, would not come in to live in Cataloochee without bringing her cord-sprung bed from Jackson County. And Miss Maria Palmer had a fine pair of spool-turned beds at the Jarvis Palmer house until Allen Davidson's daughter, Addie Davidson Williamson, once came to visit and admired the beds. She and Miss Maria traded beds, for Miss Maria fancied an iron and brass bedstead from the city in place of her good spool bed.

Later Waynesville banker, Linton Palmer, her nephew, said plaintively when told the story of the walnut spool bed, "I always wondered what became of that other spindle bed!"

Will Messer's father-in-law, Daniel J. Cook, was the one who had a real way with furniture, so his grand-daughter, Beatrice Burgess Sisk, recalled in the Park's new publication on the historic structures of Little Cataloochee.

"Cook... made furniture of cherry wood, a material he much admired... beautiful furniture decorated with intricate carvings. He provided his household with a corner cabinet of cherry adorned with a moon and star motif, as well as other pieces such as a dresser, a spindle bed, and several chairs. He also made most of the shoes worn by the family..."

Frank Stines was the main chairmaker of Little Cataloochee. He made chairs, probably of maple or oak, with green maple or oak posts to grip rungs of dried hickory. Mark's grandmother fondly called her favorite rocking chair, "Frank", after its maker.

A recipe written down by the late Flora Palmer tells of the ways some things in the valley could be utilized without going to the store or ordering from the catalogue:

"To tan ground hog hide for leather, take fresh skin and trim off all excess fat. Put in trough that has been chopped out of a piece of log. Put hickory ashes, about one half gallon water to cover hide, and put hide in, hair and all. Weight it down a little so none will be above the water. Lay plank or something over trough to keep animals out and let stay several days. Notice when hair will slip off, then put in branch and wash good till all hair is removed. Let soak in branch two days. Weight it down in water so as not to wash away. Rub and squeeze it good. Stretch it out and tack (to a) plank and set aside to dry. After it's dry, take down and work and stretch it in hands. It should be soft as cotton rag. Cut shoe strings off length of hide as needed. Strings could be used to patch harness."

Mark's comment: "But bobcat is better!"

Mark felt that chestnut oak, too, was good for tanning leather. Shakes or "boards" for a roof were best rived with a froe out of Northern red oak. An ox yoke was good if made out of sassafras or poplar. Of this he was sure because he was in the process of carving one himself, as a pastime.

Aside from toys already mentioned in a previous chapter were whistles made from willow bushes, spinning tops from spools, and whips made of hickory bark.

Harnesses were often homemade, as were bellows, and saddle bags were made of cowskin and sometimes of bearskin.

Everybody in Cataloochee whittled all the time, for fun or not. Even today in the mountains most men carry a little "wet-rock" or whetstone in their pockets with which to sharpen their pocketknives, much as city folk would carry matches or keys or such necessities. When they were not just whittling for fun while trading stories, they whittled on door latches, and such useful items, on rainy days.

ROBERT HILLIARD WOODY: "Our meal barrel, large enough for at least a bushel, was handmade, as was the mixing tray. Large trees split in half and hollowed out made excellent washtubs. Except for the barrel, our .22 calliber muzzleloading rifle was completely handmade; the same was true of the shot pouch and the bullet moulds... out in the 'lumber' room, a general storage place, was a loom on which had been woven the numerous 'coverlids' which were stacked away in 'The Big House'... split hickory brooms and a little sandstone were sufficient for scrubbing floors, and split-bottomed chairs seemed to last indefinitely. To relieve the fatigue of adolescence, however, nothing surpassed the large sheepskin spread in the shade of the porch."

"Uncle 'Tine had set up a small blacksmith shop with a hand bellows, sufficient for most farm repair jobs. If a clevis was needed or the mattock had lost its edge, it could be attended to on a rainy day. If the old mare needed a shoe, the drawing knife, rasp, and accoutrements of the farrier's trade were laid out, the shoe shaped, and the mare properly shod. The cobbler's last took care of all the bipeds."

Wooden shoe lasts were found in Uncle 'Tine Woody's old lumber house, remembered Hilliard Woody, and the old cowhide for shoes hung there, too. Hiram Wilburn found the old lasts to be such antiques by the time he came into Cataloochee, however, that he was already collecting them for his Museum.

Information on natural dyes used in the valley was hard to come by. Few remembered their names and uses, although they were known to have been used, thus reinforcing the urgency of collecting all this information before "Everything should be forgotten", including the forgetting of madder, butternut hulls, sumac berries, hickory bark, indigo (a long forgotten plant, which was once grown by the early settlers), black walnut, onion hulls, sedge grass, and bloodroot.

Cataloochee began fading in front of one's very eyes. Houses rotted or were vandalized in Cataloochee before they could be photographed. Every month one read a new obituary with the greatest of sorrow repeating fruitlessly, "I meant to go and see that person!" Informants died almost on the eve of an interview, including Sam Sutton, Eldridge Caldwell, and an old bear hunter who had gone to live in Franklin, Floyd Burgess, and others.

Nancy "Canadian" (the local name for the Ewart family who came into Cataloochee from Canada) was one who could once make baskets as well as the Cherokee Indians. She used to bring the baskets in to swap for meat. She had imparted her knowledge to her daughter, Lucy Canadian Brown, now living on the East Fork of the Pigeon River. Mark longed to go there one Sunday to learn from Lucy how she put the baskets together with splits of hickory or white oak. Alas, Lucy's son told him that his mother's mind had clouded over like a mirror breathed upon and would not be likely to remember the baskets or even her own name. It became very important to put all down on paper.

The early wooden trenchers, noggins, and spoons, for instance, had not even survived in people's memories, no more than the pewter-ware that the settlers brought in. But Neil Sutton had made wooden piggins to catch maplesap out of his sugar camp in Little Cataloochee. And some useful wooden items were also rather fun, too... such as the half-bushel measure made out of wooden staves, which had a fox-and-goose board on the bottom. Something like tic-tac-toe. Uncle Jim Hannah had one.

Like Uncle 'Tine, nearly everybody in Cataloochee knew a little blacksmithing, out of necessity, such as Jarvis Caldwell, Eldridge Caldwell, and others, but Will Messer on Little Cataloochee was the acknowledged expert and could make anything out of iron. Eldridge Caldwell claimed, being a blacksmith, that he knew all the imprints of the valley's horses, and was able to sort the house guests and valley residents from the horse tracks in front of his home.

There was an endless list of the old handmade tools that Mark could recollect being made and used in Cataloochee. He even remembered how most of them were made and used.

MARK HANNAH: "A Cataloochee flail (was made from) a small even-sized young tree. Hickory is best — about 1.5 inches at the butt. (It) should be 10 feet in length. From the butt end it should measure 3 feet to the place to be twisted. Use a pole axe or hammer and beat on each side 12 inches of the stick until it can be twisted so the flail can turn in the user's hands. Twist it when not in use and burrow in water. The flails being shown at Luftee (Oconaluftee Pioneer Farm Stead) and all books are different. They have a rope in the middle, the modern way. This is the Cataloochee flail."

"Two men, one of either side, used the flails lefthanded to clean the straw from the grain over a rack of about eight 10 inch by 8 inch rails set on four posts driven 2 feet into the ground in the thresh-yard."

A little of every profession seemed to evolve in the valley, even a few perhaps, but not in great numbers, of the "oldest profession." Tinker, tailor, soldier, sailor... Cataloochee had them all... doctor, lawyer, too, even an Indian Chief, secure in his mounded grave on which each brave used to throw a stone in commemoration as he skimmed along the trail to Scottish Mountain.

It was a small settlement, of perhaps only ninety-five families at' its height... but a microcosm, a tiny civilization, almost completely self-sufficient. Cataloochans were all things to all men, and all-powerful within their miniature world.

CHAPTER 18

Shelter

(Architecture)

W. G. B. (Will) Messer was considered a master craftsmen when he designed and built this 7-gable house in Little Cataloochee. Everything that wasn't sourced from Cataloochee was hauled over the mountain by horse and wagon. The home had acetylene piping running through the walls to provide lighting and when the park came in and bought the property, Messer had all of the materials in stock to add indoor plumbing to the home. Will and his wife Rachel raised their 11 children (10 girls and 1 boy) in this home. Messer built the coffins for Cataloochee residents in the top floor. Courtesy Great Smoky Mountains National Park Archives.

NOTHING NOW REMAINS of the earliest shelters in Cataloochee, the Hollow Log Camp, Old Smart's shanty, the Colwell's puncheon hunting cabin. And very little remains of even the later buildings of this community of over seven hundred souls.

Barnes' Old Camp did not need to be built. It was simply there.

MARK HANNAH: "(Tobe Phillips, Tom Barnes, and Maston Hall) came to a large hollow chestnut tree that had fallen over and also turned up on the roots, holding the tree trunk up in the air about seven or eight feet from the ground. The hollow part of the tree was on the bottom side and it left the round side over as a roof, making a dry shed over them. The Northwest side was a mass of roots and dirt that kept the wind from their fires."

Of man-made shelters, there had been at least two hundred log buildings here. In fact, there were once more log structures in Cataloochee than anywhere in the United States, so claimed Dr. Roy Carroll, an historian from Appalachian State College.

Hiram Wilburn, the acting Park Historian, used to fuss and fume like a mother hen, trying to protect the old notched log buildings and the old mills of Cataloochee, despite the orders of Superintendent John Needham to "burn 'em down".

A 1938 report on the proposed mountain culture program, prepared by Arthur Stupka, the Park naturalist, C. S. Grossman, the architect, and H. C. Wilburn, the curator and acting historian, commented that not only was Cataloochee rich in log and sash sawn frame houses, but there was an absence of shoddy boxed houses, probably due to the fact that large commercial interests had failed to penetrate into this area.

Nevertheless, the Park authorities made up their minds that the buildings were to be destroyed. The land was to revert to wilderness and would never again be a living community. The Park Service today has completely reversed its stand.

In the light of Wilburn's amazing research on watermills, it seems incredible that the Park Service did not save a solitary relic of these old mills other than the old mill dam of the Jesse Palmer mill. One can still see the quiet pond if one walks up Palmer Creek towards "Turkey George's" place. Ranger Jim Waldroop used to stop here often to look for salamanders.

Though Wilburn constantly reiterated that Cataloochee was a treasure-house of pioneer architecture, nowadays one does not even stumble on the old millstones which may still be buried deep in verdure, with only the memory of the hum and grinding held deep in their stern implacable rings, symbols of the beginning and the end.

Latterly the Park has had a guilty conscience about the wholesale destruction of most of these buildings. Preservation is the motif nowadays. In 1976, the Park put out a long report about the existing historical structures of Little Cataloochee, meagre though they may be, to be followed by one on Big Cataloochee.

A few Cataloochee buildings were saved, only to be transferred for the most part to the Pioneer Farmstead at Oconaluftee. Jim Conard's meat house and apiary from the head of Conard Branch in Little Cataloochee reside there now, as does Jim Caldwell's spring house from Rough Fork in Big Cataloochee. And the upper portion of the fine apple house is from the upper Will Messer Place in Little Cataloochee. Mark could remember when another apple house was built by Will Messer at the Cook Place about 1915, seven years after the death of his father-in-law, Daniel Cook.

MARK HANNAH: "I've never seen such thick walls. Thick walls and sawdust kept the apples from freezing. It was made of stone and mud (mortar). Verda's father invented a mud machine to help. The water, lime and dirt went into a vat in the center, and a horse was hitched up to walk around it and stir it, just like when you make molasses!"

The walls were as thick as 6ft 4in in some instances! Even the wooden upper story was insulated "with a six inch space between the exterior and interior walls of chestnut siding filled with sawdust", so a belated Park report goes on the historical structures of Little Cataloochee. The upper story was sold after 1950. Now only the stone walls remain.

Aside from the mills, schoolhouses, and churches, the main buildings of Cataloochee were the huge barns, of which only three remain: Hiram Caldwell's and Jarvis Palmer's in Big Cataloochee and one of Will Messer's barns in his upper tract.

Of the 139 homesteads, only four remain: John Jackson Hannah's in Little Cataloochee, Steve Woody's up Rough Fork in Big Cataloochee, the old 'Fayt Palmer Place on Big Cataloochee, and Hiram Caldwell's early twentieth century house on Big Cataloochee. Some vestiges of the fallen Dan Cook cabin, originally a fine structure, can be seen. There is a small late frame house originally built by Hub Caldwell in 1916 where the present ranger now lives, but it is of no historical consequence, except that it has beams of whole chestnut logs and chestnut paneling.

Two churches remain: Palmer Chapel in Big Cataloochee, and the Baptist Church, with a pulpit and steeple made by Will Messer, on Little Cataloochee. One school house remains: in Big Cataloochee, lately used as a horse camp, but now boarded up as a prelude, says the Park, to being restored. In the past year, the Park Service, in a fit of conscience, has also boarded up the Hiram Caldwell house and the Steve Woody house...

In June of 1975, the new young superintendent of the Great Smoky Mountains National Park, Boyd Evison, announced that the Park had received funds for rehabilitation of historic sites and would restore the Jim Hannah (Or John Jackson Hannah) cabin and the Will Messer barn on Little Cataloochee, near Davidson Gap.

When the old Beech Grove schoolhouse was burnt down on purpose by Cataloochans themselves, all of the men commenced building the new school house, the simple two-room affair which stands today.

JARVIS CALDWELL: "Old Man Chapin had a sawmill. And they hauled them logs, big poplar logs, and had all that framing to cut out, and the siding and everything, and they done all the planin' of the lumber by hand, no power planin' nor nothin.'"

MARK HANNAH: "The Little Cataloochee Baptist Church was built by the citizens of the area about 1890. The best poplar trees were selected and cut. Most of them belonged to a lumber company, perhaps it was known as Suncrest Lumber Company. This name came when the Crestmont and Sunburst Companies merged. The owners of this beautiful forest did not object to getting lumber for a church. You can readily see that the poplars were huge, and they did not contain knots. The citizens only used the Grade A lumber."

"This building was located just South of the W. G. B. Messer residence. It was a one-story building."

"The citizens bought lamps, wall type, for lighting it. About four or five, as I remember, were hung on nails that were driven into the walls between the windows, and one was placed over and hanging back of the pulpit."

There were a few log remnants scattered here and there on Caldwell Fork and Little Cataloochee. Remains of buildings might be stumbled upon near Snake Branch of the Booger Man Trail, part of Carson Messer's property. Otherwise, very little can be seen to apprise the casual visitor that this was a thriving valley of over seven hundred people for well over a hundred years. One comes upon ruins in Little Cataloochee, such as the stone walls of the Cook apple house, but often, only the appearance of roses now gone wild and purple, Spanish bayonets, and pyramidal junipers and cedars will indicate that there had been any civilization here beyond the rattler and the bear.

FLORA PALMER MEDFORD: "The house of my father, Turkey George Palmer, stood about four or five hundred feet from Pretty Hollow Creek. It was a two-story, six-roomed, frame house with two porches made of poplar lumber, with two brick chimneys made of hand-made brick. It was taken out piece by piece by a private buyer in 1943 or 1944 and relocated in Cove Creek."

ELDRIDGE CALDWELL: "The greatest thing I ever seen done was down on Cataloochee by the old pioneers with their broadaxes and their notchin' out. Be pretty hard to say which house looked the nicest because they were all good. Yeah, that's right, they did all the work together to build 'em. And when it came to this notchin' 'em and fittin' 'em together, I guess one man had the say about that, marked out how he wanted it done. They wasn't square logs. They was flat alongsides. And then they were notched together."

In 1935, a memorandum was sent to Hiram Wilburn from Willis King, the naturalist technician on Preservation of Log Cabins in the Cataloochee Watershed for Museum purposes, mentioning three old cabins in Little Cataloochee: The Weaver Bennett House on Andy Branch, the 'Tine Woody cabin on Woody Branch, and the Cook Place on Coggins Branch. But he said, "Old roads to the first two places have fallen into disrepair. And the houses and barns are going into decay. The Cook log cabin is in somewhat better condition than those mentioned above and should be restored in its present setting. There is an old apple orchard on the premises with good native grasses... On Big Cataloochee... I believe all remaining log cabins should be dismantled... placed under cover to prevent decay of timber. Since the Caldwell family played such a large part... (it is) suggested... (that the) Caldwell cabin be reconstructed; also a typical grist mill or small water driven saw mill should be shown."

This was not to be, however. In the last days of his life Eldridge Caldwell spoke bitterly about John Needham's promising him the old settler, Levi B. Caldwell's cabin, where Eldridge was born. Then he took back his promise saying the Park needed it because of its historical value.

And Eldridge said, in a rather low monotone, devoid of any emotion: "So, they wouldn't let me have it, and they let it stand there and rot down."

Now, there is only a little mound, and a few rocks of the fireplace left. Oh, Cataloochee! Oh, lost!

Eldridge continued in his rather dry old voice, low, and full of tobacco juice, "My father, after he was disabled to work, he had me to cover the south side of the building which had begun to leak some, and on the north side... it had the old original shingles on there, hand-made out of yellow, white pine, and hand-shaved. And there wasn't a leak in that side, although the old kitchen had been torn away from this building... just the body of the house was there. It had a front porch with a little side room on the end, used for a bedroom in case of company, too much company. It was a two-story building. And the beams for the overhead floor was hand-hewn and dressed down, just perfect four inch squares as could be made."

Jarvis Caldwell added that the rafters and joists were pegged together with wooden pegs. And Vick Smith said the Levi Caldwell house was built about 1858. This was the second Levi Caldwell house, the first having been a little cabin thrown up quickly when he and Dock Bennett first came into the valley, one fourth of a mile up the field.

It should be evident that this was no poverty-stricken mountain community of one-room log cabins, with the possible exception of the very earliest efforts. Many of the houses were fine by any standards, two and three-story houses, such as Will Messer's and Hiram Caldwell's, built of the best timber, and with fairly complicated architectural details, such as spiral staircases, beaded paneling, and decorative porches and balconies.

PARK REPORT ON HISTORICAL STRUCTURES OF LITTLE CATALOOCHEE: "Will and Rachel built their own log home on the upper portion of the Cook estate which they purchased from her brother, Harrison R. on Dec. 14, 1895, for $350. The house had one of the finest stone chimneys to be seen in the area. Messer added a barn, an apple house, and a springhouse to this property. The apple house was later removed and reconstructed by Park personnel at the Oconaluftee Pioneer Farmstead near Cherokee, N. C. Dan Cook continued to occupy the old homeplace until his death in 1908. From Cook's passing until the establishment of the Park, the old homeplace was occupied by tenants employed by Will Messer."

"Messer moved his family again sometime after 1905, when he purchased a 100-acre tract on Little Cataloochee Creek from J. C. Correll. This property was previously owned by A.J. (Jack) Vess, one of the pioneer settlers in Little Cataloochee, and adjoined the southern boundary of the John Jackson Hannah estate. The Messers occupied a house that had been built by Correll until a new dwelling was completed about 1910. The new house was the largest and finest structure on Little Cataloochee. It contained eleven rooms, had hot and cold water, and was illuminated by an acetylene lighting system. On this portion of his property Will developed several barns and mills, a general store and post office (Correll's old house), a blacksmith shop, and several other structures... The house and all of the other structures were later removed by the Park Service."

"... at the time of the construction of his 'big house' on Cataloochee Creek, he devised a cutting machine to speed up the process of making shingles for the roof. Dissatisfied with the unreliable nature of water power, he bought a steam engine to run his sawmill and a gasoline engine to turn his gristmill. A neighbor recalls that Messer could cut a thousand feet of lumber a day by himself..."

"Today the site that was once occupied by Messer's 'big house' is marked by a large hemlock tree which Will planted in his yard years ago. The National Park Service leased the Messer orchards to Mark Hannah for a number of years after 1930, and for this reason the apple house on the Dan Cook place and the barn on the 'upper place' were allowed to stand as reminders of what had passed in Little Cataloochee."

Often log houses, simple in the beginning, were "improved", and boarded over, such as 'Tine Woody's and Steve Woody's houses, and the old Palmer house.

ROBERT HILLIARD WOODY: "It ('Tine Woody's house) had been weatherboarded over, and it had three rooms, the big house which was a company room, you might say, where there were at least four beds in it... and the middle room which was a smaller room where there was just a couple of beds, and the kitchen, which had two beds, the kitchen table, two corner cupboards, a stove, and a big fireplace, and a meal barrel. Kept the rifle hanging over the door... the smokehouse out to one side."

"This was a hewn log house, weatherboarded from timber sawed on the place, the shingles and boards for the roof were made by hand from choice trees. The puncheon floor of poplar eventually gave way to narrow-width maple. We even cemented the stones around the kitchen hearth, and one room (the company room) got some fancy wallpaper, but newspapers and magazines (often placed upsidedown to my annoyance) sufficed for the other rooms."

In a note that was rather terse for the usually ebullient Hiram Wilburn, he reported to his superior, John Needham, the Chief Ranger, "The 'Tine Woody house on Tract 249... only the logs and puncheon floor here will probably be used. The barn, some of the logs may be wanted, frame doors with wooden hinges and possibly the hollow log mangers, a framed grain bin with wooden hinges."

But Robert Hilliard Woody wrote to Hiram Wilburn in 1953 saying that the last time he had seen the place in 1937, it was about to fall down then, the fine log barn, the smokehouse, the blacksmith shop, the mill house, the sheep house, the two log apple houses... all falling down in disrepair after the Park bought the property.

I asked Dr. Woody if most of the houses were not log which had been boarded over.

ROBERT HILLIARD WOODY: "Yes... There weren't many log houses that I recall because... after David Davis got in there with his saw mill, you could get lumber.

Will Messer had a fine big house, we considered. And Mark Hannah's father's house was considered very nice, weather-boarded. You didn't see many log houses (i.e., perhaps in Dr. Woody's time, most had been weatherboarded-over.)... now Uncle 'Tine had a fine barn built of logs that had been hewed out, you know."

"(There weren't many stone structures), nothing except chimneys, and sometimes the chimney was simple framed boards... sounds a little hard to believe. Uncle 'Tine had a field down at the lower end of his place, and he evidently rented to people for a time. They had a house there (the Maynor House); there was a fireplace with a stone structure, but the smoke stack part was boards, planks."

'Tine Bennett further described his Uncle 'Tine Woody's house as having steps about twelve inches apart, but made of logs about eight feet long and hewn with a broad-axe.

Wilburn noted that the Jim Caldwell house had been a fine log structure, weatherboarded over with yellow poplar siding, and had possessed two splendid stone chimneys with two artistic mantels. A later Caldwell house, the Hiram Caldwell house, used wood for the window sills from the wood of the original cabin.

The *Waynesville Mountaineer* newspaper, in 1971, contributed a whole page to this house because the Park had then threatened to tear this one down, also... one of the few remaining homes... saying it was not an antique historical landmark. But, for Cataloochans, in the year 1906, it was a very fine house "when Hiram Caldwell moved his wife and four children, among them Eldridge, (William, Hattie, and Dillard), into their new frame house."

"Behind them, they left a log cabin and the stereotyped mountain existence that most people associate with the backwoods, It was a two-story, frame house with porch along the front and paneling inside (made of beautiful chestnut and pine)."

"Inside was an entry hall with a circular stairway to the second floor. There was a large storage room where canned food was stored located above the heat of the kitchen. There were adjacent spring and smokehouses."

Members of the Caldwell clan had continued to lease the main house after Hiram's death, notably Lucious Caldwell, who lived in it from 1935 to 1968 after which it was left vacant... life became too lonely in Cataloochee after everyone left. "Lush" had been one of the Park's maintenance men, and was allowed to live there. His son, "Stokey", said he was a "Cataloochee Kid", and was a member of the very last school class in the valley, along with Mark's youngest son, Don.

The house was begun in 1903 by Charlie and Taylor Medford of Iron Duff, and Vaughn Massey.

"These three men built a water-powered saw mill on Ugly Creek, now called Woody Creek, and hauled in the pine flooring, the more elaborate paneling on the first floor (it looks beaded from the photo), and bricks from Waynesville. At this time, the wagon trip from town took two days coming and going. The three men, working in between their farming chores, finished the house in 1906 when Eldridge, the youngest child, helped his family move."

"Their new home featured a spring house with water cold enough to keep pork fresh. The top floor, where all the wood had been hand-planed, had a storage room along one side of the house. In this room were stored the 100 lb. sacks of sugar, dry beans and flour, and the frames for warping and quilting. Hiram's wife, the former Lizzie Howell, also had a spinning wheel and a loom in here."

"Hiram, in fact, had earned the money with which he bought the 150 acre tract for 25 cents an acre around 1879, just after his marriage, by making the trip between Haywood and Greenville, S. C. as a teamster. At that time, he earned 10 cents a day for the work. With this tract, he built a prosperous farm that eventually allowed him to move his family into the existing house."

A young Mars Hill student who studied the Cataloochee area felt that the Hiram Caldwell house was of particular interest because it resembled an Eastlake design. "Eastlake was an early architect who put together a hodgepodge of styles into a popular type which spread through the United States."

SAM EASTERBY: "The interesting thing about the Caldwell house is that it was built in this architectural style in a time when the style was just beginning to spread through the country. You wouldn't expect the style to come to the isolated Cataloochee Valley at the same time it hit the country in general. It was probably just an accident of design." Hiram's barn and the barn of the old Palmer house, with its high ramp to the second story, are both excellent examples of this period.

Hiram's barn seen on an idyllic autumn afternoon when the russet of the leaves matched the rustcolor of the old barn roof was a lovely sight. The road was lined with scarlet sourwoods, contained by a split rail fence, and it seemed as if Hiram and his boys might just walk around the bend of the road at any moment, ready for a day's work, as usual.

The Jesse Palmer house, above Palmer Chapel was originally two log cabins built in about 1840-50, remodeled by both Jarvis Caldwell and Jarvis Palmer in 1922. The fireplace was big enough for five-foot logs. The Palmer Mill, later run by Jarvis Caldwell, was above that on Indian Creek, now called Palmer Creek.

But the old Palmer house that now remains is a different one. Linton Palmer, now vice-president of a Waynesville bank, said that his great-grandfather, George Palmer, one of the original settlers, first built a log cabin in Big Cataloochee .02 mile above the now-standing Palmer house. Then George built the present one of square-hewn logs and with a dogtrot. This is where Linton was born, the last of a long list of brothers and sisters.

The Jarvis Palmer house, used by Mark Hannah as the ranger station for thirty years is the oldest standing structure in Cataloochee, and one of the oldest in the entire park. One wing of it is the old George Palmer cabin built in the 1840s.

When Mark Hannah moved into the Palmer house as one of the early rangers of the Park, the Service helped him repair it and paint it white. The dogtrot was closed up, as Mark says humorously, to keep the bears from going through. It presents a very neat appearance today... much more attractive than the present ranger's headquarters which are, however, situated in a more strategic spot for observing the incoming and outgoing visitors. The huge old boxwoods are still there, almost engulfing the house, but the road is not as it used to be. It now runs behind the house so one cannot see the long low porch where Jarvis rocked and smoked and Aunt Maria saw Dude Hannah passing by, more's the pity.

This old Palmer house, however, is apparently one of the few structures that the Park has always preserved and intends to improve by stripping the latter day siding off of it, re-exposing the good logs and the dogtrot, and, hopefully replacing the green asphalt shingles with hand-rived shakes. There was some talk of making it a nature study center for visitors. The last time it was seen, however, the outbuildings were already in great disrepair although it had not been long since Mark retired as a ranger and moved out of the valley. The old shake roof of one of the buildings curls up like winter leaves or a shagbark hickory.

The dogtrot house, of which several were standing in Cataloochee at one time, was described by historian Medford, as being "really two houses, since the smaller one (the kitchen) was on line with the 'big house', the end-doors facing each other about four feet apart. This space was bridged with broad slats or strong boards, so crossing from one house to the other was easy. The dogs would often lie on this connecting boardwalk, which was usually roofed over. The modern version of the dogtrot is, of course, the breezeway.

The little John Jackson Hannah puncheon cabin which remains in Little Cataloochee, is built of hand-hewn squared-off logs with chamfer notches at the corners. The puncheon floors have been taken up and stored among the rafters, in hopes that they can be used again one day, no longer a vain hope, according to the new superintendent of the Park. The high-pitched roof, sloping almost to the ground, has lost its hand-rived shakes long ago, and is protected by simple tarpaper. One could see tracks in the dust of the dirt floor where deer and raccoon had been "usin'". Wild vines grew through the broken panes of the one small window. Folks liked to keep their window openings small and simple in those days to keep the warmth in.

MARK HANNAH: "The logs were hewn by an expert axman, maybe Dan Cook, is my guess... I have the broadaxe that did this work. It was given to W. G. B. Messer by Dan Cook, and Mr. Messer gave it to me. It has the crooked handle in it."

PARK REPORT: "Dan Cook was primarily known in his community as a talented carpenter and cabinetmaker. He was an expert axman, and it is said that he cut the corners and hewed the logs and puncheons for several of the best houses and barns in the area."

He was a tall, slender, goodlooking man, said his granddaughter, Flora Messer Morrow, not mischievous and gay like his wife, Harriet, but more reserved and business-like. She added that he had "right smart of money" and was a "good liver".

In Little Cataloochee, he owned from the church house on Coggins Branch to Davidson Branch. One of the trails in Little Cataloochee is known as "Cook's Lane".

The Architectural Structures of Little Cataloochee refers to the John Jackson Hannah place as the Jim Hannah cabin because Jim and Melissa Hannah lived there for many years.

"The Jim Hannah cabin stands in a clearing on a gentle slope 220 feet north of a dirt park road. The cabin, which faces southwest, is reached by a footpath or trail."

"The yard was once enclosed by a rail fence. In the south corner of the front yard were bee gums. Beyond the fence to the northwest was a vegetable garden and to the southwest was an orchard which once contained what was widely acclaimed to be the world's largest apple tree. To the north, west, and south were three cultivated fields. To the east of the cabin is a small stream flowing south. Just beyond was another rail fence which ran parallel to the stream for a short distance and then crossed it and the footpath leading from the road. At that point (136 feet from the road) there was a footlog, and a slip-gap for entrance."

"The only outbuildings, other than privies whose location is unknown, were a springhouse 135 feet northeast and a corn crib with shed 185 feet north of the cabin."

"Today those outbuildings are gone. So, too, are the fences, with the exception of a few posts where the footpath entered the yard. The garden, orchard, and fields are now wooded..."

"...It is representative of the better type of log structures found in Haywood County, North Carolina. The house was built by John Jackson Hannah between 1857 and 1864, using native stone and timber which were abundant in the area — hemlock, poplar, chestnut, locust, and tizwood (or silverbell)."

"Later modifications, around the turn of the century, included replacement of the original split-board windows with glazed sashes, the nailing of weatherboarding on the exterior to cover the chinks, and the addition of a frame or boxed ell on the northeast (back) side..."

"... it has two distinguishing features: the puncheon flooring, which is in excellent condition, and some of which is 29 inches wide; and the chimney of hand-made brick, which was rare in this area."

"... the bricks, measuring 7 inches by 3-1/2 inches by 2-1/2 inches, were hand-made, burnt in the field above the house. The mud was mixed by tramping with the feet, then packed into sanded molds, and then turned out on a flat surface. A fire was built inside a kiln made out of the bricks to be burnt. It took seven days to burn one kiln. The outside bricks which did not burn completely were used to build a smaller kiln and were then fired a second time."

The Park has talked of stripping the weatherboarding off of the old Steve Woody place to reveal the original logs. It is a fine old two-story house in a lovely location by Rough Fork, though the old fields are encroaching on the house now with overgrown brush. One can just see the remains of the crooked rail or "worm" fencing. Just above the house is a magnificent hemlock forest carpeted with wood sorrel and partridgeberry.

Mark said that, in 1973, the chimney and pillars of old settler Evan Hannah could still be seen in Big Cataloochee. He was the first permanent settler, along with his father-in-law, William Noland. But there is no historical marker to commemorate the event. It's well marked in the mind of Mark Hannah, but may be forgotten when he's gone.

As the ranger of Cataloochee in the early days of the Park, Mark Hannah was under orders to burn down the homesteads and barns of his life-long friends. All this, in a time of peace. Yet, during the Civil War raid of the dreaded Colonel Kirk, only the Bennetts lost their house to the torch.

Fire or rot took all but a few of the corn cribs, apple houses, spring houses, lumber houses, smoke houses, mills, schools, churches, blacksmith shops, country stores, post offices, meat houses, out houses, beestands, sheep houses, barns, chicken houses, pig pens, bridges, footlogs, puncheon floors, rived shakes, pegged joints, wooden chimneys, hewn log siding, rail fencing, dog trots, and all. Gone.

CHAPTER 19

Plenty

(Cataloochee Cooking)

This photograph of Mrs. Sarah Parton of Cataloochee was taken in 1936, when she was 74 years old. Behind her are "shuck" beans, strung on the wall for winter food. The photograph notes that Parton had 4 bushels of these beans, 3 bushels of soup beans, and 1 bushel of pickle beans. The photograph was made by Charles S. Grossman (1900-1972). Courtesy Great Smoky Mountains National Park Archives.

W̲HEN ASKED IF he had enjoyed growing up in Cataloochee, Floyd Woody replied with fervor that he had. And his enormous girth made one believe that eating had been one of his greatest pleasures.

FLOYD WOODY: "Oh, yeah! I stayed there till I was twenty-five years old. And I loved it and we had a great time. We never knew what hard times was. And we had plenty to eat. We had plenty of cattle and plenty of milk and butter. We'us always happy."

The word "Appalachia" conjures up for some a picture of pitiful, gaunt pellagra-ridden farmers who subsisted mainly on corn meal and fatback. As this infamous Southern diet was only a portion of Cataloochee's gustatorial repertoire, this is an incorrect vision of this particular settlement.

Here there was a superabundance of natural foods! In the valley, people may have been poor by material standards, but nobody ever starved. The food was fresh, or either dried naturally, or canned without artificial preservatives. There were no insecticides. And the water was as clear as a mountain valley full of hundreds of streams and springs can be.

ROBERT HILLIARD WOODY: "I heard any number of people didn't want to leave (after the Park bought their land). Couldn't get good water. You know, get out of those hills, this water that you find is not good. You know, would be unhealthy."

At first, it may have been a trial for the pioneer trenchermen to eat heartily. The early crops required careful supervision, for, without a backlog of supplies, crop failure meant harsh times in the winter. The first permanent settler, Evan Hannah and his wife, Betsy, settled down in a cove and began their preparations for a bitter winter.

MARK HANNAH: "They used the wildlife for food, such as deer, bear, coons, squirrels, rabbits, and fish. They only needed some bread or meal, and (the mill) was about twenty miles away. After the first summer, they raised their corn, potatoes, beans, turnips, and pumpkins. Corn was stored in a dry crib. The potatoes and turnips were buried in a large four by six foot hole in the ground with weeds and leaves placed over them and a layer of soil on top to insulate them from the rough winters they had in those days. Then they placed a cover over it, made from chestnut or poplar bark. The bark was peeled in summer when sap was high, then saved to cover anything when needed."

"When Tobe Phillips, Tom Barnes, and Maston Hall came into this area and located because of the great hunting grounds, they did most of their cooking on heated stones. They would place their meat on these hot rocks and fry it. Another way they cooked meat, such as squirrels or coon, was to cut a stick about four feet long and sharpen one end of the stick and cut the meat and place the whole squirrel on the stick, then they would hold it in their hands and turn the stick to cook the meat on equal sides, barbecue style. I have done this myself many times."

ROBERT HILLIARD WOODY: "Good living was the rule. Fish in the creek, honey in the hive, milk in the springhouse, meat in the smokehouse, and an applehouse stored with a variety of canned vegetables and fresh apples was the accepted order of nature. In season, it was no trouble to step out in the morning or late in the afternoon and pick off a 'mess' of squirrels. I note for the benefit of the uninitiated that a young groundhog caught in the early summer, when he was fat on young beans and the like, and properly prepared, was a delicacy worthy of a discriminating people. Few indeed were the desperately poor."

Floyd Woody and Glenn Palmer were born the same night. Their families did not live too far apart. Floyd used to laugh at the late Glenn Palmer who was rather slim, unlike the portly Floyd.

FLOYD WOODY: "He never learned to eat enough."

That's not quite true, if the story Glenn told before he died is correct. As a young man of seventeen, apparently he had a huge appetite for fish. He and Bob "Canadian" once went over to Beech Ridge to hunt for cattle. The proper name of Bob's family was Ewart, but they had been called "Canadian" so long because of their coming from the far North on the Orr timber deal, that the name stuck, and few remembered what their real name was after awhile.

They "stole out" a frying pan and forgot the cattle. They went to Lost Bottom Creek to fish and caught ninety-seven mountain speckled trout. This was in defiance of Glenn's father's wishes, as Will Palmer, an early conservationist, had recently got a law passed in the legislature prohibiting fishing the upper streams of Cataloochee above the Turkey George place, in order to protect the streams.

They fried the fish and ate them... scared to death all the while. Young Glenn ate forty-seven, and Bob had forty-eight. The two left over had lost their appeal by then.

Glenn, always a gentle soul and well beloved by Cataloochans, felt that this was one of the meanest things he had ever done in his life. He completely abandoned the cattle, telling his father later that they couldn't be found.

Unfortunately, Aunt Laura Bennett, who was living with them, found the bait. Father William Palmer gave him a good lecture, and went off to find the cattle himself. He never whipped Glenn then or any other time in his life. Glenn Palmer remained until his death a sweet and soft-spoken man, often with remorseful tears in his eyes over the unkind thing he had done to his father.

'TINE BENNETT: "We lived good in a way, and another way we didn't have much money, but we had plenty to eat. We mostly made (i.e. grew) all that stuff."

MARK HANNAH: "My father said we made what we eat, and we eat what we made. That was his slogan."

'TINE BENNETT: "Uncle 'Tine Woody had a big ole smokehouse out there... and he'd go out there. He'd always kill a beef in the fall. And he'd hang the hindquarters up and let them dry. We could keep meat, back then. He'd go out there and slice 'im off a piece of meat as wide as my hand and get him a big onion. The dinin' room was in the kitchen... had a drawer in the table, and he'd go to that drawer and pull it up, take a case knife and cut 'im off a pone of corn bread. He had a certain place on them steps, and he'd eat that onion and that meat raw. That night at supper, he wouldn't eat a thing but milk and bread... he crumbled it in. And that's where I get my crumblin' in milk and bread now!"

MARK HANNAH: "We ate breakfast about 6 A.M. or shortly after daylight: winter and summer. The menu was biscuits, butter, honey, jellies, squirrel soup, or gravy, brown gravy, ham, eggs fried or scrambled, thickened blackberries, sometimes trout or fried chicken, and coffee or milk. Coffee mills were used to grind the coffee and to wake the family up for breakfast!"

"Dinner came around twelve noon. And the menu was cornbread or biscuits; beans dried or green; cabbage; turnips; potatoes boiled, soupy, or fried; onions; and meats which were either ham, chicken, squirrel, rabbit, deer, bear, coon, pork, in many ways, such as spare ribs, and beef, too. We also had honey or molasses with country butter, jellies, too, such as apple or blackberry, and milk, coffee, or spicewood tea."

"Supper was between six and eight P.M. after dark and after work time. The menu was (virtually) the same as dinner. (Often we would have) cobbler pies: strawberry, blackberry, apple, or rhubarb in the summertime. (Or we would have) chicken and dumplings, backbones and ribs, and soup beans. A favorite meal in the wintertime was sweet milk and shortning bread crumbled into a glass or bowl. (We) ate it by the fireside if it was baked in an oven or skillet. That was living at home. We used oak-bark or hickory wood to get good fire coals for baking under and on top of the oven. Hooks were used to remove the oven lid to see if the bread was brown. I have them now."

"A spider is a long handled type of oven with legs. It can be covered or used open top. A skillet is a long handled frying pan, maybe oven-style. A gritter is a piece of tin with nail holes punched into it, oval-shaped, over a board about 20 inches in length. Used to grate corn soft, or apples for cider. Stoneware crocks were used to put milk in springs, to keep honey in, or pickle beans. The sizes were from one to five gallons. Wooden tubs were used for molasses, or for storage of beans and kraut."

Charlie Palmer reminisced with Joe Hall, the California professor who had long studied the speech habits of Cataloochans. Hall made a note: GARDEN OF EDEN, after Charlie reported to him: "They was raspberries and strawberries and June apples and all sorts of fruit, and it was more like livin' in the Garden of Eden than anything else I can think of." It was poor Charlie, too, who agonized during World War I eating hardtack in the Argonne Forest, the worst sort of fare a Cataloochan ever had to endure.

Pearl Caldwell agreed with Charlie Palmer about the bounty of fruits. She said that a ten quart bucketful of wild strawberries was easy to pick in Cataoochee. Her husband, Eldridge, who loved his spirits, was asked if he had ever made wine out of wild strawberries.

ELDRIDGE CALDWELL: "No, I never have enough of those. Oh, there used to be worlds of strawberries in Cataloochee... more strawberries than I've ever seen anywhere else. And I wouldn't give a pint of 'em for a gallon of these cultivated berries. They don't have the flavor."

PEARL CALDWELL: "They make the most delicious jams of any."

Pearl made wine, however, out of wild grapes. She had also brought cultivated Brown Concord grapes with her to Campbell Creek when they had to leave Cataloochee. Both grape marmalade and preserved grapes were made from the grapes of the original vineyard. Visitors were also invited to taste the fine three-year-old rhubarb wine that she had made. When asked how she, a teetotaler, had become a vintner, her answer was that her preacher had taught her, on the grounds that she was doing good for her friends. So she often made a gallon or two and bottled them in tiny brown jugs for distribution.

One day when Ernestine Upchurch's Aunt Pearl invited her to lunch, she sat down to a table that included hot biscuits, apple jelly, corn, beans, beef, peaches, pickles, pineapple cake, German chocolate cake, and coffee. Something must have been left out! It was bedazzling. Eldridge had no teeth as they had all just been pulled. He had some trouble eating, but later contented himself with his 'baccy.

He was questioned as to how his mother, Lizzie Howell Caldwell, had prepared wild game. Like many men of his era, he didn't pretend to know much about the details of the kitchen.

ELDRIDGE CALDWELL: "I don't know 'specially how she prepared them, but she cooked it till it were rale (real) tender... 'course, wild meat, mostly stewed."

His wife quickly filled in a few details.

PEARL CALDWELL: "She'd cook 'coon. She 'specially loved 'coon, and she'd do that. Boil it, and then she'd take it out and roll it in meal and brown it. I never cared for b'ar meat. Now I have cooked it."

She went on to tell the embarrassment of having the superintendent of the Park turn up to take potluck with them once when they were just sitting down to a dinner of illegal bear meat. They fooled him into thinking it was beef!

The master bear hunter of them all made quite a profit in the end.

TURKEY GEORGE PALMER: "I finally went to cannin' up the extra bear meat we'd have. We'd sell it fer a dollar and a half a fruit jar."

Food was not only canned, it was also hung to dry in the kitchen. Mark described with pleasure the colorful strings of "leather-britches", or beans, red and yellow peppers, strings of onions, and sliced rings of pumpkin and dried apples also hung on strings, making Fannie Mack's kitchen look like some festive Flemish painting of a food fair.

It's hard not to feel thirsty on seeing the remains of the old white-latticed spring house that lies slumped in the spring at the Uncle Steve place. These natural spring "refrigerators" were always full of crocks of buttermilk, large yellow slabs of butter, jugs of cider, watermelons, clabber, and spring lizards which clung to the sides of the stones that lined the troughs.

MARK HANNAH: "Making apple cider in Cataloochee in my early days was quite a task. This is the way:

"Gather about one bushel of sour-juicy apples. One fourth bushel of hog sweet or any good sweet apples; wash them in a tub of clean water. Throw away the bad ones that float to the top. Get the old-time gritter (grater) and place it into a clean tub; hold the top of the gritter in left hand and an apple in the right hand and start rubbing the apple up and down over the gritter; turn the apple and keep rubbing until it is all into pomace or cider. Do all the apples this way or until you have the desired amount. We used a 25 lb. size flour bag (thin mesh as possible) to squeeze the pomace through. Put about one-fourth gallon of pomace into the bag and hold one end of the bag while twisting the other end. It presses the cider out into a clean tub; then throw the pomace away and start another run, etc. until you finish."

"Then a little later Mother bought a food chopper. Boy, oh boy, we thought we had it made until some one was turning and the other feeding the sliced apples into the chopper, trouble started — "Whoa, whoa, you are grinding on my poor old finger! Back up, please!" We learned the hard way to do our own turning."

"Then on or about 1915, a cider mill, as it was called, was purchased in Newport and hauled in via the wagon road. It had two slatted tubs to catch the pomace and a screw-type press to get the cider out. We could make several gallons in an hour. It was made to drink while fresh. None was sold at all. Sometimes we would make it on Sunday afternoon."

ROBERT HILLIARD WOODY: "I remember cornbread baked in an oven. These weren't pones. They were pancake-like things. You had, I'll call it a skillet, or a Dutch oven type of thing with a top. And you put it in the fireplace and cover it with those hot coals..."

Turkey George's daughter, Flora, discussed the eating habits of the Palmer family. One could never believe that the gossamer Flora ever ate a bite more than an occasional lettuce leaf. So light of foot that she never wore a path on the grass in front of her house, one always thought of her, in that faded house of memories where she lived all alone with her ticking clock, as ready to blow away like fern spore. The old superstition in the middle ages was that if fern seed could actually be found it would give the finder the power of making himself invisible. Quiet Flora had almost happened on this secret, even though ferns have spores and no seeds.

FLORA PALMER MEDFORD: "Had spicewood tea, they called it. And we'd drink that at table. And sassafras tea. But I never liked that. That spicewood I thought'us real good. My grandmother said, though, that the reason we didn't use no more of that sassafras was that the kind they had on Jonathan Creek didn't grow over there. Anyhow, we had the kind that didn't make good tea. Spicewood, sticks of a tree, y'know, little limbs. It grows sorta in moist places. We used to, when I can first remember, we'd sweeten it with molasses, homemade molasses. And then we got so we didn't have homemade molasses all the time, so we put sugar in it. But it was really good with that homemade molasses."

"Pumpkin butter... well, you must peel that and cut it up like you would apples and cook it a long time. And way back yonder they'd sweeten it with molasses. And later on they got to sweetenin' it with sugar, and put it in these big ole iron vats that they used to boil their clothes in out in the yard. Put some sticks under it and get your far (fire). You can't have too much far; that's why it takes so long to cook. But it's good and they flavor it with spices."

"I think sallet peas is one of the best vegetables in the world. We always grew some and made enough to can, always canned some if we could. They're as good as canned beans. They're edible pods. Some think you have to pick 'em real early before their maturity, y'know. But these edible peas, they're not too particular."

"We always kept a lot of kraut on hand. In big crocks... a long time ago. And then we got so we'd just can it up and keep it in jars... in half gallon jars."

"We didn't go in for bear lettuce that much. It's tough. Don't you think it's fuzzy or somethin'? But I like 'kilt sallet'. To make that you put onions and hot bacon grease on the greens, and a little vinegar on the greens."

"Rhubarb pie's the best pie you ever ate!"

"We didn't use to eat poke greens, but I eat it now when I can get it. It's as good as spinach. Have you eaten any? Mushrooms! We'us always afraid to... you have to know what you're doin' there, they tell me. And lots of people won't eat poke sallet because... well, I say that if you don't get down in that root, you don't get the poison. That's what I've read. And I know you don't because I've eaten tops and cooked wild poke sallet. And I think it's good for you!"

"Big hominy's the whole grain, corn, the kernel. We had grits, too. Boil grits a lot longer than we do now, and they're the best thing. We never cook 'em long enough now. Back then they cooked them a long time."

"Cracklin' bread, that's good. Have you ever had any of it? We don't ever have no cracklin's anymore 'cause don't have no hogs. Sweet potatoe pie's good... and blackberry cobbler..."

The picnic tables at Cataloochee Homecoming each August are living testimonials to the love of good food stretching out for endless yards by the fringe of creek and hemlocks behind the church, bending under the weight of copious outdoor delicacies.

A young descendent of old settler, George Palmer, wrote about it.

JOHN PALMER: "Joy and laughter grew in volume as the families left the chapel and assembled for their dinner-on-the-ground. Out under the shade trees, just a few feet from the rushing creek were the longest tables I had ever seen, each covered with a bright gingham table cloth. The merriment was contagious. Everyone was hugging each other and everyone was hungry... as they unloaded their picnic baskets."

"Oh what a joy to wander indecisively among the dishes of devilled eggs, fried chicken, potato salad, squash casseroles, baked apples, bean salad, apple stack cake, lemon pies and pink lemonade!"

But the accumulation of food at these gatherings is not entirely typical of older Cataloochee. Much of the present day picnic fare is duplicated at church affairs throughout America. Who, nowadays, gets bear meat stew and fried bear liver, or squirrel soup, baked groundhog and coon at a picnic? And what has happened to the Cataloochee sweets of yore: persimmon and sweet potato puddings, vinegar pies, and fried dried halfmoon apple pies? Where are the pokeberry and bearberry jellies, pumpkin butters and corncob syrups? For us, no longer, the gritted breads, pone breads, cracklin' breads, big hominy, or brown meal mush — no more wild greens and "kilt sallets", or year-old kraut in brine.

One could forego some of that, but the final word on esoteric Cataloochee cookery was found in a recent article in The *Waynesville Mountaineer* entitled, "Rattlesnake Patrol Cooks Best Meal":

"Twelve Boy Scouts and four leaders of Boy Scout Troop 318, Waynesville, enjoyed an overnight camping trip into the Cataloochee section of Haywood County recently."

"Highlight of the weekend was a meal preparation contest between patrols with the Rattlesnake Patrol winning with a menu of bean hole beans, barbecue chicken, tossed salad, tea, and Jello congealed in the creek."

It would surely have given Miss Maria a turn to have stepped on Jello if she had happened to be wading in the "only safe part" of Cataloochee Creek, the Sycamore Pond, which is not too far from where the Rattlesnake Patrol camped that night!

CHAPTER 20

The Food of Love

(Music)

Music was the main form of entertainment in Cataloochee and you had to make your own. If you were fairly talented, you could earn extra money from playing at square dances and events. From L to R: Burt Denton on the guitar, Mark Hannah on the autoharp, and Cal Messer on the fiddle, circa 1936. Courtesy of the Mark Hannah family.

AT THE ANNUAL Cataloochee reunion at Palmer Chapel, nearly always the opening hymn is "Shall We Gather at the River". The real river conducts its own counterpoint to the singing as it rushes by outside the windows, roaring and tumbling over the mossy green stones between the banks of rhododendrons and hemlocks.

Music in old Cataloochee always flowed like the mountain creek — or like wine — or like moonshine. It was unstoppable and effervescent. For in this closed community, a little fiddle, banjo and guitar-playing was the greatest entertainment ever devised. It brought old and young together in a kind of back-slapping, hopping, rollicking enjoyment of life. Or, if it was a good round of church-singing, then the heat of brotherly love warmed every heart even on a cold winter's day.

At the reunion, after the hymn-singing of traditional favorites, and a little praying, and a little exhorting... one year from the lieutenant governor of the State, another year from the chancellor of Western Carolina University... and after the eating, the serious instrumental music of the mountain banjos and guitars used to begin with Mark Hannah's family as the focus, though other musicians could join at will. When Mark was ranger of Cataloochee, he said they all used to retire to the ranger station after the festivities were over, and would play for the rest of the day.

A typical audience one year included an old woman in her nineties who asked to be brought close to the music and singers in her folding deck chair. Eldridge Caldwell, then painfully crippled, wearing a bright red peaked cap, leaned toward the musicians on his old walking stick. Another old man, sitting on a picnic table, patted his thigh in time to the music as he looked upwards with rheumy dreaming blue eyes, thinking of other times, other music. And a tiny child, jogged to the tunes, surrounded by a circle of amused adults.

Music was always a big and sentimental part of Cataloochee life. But the old ways have passed. The English and Scottish ballads of their ancestors have almost disappeared, and could hardly be recollected even when a visiting balladeer in recent times tried to evoke memories with a new rendition of "Lord Randal". Hardly anyone living could remember these old "song-ballets" being sung in the Valley, though everyone could remember hymns and more recent Grand Ole Opry music within this century. No one could ever remember having heard a dulcimer in the old valley days.

How had this tragedy happened? Why had the popularity of the ballad declined, and why were so many of them lost to memory?

John Jacob Niles, the noted folksinger, suggested that preachers had condemned the "love-ballets" and guitars as instruments of the devil. Newer music came from the radio and people were ashamed to be caught singing the old-fashioned ballads. Revivalists brought in books of "jerry-built" hymns — and the worst damage was done. That is, until many years later when people were encouraged to compete for prizes in ballad and folk singing, in fiddling, and in the old-time shape-note singing.

Mark displayed some of his old worn shape-note songbooks which had obviously had good usage in Cataloochee. Some of the better religious folk songs later came to be known as the white spirituals of the Southern Uplands, rather than as hymns, and the signers came to be known as the fa-so-la singers.

A simple system had been devised in old England whereby the sound of a note could be understood by its shape rather than its position in a musical manuscript. Nearly everybody could sing from shaped notes without much instruction, or without knowing how to read or write.

Some people had fanciful names for the shaped notes. They were known variously as "buckwheat grains, three-cornered sounds, measle-toed, and square-toed music", though Mark never heard these names in Cataloochee.

The shape-note songbook which Mark has preserved uses the seven shapes method. *Carol Crown* is the name of this book, published in 1915 by James D. Vaughn, who

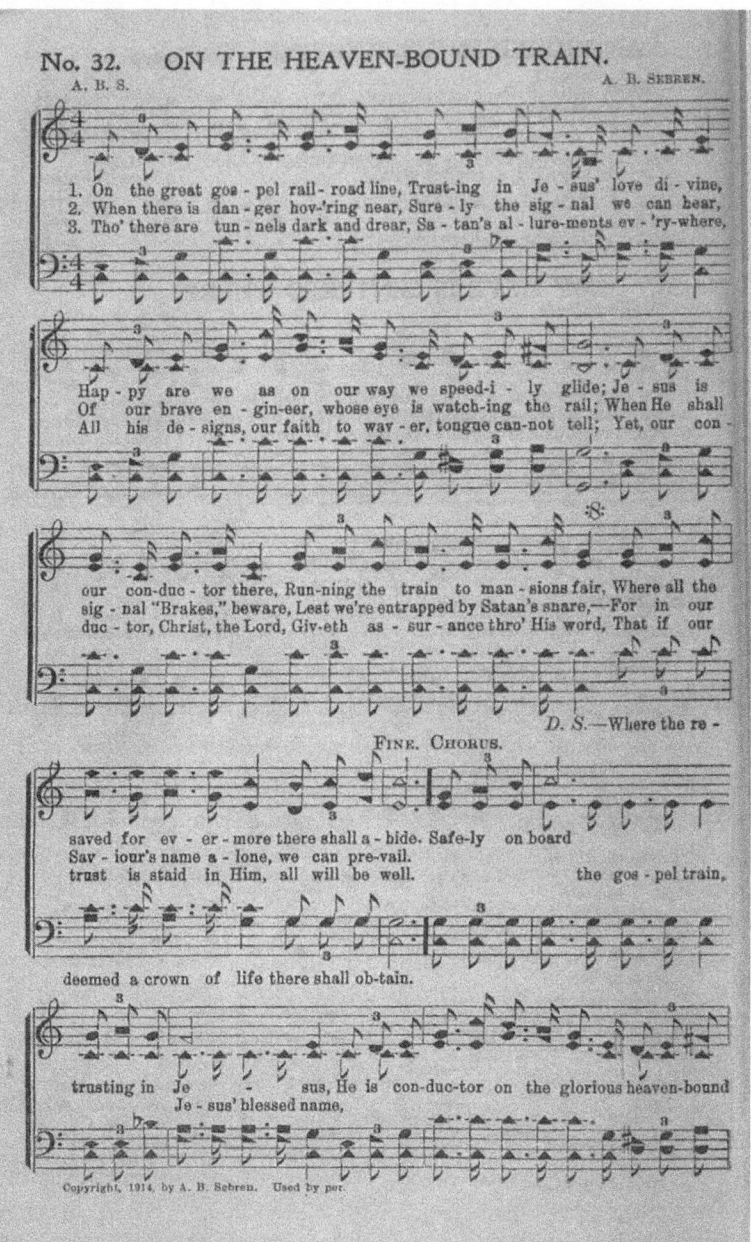

Shape note sheet music for the hymn On the Heaven-Bound Train.

published subsequent songbooks with splendid titles like: *Glorious Refrain, Gospel Hosannas, Harp of Gold, Crowning Praises,* and *Silver Trumpet.*

A second, older, quite dog-eared book of 1886, was evidently used for Sunday School singing lessons only... Hymns, such as "Amazing Grace", "Rock of Ages", and "Jesus, Lover of my Soul", were so familiar that only the words were given in this version, and not the shape-notes. It also included many of the old favorites: "Work, For the Night is Coming", "Are You Washed in the Blood", "The Lily of the Valley", "By and By", "What a Friend We Have in Jesus", and "Bringing in the Sheaves".

The shape-note book includes such familiars as "From Greenland's Icy Mountains", "My Faith Looks up to Thee", "He Leadeth Me", "How Firm a Foundation", "Old Time Religion", "Nearer My God to Thee", and "Blest Be the Tie That Binds", as well as some astonishing hymns which were carefully tailored to the times, like "On the Heaven-Bound Train", which goes on to mention "Tunnels dark and drear, Satan's allurements everywhere... when he shall signal Brakes, beware, lest we're trapped by Satan's snare."

The theme was evidently popular because it occurred in another hymn entitled "The Gospel Railroad," which contains a verse with astonishing metaphors: "Get your ticket, God's forgiveness, Jesus paid the fare, you know, And his telegrams of mercy, Up and down this railroad go, etc. etc."

Imagine a popular hymn of today, trusting to the Thunderbird or the Kawasaki as the angels of fate?!

A personal note in pencil was found after Hymn No. 33, "Only Trust Him" "if you can", someone from Cataloochee has pencilled in the warning.

Mark claimed that much of his social life was bound up in the church and singing.

MARK HANNAH: "We looked forward to our Sunday singing. And they came from Big Cataloochee, Little Cataloochee, White Oak and Big Creek... everywhere... to hear us sing. In other words, we got to be pretty good for a country choir. Yep."

"We used shape-note songbooks altogether. We'd have singing' school every year... a week, sometimes two weeks. Oh, some of those old timers liked "Amazin' Grace", "Sweet Bye and Bye", and all those old songs. And then we got into the new ones as fast as we could keep up with them. Each year they brought a new book of new songs."

Another old-time perennial was "I'm a Poor Wayfaring Stranger", which was often sung by Verda Hannah's uncle, John W. Burgess, at revivals, and which, Raymond said, his Aunt "Ellender" Palmer sang at her daddy-in-law's funeral. Flora Palmer remembered that her mother, while quilting of an evening, might sing hymns to the family. Aunt Lizzie Caldwell loved, "Oh, Prepare to Meet Thy God", and it was, accordingly, sung at her funeral.

JARVIS CALDWELL: "(Some of the favorite hymns were) 'God Be With Us till We Meet Again.'"

RAYMOND CALDWELL: "'On the Uncloudy Day'... that was Aunt Ellender Palmer's!"

Verda's father, Will Messer, usually led the singing at Little Cataloochee church, while her Uncle John Burgess did the revival singing. Robert Hilliard Woody remembered the revivals as rather emotional events. There is a strangely affecting song, in the manner of an Indian chant in the *Carol Crown* songbook. One can imagine that it might have been sung at a revival in order to whip up feeling. It was called "Now I Feel the Sacred Fire" and ends with the descant:

> I was dead but now I live, Glory! Glory! Glory!
> I was bound but now I'm free, Glory! Glory! Glory!
> For I feel it saving me, Glory! Glory! Glory!
> Let the Pilgrim shout aloud, Glory! Glory! Glory!

Little Cataloochee church must have nearly burst its bonds if this were sung with the fervor of the ritual fire dance that the words imply.

Mark's grandmother, Rebecca Hoyle, who used to sit on the front porch with his Grandmother Hannah, as they comfortably smoked their little clay pipes, had a special song which Mark remembered as "Rosim the Bow". Investigation turned up an old tune called "Old Rosin the Bow" from which a religious parody was made called "Sawyer's Exit". According to a compiler's note in 1859, these words were composed by the Reverend Sawyer on the day of his death with a request that they be set to this profane tune.

But as the search for Cataloochee ballads continued, it struck mostly barren ground. One has listened, as John Jacob Niles might have, all evening, to a bunch of mountain musicians, waiting, in vain, for the old English ballads to turn up... and, finally, at 3:00 or 4:00 a.m. when hardly anyone was awake, a shy voice to a low guitar accompaniment might sing haltingly, so low that one could scarce hear, "Down in the Willow Garden." This, after a rousing night of "Foggy Mountain Breakdown" and "The Bugle Call Rag"!

One afternoon, Mark Hannah and his late brother Fred, two of the foremost musical arbiters of Cataloochee, were probed for what shreds of old song ballads they might have saved. Although they had compiled an impressive list of sixty-eight songs and instrumental tunes, not even counting hymns, they remembered only two real ballads. Their brother, Robert, contributed the words.

Only one, "Ellen Smith" seems to have overtones of an English ballad, though the noted collector, Cecil Sharpe, claimed that he found <u>nothing</u> but Elizabethan ballads in the mountains not too many years ago.

> "Poor Ellen Smith
> Just as true as a dove

Oh, where did she ramble
And who did she love?"

Sounds English enough, but historian Manly Wade Wellman of Madison County claims that "Poor Ellen Smith" concerns a Forsyth County murder in the 1890's.

Bascom Lamar Lunsford, of Buncombe County, over the years collected "more than three hundred songs for the Library of Congress and Columbia University, a truly phenomenal achievement, writing down and arranging many of them for the first time." He is certainly the outstanding collector in this part of the country, continuing the work of Cecil Sharp, the English Ballad collector, who lived in Appalachia in 1918.

One day he came to see Mark Hannah in Cataloochee. They played and picked and sang all day. The outcome of which was that nothing Mark played or sang was unknown to Lunsford, with the exception of a tune from Madison County which is now a classic, called "Shelton Laurel". This tune was often played on the five string banjo by Nick Hannah in Cataloochee.

MANLY WADE WELLMAN, the historian of Madison County said that "Os Deaver, a master fiddler before the Civil War, improvised a hauntingly lovely tune at a hilarious party in a Shelton Laurel cabin. A woman, half-drowsing on a cot, sat up to cry, 'Oh, play that lonesome thing again!' His tune was called Lonesome Laurel thereafter."

In his list of sixty-eight "old" songs and tunes, Mark included one called "Smoky Mountain Blues", which he himself had written. But he refused to sing it outside of his family circle as it had not been copyrighted.

Things still come to Mark's mind. One night he was singing to his family and sang an old ballad which made his son, Don, (who is no mean musician himself, having won prizes for his banjo-picking) say, "Why, Daddy, I didn't know you knew songs like that!"

Mark admitted that he hardly ever sang the ballads anymore, and had forgotten many of them. He was chided for this and told it would be a great loss for his grandchildren. Therefore, recently his two sons, with guitar and banjo, made a tape which included all of the old tunes that Mark could recall.

The following is his reconstruction of a musical scene from Old Cataloochee.

MARK HANNAH: "(At the box supper in Little Cataloochee church), when the boxes were all in and about ready for sale, the banjo and the fiddle were tuned up; this was a hard job to tune with those old wooden pegs. Some would take them out and put it in his lips to wet it with saliva, to make the pegs swell and tighten so they would hold the strings in tune."

"Mark Putnam was the top banjo-picker in those days. Squire Mitchell Sutton, Jim Sutton, and Nick Hannah were others. The fiddler was 'Mericus Hall, who married

'Tine Bennett's sister, Alice, and you should have heard and seen him putting rosom (resin) on the bow. When they got going' with 'Wildwood Flower', my hair would start rising... How sweet was the sound, to my ear..."

ROBERT HILLIARD WOODY: "Mitch Sutton was the best (banjo-picker) I ever heard on Cataloochee. Uncle Blaine could play pretty well."

ELDRIDGE CALDWELL: "We didn't have a whole lot of music there in Big Catalooch'. Suttons... ones raised there at Catalooch' and Hemphill together, ole man Sol Sutton's family. Several of them would make music. And sometimes there would be musicians that would come in. But there was very little music on Big Catalooch'. Now Little Catalooch' had plenty of music. They had a talent for it, and Big Catalooch' didn't. We'd attend revivals together."

Since the preacher came only once a month, the other three Sundays were spent in singing and Sunday School.

ROBERT HILLIARD WOODY: "(Palmer's Chapel in Big Catalooch' was) graced by a belfry tower from which went forth the melancholy and lonesome and mysteriously moving call to worship... where several songs of Zion are sung with the aid of the tuning fork."

He perfectly describes the sound of that Sunday church bell. If the bells of Cataloochee can be said to be musical instruments, then one should include the sheep, cow, and hog bells as well. The far-off tinkle, a pleasant and sentimental sound on a summer's day were all a part of the musical scenery.

A memorable passage from one of the contacts from Nantahala in *Foxfire 3* says it best.

FLORENCE BROOKS: "I like to hear cowbells ring at night. People used to keep bells on their cows, y'know. You get out an' you could hear all sounds of them. Some of them'ud be little, some of 'em 'ud be coarse, some of 'em 'ud be kind of music-like. You could hear the little ol' bells go 'ding, ding", and then you could hear a big ol' coarse one... hear all kinds. They go 'ding, ding, ding, ding', just like someone's heart a-beatin', just as reg'lar, all th' time."

MARK HANNAH: "We ranged or grazed our cows in the mountain fields during the day. Each evening we drove them to the barn to milk them. We would leave them in the barn during the night. Many a night I have lay in the bed and heard the cowbells ringing — ding-ding — as the cow chewing her cud made the bells ring. Some three or more cows would have bells; their names were 'Cindy', 'Bonnie', 'Red', 'Old Little', and 'Half Pint'. They were real good cows, too. Those gnats were terrible while milking."

'TINE BENNETT: "Who made the music in Little Catalooch' in my day? Uncle Umph White. He was a fiddler. Jane Jolly picked the banjer. Seems like there's two banjers there. I don't remember now who the other'n was."

FLORA PALMER MEDFORD: "Squire Mitchell Sutton lived there at the Kerr Place for several years. We always liked to go down there because he'd pick the banjer and sing. Now one ole song we used to like to learn to pick and sing was 'Ticklish Reuben'. You never heard that? Well, now, that's funny. It just pleased us to death to hear that!"

Floyd Woody had told, too, about the Indian, Jess Swayney, who would sometimes come all the way in from Big Cove and pick his banjo for them in Big Cataloochee.

Actually the Cherokees traditionally used a kind of mandolin or guitar-shaped instrument, perhaps made of gourd; it was also used for a rattle and a drum. They also made horns out of gourds, and bugles to call sheep or to call people to dinner.

There's a quaint picture of Hilliard Woody as a young boy, looking as cool as Steve Woody's springhouse, with a straw hat on his head, a corncob pipe in his mouth, and Uncle 'Tine Woody's home-made banjo in his hands. Dr. Woody confessed that it was a put-up job, as he never knew much about playing it.

'TINE BENNETT: "Uncle 'Tine's banjer? Oh, hit 'us made there. I don't know who made it, but hit'us made there. It had a groundhog skin over the top of it. And he put it on the top of the banjer and pulled it tight, and nailed it down everywhere with smooth tacks. (wistfully) I wonder what ever become of that banjer?"

It's been said by Manly Wade Wellman that banjos were made popular by minstrel shows before the Civil War. Prior to that, the fiddle was the main mountain instruments and were played way back then laid flat in the lap or against the belly.

One of the finest fiddlers of Cataloochee was Elijah Messer, grandfather to Verda Messer Hannah. He deserved his nickname of "Fiddlin' 'Lige" when he came into' this valley from Cove Creek right after the Civil War... tall as Lincoln, impressive in his high hat, impressive, too, to Tom Porter, the surveyor who conversed with him, thinking him an educated man. Self-educated, said Verda... he read lots of newspapers. What's more, he was allowed to stay in this valley of Confederates although he had been a Union sympathizer during that hard and bitter time. Like Elijah of the Bible, maybe he was fed by the ravens when rations got scarce back then. He seemed to have a lot of the answers, with those newspapers in hand. And he had that all-mighty fine fiddle which set them to jigging just to hear it. One of his fiddles has been preserved in Maggie Valley.

Another Messer, Cal, a nephew of Elijah's, just out of Cataloochee in Tobe's Creek, Tennessee, on the other side of Mt. Sterling, was another famous fiddler in these parts. He would travel a long way to play in Cataloochee, or on Fie Top for square dances, or to any folk dance gathering or fiddler's convention. Only poor eyesight and poor health kept old Cal from playing toward the end of his life. He recently gave up the ghost and is sadly missed at all mountain doings.

Possibly the most famous tune ever played on Cataloochee was "Bonaparte's Retreat", fiddled by the hapless Groom at Mt. Sterling before Teague's Scouts killed him during the Civil War. "It is a sad one, running much to the minor key, musicians say. Dogs often begin to howl when it is played."

Manly Wade Wellman said that many of the jig and square dance tunes, rendered in lively tempo by banjo and fiddle, hark back to Scottish and Irish jigs and reels. (But) something of an insinuating bagpipe wail persists in songs like "Wildwood Flower" (sometimes called 'Raven Black Hair' in the Western South), and 'Poor Ellen Smith', which Mark Hannah could still sing. Guitars came later still, Wellman said, perhaps from the Spanish-influenced deeper South. "For a time they were considered more or less a lady-instrument."

MARK HANNAH: "We'd go up some of those creeks, went up to Carl Woody's and had a few good plays there. Sometimes up to Willie Messer's up near the Davidson Gap. He played the git-ar, he and his wife both. We'd play whatever came to our minds, just whatever anybody wanted to hear. We'd play and sing, too. Fiddle, banjer, autoharp and git-ar was about it then... about four instruments. 'Goin' Down the Road Feelin' Bad' that's the Lonesome Road Blues, they call it now. 'Cripple Creek' and 'Ground Hog', and 'Cindy', and I don't know all those old pieces we used to play... all of 'em... 'Casey Jones'...'Shout Old Lou', 'Free a Birdie', 'Cackle Old Hen', 'Buckin' Mule'."

The banjo, the fiddle, and the guitar were the usual, but not the only musical instruments played on Cataloochee. Little boys played the French harp, or harmonica, at school. Mark's family, musical to this day, had a wide range of instruments to choose from, including the autoharp and the harmonica. Even homely objects like the comb were played upon. There were organs in the Valley, too. Will Messer, a substantial landowner in Little Cataloochee, owned one as well as a phonograph. The spoons were played as a sort of percussion instrument. Some children grew up with these as their very first musical plaything, just as a kindergarten of today would use in their percussion band toys of triangles and sticks.

HAROLD HANNAH: "Dad always encouraged us to play music. Since he could play auto-harp, banjo, guitar, fiddle, harmonica and Jew's harp, we nearly always had one of each available to learn on. Long evenings before TV was known were spent playing... sometimes as a group, sometimes as individuals. All of us learned to play at least one of those instruments."

"We used to tune up and play just anytime the notion struck. Of course we could not read music but played by ear the tunes Mom and Dad taught us or those we heard on the radio. Both Mom and Dad can read shaped notes to sing the old hymns by, but I was in college before I knew that people played string instruments from written music."

"Most people that visited us requested music... sometimes for special events, reunions, etc., Dad would get Cal Messer to come play the fiddle. Sometimes several people would come that liked to play. Most of us learned to play at a fairly early age. I started with guitar but changed to banjo after hearing Earl Scruggs on the radio with the new three-finger method."

"Even when any of us go home we have many sessions of playing and singing, and at my own home I play the banjo three or four evenings a week. Mr. B. H. Oates... a very special friend of my Dad's, gave me the banjo I still have after twenty-three years."

The advent of radio,... Mark had the first one in Cataloochee, about 1926... brought in the Grand Ole Opry from Nashville, and soon the radio singers were idolized by everybody in the Valley on a Saturday night. Mark named one of his sons, Harold Dean, after two of the Bluegrass Singers. Some of the great old groups on the radio in those days were The Possum Hunters, Sam McGee, and The Vagabonds.

A group sat around a campfire in Cataloochee one recent summer night to hear Debbie Gaddy from Waynesville play her dulcimer to a group of Pony Club members, and to sing old English folk songs which, alas, have rarely been preserved in Cataloochee, with the possible exception of 'Barbara Allen' and 'Down in the Willow Garden'. The dulcimer, of course, was not used or remembered in old Cataloochee as an instrument in common use at all.

Even so, it seemed a hopeful sign that people like Debbie were spreading the old songs. And hopeful, too, when modern balladeers write about Cataloochee, as did young Sam Parsons up from Texas, and about the Smokies, as did Mark in his 'Smoky Mountain Blues'.

Sam Parsons' modern ballad "Cataloochee Wild Man," about the fellow who was tracked down by rangers and bloodhounds in Cataloochee recently is in the best tradition of old English ballads. It deserves a place in history, for the forests of Cataloochee, and the coves in all the Smokies still throb from the strings of his guitar. It begins with the verse:

> "Cataloochee Wild Man"
> Well, they say you got a wild man
> Livin' down in the Catalooch'
> They say he's just tricky as a fox
> And livin' on the loose.
> Well, the rangers they don't like this,
> They say it ain't fair
> That other men should have to work
> And he just lives down there.

Echoing, as the strains of the guitar and song die down, the sentiments of Julius Caesar, who said "Montani Semper Liberi!" (Mountaineers are always free!)

CHAPTER 21

Tom-Walker-Nation-on-the-Devil!
(Speech, Folkways, and Superstition)

Vernon J. Palmer, son of Will Palmer, feeds chickens at their home in Cataloochee. Almost every farm had chickens to provide eggs and meat for their family. The hens roamed loose during the day and were shut up in the hen house at night. Broody hens took their chances when they nested in surrounding trees. Courtesy Great Smoky Mountains National Park Archives.

To begin with, the original Cataloochee tongue was Cherokee. The eloquent circuit-riding lawyer, Allen Davidson, said it was the most beautiful sound in the world. He had listened to the Indians ever since his boyhood of herding cattle near the Indian borders.

ALLEN DAVIDSON: "There is a striking peculiarity about the voices of Indians, big and little; and if their chants and war songs have not been reckoned by musicians as a very high order of music, to me they have always been suggestive of the voices of nature. They have no labials or lip sounds, most of their utterances being guttural; but, notwithstanding that, does any language, not excepting the Italian and the Spanish, contain more pure liquids than the Cherokee? We try to give their pronunciation to those names of streams and mountains which they gave; but to one acquainted with their pronunciation, it is evident that we fall very short of giving to their words the music their voices imparted to them. Nantahala, for instance, loses much by the "e" or "y" sound we give the second and fourth syllables. Yonalossie, or grandfather, also loses much in our hands or lips. Swannanoa suffers likewise, for they give it a breathing sound we do not even attempt. To me it has always seemed that their voices were splendid imitations of the most musical sounds of nature, as uttered in the falling torrents, the rushing winds in the wilderness, the tinkling of the brooks over pebbly shallows, or the very silences of the mountains, which at times are really vocal. They are crisp, crackling, undulating, soft, romantic as the wild wind."

"How much I wish I could remember the Cherokee name for Long Creek. There is another jewel of a name lost to the world because of the want of music in the soul of an ordinary landgrabber, as most of our early settlers were. "Long" Creek, to be substituted for some Cherokee liquid to designate a regular necklace of a mountain stream which sparkles in the sunlight or glooms in the shadows more perfectly than the rubies and diamonds of fashion."

When the whites came into the valley, they brought their own habits of speech, corrupting the Indian word for their region, Gadilusti, which they spelled in various ways, Cataloochee, eventually shortening it to Cattylooch', Catalooch', Catalucha, or Cataluche on various deeds, documents, and maps. Actually, except for this word, there seems to have been little influence of the Cherokee language on Cataloochans, and almost none of the original names have been kept, though one of Mark Hannah's girls married a descendant of the noble Cherokee chief, Nimrod Jarret Smith, from Big Cove. But his name is Sam Smith, instead of Owl-who-sees-in-Dark, or what it might have been in the old days.

Horace Kephart corroborated the general theory that the Cherokee language did not flow over into mountain dialect to any extent. However, Judge E. J. Sutherland, in 1961, says that certain Indian words <u>have</u> survived to become part of the mountain language, indeed, part of our general everyday speech. Words like hominy, hickory, chinkapin, possum (opossum) and coon (raccoon), for instance, are all of Indian derivation.

Jarvis Caldwell swears that he can tell a Cataloochan from someone of a neighboring community simply by his habits of speech, but this was only an instinctive feeling, and he could not, for the life of him, give a definite example. However, the repetition of phrases for emphasis, and even of whole sentences, seems typical of the valley, as in Mark Hannah's and 'Tine Bennett's conversation about a coon-hunting gun owned by Mark's father.

MARK HANNAH: "He had a .38 Smith and Weston (Wesson) short. I have it yit."

'TINE BENNETT: "It broke down like that. What ever become of that gun?"

MARK: "I've got it yit. He gave it to me."

'TINE: "Well, you've got it?"

MARK: "I've got it yit."

There is also a tendency among Cataloochans, all of them, to use more prepositions and adverbs than one would have thought possible, as in the following sentence of Eldridge Caldwell's, describing a hurricane.

ELDRIDGE CALDWELL: "And sure 'nough, there come one right up in above where he lived over there on Little Catalooch'!"

And in Mark's descriptive passages, too.

MARK HANNAH: "And then I found the original Indian trail leading right off down through there on both sides."

Dr. Cratis Williams has an interesting theory of mountain pronunciation which might fancifully be called "The jutting jaw syndrome". He claims that the whole sound of mountain speech is affected by speaking with a half-open mouth and a fixed chin thrust slightly forward. It actually seems to work until one recalls many Cataloochee friends whose jaws seem perfectly normal or even underslung, but whose speech has the right twang!

A more scholarly approach than this was followed by a young Columbia University graduate, Professor Joseph S. Hall, who first came into Cataloochee in 1937 when he was sent into the Smokies by the U. S. Government to collect records of the speech and oral lore of the 1200 people who were still in the area at that time. He spent much of his time going from one CCC camp to another, cadging rides and going further into the hills. Cataloochee was only one of his many stops, but it figured largely in his subsequent book, *Smoky Mountain Folks and Their Lore*, published by the Great Smoky Mountains Historical Association. He has authored several small volumes on mountain speech and stories. His inevitable conclusion, along with many other speech experts and etymologists, was that there actually was not too much original expression among the mountain folk, that nearly everything was derivative (They are very fond of stressing the Elizabethan aspects, of course)... from English, Irish, Scotch, German, and even other nationalities. Nothing new under the sun of Old Smoky.

One might dispute this when said of Cataloochee. It's hard to believe that anybody else in the world ever thought of such an apt way to describe Clay Batchelder with a hangover as the following oft-quoted remark of Turkey George's:

TURKEY GEORGE PALMER: "Your eyes looked like a red fox's ass in a pokeberry patch!"

Eldridge Caldwell quoted this, and it was also included in a later book of Joe Hall's called *Sayings from Old Smoky*, published in 1972, which deals a great deal with the Cataloochee area.

The following expressions are directly attributed to Cataloochans, or people temporarily in Cataloochee, from *Sayings from Old Smoky*, collected by Joe Hall, unless marked as Elizabeth Powers.

AWFUL... "My daddy... he was an awful hoss-trader." Jim Sutton, Cataloochee, 1939 (Disc 103B).

BAD... "He was awful bad to drink." Said of a Cataloochee bully who was the "meanest of the lot", John Jones, Ravensford, 1937 (IV, 81).

BOOT HILL... "When a guy comes and steals my stuff, he better be ready for a wooden suit on Boot Hill (coffin in the cemetary)." Heard at Cataloochee Homecoming Day. 1962.

CHUNK... Bill Barnes, Hartford, said that his father, the well-known hunter, Uncle Tom Barnes (of Barnes Old Camp, Elizabeth Powers) went to the Cataloochee side (of the Smokies to hunt) at chestnut time. "I was just a chunk of a boy." 1937 (III, 98).

COUNTRY... "My Country!" exclaimed Mark Hannah to Elizabeth Powers in a story he wrote about Uncle Hiram's last bear hunt, 1973.

COW-BRUTE... (euphemism for both bull and milk-cow. It was bad form to use the word bull in front of ladies). "The snow was fallin' from the bushes like a cow-brute had walked through." Will Palmer, Cataloochee, 1939.

DADDY MAN... "Will Messer was the Daddy Man of them all!" exclaimed Jarvis Caldwell about W.G.B. Messer's many accomplishments, to Elizabeth Powers, 1973.

DEVIL... "Tom-Walker-Nation-on-the-Devil!" shrieked Sheriff Palmer when desperately trying to escape a lynch mob with his Cataloochee prisoner, remark repeated to Elizabeth Powers by Jarvis Caldwell, 1973.

DIME... "I wouldn't miss it (Cataloochee Homecoming) for a Yankee dime!" Mark Hannah to Elizabeth Powers, 1973.

FOXY (drunk)... "You was sure foxy last night when we left you." Dick Owenby, Gatlinburg, Tennessee, 1939, meaning deciphered by Dinty (Dinny) Nichols, blacksmith, Cataloochee CCC Camp: "drunk, too drunk to be in public." Term much used in 1939-41, and also in 17th century England.

GREEN... "The long green!" Mark Hannah referred to the money that the loggers had to put out at the box supper for the church lamps, Cataloochee, 1973, Elizabeth Powers.

HAND... "Mont Hannah is a good hand on stories." Will Palmer, Cataloochee, 1939.

HEAP... "There's a heap more hard work an' slavish runnin' and trampin' in bear-huntin' than in coon huntin'." Major Woody, Cataloochee, 1937 (III,109).

HEELS... The Canadian logger in Cataloochee, John Ewart, sometimes known simply as John "Canadian", often had a terrible temper. In a black fury, he encountered a man one morning. When asked why he looked so angry, he replied that he had just had an argument with his wife and had "Turned her heels towards the sun!" So said old Glenn Palmer, Elizabeth Powers, Rush Fork, 1973.

LAW... "They said they would law ever who 'done it,'" Floyd Woody, speaking of a prank he and others had played on Andy Caldwell, Elizabeth Powers recording, Canton, 1972.

MAKE... Meaning "grow", as in Flora Palmer's remark, "Make enough sallet peas", and Mark Hannah's remark, "My father said we make what we eat." Elizabeth Powers, Iron Duff and Maggie Valley, 1972-73.

MASTER... "I owned 400 acres. We had the masterest law suit you ever seen." Steve Woody, Cataloochee, 1939 (XI,5); he contested the value of his land set by the Park Commission.

PERT-NEAR... (pretty nearly)... "I pert-near got my eyes beat out last night!" so said Tom King, according to Mark Hannah (to Elizabeth Powers, 1976).

POUR... "Uncle Steve took his shot gun. The bear riz. He turned the shot gun loose and poured the shot into him." Will Palmer, Cataloochee, 1939 (XI,137).

RIZ... see definition above, (rose up).

SHOE... "They said he was a-steppin' on the ground so hard (in running, he thought, from a bear) that he went in shoe-mouth deep." Mack Hannah, Little Cataloochee, 1939 (Disc 3B-1). Elizabeth Powers notes "Shoe-mouth deep" was also an expression used back in the 1780s by the Western Carolina men en route to the Battle of King's Mountain, Sept. 1, 1780, to describe the snow on Roan Mtn.

SKIFT OF SNOW... "They was a little skift of snow a-fallin' like a cow-brute had walked thu'u." Will Palmer , Catalooch, 1939 (VI, 135f).

SORRIEST... "The wust sorriest things they is like bobcats you cain't kill!" Major Woody, Cataloochee, 1937 (III, 110), chafing over restrictions in the National Park.

SPELL... Turkey George cut down on (a turkey) with a muzzle-loadin' rifle. That thing just got to floppin' and jumpin' about, 'hit tuck an awful spell." Mrs. George Palmer, wife of Turkey George, Cataloochee, 1939 (VI, 143).

SHACKLEY...(loose-sounding) "That's all shackley, must be a punkin' ball loose in your gun or your gun part's loose." Old man's remark to Elizabeth Powers, 1972.

SHACKELTY (loose-jointed)... Elizabeth Powers heard Weldon Williamson of Asheville, 1972, tell of a simpleton who worked for Jarvis Palmer in the 20s. He saw girls bathing in Cataloochee Creek, when they took their clothes off, he said he "went all shackelty and laid down in the corn rows so's they wouldn't see me."

TEE-TOTALLY... "My daddy yelled, 'Mother (Aunt Easter Sutton), come here, come now. That cussed old cat scratched my hoss, and he's tee-totally ruined.'" Jim Sutton, Cataloochee, 1939 (Disc 103-B).

THING... "I'll trade that thing (a windsucker horse) if I don't get nothin' but a bull yearlin' fer it. That was about the cheapest thing in the market in this country at that time." Jim Sutton, Cataloochee, 1939 (Disc 103Bo, used as a derogatory remark. Sometimes meaning well-done, or in large quantity. "He can mimic Windy Bill just like one thing." CCC enrollee, Catalooch', 1939 (IX, 1). Another CCC man thus described preparation in the camp kitchen for an inspection day dinner. "They're bakin' just like one thing!"

YAN (yonder)... Floyd Woody speaking of one of the many pranks he played on Andy Caldwell. "Well, they'd be way at the other end. They'd ring their bells. Well, he'd go yan (yon) way." Elizabeth Powers recording, 1972, Canton.

A lovely name for rattlesnakes in Cataloochee was "belltails", called so with good reason, for they rang out, or were supposed to ring out, their warning. John Strother, while surveying the Tennessee—North Carolina line, came upon some snakes near Cataloochee vicinity and called them, in his journal, "rattlebugs".

"Skybugging" has a certain charm. It means scanning the sky aimlessly as one's trusted old horse walks along a Cataloochee trail. Or, it can simply mean "not paying attention".

In Cataloochee, the "dead man" is not something scarifying but merely a heavy post which is set in to hold up cables for a footlog or bridge.

An "owl-head" is not for a chapter on natural history, but refers to a cheap pistol which was used locally. Jess Swayney brought one in from the Indian Nation for the mock shooting of Andy Caldwell. Floyd Woody, who participated in the prank could not tell me why it was called an "owlhead", but Dick Hughes, from Wyoming, said that this was a pistol made by the Iver Johnson Co. and actually had a bas-relief of an owlhead on its handle. Nowadays it probably would be referred to as a "Saturday Night Special".

A mule was sometimes called a "jarhead" according to Glen Messer. Mark said it was because it was empty minded. A mule was also called a "pencil tail".

In Cataloochee, people's nicknames usually indicated some event that had occurred to this person, or to some physical characteristic, such as "Mink Henry" Grooms who was dark-skinned and black-eyed, as opposed to "White Henry" Grooms who was a fair Anglo-Saxon. "Polecat" John Cagle had, of course, the misfortune to come up against that creature (a skunk) and could never live down his nickname. John "Canadian", or Ewart had come from that far-off country. "Boogerman" Palmer's name has been explained earlier, and he was called that till his dying day. There was a little girl called "Little Bluehead" (Grace Sutton), according to Floyd Woody. Did she fall in the indigo dye pot when she was small, one wonders? "Flora" was a favorite Christian name for Cataloochee girls. It seems entirely appropriate in this abundant paradise to have had a daughter called Flora, but why not, also, Eve, or Ceres, or Persephone?!

One heard many stories about why "Turkey George" Palmer got his name, but Professor Hall came up with a classic folk tale on the subject. It might be called the Appalachian Peer Gynt.

PROFESSOR JOSEPH S. HALL: "Why do they call him 'Turkey George', I asked Mrs. Lackey of Mt. Sterling when she mentioned him. 'Hit's soze a body kin know him from 'Creek George' Palmer, I reckon,' she replied. It was not until I arrived in Cataloochee that I heard the fantastic tale which explained, to the satisfaction of some, the reason for his unusual name. Uncle Levi Caldwell (a later descendent of the early settler), the genial blacksmith of the Mt. Sterling CCC Side Camp in Cataloochee, told me how Palmer was once walking on the mountain without a gun and saw a 'gang o' wild turkeys'. He tried to catch one and chased it as it fluttered along. Finally he managed to grab hold of its legs, but as he did so, the turkey 'riz' in the air and carried him across a 'swag' (gap) to the next mountain and courteously dropped him. After hearing this or similar accounts from several others I was surprised upon meeting the man himself, to find so softspoken a person was the subject of such an extravagant story. He was about eighty years old, and, with his wife, lived on a well-kept and prosperous little farm in Pretty Hollow. Here they cultivated a portion of their original property and kept some livestock. He was strong, considering his age, and didn't mind working."

"Asked how he had acquired his strange nickname, 'Turkey George', he gave the following more credible account, 'I had a patch of land in corn. The wild turkeys was about to eat it up, so I built a pen to try to catch them. The pen was ten foot each way, and I covered over the top. Then I cut a ditch and run it into the pen and covered the ditch with bark. I scattered the corn in the ditch so as to draw the turkeys into the pen. Next mornin' they was nine big gobblers inside, an' one outside. I stopped up the hole an' got me a big stick to kill 'em with. When I got in the pen, they riz up and mighty nigh killed me instead; so I got out and fetched a hoe. When they stuck their heads betwixt the slats I knocked them with it. After that I built about three pens in the mountains an' caught two or three turkeys. That's why they call me 'Turkey George', I reckon.'"

Place names are now mostly descriptive, as many of the old Indian names have been lost. Consider the name of the rock which memorializes the fate of the Reverend Camel who lost his life near Falling Rock Creek when a cliff face fell on him as he slept. Shanty Branch was named after the shanty built by Ole Smart, the Davidsons' negro slave of olden days. Pizen (Poison) Cove near Turkey George's place, was where the cattle got the staggers, grazing on a poisonous weed, possibly white snakeroot. Prettyland Mountain and Pretty Hollow Gap must have looked just that way when they were named by some fond mountaineer with an aesthetic sense. Lucky Button Hole, a deep pool in Cataloochee Creek may be a misnomer as it is quite near Lucky Bottom where some deer hunters in the old days found some hides they thought they had lost. The Muster Ground up near Cove Creek Gap on the original road is where the early settlers mustered out for soldiering, drilling, electioneering, rifle matches and the like. Poll's Gap, sometimes misspelt Paul's Gap, was where Polly Moody's husband, against her will, took her milch cow up to the summer pastures when she was calving, and the calf died. Polly's wrath became a legend, hence the name of the gap. Dude Branch was named after "Dude" Hannah who lived on it, as was the Booger Man Trail named by Mark Hannah after "Booger" Palmer.

When the N. C. Nomenclature Committee took over the renaming of mountain sites after the National Park was in situ, even more of the colorful old names were discarded in order to honor family names and to perpetuate the names of the pioneers in the park. Maggot Spring Gap remained the same, however, as did Onion Bed Branch, and Strawberry Knob. One wonders about the story behind the naming of Whim Knob. Perhaps it was named so because a logging company had a machine sitting on this knob with a wire cable on a drum that pulled logs up the steep slope, at the whim of the loggers, just as the Lazy-gal did the water for Lush Caldwell on Messer Fork Creek. But Den Branch was named for a huge den of nearby rattlesnakes, and Pig Pen Flats and Sugar Tree Licks are self-explanatory, as are Ugly Fork, Rough Fork, Winding Stair Branch, Lost Bottom Creek, Sheepback Knob and Horse Pen Ridge. Canadian Top was named for John Ewart, the Canadian logger.

The imagination of the mountain man in telling a story, such as the one about Turkey George's being snatched up into the air by a turkey, could lead him to Paul Bunyan heights. Floyd Woody, who is still, at eighty-nine, noted for his humorous telling of tall tales, said it was "so quiet in Cataloochee that I could hear the dynamos in the fireflies on a quiet summer evening".

FLOYD WOODY: "One time I was fishin' with a live minnow. And I'd seen people spit on their bait. And I had me some whiskey with me, and I decided I'd pour it on that there minnow and then th'ow it back in there — in the big hole water. I threw it back in there. Directly my pole line went down, and I kept pullin' and got out. And that minnow had caught that big trout right in the neck! Draggin' that fish out! He held that liquor!"

And many a Cataloochee man will give you a version of the old mountain expression that Cataloochee (or some other settlement) is "so far back in the hills that owls are the alarm clocks", a step better than the usually heard "roosters are the alarm clocks", denoting taller mountains, darker areas, more mysterious glooms.

Unfortunately, many of the elder informants died before they could enlighten one on Cataloochee speech. Hence the reason for this book. Information slips out of our fingers like sand through an hour glass.

The whole area of mountain speech and native dialect is of great interest to the Professor Higginses of this world as in Shaw's "Pygmalion;" a real afficionado will pounce on a rare word the way an ornithologist will greet a prothonotary warbler or an ivory-billed woodpecker. Imagine the joy of detecting a far-off Scottish Highland inflection of a mountaineer to whom a fern was once given. He smelled it, then said delightfully, with his nose lifted in the air at the sweet scent, "Oh-h-h! It's a nice feer'rn!"

High Sheriff William Palmer used the phrase Tom-Walker-nation-on-the-devil when he was flustered or annoyed, so said Raymond and his father, Jarvis Caldwell. He said this when the wind blew his hat off as his son sped away with him and the murderer of Rudolph Caldwell, trying to escape a lynch mob. The story of Tom Walker and the Devil was one that Washington Irving used to relate, and the High Sheriff had undoubtedly heard it through his forebears.

The Devil was a tangible thing in these mountain coves, as an author from Duke University pointed out in her article, "Devil in the Smokies; The White Man's Nature and the Indian's Fate".

MATTIE U. RUSSELL: "To explain natural phenomena, the Indians had created a world of spirits and woven many a tale about them. The dark, dense areas of the mountains and the roaring cascades had stirred their imaginations until they came to believe in a personal devil whose footprints were the barren spots or balds on the mountain peaks. Old Field Mountain in the Balsams was his bedchamber. He was seen there many times. With the advance of civilization, spirits were no longer necessary to explain natural phenomena, but in the unfolding struggle between the whites and Indians for survival and mystery of the area, the legend of a personal devil might wreak havoc upon those who intruded among his hills became increasingly appropriate.

The Old Field Mountain referred to here may be Mt. Sterling in Cataloochee, as it was often referred to by the locals as having the Indian Old Fields, the "Fur" Field, and the "Nigh" Field, and it is certainly one of the Balsams.

Raymond Caldwell's great-grandfather, Hosey (Hosea) Mauney, a very religious old man who lived just over the hill from Catalooch' knew the Devil from close experience.

JARVIS CALDWELL: "I'll told this little joke on Granddaddy Hosey. He was livin' down in Davis Cove, in Iron Duff, on Old Man Davis' place. And they's ploughin' somewhere down in the field. Come time of the evenin' he had to go to this meetin' over at Hyder Mountain, at Fincher's Chapel. They was holdin' a meetin' over there, and he had to go, didn't make no difference what was to do or not, he just left, tied up his mule, the one he was ploughin' corn with at the end of the row and left him."

"He got that scissortail coat and put on, a long-tailed coat, and walked, and, as he went across Richland Creek, he said he met the Devil on the bridge. And he said the Devil said to him, 'Hosey, now there ain't no use you goin' up yonder to that church tonight.' And says, 'Well, I'm goin' to keep you from goin'. And he says, 'Well, you're not goin' to keep me from goin'". And he said, 'I grabbed the Devil and threw him in that creek'. And he said he just seared like a hot rock in cold water. And says 'I went on to that church.' They told that on Uncle Hosey."

ELIZABETH D. POWERS: "I wonder who he threw in the creek?" (much laughter)

JARVIS CALDWELL: "Thought it was the Devil. For him, it was just thinkin' about it, y'know." One will not find too many old Cataloochans left who profess to be strong believers. There are still remnants of superstitions about, though few will talk about what was believed, perhaps for fear of being laughed at. A belief in many mountain communities was the use of the Bible verse to dispel evil. This was commonly used for "taking the fire out of burns", for instance. And Fred Hannah's widow can still do this, though none can say how. One old Cataloochee lady used the Bible verse to keep bugs and worms off her beans! Sad to relate, this particular verse was not remembered, as one would find it very useful in these days when we are advocating the obliteration of DDT and other harmful pesticides!

Many planted by the signs in those days. Jarvis Caldwell, now settled on Allens Creek, still plants by the signs, says his son, Raymond. The Farmer's Almanac was almost like a Bible in the way it was consulted. This "oracle" decreed that one should plant on the dark of the moon, or the first quarter of the moon. Seeds could be planted when the signs were in the legs, neck, arms, knees or thighs, but not when the signs were in the feet, bowels, head or heart. This applied to seeds only. Plants could be set in the ground at anytime.

When the word 'witch' was broached to Cataloochee informants, they merely shook their heads. No, no one had really believed much in witches. And yet Allen Davidson had recorded a classic story about witchcraft in Cataloochee.

ALLEN DAVIDSON: "I remember that on one occasion Ned (McFalls) shot at and missed a large buck. He immediately concluded that his gun had been 'spelled'. By that he meant it had been bewitched. 'I told Annie (his wife) not to let that woman touch it', he said; and no doubt he believed that the mere fact that his gun had been touched by some woman whom he probably did not like, convinced him that she had put a spell of bad luck on his gun for the purpose of annoying him. Once this notion found lodgement in his brain, nothing would do but that he must leave the cattle unsalted and uncounted and walk forty-five miles over several steep mountains to old John Bryson's on Cullowhee for the purpose of having the 'spell' taken off. I was opposed to this for the reason that it obliged me either to remain in that wilderness alone, or to go back home before I had had my fun out. So I determined to convince him that his gun was not 'spelled' at all. I persuaded him to lend it to me, while he took mine. He reluctantly consented to do this, and we parted for a time, I going down one ridge, he the other. It had been agreed that if he heard me fire he would come to me, and soon I saw a young doe and shot her squarely between the eyes. 'What did you shoot at that sap-sucker for!' shouted Ned from his ridge, for sap-suckers were always 'using' about the lick logs near where we were then. I answered that I had not shot at a sap-sucker but a deer. This brought him running, and pointing to the spot where I thought the doe would be found, he went there and sure enough! it was shot between the eyes. But when I tried to show him that he had only imagined that his gun had been 'spelled', he turned upon me with the statement that the doe had spelled it, and that since the doe was dead the spell had been removed. Some of our primitive people undoubtedly believed in witches, and thought that the witch would get into anything imaginable. He concluded that it had got into the doe, and that in killing the doe, I had killed the witch. But he never doubted for an instant that his gun had been 'spelled' by someone or something. I remember that his gun was one we had got from a man named Aaron Price, an old neighbor. (ELIZABETH POWERS: I believe it was a Gillespie rifle)."

Stories of witches were also told by "Climbing Bear", one of "Little Will's" Cherokee scouts in Cataloochee during the Civil War, who was a descendent of an old lineage of Indian medicine men or shamans, according to the Swimmer Manuscript. In this manuscript, "Swimmer", the most famous of all Cherokee medicine men, had written down all the secret formulas and translated them for James Mooney and the Smithsonian. "Climbing Bear" apparently had the power of seeing witches when he had drunk the medicine by which one could see witches. He once dispersed a witch by touching it with a burning switch. The third day the witch, J. B., died and the patient, T., who was suffering from a spell the witch had concocted, recovered. One wonders whether the young "Climbing Bear" tried to use his magic in dispersing the infamous Colonel Kirk when the two met in battle in Cataloochee! In any case, the Indian's magic preserved his own life for a very long time, for he lived until 1928! — a good sixty-eight years after the beginning of the Civil War.

When Cataloochans were asked if they ever heard ghost stories, or 'hant' stories, or if they had ever believed in them, they gave very little response at first. Raymond Caldwell wanted to believe in ghosts. The very thought gave him a thrill of excitement. He said he thought he saw one once in the Cataloochee bottoms at night and he pursued the white will-o'-the-wisp on horseback until it proved to be only a shred of fog. He said he was most disappointed!

On the other hand, Mark Hannah could remember folks talking about ghosts, and he used to scare his own children telling them stories around the fire at night. When asked if he personally had ever been fearful of ghosts, even as a child, he denied this vigorously. Then, later on, with a ruminative smile, he added: "Our road went by the cemetery, and I always looked the other way, that's the way to keep from seein' anything in the cemetery... just look the other way!"

ELIZABETH POWERS: "Oh, you were superstitious, after all!"

MARK HANNAH: "I think we were all suspicious of cemeteries! Well, there were several people who believed kinda in seein' ghosts, I mean, had seen ghosts. There used to be something people would see occasionally up near the church house. There was an old road came off before they built this one there now. It came more down the hill by a big hickory tree they called the Dry Hickory. You could get there and shelter from a storm or anything. Well, people would get there some times of a night and were ridin', they'd see things like women with white gowns on, floatin' around. And they'd run. I don't know what all happened!"

"My brother-in-law, Vernon Palmer, was at Big Cataloochee near the campground there. He was comin' down there one night and met a woman dressed in white... and she didn't have no head! (laughs) He went around and run back up the road... like to run hisself to death gettin' away from there! I don't know what all! She was in a white dress and didn't have any head..."

At that point in his story, fierce noises, as if of frantic spirits, sounded in his chimney. Mark dismissed it, saying it was only chimney swallows.

"Uncle Rhode Hannah's house, away up on the north prong of what they call Andy Branch, in Little Cataloochee. They had a noise that used to be heard in the house there, an old log house they lived in. And my brother, he didn't believe it, that there was anything to the noise, so he went up and spent the night with his cousin, Eustace."

"During the night they heard... sounded like somebody diggin' down in the ground, or in a grave or somethin'. Then for a little while something rolled around the floor. And they got up and couldn't find a thing... wasn't anything there whatsoever. So they kept that up for a long time. Once I was up there myself, long about two o'clock in the day... and we were just sittin' there talkin', and my cousin said, 'Listen, now, and you'll hear that noise! says, 'I hear it.' I listened and heard it myself... a very thumpin' sound like it was in the dirt or somethin'. We never found out what that was... yet. They lived in it for years and had that sound and never did discover what it was... It wouldn't sound every day."

"Well, at Mossy Branch, near Nellie Post Office, flows off that cold Mossy Branch... used to be a story goin' round that people would be comin' and goin' on that branch. They'd hear somebody talkin'. And you could hear them talkin'. I never did believe that story till one day I was comin' up through there ridin' a horse, and

I heard somebody comin' down the branch, talkin' just like... kinda jolly-like. And I says to meself, I'll meet them up there pretty quick. I hadn't even <u>thought</u> of that story 'bout hearin' things. Just kept ridin' on, and I thought when I got a couple of hundred yards out there now I'd <u>sure</u> see 'em. And I... all ready to meet 'em, y' know. And never did find anybody... and I looked, and there's no tracks goin' up the road away from me... I couldn't figure it out... studied about it all the way home. I thought of it then after I didn't meet anybody that maybe that was the same story that had been goin'. But I tried to track and find out. I wasn't scared of it in the world. I just thought it was somebody sure comin'."

MARK HANNAH: "One time when Cal Messer and Johnny Hannah were tearing an old chimney down at my father's house, they decided they were doing something aginst their will. Johnny didn't like to work, too well, at anything, so he kept saying to Cal, 'I don't feel right about tearing a chimney down at this old house, do you, Cal?' 'No, by George!' (said Cal), 'Let's leave here!' And they did. Cal told me several times that he would never do that again. 'I jest don't feel right about it!' They agree that they did not run but they <u>walked fast</u>!"

The imagination really takes hold in this lonely wild country where so much has happened in the past. Like Cal Messer and Johnny Hannah, one often has a strong and palpable feeling of some tangible presence whenever one wanders through Cataloochee alone. Those ancient boulders and tall hemlocks cannot be forgiven for keeping so silent when they've seen so much. What one would give to have laughed and lived with those people who now lie under bleak markers in the Palmer Graveyard, the Caldwell cemetery, or the Hannah cemetery, surrounded by bear fences.

The sense of the people who lived there is never erased; there is always an emanation of some sort. One often feels like looking behind oneself, not for fear of bears or the Cataloochee Wild Man, but because there is a sense of an unseen presence there. Hiking through the long damp grasses of Mt. Sterling's balds, one half expects to hear the bell of Dudley, Mitchell Davidson's lead bull, especially when the clouds are rolling up the mountain, and the bulky shape of a wind-stunted rhododendron could resemble anything.

Or, walking near Shanty Branch, one might imagine he hears a mournful African song of longing for home from Old' Smart, the slave of Mitchell Davidson, who lived up there alone and tended the cattle long before the settlers came in.

Is that the sound of the stream burbling, near Rough Fork, or is it the sturdy spirit of Uncle Steve Woody who mounts his black horse flat-footed from the ground and rides so merrily up the hemlock-dark avenues, cracking his hickory stick at unseen foes, laughing a chuckly, bubbly laugh like the stream itself?

If Jesse Palmer were to come back some night to see what had happened in Cataloochee, he would surely bring with him a ghostly choir of turning wheels, rushing water, and grinding stones,... very easy to hear even now as one walks past the old mill dam.

There's no reason to doubt who that old lady in the little black cap is, wandering by herself, humming as she picks dogtooth violets, heedless of the cries of dogs and a great company on her heels. Granny Pop was never lost. One is quite sure of that.

Mack Hannah's spirit is apt to be a bit more mischievous. If of a night, one listens to some yelping hounds, who is to say that Mack has not, as a joke, set them to cold-trail you. And Fannie might happen upon an unsuspecting hiker, struggling up by the Indian Grave, as she silently urges her mule on through the moonlight up that steep path, going to some birthing up some forgotten road to a cabin now in ruins.

If the old cradle seems to rock by itself, on a winter's day by the fireplace, one may be sure that the unseen foot of that little old woman, Mag Mauney Caldwell, has carried on to her other life what she began before and absentmindedly continues.

Dude and 'Ras Hannah: their ghosts are most certainly lurking high up in the coves now, laughing great hollow laughs over their latest escape.

That will-o'-the-wisp shred of fog that Raymond was pursuing one night... who's to say it was not the long shredded white beard of old Lafayette Palmer floating there, cannily disappearing when Raymond came into view?

The sound of the wind soughing through the hemlocks way up on Caldwell Fork might well drown out the eerie music of a taut bow being drawn against cat gut. Is it tree limbs rubbing against each other, or is it all the earthly sound left by "Fiddlin" 'Lige Messer?

The Devil need never be feared in this valley, for Lizzie Howell Caldwell, the Angel of the Valley, has surely put Beelzebub to rout, smothered by her wide black circled skirt as she floats over this old Paradise Lost, seeing only the good sights she left behind her.

But Daniel J. Cook will never be seen again. He played ghost during his own lifetime, scaring the suspenders off anybody who was with him for his death watch by suddenly coming out of his coma and rising from the cooling board. He's lost his second chance.

Hiram Caldwell's spirit may still be concealed by the foot-bridge to the fine house he built in the earliest part of this century. There he surely waits, as he waited in other days, for an unsuspecting young-un to come by and be impressed as a worker. Nowadays, tip your hat to the unseen squire, whispering, "Howdy, Hiram." and run as fast as you can past that footlog, or Hiram will surely trip you!

If one hears a dragging, reluctant footstep behind on the path, it may be a belated memory of the old crippled Major Woody. But there is nothing to fear, for Major is everlastingly after the coons in the moonlight with his dogs way ahead, barking high and sharply.

Have a care, though, that one doesn't fall in a dead-fall trap of Turkey George Palmer's, set for some unsuspecting mortal, as he used to do for the bears during his lifetime. If an unwary camper at Pretty Hollow Creek should be frightened out of his wits one night by a mighty bawling and a bellowing, it might be only the echoes left of Uncle Turkey, hallooing home from Big Butt Mountain, announcing his victory over a bear.

Ghost doubters may laugh and refer to the funny story that was told about a man in Cataloochee who was scared to death by his own tie flapping in the wind, so they said. The more he ran the more it flapped, as he thought he felt some unseen force pulling and picking and pawing at his throat. But who can say differently? For who saw what happened? The owl? The panther? The rattlesnake? The Great Buzzard? They'll never tell.

PART III

The Place

Cataloochee

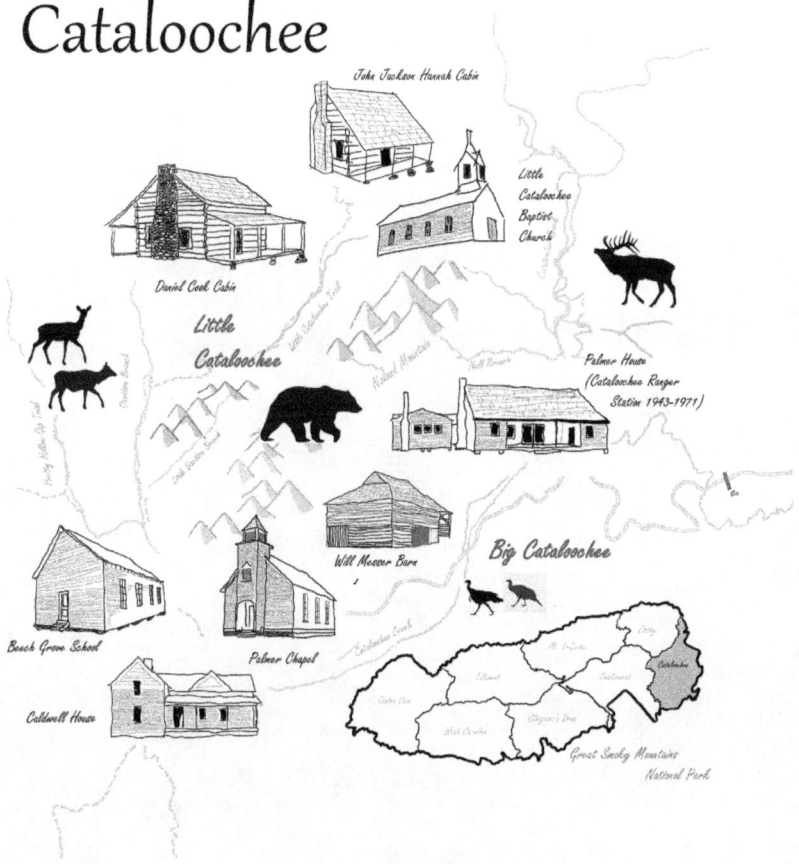

A hand drawn map of Cataloochee valley shows both the remaining structures in their relative positions, as well as illustrations of animals currently found in the valley- deer, bear, turkey, and elk. A map of the Great Smoky Mountains National Park shows that Cataloochee is located at the far eastern border of the park. Artwork by Rebecca Mendoza.

CHAPTER 22

Once an Inland Sea

(Geology)

Eldridge Caldwell was born in this cabin, built by Levi Caldwell in 1858. It was one of the many old structures burned or allowed to rot down after the park came in. The park's original intent was to return Cataloochee to its wilderness state and most of the old structures were destroyed or neglected. Subsequently, the park service realized the historical value of the Cataloochan's homes and way of life and a few remaining structures were saved. Courtesy Great Smoky Mountains National Park Archives.

IT IS IRONIC that any flatlander growing up in the eastern foothills might have languished for those Cataloochee peaks, a hundred and forty miles away to the west, envying Mark Hannah his mountain boyhood. For it is quite possible that, eons ago, the Smokies were but an inland sea, a long narrow geosyncline or trough, and that the Piedmont further East was then part of a long mountainous chain which reached higher than the Alps!

This early stark, unclothed range, known as the true Appalachia, was later cut away by streams which deposited sediments in the westerly sea trough up to 40,000 feet, say some geologists. Eventually this ancestral plain, containing the germ of

Cataloochee and the Smokies, was forced upwards, buckling towards the heavens almost five miles high.

This was during the Appalachian Revolution which is not, as it sounds, a shoot-out at high noon, but is a geological term describing the epoch of mountain-building which transpired some 200 million years ago.

Though the valley walls of Cataloochee still seem high and fearsome to Easterners, they are actually only the "erosional remnants of roots or stubs of mightier mountain masses", perhaps higher than the Alps at one time. The mind boggles at the thought of a Mt. Blanc in Cataloochee, yet is even more stupefied by the thought of an earlier Cataloochee as an inland sea, connected to the ocean at both ends. The sound of the great hemlocks above Steve Woody's place, soughing in a heavy wind, now supplants what might have been waves breaking on a bleak shore!

The process continued by pushing the early Precambrian stone partially over the later limestone mass formed by the animal life in the inland sea, particularly in the western part of the Smokies. Slowly, inexorably, the old stone slid in a northwesterly direction over the new for nearly a hundred miles until it reached what is known now as Little River, Tennessee, or roughly, the western boundary of the Smokies. The old Appalachia was no more, washed away to a mere peneplane, or partly falling away into the great sea to the East.

So it is that a flatlander from the eastern outcroppings might grow up with an instinctual feel for lost mountains as Mark Hannah wandered the steep-sided Cataloochee which had risen from the ancient drowned valley!

Mark was most disgusted with a man who was sent out from Asheville in a Model T to appraise Cataloochee land for inclusion in the Park. He said scornfully to Mark: "Why, I wouldn't give my house and lot in Asheville for the whole of Cataloochee. It's nothing but a bunch of shale!"

Mark should have confounded him by explaining that the late Precambrian stone was actually made up from sediment, now hardened into sandstone and conglomerates, which had washed down from western slopes thereby diminishing what was to become Asheville and the later Piedmont of old Appalachia.

What makes up these venerable stones of Cataloochee that know so much and reveal so little? More ancient than the Nile, those rocks felt the turbulent waters upon their breasts and so melted away, felt the thunder of buffalo upon their backs and so received the notched gaps, felt the springy steps of the early Indian hunters along their stony spines. They alone mark the nameless corpses of diphtheria-stricken children and black slaves in the burial grounds; they alone fell on the Reverend Camel as he lay sleeping; they alone tripped the unsuspecting Jarvis in the creek and broke his ankle.

Shale, indeed!

It is true, however, that many of the geologic mysteries of the Smokies had eluded man for quite a long time. Full scale studies of the area only came to conclusion after World War II.

The bulk of Cataloochee, as in most of the Eastern side of the Smokies, consists simply of Thunderhead Sandstone, a later Precambrian mass of the Ocoee Series, Great Smoky Group.

Somehow, though, Little Cataloochee, with its usual predilection for originality, thrust its tongue at the Thunderhead sandstone in a most complicated upheaval known as the Cataloochee Anticlinorium. This impertinent tongue was composed of folds and arches of stratified rock in which the strata dip in opposite directions from a common ridge or axis.

Thus, much of Little Cataloochee, from Big Fork Ridge, Noland Mountain and beyond to Scottish Mountain belongs to the Snowbird group of the Ocoee series. Big Fork Ridge and Mt. Sterling Gap are made of Roaring Fork Sandstone; Canadian Top and Noland Mountain are of Longarm Quartzite; Scottish Mountain has bits of what are called Wading Fork Formation. There are even slivers through Scottish Mountain of the earliest Precambrian rock, or Basement Complex of gneiss, schist, and granitic rocks.

But Indian Knob and Long Bunk Mountain, as well as the lower eastern slopes of Mt. Sterling are of Rich Butt Sandstone in a sequence broken by fractures or faults, and therefore subject to earthquakes. In fact, the Greenbrier Fault completely encompasses this tongue of Little Cataloochee, rendering the whole area of more than considerable interest.

There have actually been earthquakes, too, in Cataloochee environs though far less frequently than those in the West coast area of the San Andreas fault, and nothing to compare with Japan and New Zealand.

In 1776, Captain William Moore and Captain John Harden, of General Griffith Rutherford's expedition, after burning an Indian camp on Oconalufty River "crossed prodigious mountains, which were almost impassable, experiencing there a severe shock of an earthquake, reached Richland Creek Mountains, and then returned to Pigeon River." This was on the Balsam Mountain in the immediate vicinity of Cataloochee. But no Cataloochans recorded it, as the valley wilderness was, at that time, only frequented by Indians hiding from the British, and perhaps a very few, intrepid white hunters. No doubt the Cherokees thought the earthquake was due to the wrath of their gods, rising against the cruel expedition which burnt many Indian towns!

RAYMOND CALDWELL: "Story about my great granddaddy, Hosey (Hosea) Mauney. Anyhow, they's holdin' a revival. Some preachers always preach that the end of time is goin' to come next day, next week, get ready. And they'us havin' one of these here meetin's goin' pretty strong. There's a lot of interest and quite a bit of activity goin' on. That was during the earthquake that shook this country so bad... Charleston, back in 1886 sometime. When that happened, the windows started shaking right in the middle of that. And everybody thought the world was comin' to an end. Says Uncle Hosey: 'Let 'er come! Hosey's ready!'"

JARVIS CALDWELL: "He went up behind the pulpit and said: 'I'd rather die here than anywhere.'"

BONNIE CALDWELL: "That was the old log chapel church."

Mark lived at the Flats of the Bank near the Greenbrier Fault.

MARK HANNAH: "There was an earthquake in 1914 when I was a little boy. The rock chimney rattled! The dishes rattled! The two grandmothers ran to look at the dishes!"

Cataloochee has quite a different geologic character from Cades Cove, the only other well-settled valley in the Smokies now preserved by the Park as a pioneer community with its buildings still intact. Cades Cove is a limestone cove, having been worn down into a vast broad bowl which makes the area extremely well adapted for farming and cattle grazing.

Here the Old Smoky Mountain conglomerates of the Ocoee series had pushed over the newer limestone and dolomite along the Great Smoky Fault. Erosion subsequently revealed the Lower Ordovician limestones, creating what geologists love to call a "fenster" or window, through which might be found later Paleozoic and Ordovician fossils.

But Cataloochee remains stubbornly Precambrian, of the ancient times more than 500 million years ago when animal life did not exist. No fossils here. Cataloochee had no soft limestone to wear away into comfortable warm valleys. As a much narrower and older valley with rather precipitous mountain walls surrounding it, it wore down into chasms more gradually than did Cades Cove. Even now, one thinks of it as a fortress, guarded by its high, fir-covered parapets.

North Carolina and its mountains have long been known as a mineral hunter's paradise, not because of the quality or quantity, particularly, but because of the diversity. De Soto's men hunted in nearby mountains for gold, and some of their early mine shafts have been found, it is thought. In other areas of Carolina, people sometimes paid their taxes by panning for gold. And not far south of Cataloochee are the Cowee ruby mines where rubies are still found everyday by amateur collectors.

Allen Davidson, the late Cataloochee cowherd, swaggered around in beautiful cufflinks made of huge Carolina amethysts. And his daughter, Bettie, once had a fine bracelet made for her in Switzerland, out of North Carolina garnets in the shape of a serpent — while his grandson, Weldon, once mined for mica in the mountains during the second world war. But Mark said that, aside from an abortive silver mine at the Cagle place in Cataloochee, there was little of commercial value there. No fossils. No gemstones.

If great gems are to be found in the implacable stones, their secrets are well kept. Water, not minerals, was the great treasure of the valley. Meanwhile the Thunderhead Sandstone is now hidden by a clothing of black dirt and luxuriant forests and streaming rivulets.

CHAPTER 23

About As Far As New York to California
(Geography)

The Cook Cabin is preserved in Little Cataloochee in the Great Smoky Mountains National Park. A short walk from the Little Cataloochee Baptist Church, the cabin was built in the 1850s by Daniel and Harriett Cook and restored in the late 1990s through a grant with the Friends of the Smokies, the Great Smoky Mountains National Park and Aurora Foods (Log Cabin Syrup). It was then reworked again through a joint project between the Friends of the Smokies, The Hands of Sean Perry (donated all the labor), and the Park. Photograph by Brian Stansberry, September 4, 2007. Used under a CC-BY license.

IN 1859, THE famous wandering Swiss geographer, Arnold Henry Guyot, first set eyes on Cataloochee at age fifty-two when he left with a party from Waynesville and reached the top of Balsam Mountain via the Straight Fork of the Oconaluftee River. Now known as Luftee Knob, he called the peak The Pillar. The purpose of his trip was to measure the Balsam Range and the Great Smokies and other mountains in Haywood and Jackson Counties. Colonel Robert Love, who owned and sold so much of the Cataloochee territory, and with whom Guyot was staying, had loaned him a horse during some of his measuring visitations. And, in return, Guyot had honored his benefactor by naming a knob Mt. Love.

The summaries of his findings were published in 1860 and 1861, resulting in a new map of the whole Appalachian chain and his paper, entitled "On the Physical Structure of the Appalachian System of Mountains".

In his letter to the editor of the *Asheville News*, Guyot also expressed his appreciation for, among others, the aid of a Mr. Brown of Waynesville, who helped with the triangulation of "the mountain of Pigeon Valley", which may have included Cataloochee and environs, as his triangulation was of the chain of the Great Smoky Mountain from northeast to southeast from the bounds of Haywood County to the gap of the Little Tennessee River. But it is doubtful if Guyot ever ventured further into the interior of Cataloochee, for he ends his letter of 1860:

"As I intend this summer to visit the high group of mountains of the Cataluchee and those south of Haywood County, as well as the Nantahala and others to the boundary of Georgia, I shall be happy to give you for those who may be interested in my researches, the results of my further investigations.

> I remain, very truly yours,
> Arnold Guyot
> Professor of Geology and Physical
> Geography, Princeton College, N.J."

He may have slipped quickly in and out of Cataloochee at some later date. There is no record. But it is much more likely that the Civil War simply put a sudden end to all scientific research. Mt. Sterling Gap, for one, was thick with Yankee soldiers at the end. Even in the wildest parts, a professor could easily be mistaken for a bushwhacker.

PROFESSOR JOSEPH S. HALL: "(Cataloochee) has an appeal not easy to define, but one that probably has to do with the steep wooded slopes rising suddenly from a smooth valley floor, with its early morning splendor when fragments of clouds become tangled in the upland thickets; and with the majestic, ruffled surge of its river."

Too bad Guyot undoubtedly missed that early morning splendor!

"The majestic ruffled surge" to which Joe Hall referred is a characteristic song of Big Cataloochee Creek, one of the largest streams in the Smokies and, next to the Pigeon River, one of the boldest mountain streams in Haywood County.

Little Cataloochee Creek runs into Big Cataloochee Creek several miles from its junction with the Pigeon. Caldwell Fork is another which joins Big Cataloochee to increase the surge.

The watersheds of these three bounding creeks are fed by dozens of other little tributaries with their intricate webs of springs and trickles like the blue-blooded veins of aristocrats draining down from the foggy, cloudy uplands which were like the rain forests of the tropics with their luxuriant, damp vegetation. The streams brought in thousands of fishermen. And the unsurpassed spring waters, like wine to one who has tasted only the chlorine-tainted water of a city tap, have been converted into thousands of gallons of pure corn liquor in the past.

MARK HANNAH: "There's no other place in the Park that's like Cataloochee exactly. There's differences. It's cooler in summer than any other district of the Park. The good water is the one thing. Any where you can find a spring there, it's good drinking water."

"And there's one place over there that's different from anything I've ever seen. We have a branch they call Mossy Branch on Big Cataloochee. It flows into Cataloochee Creek about one mile below Palmer's Chapel. I've been there thirty-one years, and I never saw any water freeze in it anywhere. The Creek would be frozen over... Big Cataloochee would be frozen over, and that branch would still be running warm nice water with no ice in it... warm enough so that it wouldn't freeze. I think that was due to the springs flowing into that thing. Spring water won't freeze, you know, until air gets to it. And many a time I went up there in the winter time, and there'd be a vapor up... just like a fog... over that branch. And you'd think you had to turn on the lights or something... it's dark and misty, just like a light fog. I never saw that anywhere else."

The listener felt a slight chill coming on, suddenly remembering his ghost story about the Jolly Company on the other side of Mossy Branch... the unseen party of travellers, shrouded in mist.

Cataloochee Creek flows northeast into the Pigeon River which flows north to Newport, Tennessee. The engineering feat which bisected the cliff faces of this area in order to make the Grand Canyon-like North-South section of Interstate 40 with terraces like Mayan temples, from North Carolina into Tennessee enables the driver to see the lower Pigeon River along most of its route, including the Waterville Lake into which Cataloochee Creek flows along an eight-mile tunnel bored through the mountains of Cataloochee.

Carolina Power and Light began the huge Waterville Plant in 1925 at a cost of twenty million dollars, which was a lot of money at that time. It was near the mouth of Big Cataloochee Creek and was not finished until 1930. The power plant is at Waterville, near the Tennessee line, but the water comes from the mouth of Big Cataloochee through the now famous tunnel which was bored through the mountains of Cataloochee.

MARK HANNAH: "Waterville was just a wide place in the road until a fellow flew over it in an airplane and said, well, we're going up the river here and make a dam across the mouth of Cataloochee and Pigeon River and back all that water up here. And then we'll be able to tunnel through the mountain and let it come out here at Waterville."

"The power plant is not strictly Cataloochee watershed, but the dam comes off out of Cataloochee and gets on the Cataloochee side and actually up Cataloochee Creek' above the intersection of the River... They bored a hole through there about fourteen foot square, square through that mountain. And, at one place, it goes 500 feet straight down through a shaft and then goes out again through Long Arm Mountain."

"In 1927-28, it was a pretty rough place down there. It was hidden and a lot of desperadoes, so to speak, come in there, running from the law. And they got down there in those places, hide, work right on, working most of the time. They caught a few of them, not very many."

"Quite a few lives were lost in building that tunnel in and around there. That's a very interesting thing, that tunnel. Some of the best engineering by Luke Runions that I heard of. They started in one end and went in seven different places to dig in that tunnel and they never missed center when they connected over 3/4 of an inch in any place."

The Pigeon River thence flows into the Little Tennessee River which flows west to Deal's Gap and drops from 2,200 feet into the drainage of the Mississippi Valley and thence to the Gulf of Mexico – a long trip for the water courses of Cataloochee.

The indefatigable Hiram Wilburn often corresponded with Dr. E. W. Gudger of the American Museum of Natural History. Gudger, who loved the mountains of North Carolina and took a deep scientific interest in them, wrote Wilburn that Haywood County, of which Cataloochee is the most mountainous part, had the highest elevation of any county east of the Mississippi, with an average elevation of 4,787 feet, the highest reaching 6,621 feet, the lowest 1,396 feet.

Although the elevation of Cataloochee's valley floor is only 2,500 feet, it is surrounded by mountains many of which are more than a mile high. The Balsam Range where the soldiers experienced an earthquake in 1776, is the western flank of Cataloochee, dividing the counties of Jackson and Swain from Haywood County in the East. Luftee Knob where Guyot gazed into Cataloochee, and Balsam Corner, within this range are over 6,000 feet high. Big Cataloochee Knob rises to 6,122 feet. There are two or three gaps into Cataloochee from this westerly range: Laurel Gap between Balsam Corner and Balsam High Top, also Poll's Gap where the milch cow died, and Pin Oak Gap, earlier called Spanish Oak Gap where a fire once raged. Poll's Gap, at 5,110 feet once had a logging railroad through it. It lies between a branch of Bunche's Creek of Swain County and Warm Cove Branch of Caldwell Fork of Cataloochee Creek. A logging railroad was also built through Spanish Oak Gap at the elevation of 4,428 feet. This gap is between Ledge Creek, near the old grazing grounds, of Straight Fork in Swain County, and old Indian Creek of Cataloochee Creek. Indian Creek is known as Palmer Creek now because "Turkey George" Palmer lived up that way.

On the Southeastern flank of the Valley is the long mountain range between Jonathan's Creek and Cataloochee Creek known as The Cataloochee Divide.

It includes such famous high mountain meadows and peaks as The Purchase, where one of the Fergusons died of milksick, which has one of the finest views into North Carolina and Tennessee that can be imagined; Purchase Knob; The Swag, which is typical of the saddle balds; and culminating in the imposing Hemphill Bald, with a herd of Black Angus from the now transported Cataloochee Ranch grazing among the impressive tall snags of dead chestnut trees. Beginning at Cove Creek Gap, the Cataloochee Divide trail runs left with the ridge, punctuated by Panther Spring Gap, Double Gap, and Pine Tree Gap. The trail of the indomitable Bishop Asbury runs off to the right of Cove Creek Gap.

To the North, the great Mt. Sterling Ridge overpowers all the others with its massiveness and its prickled Fraser Fir and red spruce silhouette. This massif, which completes the boundaries of the Cataloochee watershed, is gashed only by Pretty Hollow Gap at 5,179 feet to the West, and the lower Mt. Sterling Gap at 3,894 feet, which was the chink in Cataloochee's armor during the Civil War.

It is understandable that, until 1928, Cataloochee was only remotely connected with parts of Haywood County, too, when one views these tall mountains and considers the sweat of road making and maintenance, and the effect of rainfall on the finished product.

The earliest areas to be cleared and farmed were along the largest bottoms of Cataloochee Creek. All else, except where an occasional field had been cleared, was covered with virgin forest. The sheer slopes of mountainsides were imperfectly suited to farming, but as more of the rich soil was carried away from the lower fields by runoff, more of the upper land was cleared, some of it right to the top. Abandoned fields were reforested by nature, or used as indifferent pastures.

But most of the good farming, of necessity, was carried on in the fertile coves and bottoms. Steve Cove and Turkey Cove are typical examples of mountain farming in Cataloochee.

Cataloochee was never known for its broad valleys full of grazing cattle, as was Cades Cove in the western part of the Smokies.

For one thing, it was almost totally bisected by Noland Mountain, quite a substantial barrier of nearly 4,000 feet. It was this mountain which divided the settlements into Big and Little Cataloochee. Davidson Gap, named after the pioneer cattleman, Mitchell Davidson, was the narrow passage from one community to the other. It was along this pinched way that Homer Lockman's coffin was so laboriously carried.

Not as large was a third settlement of Cataloochee in the southeastern ranges known as the Caldwell Fork Community which had, nonetheless, a mill and a school which sometimes doubled as a church. Caldwell Fork's main path out of Cataloochee led right across the divide through The Purchase.

So near as the crow flies, but so far for a small boy.

RAYMOND CALDWELL: "Well, it was quite a chore to go through Davidson Gap... it would take more than a day to go over to Little Cataloochee and back... so, in one respect, it was separated about as much as New York City and California are today (by airplane). Had to go across Noland Mountain. I was an eight or ten year old, no older than that before I can remember havin' been into Little Cataloochee. Just one ridge separatin' it."

CHAPTER 24

Herrycanes and Sech

(Meteorology)

The Hall House in Little Cataloochee circa 1946 was a short distance from Little Cataloochee Baptist Church between the church and the Cook cabin. One rainy Decoration Day, the food was transported down the hill from the church and tables were set up on the wraparound porches so dinner could be enjoyed out of the rain. Now when it rains, the descendants have to set up and eat on the pews in the church — the food is still grand! Courtesy Great Smoky Mountains National Park Archives.

THE CHEROKEES, WHO worshipped things in nature, thought of the thunderbolt and the lightning flash as tangible evidence of gods. Some of these weather gods were powerfully incorporated into the tapestry of Indian life and lore.

Leaves of the white rhododendron, for instance, if thrown on a fire around which Indians are dancing are supposed to bring cold weather, by the invocation of a special god.

In the early morning of the thirteenth of November, 1833, stars fell on Cataloochee and all the vicinity. They were visible in all the western mountain counties, if not elsewhere. Colonel John C. Smathers remembered them distinctly. He remembered hearing women wailing and men praying. It must have startled any Cataloochee cattle herders or hunters in the early morning hours, if they still had any cattle grazing up near Mt. Sterling in early November. What the Indians made of this is anybody's guess, as falling stars are normally seen in August, a natural month for this phenomenon. There must have been a flurry of conjecture about the Star People, as the Cherokees call them.

The later white inhabitants of Cataloochee apparently confined their weather-lore to superstitions, and did not deify events. They spoke of blackberry winter, dogwood winter... or unusual cold spells which concurred with the fruiting or blooming of these species. They believed, and still do in some parts, that the 'wooly bear' or furred caterpillar could foretell whether the winter would be hard or not by the thickness of its furry coat, or the width of dark bands around it. Their expressions about weather were colorful. Mark still writes of winters in Maggie Valley, where he now lives, as 'whizzin' cold', or 'cold as whiz'.

MARK HANNAH: "When our corn had lots of shucks on it, that meant a bad winter coming. If the hornet nests were found hanging high in the trees, (that also meant a) bad winter. When the turkeys started feeding, scratching and were real busy all day, we expected the snow to be on the ground soon. If we heard a bird (which we) called 'raincrow' coo-ing, one just knew it was going to rain within forty-eight hours. The first thunder in the springtime awoke the bears, and they were to be prowling through the forests soon."

Anyone who has hiked in these mountains knows how changeable the weather is. The unwritten law is: "If you don't like it, just wait a bit." Within a short space in one single day, one may put one's sweater on and take it off many times on a winding, climbing path because of the quixotic changes of temperature.

This is because the mountains of Cataloochee are not simple walls or ridges like the Alleghanies, with the possible exception of Mt. Sterling, but are, as Donald Culross Peattie characterizes most of the Great Smokies, "tossed in a congested mass; the axes run in every direction and each axis has been carved by a mature erosion system fed by heavy rainfall. As a result, each range is dissected to show exposure to every quarter of the compass, and there is an astounding difference between the north slope, with its many hours of shadow, its greater humidity, its severer winters, and a southern exposure with conditions corresponding in summer... to those of the tropics at the same season."

In short, one might shuck one's clothes and shoes as if it were midsummer on a balmy April day in the sheltered hollow of Steve Cove while picnicking along Rough Fork. Obviously the Woodys elected to build here because it was so protected from the winter cold. Later, upon walking only a short distance up towards the dense shade of the giant hemlocks, crossing an icy stream, one experiences a deep chill in the darkness of this virgin forest. Sweater, jacket, and hat are put on again, only to be hastily doffed when one rounds a corner and feels hot sun in a clearing or on a different slope.

Unexpected walks in the rain might change just as quick And soon one is drying one's hiking socks on a hot boulder in the blazing sun.

But how very nearly like a rain forest Cataloochee is in some seasons, with almost as much rainfall as the Pacific Northwest. Watching the damp behemoth clouds rolling up the valley every day is to glory in this excess which softens the skin and luxuriantly festoons stream banks with ferns and cushions stones with a mossy velour.

Indeed, flash floods are not an unusual occurrence. There is an extant photograph of a wildly rampaging Cataloochee Creek in the 30's. The ground can hold only so much moisture, and the excess must be dispersed in some manner, even if it means Nature's playing havoc with the footlogs and stony roadbeds. The Cataloochee Bottoms, for instance, were pretty much covered with water during a large part of the Spring of 1973. The Park's maintenance men had almost more than they could handle in re-establishing some of the old roads, ditching the trails, and making fords passable once more.

Occasionally a freak flood might even happen in the winter.

HAROLD HANNAH (Mark's son): "We had had several days of zero degree weather. The creek was almost solid with ice. It was about six inches thick except where the water was swiftest. The 'still hole' known to others as the Sycamore Hole just below our house was solid with this sheet of ice. Lowell and I had been riding our bikes on the ice all morning. We'd had a warm rain all night and this morning was the first time we'd had temperatures warm enough to get out in comfortably."

"About ten o'clock, we had tired of the game and gotten out on the road to start home. We heard this roar which was gradually getting louder and were looking at the sky and all around trying to figure what it was... sounded like an airplane in trouble."

"Suddenly there was a series of loud cracks like thunder and only then did we realize what was happening. The popping came from the ice cracking, and the roar was really loud, thrashing and thumping. Looking upstream we saw the ice being tossed into the air and a wall of water, and great sheets of ice tumbling down the creek. Within a matter of seconds, the great sheet of ice on the 'still hole' was a conglomeration of big pieces of ice and swift muddy water. Some pieces of ice were ten and twelve feet square and shoved up onto the bank. We were almost too stunned to move. I've always wondered what we would have done had we still been on the ice when the first abnormal sound was heard."

Hurricanes were not unheard of in Cataloochee. All the same, hurricanes are extremely rare in the area owing to the fact that they are broken up as they approach the lowlands east, west, and south.

J. PRESTON ARTHUR: "There is a place called 'herrycane'... on Indian Creek just above its junction with Ugly Creek, thus forming Cataloochee Creek in Haywood County... a whole mountain side in front of Jesse Palmer's residence is covered with the 'rent fragments of giant trees which have been uprooted or twisted from their trunks bodily... (This) Haywood hurricane (occurred) about 1898."

ELDRIDGE CALDWELL: "There was a storm tore my father's apple trees down when I was just a kid. Had a hurricane strike up there right below Turkey George's, and come right around side of that mountain that run down their home, and cut across it, turned up the stream by our house. I was about six years old when that hurricane struck up there (about 1904). It just blowed... It just twisted them apple trees up by the roots, all of 'em's any account. I think there was just three left, we let stand. It blowed some of them big trees right below the house almost into the house, wrung them off, right to the ground. That's the worst one I've ever knowed to hit in this part of the country."

There was a branch named Hurricane Creek on Rough Fork of the Cataloochee because so many trees were felled about 1910.

And then there was 'Major' Woody's famous invocation when he got mad at the U. S. Park Service because they wouldn't let Cataloochans use any timber after the park had taken over.

ELDRIDGE CALDWELL: "He said he wished they'd come a herrycane and blow the cranberry bushes out of the ground. They'd let you take it (fallen timber) up now and then, y' know. And, sure nuff, there come one right up in above where he lived over there on Little Catalooch'. Just flattened out a strip..."

Electrical storms are more frequent than hurricanes and can be quite frightening in these mountains during the summer. One often hears a phantom telephone ring though it is only the electricity in the air causing the magical 'ting'. Fortunately, most have never had the experience Mark Hannah's family had. A bolt of lightning once struck their ungrounded bathtub in the old George Palmer house where the ranger was then housed, blackening it ominously. No one was in the bathroom at the time, but the impact was terrifying on the family and some guests they had for the weekend.

Old timers always talk about how they endured hard times and frigid winters worse than any we know now. There is some evidence to make us believe that winters were indeed much colder in Cataloochee in earlier times, not counting, of course, the ancient Ice Age which never quite reached Cataloochee but blew its Arctic breath on the upper heights, causing a Canadian climate and vegetation to remain in this part of the Southland. The Ice Age actually benefitted the valley because it pushed all of the northern plants down into this southern region, where they melded with the more exotic southern plants, forming a huge collection, as a result.

Tom Alexander, the younger son of old Tom Alexander, late owner of a ranch in Cataloochee Valley and Fie Top, wrote an article on the world's weather for *Fortune* magazine, of which he was once science editor. As a small boy, young Tom had ranged about the existing world of Cataloochee. There is a photograph showing him grinning, bundled up against the snowstorm as the horses bear him and his parents in a sleigh over stony roads softened by the drifts along the Cataloochee bottoms. Yes, winters <u>were</u> worse in old Cataloch'. The oldtimers weren't complaining for nothing.

TOM ALEXANDER: "... Now there's good reason to believe that the world's climate is reverting rapidly to its less beneficent norm."

"The changes began with a pronounced warming trend after about 1890. Mean temperatures peaked in 1945 and have been dropping sharply ever since... There seems to be a return to the more extreme and variable weather conditions... including floods, droughts and great winter blizzards... that were typical of the nineteenth century."

'When Grandpa said the weather was different in his day, he wasn't kidding,' remarks one climatologist."

The winter and summer of 1977 seem to prove that there's a sudden return to the weather that Robert Henry used to know.

He was born in 1765 and lived in nearby Waynesville, faithfully recording in his diary that in "the summer of 1815 no rain fell from the 8th of July till the 8 of Sep."... on 28th day of August, 1830,... creeks ceased... and the corn died from the drouth... The summer of 1836 was the wettest summer in seventy years in my remembrance... Thus., Fri., and Sat., next before Christmas 1794 were the coldest days in 70 years." He had been around long enough to remember how the snow was "shoe-mouth" deep before the Battle of King's Mountain and how wet it was on the survey of the Tennessee-North Carolina line when he and Colonel David Vance had reached the Cataloochee stone in the turnpike. General R. M. Henry and Allen Davidson read law together with the Scotsman, Michael Francis, in Waynesville, undoubtedly with many a discussion of weather along the way. The lives of so many farmers and soldiers depended on the weather. Neither did a circuit-riding mountain lawyer take weather lightly. No wonder he kept weather records.

The year 1816 was called by some, The Year Without a Summer. But there were few traversing Cataloochee then aside from some Cherokee hunters, and the Davidsons and the Caldwells (they called themselves Colwell back then) who were merely ranging cattle, hunting, and clapping cold hands together in front of a campfire. Camping out at Turkey George's once in July, a rider recalled feeling the chill of winter in the early morning air as his teeth chattered around the breakfast fire. V. A. "Tot" Henry from Cataloochee Ranch, a descendent of Robert Henry's, warmed the group up with some hot oatmeal and coffee from a huge blackened pot.

In the second quarter of the nineteenth century the rivers in that area froze solid enough for teams of horses. In times such as these Eldridge Caldwell's great grandfather Ferguson, who was something of a 'yarb' doctor over on Laurel Branch down below Cove Creek just on the other side of Cataloochee, would cross the river on the ice in order to treat the sick.

In those old cold days, deer were easily pursued because their sharp hooves plunged through the crust of frozen snow, rendering locomotion impossible. In January of 1879, this was repeated.

In 1866, a huge three foot snow fell in Cataloochee and stayed for two weeks. The snow came to the top of John Jackson Hannah's fence, and he was finally forced to burn rails for firewood.

There was snow in Cataloochee on June 10, 1913.

Hiram Album's notebook says there was a forty-two inch snowfall in 1896, and another unusually heavy snowfall in 1936.

MARK HANNAH: "I have seen my father return from feeding hogs on winter days with his shoes and pants frozen in ice and snow, his mustache with icicles hanging. We had bad winters and many deep snows in those years, and it was rough going on the hogs and the owners. We had to carry corn in a bag to them until the snow melted enough for them to root the leaves off and get the acorns or nuts, called 'mast.'"

During January and February of 1918 the ground was consistently covered with ice for 2 months, which must have made it very hard for horses to gain a footing. One of the earliest settlers in Cataloochee, Creighton Bennett, was forced to use a pick and mattock in order to make ice steps for his horses one bitter winter on the steep Cataloochee Road, undoubtedly the reason for the naming of the famous Bennett Turn.

Now a retired Park naturalist, Arthur Stupka, recorded two extremes in the Smokies beginning with January of 1937, when very few people other than Mark were still living in Cataloochee. Apparently no snow fell on the mountains for the entire month, and the temperature actually reached 81 degrees one day. Hibernating animals left their dens and some flowering trees came into bloom.

But a few winters later in 1940, it was a stunner, not only in Cataloochee, but throughout the mountains and the East coast, in general. Sub-zero temperature readings were not unusual and birds were frozen. Frost penetration was unbelievable. Drifts were higher than five feet on some cross-mountain roads. Rainbow Falls, in another part of the Park, became "a great ice cone above which were suspended huge stalactites of ice." Stupka also reported sharp reports and explosions when trees burst from the expansion pressure resulting from the freezing of the moisture-filled cells of their cambium layers.

HAROLD HANNAH: "There is nothing quieter than a quiet, still winter night in Cataloochee. Sometimes you could not even hear any wind in the trees on the highest peaks. Not even the hoot of an owl nor the bark of a fox."

When Mark was a ranger, he had been asked to search for a lost plane one winter's day in Cataloochee. Without noticing how cold it was, he went out and began trudging the paths to obscure parts of the Park. However, when he got to the falls at Sinking Creek he found it distinctly sinister that he could hear no noise of falling water. The waterfall was completely frozen. That sobered him, and he quickly returned home before he froze in the deadly cold.

MARK HANNAH: "I spent my last Christmas in Cataloochee up at Mt. Sterling fire tower. My sons-in-law and all were there and wanted to go up and spend a good Christmas Eve. We finally got to Mt. Sterling Gap. The snow started falling and some of 'em wanted to change the course and go back home. Ten of us... grandsons and sons, and sons-in-law. By the time we reached the tower, there was about four inches of snow on the ground, and it was whizzin' cold, and the wind a-blowin' off from the north."

"Well, we stayed in the cabin there, stayed the night. One of my grandsons got excited, my namesake, Mark E., so he said, 'We better go out and get the thermometer... it might burst!' It was six above zero. We got up the next morning, and the snow was still pilin' up and windy, so we decided we'd better get out of there. Boys didn't have any boots on. We got an old blanket, cut it up, made strips, and made leggin's out of it for the little boys. Came down the mountain thataway. We thought it was a bad time. Met a family comin' up, just enjoyin' the snow, just the same as if the sun was a-shinin'! Tourists! Just goin' up towards Balsam Corner. We were runnin' from it and they were runnin' into it!"

"But that was about the worst storm I saw in all my years in Cataloochee, (with the possible exception of) March 17, 1936, when I was called on by a neighbor to go to Mt. Sterling depot to pick up a country doctor that was good to attend sick patients that were suspected to have fever. It started snowing and we made it to the Vess Camp Branch before we had to put chains on the pickup truck. We arrived at the depot on time but the wind and snowstorm had blown a tree across the railroad delaying the 'Jitney' some two hours.

"When the doctor did arrive the snow had a depth of six to eight inches and it was being blown away at places. We piled rocks into the rear of that pickup (for weight) and headed up toward Sterling Gap. Deeper and deeper we were hitting snowdrifts, limbs, tree tops and all kinds of things in the roadway. We made it to the 'Joson Hill' and my truck went toward the upper water ditch in a snowdrift some two feet deep under a chestnut tree that was weaving from the wind."

"I said, 'Fellows, get out of there and hit the road toward Cataloochee before you freeze to death.' They were shaking like a leaf in a whirlwind. We were already parked well out of the road and the amount of snow that was falling would soon cover the truck so that it wouldn't be found until the snow melted."

"Dr. Cates and C. Ramsey started hiking, I followed; walking was as tiresome as I have ever tried in that snow and up hill every step. At the Sterling Gap entering Little Cataloochee, the snow had been carried by wind out of the gap and piled high as your head in places. Off went the doctor's hat and I went for it — landing in a snowdrift waist-deep, but I caught it. We headed down a nearway into the forest, and I believe we heard and saw the most trees falling close by us. My, it looked as if we would be killed any minute."

"We fought our way through snow and fallen trees to a neighbor's house, Irving and Dollie Messer's, they had a good fire and invited us to a late lunch. Man, oh, man! That sausage and other good food surely was consumed rapidly. After thanking the neighbors for their hospitality, we again headed towards Mrs. Ramsey living at the George Bennett place, four more miles through the forest — no trail to follow as it was covered in deep snow. I knew the country and led or went in front to break the snow. We made it before dark."

"Dr. Cates stayed with the patient from Tuesday to Sunday; she had the fever. The patient was almost well before the roads were cleared by the CCC crews and they gave me and the doctor a ride back to my truck and to the 'Jitney' so he could go home. Only one man, the lookout from Sterling Tower, Mr. Wade Hopkins, had passed my snow-covered truck in the six days. The snow was 24 inches any place and up to 18 feet in the drifts. March 19th, being my oldest daughter's and oldest son's birthday and a photo of them in snow helps to remember this so vividly. 'Snow on top of snow for two weeks'".

With changing weather patterns, it's hard nowadays to say what is normal in Cataloochee. But usually September, October, and November are the driest months here. July, curiously, is the wettest, with August running a close second. The last frosts are usually in mid to late May, and the first in September. There are variations in frost times, according to elevation and exposure, of course.

MARK HANNAH: "The first dry summer that I have heard (of) in Cataloochee was prior to 1861. Creighton Bennett was living in the house that the soldiers burned to the ground during the 1861 war. He was getting water at a spring-branch just east of The Bennett House Place and during the summer the water ceased to run (dried up). It was almost a mile to carry water to his home. It was then that he decided to dig a trench or ditch to a point above his house, in the branch, so that gravity would bring the water to his home or near by. He dug it about 24 inches in depth in some places. It proved successful and the branch was later named for him "Bennett Branch". This is the first record we have of any man bringing the water to his house. They usually took the house to the water. The abovementioned "Man Made Water Ditch" is still visible. The Creighton Bennett house was only about three hundred yards north of the first house built in Cataloochee by Evan Hannah."

In spite of the immense rainfall of the region, old Tom Alexander, interviewed only a month or so before he died, remembered that August 1925, was one of the driest seasons Cataloochee ever saw. He was working near Cataloochee as a young timber cruiser at the time when Ravensford Lumber Company had a cabin at The

Ledge on the rim of Cataloochee and had built a railroad from Round Bottom, near Indian Territory, through Pin Oak (Spanish Oak) Gap.

A disgruntled employee who had been fired by Ravensford deliberately set a blaze in Cataloochee on the east side of the Balsams near Pin Oak Gap. Tom recalled their fear because of the dry season. He said he never would forget having to rescue a sick mountain woman by toting her across a railway trestle to safety. She had just had an appendectomy, and Tom was terrified that all her stitches would come loose!

ELDRIDGE CALDWELL: "Yeah, it (the fire of 1925) started between this Ledge Mountain and Butt Mountain on what we called Beech Ridge. They was families lived all along there, y' know, in shanty cars, we called 'em. Loggers. The men logged and the women kept house."

RAYMOND CALDWELL: "Go right around to Heintoogy (Heintooga) to Pin Oak Gap where that's all that country where the big far (fire) was at what we refer to as The Ledge."

Mark recalled that particular dry season with sorrow also, because it spread the fungi disease to the native chestnut.

MARK HANNAH: "Didn't have any bad fires in Cataloochee while I was ranger. Well, there were two or three little ones set by lightnin', but the biggest one I had wasn't over five acres. I believe I had five lightnin'-set fires... no mancaused or accidents (while) I was a ranger. Now, John Carroll (Mark's immediate predecessor) had some bad fires comin' from the outside, burnt in on him. But we were lucky about people settin' fires out in the middle of the Park. If we hadn't had good cooperation... 'cause I couldn't keep them from settin' (campfires)."

HAROLD HANNAH: "Mom was always home (when Dad was ranger) and 'caught the hourly schedule' for Dad if the fire-guard was on tool maintenance, trail maintenance, foot patrol or other work. Mom, also, was adept at 'taking the weather' and relaying that at the proper time to headquarters. That is what we called the process of determining fire danger by measuring the fuel moisture, wind velocity, days since last rain, and condition of vegetation."

"If the towerman (in fire tower) sighted a smoke near the park, it was checked out by patrol and assistance given to State forestry fire fighters if needed. The two or three fires that occurred in Dad's district that I remember really caused quite a stir. Two of them lightning-caused were very difficult to get to with crews but did very little damage. The one that I remember best started one night outside the Park on the Big Creek side of Mt. Sterling. Dad and the crews were gone two or three days before getting it stopped. The damage is still evident after thirty-three years."

"Fire season meant that we could not go anywhere as a family unless it was raining. Of course, we rarely went anywhere out of the valley anyway. Nowadays the average family could not tolerate staying so close home for two months (March and April). Another thing that is hard for most people to believe is how quick that the forest will dry out after a rain. I've seen Dad leave for Waynesville in the morning after a night of rain and hurry home by three P.M. because high winds and bright drying sunshine had made south and west facing slopes burnable. Then there would be times that it would rain every day for a week or more. That's when the tools were put into the best state of repair and other projects could be done."

A little weather never daunted mountain people, though. They are never seen with raincoats, golashes or umbrellas. Horace Kephart used to marvel how "the native hunters would lie out in the open all night without a sign of a blanket or axe... they sleep out wherever night finds them, often in pouring rain or flying snow... only eccentrics carried umbrellas!"

CHAPTER 25

Flora's Ark

(Flora)

This photograph of rhododendron was made by George Alexander Grant (1891–1964), first chief photographer for the National Park Service. Grant began work in 1929 under Horace Albright, second NPS director, who hired him to create a documentary file of images for use in reports, interpretive projects, education, and public information. Considered an Eminent Photographer, many of Grant's photographs were published without his name, instead, being credited as an "NPS photo." Before his retirement in 1954, Grant created approximately 30,000–40,000 images for NPS. Courtesy Great Smoky Mountains National Park Archives.

Towards mid-April the bare bones of silvery oak groves on the higher slopes of Cataloochee are tipped with incredibly delicate shades of pink. These are the tiny buds which will soon break into leaf. In the early heat of lower elevations, a lava-like flow of palest green leaves surges upwards as temperatures climb, streaking the upland sea of silver and pink like jade-colored tidal rivers in full freshet.

Quicksilver water runs everywhere. In the noonday sun, meadows glitter with watery veins as the tiniest springs gush forth in torrents. It is still a Gothic winterscape on the highest reaches, traced with paths that are never seen in summer.

By April 20, the whole valley has an overpowering sweet smell of black earth and burgeoning vegetation. Though this small world has been skinned by winter's depredations, it is now filmed over with a green mist which softens the severe spines of the mountains. Landscapes have been rearranged. Spring floods have washed Uncle Steve's road down to rockbottom. Frogs croak in Rough Fork. And tender young greens such as bear lettuce bring a welcome relief to the winter diet.

In midsummer the valley lies like fair Ophelia among the streams and flowers, half-drowned with sleep and warmth. Summer rains swell the streams as a shroud of clinging wetness envelopes Cataloochee with clouds, and the foliage becomes that of rain forests. Now the growth rate is palpable, rising before one's eyes, a fine living mass, sending out tendrils, stems, leaves, branches faster and faster as though in some speeded-up time-growth movie sequence.

Naturalists liken this part of the world to a botanical ark. They account for the extraordinary number of plants in the Smokies by saying that the Ice Age pushed the Northern species all the way down to join forces with the Southern ones here. The earliest plant life of Cataloochee may be much older than the Smokies themselves, for there was apparently life on the vast peneplain that rushed over the Inland Sea long before the ancient rocks of the plain, erupted into the great early peaks of Appalachia. One writer-naturalist thought of Cataloochee and the lower slopes of Mt. Sterling as a sort of Temperate Zone Tropics, as he walked in its vast humid greenery.

CHARLTON OGBURN: "Rhododendron grew in jungles 20 feet high and its long narrow leaves against the light overhead reminded me of looking up through bamboo. Lianas of grapevines hung from the treetops, the stocks as much as 6 inches in diameter. And there were plants of paired, deeply-cleft leaves, some two feet across, the largest I have seen in wild vegetation north of Florida. Umbrella-leafs they were..."

The superfluity of wildflowers in Cataloochee recalls the complex tapestried understory in a Botticelli painting, especially the opulent groundcovers of partridgeberry, moss and wood sorrel, and the meadow carpets of wild strawberries. William Bartram, that intrepid 18th century traveller, wrote with enthusiasm of crossing Appalachian mountain meadows where his horse trod in wild strawberries so thick that it was crimson to the fetlocks.

Nowadays there seems to be a renaissance of interest in Cataloochee's flowers. There have been official wildflower pilgrimages to the valley under the aegis of Mondamin Wilderness Adventures and Dr. Ritchie Bell who is a professor at the University of North Carolina and director of the North Carolina Botanical Garden.

No longer is the shy orchis overlooked or trodden on by hikers and horses on the trails. Nowadays these New Pilgrims dismount from their horses, with magnifying glasses in hand.

One of the most indefatigable of these Pilgrims, "Dr. Doris", a pediatrician from nearby Waynesville, rides her horse into Cataloochee on every fine day that she can take off from her busy practice. The Sierra Club's Hiker's Guide to the Smokies published her careful notes on the Cataloochee Trails, with specific botanical references.

DR. DORIS HAMMETT: "... Palmer Chapel is located on the left, and the old church graveyard on the hill to the right. There is an excellent show of pink lady's slipper at the cemetery in the springtime."

"... The Caldwell Fork Trail follows from the main stream (of Cataloochee Creek) and thus is a valley trail. It is graced with an abundance of flowers... dog-hobble, violets, hepatica, bloodroot, Mayapple, wood anemone, spring beauty, trillium, and Solomon's Seal. The largest single-stem rhododendron in the Park can be seen from this trail..."

"The trail continues through this relatively open area (The Deadnin' Fields) to... where the Double Gap Trail begins on the left... This section has one of the largest shows in the Park of wake robin trillium, galax, partridgeberry, Turk's Cap lily, azaleas, Indian pipe, and wood sorrel."

One can spot showy orange orchis along the Rough Fork or Poll's Gap Trail where it follows the road to Steve Woody's house. Dr. Hammett also saw jack-in-the-pulpit along this trail as well as wake robin trillium, Solomon's Seal, Clintonia, azaleas, rhododendron, mountain laurel, trailing arbutus and Dutchman's Pipe, among others.

Cataloochans called rhododendron "laurel" — the purple variety being known as "blue l'arl", whereas the true mountain laurel was called "ivy" by them, causing great confusion among outlanders.

DR. HAMMETT: "At 1.9 mi. (Rough Fork Trail) enters the clearing of the Steve Woody house... Continuing to run between old rail fences and the creek, the trail passes through a grove of large trees (virgin hemlock and oak) where excellent painted trilliums grow on the forest floor."

The Big Fork Ridge trail, so designated because it crosses that long, low ridge of Big Fork which separates Caldwell Fork and Rough Fork, has an unusual display as the trail crosses Rough Fork via a footbridge.

DR. HAMMETT: "The area to the right has been cleared and still shows the effects of farming (Steve's Cove) — about 1918. On the left bank beautiful purple fringed orchids are growing."

Turkey George Palmer, had he ever noted anything besides wild game, would have seen many flowers along Palmer Creek (or Indian Creek) as he ambled along with "Old Sank" the horse. Here "Dr. Doris" paused to examine hepatica, violets, white fringed phacelia, rue anemone, bloodroot, trout lily, and wild geranium, noting a large bed of yellow lady's slipper at 4.3 miles on the ridge.

She followed the trail where it joined Pretty Hollow Creek and found an excellent bed of pink lady's slipper on the right of the trail just below the site of Turkey George's house.

The incredible blue of lobelia in August is sometimes found at Cove Creek Gap where the boundary of the Park begins.

Late one September a writer for *The National Geographic* headed northeast along the crest of the Cataloochee Divide in the general direction of Cove Creek Gap. Her article (October 1952) on this autumnal ride, which was called "Pack Trip Through the Smokies", mentioned some of the late season flowers.

VAL HART: "The trail narrowed suddenly, and we passed through a jungle of rhododendron, the first of hundreds we would see. Masses of doghobble (Leucothoe) dense and intertwined with the trunks and branches of rhododendron, covered the forest floor. So thick was the growth that only occasional patches of sunshine lit bright red partridgeberries growing along the trail... From the quiet darkness of the jungle mass we emerged into the full sunlight of a meadow of goldenrod, sunflowers, purple and white asters, and vagrant butterflies. Ripe blackberries and blueberries dotted our trail; at lower levels the fruit has ripened several weeks earlier."

"... on our last day's ride we stopped for lunch at Rough Fork of the Cataloochee... our route home on the trail which had been so hidden in the mist now lay open and appealing in the sunlight and warmth of goldenrod and asters."

On April 28, 1973, a late snow covered blooming violets and white strawberry blossoms with a glaze which melted in the noonday sun. One could see the white jagged snowline of faraway Mt. Sterling through the branches of a huge sarvis tree in full flower like a bridal bouquet. Cataloochee apple orchards were just on the brink of blooming, as was the pear tree that Steve Woody planted by his house. Pink and white silverbells, called "bellwood" locally, embroidered the middle slopes almost as delicately as the smaller sarvis trees and wild cherries, but not as stunningly as the great starry splotches of the mountain magnolia blooms. Later these would shower their white petals on the rich black earth, in luscious display, even in death.

Winter may still reign through most of May on the mountaintops, holding back leaves until early June. The profusion of May flowering trees is what assaults the eyes rather than the tender young wildflowers of the forest floor in April. Early galaxies of dogwoods bloom at the base of the woods bordering the meadows. The Palmer cemetery is radiant in spring with these trees.

There was a very late spring in Cataloochee on May 27, 1974. The woods were still as pale green as a new lettuce leaf. The wind twined sinuously in the feathery trees, giving off sonar waves as a fish might while swimming through tangled seaweed and coral forests of the ocean depths.

Allen Davidson and Ned McFalls would long ago have had their cattle in their spring pastures by this time of year if the "sugars" (maples) had leafed out. Men of today would be ashamed to spout some of the sheer romantic nonsense that Allen wrote in 1847 about the early nineteenth century forests. But his writing was typical of the lyrical, lush prose of his day.

ALLEN T. DAVIDSON: "(I was) passing through a lovely country, by glades, benches, and hillsides in the then primeval forests, a wild and romantic country well calculated to attract the attention and interest of anyone not utterly dead to the chorus of nature whose beauty unadorned adorned the most."

The mere sight of the Bunk Mountain licklogs at sunset would move him to tears, reminding him of his boyhood as the young cattleherd of lost Cataloochee. If he were alive today, the tears would be streaming down his furrowed cheeks in deepest sorrow for what else has been truly lost.

As late as 1905, native chestnut trees made up 40% of the ridges of Cataloochee. By 1940, all these splendid cockaded trees were totally lost to the chestnut blight, which Mark Hannah recalled as beginning in 1925. A few scattered root sprouts still grow for as long as 3 years, then succumb. Now the tulip poplars are taking their place. No one who knew those old chestnut forests could ever forget the sight.

DONALD CULROSS PEATTIE (writer naturalist): "... I recollect gazing down once, in July... upon the whole forest, far as eye could see, tossing with the creamy blooms of the chestnut, which in those days was king of the cove hardwoods. There were so many, the chestnuts, and each crown bore such a myriad of long shining catkins, that as the wind threshed those woods the whole sea of waving leaves seemed breaking into whitecaps. It was a sight one would not have beheld by looking up under the woodland canopy; only by gazing down, from the vantage point of a hawk, did one see this grand primeval treetop flowering..."

The hemlock, known locally as "hempine", covered 60% of the bottoms of Cataloochee in 1905. Fortunately a great deal of that still remains — even large virgin tracts such as the one above Steve Woody's farmhouse.

By contrast with what Charlton Ogburn calls the Temperate Zone Tropics, the ridges of massifs over 6,000 feet high, such as Mt. Sterling present a peculiarly Canadian appearance, clothed as they are in prickly evergreen firs alone.

VAL HART: "The vastness was overwhelming... In a few hours' climb horses carry their riders through sweet gums, (Mark says they were blackgums), umbrella magnolias, and shortleaf pines, common in our Southern coastal states; then upward under maples, oaks, and hemlocks familiar in more northerly states, and finally into the stands of red spruce, fir, and mountain ash atop the highest peaks."

Unfortunately, the beautiful Fraser fir which is rare and indigenous to this area, has very largely succumbed to the attacks of the wooly Aphid, but not the red spruce. The Fraser fir has traditionally dominated the mountain slopes of the central and eastern half of the Great Smoky Mountains from their crests down to altitudes of 5,000 feet only. Where only a few years ago were massive stands along Mt. Sterling Ridge, there is very little except grey skeletons.

However, there is still a lusty nursery of tiny Fraser fir and spruce seedlings along with beds of pink turtleheads growing under ghostly giants of the racked species, still redolent of the resinous needles from which the ever popular balsam pillows of Victorian parlors were made.

Once the Eastern white pine made up 40% of the ridges of the Cataloochee district. There are still many magnificent sentinel pines standing, but they seem to be isolated rather than in great stands except where the CCC boys planted them in soldierly rows. These thick-massed pines are their tidy efforts at reforestation after the Park took over. However, they represent man's systematic, but not very aesthetic attempt at reclaiming the forest from the old fields.

At other locations, the pinebark beetle has taken a bit of a toll with the white pine.

All but one known specimen of the Allegheny Chinkapin at Mt. Sterling on the Park's northeastern boundary have been destroyed by the chestnut bark disease. The imperturbable Mark Hannah, however, views this decimation of the forests in a detached manner. Quite philosophically, he considers these fluctuations of disease and destruction as natural happenings which occur periodically in the scheme of things, just as human populations were decimated by the Black Death in the Middle Ages and by the Great Influenza Epidemic after World War I. Yet we now have a population explosion!

Though experts are less optimistic than he is, Mark claims the chestnuts are "coming back", and that he has even picked chestnuts from three year old trees. This unflappability is what made Mark one of the great park rangers, combined with his truly steadfast love of the forest.

MARK HANNAH: "Getting (the people) out, I think it was one of the great things the Park did, getting them out of there. And, of course, to protect that fine virgin timber. That was wonderful. I always enjoyed them most of anything. I knew that I was protecting one of the best forests in the United States, right in Cataloochee."

Possibly one of the first forest rangers and game wardens in nearly any North American forest was 'Fayt Palmer, who, in 1894, was made custodian and controller of the waters of Cataloochee Creek, representing the Love Speculation Lands. His job also was to prevent trespassing and cutting of timber.

Lafayette Palmer knew all of Cataloochee's forests. He knew the wild, steep Caldwell Fork area with its romantic air, engendered by the moisture and mist about the cloudy ravines which are filled with rhododendrons of Himalayan proportions, higher than cabins and with twisted, tangled rooms twice as intricate. Bears hide here. And many a dog or human being has become lost while crossing and recrossing Caldwell Fork as the path turns and zig-zags once again. Here, too, is the Big Poplar, in a forest so dim and dense in its upper story with vintage trees that one reins in the stumbling horse from that inexorable headlong path long enough to ruminate on how many horses and men it took to girdle that one tree. Raymond Caldwell's brother has a photograph of men holding their horses' tails and manes as they surround the Big Poplar.

DR. DORIS HAMMETT: "... after passing through... (Double Gap Branch), the trail begins to climb and is known thereafter as the Big Poplar Trail.... An unmarked trail (off the Caldwell Fork Trail) leads downhill to the right into a heavily wooded area along a small creek. At 300 yards down this side trail grows the largest of three yellow poplar trees, which has given this section of the trail its name. It takes seven men with arms outstretched to encircle this tree at its base. In 1968 a vandal cut his initials on the far side of the tree at six feet above the ground, and it bled throughout that summer. The scar is healing, but it can still be seen."

The thing that strikes the casual visitor is the remarkable variety, more than anything else. There is no one typical woodland, though tall hemlocks and giant rhododendrons with a groundcover of wood sorrel and partridgeberry spring to mind when one thinks of deepest, darkest, most inaccessible Cataloochee. Mark says the most typical of these hemlock forests are above Uncle Steve Woody's house on Rough Fork, also the forests along Messer Creek and Dude Creek. But a 15-foot circumference hemlock was recorded at 5,700 feet on Mt. Sterling Ridge. The cove hardwoods, which include beech, oak, ash and poplar join the hemlocks just above the Steve Woody place, and are also quite spectacular by the new Cataloochee Road, also along Dude Creek in Little Cataloochee, and in Poplar Cove, just below Coggins Branch. American sycamores are common along streams in low altitudes.

Typical of the heath balds are the Hiram Yellow Patch and the Mack Yellow Patch at Mt. Sterling Gap. There was also another between Wolf Creek and George Ira Creek on the head of Rough Fork, to the east of Spruce Mountain. It can be seen from the trail on the northwest side of Spruce Mountain. These were called "yaller patches", "woolyheads" or "slicks" because the rhododendron and laurel comprising them turned yellow in the early fall, dropping some of their leaves, even though they are known as evergreens. Beartraps were often set on these heath balds.

The grassy balds are found at Ledge Bald, above Pin Oak Gap, though it is fast growing up now, and on Mt. Sterling, comprised of the Indian old fields locally called the "Nigh Field" and the "Fur Field", and on Hemphill Bald, which was cleared, however, in fairly recent times, as were The Purchase and The Swag fields along The Cataloochee Divide. The Alleghany Serviceberry, or "sarvis" is the most common deciduous tree on the balds.

The best northern hardwood forests can be found above the Turkey George Place, with prime stands of yellow birch on the Northwest slope around The Purchase on the Divide. When the spruce is burned, as it was at Poll's Gap towards Heintooga and on the backside of Mt. Sterling, blackberries, fire cherry, and yellow birch come in their place. When the yellow birch dies, then the spruce comes up again. So much for Mark's equanimity. The black walnut grows at the highest altitude. It is known to occur at approximately 3,850 feet on the old J. M. Conard place in Cataloochee.

Closed oak forests may be found on any Southern slope in Cataloochee. The greater part are Northern red oaks and chestnut oaks, as are found on the little ribs of Southern slopes. There is a huge white oak above Steve Woody's house. One can hardly see its leaves, even with binoculars, because the branches begin so high up. A very good example of these forests can be seen from Cataloochee bridge to Sterling Gap on old Highway 284 clear up to High Top (Scottish Mountain). The South side of Bunk Mountain provides the same forest. A good showing of Northern red oaks may be seen on the side of Indian Knob, and on the trails to both Mt. Sterling and the Caldwell Forest. Northern Red Oaks, not Pin Oaks, abound at Pin Oak Gap. The leaves stay on them longer than any other oak in the area, although their acorns are quite small.

Noland Mountain, above the Preacher Hall Place, presents a good example of open oak and pine stands. Here the white pines give way to pitch pines, pin oaks, and blueberries.

Though the wooly aphid has killed nearly 90% of the Fraser fir right up to the tower at Mt. Sterling, there is still a fair example of the spruce-fir forest below Birch Bear Pen, which was built by Tom Barnes, about one and a half miles from Mt. Sterling, on Sterling Ridge, over to Spruce Mountain, on all the high peaks, including Cataloochee Balsam.

Another man who, like Allen Davidson and Mark Hannah, spoke unashamedly of the forest's beauty was old Tom Alexander who had once run a ranch in Cataloochee before the Park ran him out. Back on Fie Top, he had planted so many species of evergreens about his Japanese-style house that in his old age he slept in a soft cocoon of firs and pines and spruces which murmured to him like the waves of the Inland Sea on breezy nights.

Shortly before he died, Tom talked at length about the Cataloochee forests and his youthful stints as forest ranger and timber cruiser. His ranch house on Fie Top was a warm haven on a particularly snowy December day. "Bear Dog", the feist who was his faithful companion, lay on the sofa beside him, his grizzled head showing the recent scars of a horse's well-aimed kick. Old Tom held his own head carefully, too. He had had a series of strokes and moved gingerly as though his fragile life would crackle. His massive head, with its fine platinum hair and eyes the color of blue-eyed grass, faced the fire impassively.

He didn't seem to see or hear anyone as he stroked "Bear Dog" absently while his wife, "Miss Judy", made tea. At first she answered all questions which were directed towards him. Then his eyes began to flicker and come alive. Then, for two hours he looked into that other lost world of Cataloochee past — a world he had known during the Depression years — and talked without ceasing, of the trees, of the frozen rivers, and of the fires that destroyed some of the finest forest.

He ended abruptly, looking at the interviewer piercingly. Then his mind seemed to fade away. He died a short month later, from a final stroke which left him violent and incoherent, calling out fitfully, remembering fragments of an earlier time and the mighty forests that had been his life.

When Tom Alexander was a young man, the fine virgin forests of Cataloochee were beginning to be very much coveted by big timber barons. Until then, very little had threatened this magnificent isolation. Little by little, however, logging companies ringed the area.

Crestmont, operated by Champion Lumber Company, almost penetrated Cataloochee at Pretty Hollow Gap. The only advantage was its famous logging railroad over in Big Creek, which enabled Cataloochans to catch an occasional emergency ride and to ship apples and other produce from Mt. Sterling into Newport, Tennessee.

PROFESSOR JOSEPH HALL: "The Cataloochee Company was the name of one of the timber operations connected with Crestmont, which was really in the Big Creek section. Fortunately for the valley, it went broke at Mouse Creek before it ever reached Cataloochee."

DR. ROBERT HILLIARD WOODY: "Champion Lumber Company had their operation behind The Balsam, we called it — Mt. Sterling, the principal mountain — we used to go there for picnics. The lumber company carried the stuff down to Big Creek where it was dumped into a tremendous pond and held until they sent it into the mill. They built their own railroads up in the mountains, you see. But some of those railroads came up very nearly to the top of The Balsam, and the logging came practically to the top."

"Now they brought in a lot of Italians. These Italians would set up their own logging camp, and they were quite sociable and friendly. Some of them used to come over to Uncle 'Tine's...'"

"I remember being at Crestmont which is (was) the little railroad station up above Big Creek. I had a distant relative (Arthur Ford) by marriage who was the station agent. I was there once in the summertime when the train came up from Newport. But, of course, they took up those tracks about 1928. The train came up, and there was a colored boy on the train selling things — some kind of ice cream affair. And the people flocked around... not because they were interested in the ice cream, but to see this boy. He was a curiosity. Some of these people had never seen a colored man before."

"The last time I rode out, they had done away with the passenger coach so I rode out on the freight car, sitting on some freight. Then once we rode out, maybe a year or two before 1928, on a kind of bus that they had put railway wheels on."

After Cataloochee was designated as a Park in 1927–28, The North Carolina Park Commission began buying land by about 1930. One of its first actions was to shut down the Suncrest and Ravensford Lumber Companies by court injunctions before they encroached on Cataloochee territory.

The Ravensford Company had a cabin at the Ledge, and its railroad ran from Round Bottom, near Big Cove on the other side of the Balsams, to Pin Oak Gap to Ledge Bald, just skirting the Big Cataloochee area. Lumbering never got as far as Poll's Gap which still has some virgin timber though a railroad was once built through there at 5,110 feet.

ELDRIDGE CALDWELL: "The grade and the railroad went out to what we call Pin Oak Gap, to The Ledge Mountain out there. They got a building there. They was families lived all along in there y'know, in shanty cars, we called 'em. Loggers. The men logged and the women kept house... seemed like they enjoyed it..."

PEARL CALDWELL: "They always made good money, and you could see 'em all dressed up and leave out for the weekend."

Jarvis Caldwell recollected how Ravensford Lumber Company had come out from Smokemount with its railroad through Pin Oak Gap to Little Cataloochee and Indian Knob through Poll's Gap at 5,110 feet above Steve Woody's. He said the band mill was where the new shopping center is in Waynesville.

'TINE BENNETT: "We had a place over there (in Little Cataloochee) we called The Indian Knob, too (just northwest of Short Bunk Mountain). (Ravensford) got over there. They got across the mountain gettin' the balsam timber out of there, and they (The Park Commission) stopped 'em. They was right on the head of Big Catalooch'. They just got started. I think they had a skidder over there at the time. And they pulled the logs from down on the Catalooch' side up the railroad and loaded 'em. But they didn't get very much of it. I think they had the railroad round The Indian Knob, am I right?"

MARK HANNAH: "Yes, round on the East side of Indian Knob."

'TINE BENNETT: "Ravensford Lumber Company just got across, we call it The Ledge Mountain, and the balsam timber come down so fur on the Catalooch' side."

MARK HANNAH: "Suncrest was hiring local Cataloochee folk. Suncrest Lumber Company went up Maggie Valley and through Poll's Gap into Cataloochee above the Steve Woody Place. Also, this company had a survey through Caldwell Fork and the virgin forest to Cove Creek Gap when the Park stopped them. The band mill was in the area of the shopping center of Waynesville."

"Ravensford Lumber Company came up the river via Round Bottom to Pin Oak Gap and then through the head of Big Cataloochee and into Little Cataloochee at Low Gap of Indian Ridge to the J. M. Conard Place."

'TINE BENNETT: "All of it was done with axe and crosscut saw, too. Didn't know what a power saw was at that time."

Now that the logging brouhaha has subsided, the Forestry Service has made a survey for the Tennessee Valley Authority, marking superior trees in the Cataloochee area for use as seedling trees. "Dr. Doris" verified these marked trees recently by personally searching for each one. William B. Buckley, the staff forester for the TVA work wrote in 1971:

"Seedlings and grafts from these trees are currently being used in our hardwood improvement program, aimed at the ultimate production of a better grade of hardwood seedlings for valley landowners. These genetically improved seedlings will eventually produce more timber faster than the seedlings in current use, and hopefully reduce somewhat the pressures of increasing wood demands on our diminishing forest base."

Aside from reducing the pressures, the idea of perpetuating Cataloochee's splendid forests in other parts of the country is an intriguing one. Genetically controlled! Test tube babies out of Cataloochee! Little bits of Cataloochee everywhere. Nothing lost.

Not everything growing in Cataloochee is wild. There are still some domestic plants which survive the former efforts of the Park Service to eradicate all indications of civilization. Sometimes all that remains of the traces of the old pioneers is a few straggly conical cedars, some old purpled climbing roses on a rotting rail fence, a mat of periwinkle, a clump of daylilies, scattered boxwoods, or stark, prickly Spanish bayonets. Balm-of-Gilead trees, used by Eldridge's mother for medicinal purposes, can still be found near the old Kerr Place in Catalooch'.

Remnants of the apple orchards which were introduced into Cataloochee can still be seen. Hiram Wilburn said that the apple tree on the old John Jackson Hannah place in Little Cataloochee was the largest ever recorded. It was 30 inches in diameter, growing at an altitude of 3,150 feet. By 1948 this tree, by then only a shell, still had a few living branches.

But the best thing about Cataloochee, so the surveyor, Tom Porter, said, was the smell... the ineffable smell of the greenery, the damp earth, the black dirt, the rank but exotic smell of galax, the rhododendron, the rotting verdure that left such a rich treasury behind for the plants to come. Perhaps, if old Tom Alexander couldn't see at the end, he could at least smell, or remember that smell of the forests and flowers of Cataloochee.

CHAPTER 26

Klandaghi and Other Lords
(Fauna)

Timber rattlesnakes, *Crotalus horridus*, were very common in Cataloochee.
You were smart to watch your step as you walked in the roads or in the woods,
and especially playing in and around the old barns and chicken coops.
Courtesy Great Smoky Mountains National Park Archives.

THE SHADOWY MEMORIES of birds and beasts now extinct in Cataloochee keep good company with the burned cabins, the forgotten ballads, the lost crafts, and the ghosts of Indian chiefs.

Among the non-survivors of the valley was the shaggy eastern mountain or woods buffalo, never very prolific here, in any case as, being herbivorous, it preferred grassy rangelands rich in peavine. These early buffaloes, like the Indians themselves, supposedly came to North America between 200,000 and 800,000 years ago on the land mass which then connected Asia with Alaska. By 1000 A.D. there was a type called the Pennsylvania Bison which might have frequented the Appalachian mountains.

Although it is known that buffalo trails once crossed the North Carolina mountains into Tennessee at several strategic passes, some say that there was a virtual extermination of the bison in the Appalachians by 1769 partly by the Cherokees, partly by the long hunters.

"At first buffalo were so plenty that a party of three or four men with dogs could kill from ten to twenty a day; but soon the sluggish animals receded before the advance of the white men, hiding themselves behind the mountain walls," so said Thwaites in his biography of Daniel Boone, recalling the year 1769.

Certainly by 1815, these early trailblazers had not only completely disappeared from Cataloochee but also from the area east of the Appalachians where the last buffalo was killed at Buffalo Gap near Asheville, nearly fifty miles east of Cataloochee.

Where then, did the early doctors who rode into Cataloochee get the buffalo hides which kept them from freezing on bitter wintry nighttime rides?

In the year 1976, in Haywood County, there was a totally unexpected buffalo stampede. The animals had escaped from a wild life preserve not too far from Cataloochee. They roamed freely about a local golf course, terrorizing the golfers. The sheriff got up a posse which quickly commandeered some golf carts. They took off like the Keystone cops over the greens with tranquillizing guns… The startled populace rubbed their eyes in disbelief as buffaloes charged through the breezeways of suburbia. Some of the animals had to be killed because they tried to demolish the sheriff's car. Others finally succumbed to tranquillizer shots after two hours or more and were rounded up. Two totally escaped that first posse. Of these two, one was seen heading for wild Smokies country by a flabbergasted motorist driving in from Cincinnati. And the other was finally captured a few weeks later near Utah Mountain, a very short distance from the Cataloochee Divide. With some luck, he might have made it back to a wilderness that his glorious ancestors once knew.

Not so very long ago the elk, the panther, the fisher, the wolf and the river otter, as well as the beaver were safely dwelling with the buffalo among the high meadows, the coves and crags of Cataloochee, and by the swift streams that roared over boulders. Darting among the trees was once the passenger pigeon, too, in droves so huge they darkened the sky. The ivory-billed woodpecker, beloved by the early 19th century Scots ornithologist, Alexander Wilson, was once seen in great numbers, as was the beautiful green Carolina parakeet in the warmest part of the year.

Now all but one of that number are extinct, having been trapped or shot out of existence. And that is the Eastern panther (*Puma concolor cougar*) or, as the Cherokees reverently call him, Klandaghi, Lord of the Forest. No longer is Klandaghi considered extinct though the buffalo had completely disappeared from the surroundings by 1815, with the elk following soon after. The river otter, known locally as an "orter", held sway in Cataloochee until the last sighting in 1927.

HAROLD HANNAH (Mark's son): "A thing that used to hold us kids spellbound were the stories that Mom and Dad and others would tell about the thrills of the old days. Stories about hunting, hants, headless people, wolves, tragedies, and worst of all the panther. The tales of the big cat always made my hair stand on end. I always dreaded the day I would come face-to-face with one, or worse yet, have one leap on my back from the road bank or a tree limb. It was a fear I didn't conquer until I was about fourteen years old. I still believe there are cougars in those mountains."

There have been several rumored sightings of the panther in recent years. The late Glen Messer, of Hemphill Valley, swore that, a mere twenty-five years ago, he ran into a panther at Pin Oak Gap in Catalooch' territory... not once, but several times while on pack trips out of Cataloochee Ranch.

Then, in August of 1975, park employees working in Cataloochee Valley claimed they saw a panther chasing a deer across a meadow at dusk. They later checked and found its tracks in the mud at the edge of the clearing. A local newspaper wrote their story.

WAYNESVILLE MOUNTAINEER (Jack Horan): "Dusk was settling in the coves and hollows of the Great Smoky Mountains National Park in Western North Carolina last July 23 (1975) as five park maintenance workers sat smoking on their bunkhouse porch. The men amused themselves by watching three deer frolic 50 yards away on a gravel road that ran through the hardwood forest of the park's Cataloochee section."

"Suddenly the men noticed the deer's easy play turn to apprehension. 'Two of the deer,' recalled Emmitt Wiggins, a 54 year-old pipefitter from Bryson City, 'started running away and looking backward.' Seconds later a grayish animal the men described as a cat with a long tail sprang from the trees, bounded across the road in one leap and vanished in the forest in apparent pursuit of the deer."

"Wiggins and another workman, Walter Laws, 41, of Bryson City, said the men concluded that the five-foot-long animal was a... panther... Both men agreed the animal definitely was neither a dog, nor a bobcat, which has a stubby tail. 'I've seen a lot of bobcat,' Wiggins said. 'It wasn't even similar to a bobcat.'"

"Gilbert Calhoun, then acting park superintendent, reviewed the workmen's report on the animal and said the sighting was the first substantial account indicating cougars, thought to have been extinct in the Park for fifty-five years, may once again roam the Smokies."

Panther stories of old are still rife in these mountains. Panther Spring Gap, along the Cataloochee Divide, was so named because of a young girl who was dragged, screaming, into Cataloochee by panthers. That is possibly the earliest known panther story of this region, as that side of the mountain was settled earlier than Cataloochee Valley.

Two of the earliest pioneer women, Mrs. Bennett and Mrs. Caldwell, were harrassed by panthers the very first year of their settlement in Cataloochee. These animals must have been quite a scourge in the 1840s, for Allen Davidson's wife, Adeline Howell, in her old age, would recall for her grandchildren the terror of hearing panthers scream around her Jonathan's Creek home, just over the ridge from

Catalooch', on nights when Allen had left her alone while he studied law in Waynesville. She remembered, too, a panther in the moonlight which sprang onto the rump of the horse she was riding, sending it galloping wildly home with its terrified rider clinging to its back.

No wonder that Cataloochans feared Klandaghi so. His call alone was enough to freeze the blood, according to the author of *Discovering the Appalachians*.

THOMAS CONNALLY: "From the Catskills to the Rocky Mountains, the panther's scream has terrified men. This weird sound has been variously described as resembling the cry of a child in pain, the scream of a woman in distress, the growl of a lion, the screech of a parrot, or the hysterical laughter of an insane person."

Floyd Woody is fond of telling the following story, with variations, according to his audience. The "Granny Pop" referred to was his grandmother, Mary Nailon Caldwell Woody.

FLOYD WOODY: "Yeah, well... Granny Pop was visitin' on Little Catalooch', and she'us started back home to Big Catalooch'. And, up on the mountain at Davidson Gap, why, she saw a pant'er settin' up on a tree, gonna jump on 'er when she come under the tree. She saw it and got around it and got into the trail a'gin. And the pant'er got after her. She'd been told to leave part of her clothes at a time, not all of 'em, and she commenced to sheddin' her apron off. And then she went on to give that pant'er time to tear that up. Right in 'bout time she thought it was gonna overtake, she'd pull another part of her clothes off and leave them. And he'd tear that up. When she got home to the Uncle Hiram place, why she didn't have much on (sometimes, his eyes popping wickedly, Floyd will suggest that she came in like Lady Godiva, without a stitch!). And the pant'er got away. Yeah, he ran 'er in home there! And that saved her life, was leavin' her clothes."

"Back then they were a lot of home made stuff, was strong sort of like jeans and stuff like 'at that they couldn't tear up. It took stren'th to do it. And it delayed the pant'er. All the ole people got together, you could hear 'em talk about it... there was a great talk in the community about that pant'er gettin' after Granny Pop and runnin' her from Little Catalooch' to the Uncle Hiram (old) house. She lived there with her son after he (Levi Caldwell, her first husband and one of the first settlers) died."

No wonder children such as Harold Hannah had nightmares if their parents related stories like the following:

MARK HANNAH: "When Old Man Wiley Caldwell was a little boy about six years old at the time... I'm not for sure who his father was, seems to me he said Elsey (the one who got shot in the Civil War)... he lived near the William A. Palmer Place. The cabin sat there, very close to the old Nellie sign, the old post office is where he told me it was. He said he was there early one morning. And a panther got on the roof. The roof didn't have nails in it then, just boards (rived shingles) layin' up there, heavy weights on it. And said that panther got up on top of that house and was tryin' to tear in. His mother was screamin' for help. Old Man Dock Bennett was somewhere nearby and heard it, and he ran to the house and got close enough to shoot the panther off the roof of the house and killed him."

For better or worse, the panther seems to have returned, though the settlers themselves are now extinct! Soon even the wolves may roam again in Cataloochee. The Endangered Species Act of 1973 has authorized the reestablishment of the eastern timber wolf with the Great Smoky Mountains National Park as one of the six target areas. The former Superintendent, Boyd Evison, thought that wolves would do well back in the Park because they would have plenty of deer and wild boar to feed on. The exotic Russian wild boar, not indigenous to the Smokies at all, but an escapee from a wild game preserve near Santeetlah at Hooper's Bald, has now proliferated out of all reason in the Park.

Wolves used to be a terrible scourge in Cataloochee. Bounties were given by the state for wolf heads. Jonathan Woody, II, said that his father, Steve Woody, rode all the way to the state capital at Raleigh as a boy, with Jonathan's grandfather, the old settler, the first Jonathan Woody, and 'Fayt Palmer, who was destined to become Steve's father-in-law. The bounty on wolves at that time was high...$20 a head. 'Fayt had killed a female wolf and all her whelps, which fetched him the princely sum of $160. With the bounty money, he was able to buy 125 acres of the Love Speculation Lands at $1.00 an acre.

This reminded the present Jonathan of a story that had often been recounted in Cataloochee, told earlier by Colonel Bryan in his *Primitive History of the Mountain Region*, about the Lewis family of Western North Carolina in 1794.

COLONEL W.L. BRYAN: "Gideon Lewis and his family were great hunters; but his sons, Gideon and Nathan, were for years the great wolf hunters of Ashe County. They would follow the gaunt female to her den, and while one waited outside, the other brother crawled in and secured the pups, from six to ten in each litter, but allowing the mother to escape. The young were then skalped, the skalp of a young wolf being paid for the same as that of the mature animal. For each skalp the county paid $2.50. When asked why he never killed grown wolves, Gideon Lewis answered, 'Would you expect a man to kill his milch cow?'"

Old Man Messer outwitted wolves once when he was late returning from a hunting expedition and had to sleep in the open. He sat inside the classic ring of fire to keep the wolves at bay.

Catalooch' wolves were great predators in their day. No wonder there was a bounty on them. They almost plagued Turkey George to death until he decided to do something drastic about it.

TURKEY GEORGE PALMER: "They used to be wolves in these mountains. They came right down in the settlement and killed sheep. Like fox, they're too smart to be trapped, so I went to poisonin' them with strychnine. I put poisoned sheep meat in bushel baskets an' took 'em back in the mountains. I went back sometime later an' found two dead wolves."

There is seldom anything as dramatic for the horseman as meeting a big bear plunging down the wild steep virgin slopes of the Caldwell Fork area. He would have to rein in his horse as the poor beast snorted in terror, prancing sideways up the slope. Gradually the shiny green canopy of rhododendron leaves would stop shaking crazily as the bear crashed like a Juggernaut down and through to the creek... ungainly as he may look, he can outrun a horse. A Juggernaut god... along with the silently moving Klandaghi, the panther... all lords of the forest.

Because of such mighty hunters as Uncle Turkey, as well as poachers in later years, and because of the terrible chestnut blight which took away mast from starving animals, there were, as of 1978, estimated to be no more than three hundred bears left in the Park.

MARK HANNAH:" When bears can't find anything else, they will go down to lower ground and leave. I don't know how many hundred miles they'll go... just till they find some food. I remember very distinctly when we didn't have any food over there in the fall of 1946. There just wasn't any acorns, no grapes, nothin' for the bear to eat. And they had to come out. People just slaughtered them out in their fields nearby, found them in their cow pastures sometimes. One bear was killed in Waynesville inside the Incorporation, one in Canton, and one in Asheville, huntin' for food."

In the early 1940s, Tom Alexander over on Fie Top out of the Park won a celebrated case after setting bear traps just inside the Park to catch a culprit bear who had been killing the fine cattle on his ranch which adjoined the Park. His peers judged him blameless, and *The Saturday Evening Post* wrote up the sensational jury trial.

It's hard to guess just how many bears now remain in Cataloochee. They often loiter near the garbage cans and the campgrounds, which spoils them for foraging for their own food.

Mark was asked how to ward off aggressive bears while hiking or camping in Catalooch'. He proposed the classic remedies of hanging your food high on a rope between 2 trees, keeping a campfire going, beating on a tin pan to scare the bear away, and keeping food and cooking away from the camping and sleeping areas. Then he mentioned his personal theory that spraying liberal amounts of household ammonia around garbage cans will make any bear hold his nose and detour. Apparently they can't abide the smell!

Maybe because Ned McFalls was felling bucks and does all over the place with his trusty Gillespie rifle in the old Catalooch' of the early nineteenth century, Virginia deer became scarce there by 1855 and did not multiply until later. Mark said nearly all the deer had left when his father was a boy. By 1931, the U. S. Government actually had to restock Cataloochee with Virginia deer, though this had once been the staple food and clothing of the early Cherokee hunters.

In the fall of 1973, a fine herd of them came down by the side of Cataloochee Creek at the old bridge in the late afternoon sun. Light dappled their coats, camouflaging them from the casual eye. Even when one knows they're there, they are too elusive to be seen.

They seem to like the old settlers' fields, and it was near here that the panther was seen chasing deer in 1975. Deer tracks could often be seen, too, in Little Cataloochee inside the old John Jackson Hannah cabin on the dirt floor after the boards were taken up. Now the cabin has been restored, and the door is shut against the raccoons and deer who were "usin'" there. On the trail from Mt. Sterling Gap to the fire tower, deer tracks were seen in 1976 along with panther-like tracks, as if in hot pursuit. Mark Hannah thought that deer now went often to the Latham Hole in Cataloochee Creek to drink, below the old Kerr Place, where Bill Latham of Newport once had a camp.

MARK HANNAH: "Deer Lick Gap is on the Rough Ridge, one half mile north of the 'Tine Woody farm in the Little Cataloochee area. The first cattle herders used to salt their cattle on some maple roots, and deer would lick there, too. I guess the Davidsons and McFalls may have started this lick."

Turkey George's diary, now unfortunately lost, recorded twenty deer that he killed during his most active period as a hunter. Once the usually benign deer turned the tables on him, much as the turkeys had nearly done him in. In this instance, he and his brother, Will Palmer, were at a stand waiting for deer when a big buck ran up, jumped over his brother's head and, as he turned to get away, struck Turkey George with his buttocks and knocked him down, vanishing in the forest. The story goes that this was "the only time George acknowledged defeat at the heels of a deer."

One night at the Turkey George campground on Pretty Hollow Creek, a pack trip party slept under tarps. In the morning, one horsewoman complained bitterly that so many tiny shrews had run over her in the night she could hardly sleep.

MARIELLA DUMONT: "I imagined that one actually crept up on my eyelid, pulled it open and peered in my eye!"

If the bear is the largest mammal in Cataloochee, then the shrew, in its many varieties, is the smallest and probably the most numerous of the mammals there.

The panther and bear may have shared the supremacy as the great lords of the mammal kingdom of Cataloochee, with the fleet deer as their couriers and the wild boar as their generals, but the wily underlords were surely the fox, the raccoon, and the bobcat, while the myriad tiny shrews, bats, moles, two kinds of skunks, four kinds of squirrels, chipmunks, groundhogs, mice, slow opposums, and fearful rabbits were their subjects.

Allen Davidson's Scottish ancestors of the Clan Chattan up on the Firth of Moray, emblazoned the wary mountain wildcat on their heraldic designs, fiercely proclaiming their motto: "Touch Not the Cat without the Glove." With that as his emblem, no wonder Allen felt at home hunting and herding in Cataloochee. But Major Woody had no respect for these spitting animals with their wild cries which he called the "wust, sorriest things they is". He told Joe Hall that he used to kill them by "breaking them down", that is, by breaking their backs, saying, "I kilt five that-a-way."

Major Woody, Uncle Steve's nephew, and son of Jack, was a great source of hunting tales, some that he told, and some that were told about him. Major was his given name and not a military title. In fact his looks and bearing quite belied the name "Major" because he had been a cripple since his early days when, according to various accounts, he had either had polio or caught his foot in a threshing machine. In any case, one foot was so grotesquely deformed that he wore two rightfoot shoes.

PROFESSOR JOSEPH S. HALL: "... he presented an odd appearance in his bedraggled, worn-out clothes and his broken-down shoes... Even to his dying day he wore his right shoe on his left foot, a circumstance which gave an effect at once odd and pathetic."

"Although he was a born hunter, his lameness prevented him from taking part in the arduous exertions of bearhunting which ordinarily required the combined labors of several men. He could not keep up with them on their drives over rough country."

MAJOR WOODY (talking to Joe Hall): "... There's more real sport in coonhunting (than in bearhunting). Hit takes only one man to coonhunt, but when ye bear hunt ye've got to have a passel of men, some for the stands and some for the drive. When you tree a coon, you've got him, 'n there's a heap more hard work, 'n slavish runnin' and trampin' in bear huntin' than there is in coon huntin'."

Indirectly, however, Major was probably responsible for the demise of several bears. He was, after all, quite a craftsman and could make almost anything that took to a soldering iron.

MARK HANNAH: "Major Woody was good at making home-made bear traps from car springs."

PROFESSOR JOSEPH S. HALL: "Major Woody once saw three raccoons enter a hollow log. He crawled in after them and shone his light into their eyes as he prepared to shoot them."

MAJOR WOODY: "They made for me, and I twisted a right smart bit to keep them from biting me. Then two went out t'other side, and I mashed the third one to death. Jonathan Woody got one, and the dog t'other. The oil from coons is wuth more than lard and has 'most the same taste."

RAYMOND CALDWELL: "I, as a young chap, went possum hunting with (Major), and he always kept some good coon dogs."

Old Turkey George Palmer was a gentler soul than Major, in some respects. He used to keep pet coons for several years. Apparently he worked out all his violent feelings on bear alone!

A noble portrait of Mack Hannah, another great bear hunter, was taken when he was an old man. It shows him as a benign, long-bearded patriarch, now white-haired, seated on the ground with the limp body of a fine fat coon in his lap, and all the accoutrements of the hunter scattered about him... a hunting horn and his favorite dog, "Old Moove".

MARK HANNAH: "My father, Mack Hannah, one crisp fall morning decided he and Old Moove, his great coon dog, would go down to the Poplar Cove and hunt for a coon. They travelled via the Big Hill to the mouth of Dude Creek. There the dog found a real hot coon track. He chased the coon into a den along the creek bank. Dad threw out several loose rocks and made way for the dog to get into the rock cliff. There was a little crack in that cave that Dad could see the coon (through), but the dog could not get any closer for the rocks. As usual, he had his .38 pistol in his pocket, and he crawled into the den, making the dog stay outside. With a small little stick, he punched the coon."

MACK HANNAH (as Mark recalled history): "Good gosh, that coon came at my face like I've never seen a coon move. I slapped at him, and he caught one finger. I slapped with the other hand. He caught another finger, and I changed hands again, and a new finger went into his mouth. This was all so fast that I didn't have time to get my pistol. That coon was trying to bite me in the face. This lasted until every finger was bitten and I was bloody as a stuck hog. Finally that coon shet down on my thumb, and I got him round the neck and choked him to death. I kept my knee and weight on his body. Old Moove was very disappointed because he could not get to assist."

MARK HANNAH: "Dad came home that morning about 9:30 A.M. bleeding. Out of the ten fingers, only one was unbitten. I remember the word he said. He said, 'I shet its wind off!' He had a .38 Smith and Weston (Wesson) short. I have it yit."

'TINE BENNETT: "It broke down like that. What ever become of that gun?"

MARK HANNAH: "I've got it yit. He gave it to me."

'TINE: "Well, you've got it?"

MARK: "I've got it yit."

'TINE: "Well, first time I'm at your house, I want to see it. I had it in my hand, I don't know, lots of times. I just hunted... me and Major Woody. Major used to stay at Uncle 'Tine's, y'know. He had a little black hound called Ole Muse. And me and Major'd go possum huntin' and take us a sack. And Major Woody would take a groundhog string, and we'd cut holes in the possum's lips here and tie a string through his lip... and come in with 'em. A live possum, yeah. Oh, I've seen him tie a many a one down."

Though fox hunting was a sport of the Cataloochee men, it was not the elegant blood sport that reigns supreme in England or in fashionable Virginia. Hounds were used in the mountains, but no horses were employed, and no hunter would be caught dead in the traditional pink coat. Indeed, the very term, fox-hunting, is an ambiguous one; the correct one is fox-chasing, for there is rarely a kill at the end of it. The men who own the fox hounds or fox dogs, love merely to hear their dogs' musical voices, like the horn of Roland, baying up and down the coves as the men sit yarning around an open fire, often passing a jar of white liquor among themselves to ward off the cold and damp of a night.

One often hears the foxes themselves barking in the night up near the Cataloochee Divide. There's nothing quite like "the lonesome bark of a fox on the prowl", wrote Harold Hannah. And once in awhile, a fox with a big brushy tail will whisk across the path of one's car so swiftly that he seems an apparition. Once a fox tarries, he is assumed to be rabid and is avoided assiduously. That the fox, grey or red, was an underlord of Cataloochee, one has no doubt, for did not Turkey George himself say that foxes were too smart to be trapped?

Uncle Turkey apparently had his gunsight on everything that moved, including squirrels, according to his son Robert.

ROBERT PALMER (as told to John Parris): "He was a mighty fine shot. As I say, he never wasted much lead or powder... One time he was out hunting and killed nine squirrels without missing a shot. He shot off the heads of six of them, and drew no blood from the other three."

One old mountain man who knew the paths of Cataloochee like the life-line in his palm, loved the taste of squirrel so much that he maintained, "If I lay a-dyin', I'd raise up fer squirrel soup!" He recently died, just before setting out on a final squirrel hunt. A member of the family, sitting up with the corpse, half-laughingly proposed that they make a plate of squirrel soup to see what the old man would do.

He surely loved hunting the tantalizing little animals that chattered at him from tree to tree. There are four types of squirrels in the valley; grey, fox, red, also called the Boomer, and the flying squirrel, one of which spread-eagled on a screen door so hard in the middle of a night that both a dog and its owner jumped plumb out of their warm beds in fright.

Shooting chipmunks, or ground squirrels, as they are called here, was a common sport for the younger boys of Cataloochee. Even so, it was quite a feat, considering some of the weapons they had.

ROBERT HILLIARD WOODY: "The muzzle loader that I used was handmade except for the barrel. The barrel we found in somebody's house when they were remodeling. No telling how old it was. And this Vick Smith, who was quite a carpenter, made the whole stock and the triggers... It had two triggers.. and the whole apparatus. And along with it, I had a leather pouch that held the powder, bullets, and the bullet mold... I've made bullets out of the bullet mold. Just melt the lead and pour it into the mold, and knock it out, and then you have to cut the neck off to make it round. This gun was light. The big ones were real heavy. You could hardly hold them up without a rest. I've shot ground squirrels with it, sitting on a porch, seeing a ground squirrel run down the fence."

Harold Hannah, Mark 's son, wrote that he will always remember the mysterious sound of a purring or snoring animal underneath the house that turned out to be a skunk with little ones. Nobody shot skunks very often and even then, not unless they were a safe distance away. "Polecat John" Cagle, as his name implies, had a very bad experience with one once.

FLOYD WOODY: "He was called Polecat because it got all over 'im, the perfumes did. They thought he'd die. Come a hair a-killin' 'im. Got 'im hemmed in a smokehouse. It was at the front, and he couldn't get out over it."

Though it is true that skunk fumes, if sprayed directly into the eyes, can cause temporary blindness, it was startling to read recently in a book of Edwin Way Teale's, that eye specialists have actually used the spray as an aid to helping certain eye diseases!

Less odiferous would be a rabbit hunt in Cataloochee on Christmas Day, with a great yelping of feists, instead of the better-known sleigh bells.

Minks and weasels were killed as predators of the chickenyard. "Mink Henry" Grooms was so named because of his dark coloration, and not because a mink had attacked him, though they are known to be fierce when cornered. The Cataloochee mink did not turn white in winter, as its more northerly cousin might.

The groundhog, known locally as a "whistlepig", was eaten as a delicacy, particularly the very young fat ones, though one had to make sure that the proper underforeleg glands were removed before eating. Their skins were sometimes used for the drums of home-made banjos, or as shoe laces. One used to hear dire stories of the Great Depression when the folks had to live on groundhog meat. But that is no deterrent. It's as good as beef, if cooked properly. Hubert Burgess and his wife had a fat little groundhog for company to eat over at his house on Rabbitskin Road not long ago. They enjoyed every single morsel of it, with hardly room for the blackberry pie to follow. Hubert's ancestors came out of Catalooch', and had relished groundhog and blackberries many a time there, too.

Nowadays the golden eagle and the wild turkey, as well as the panther, are increasingly rare to absent, although Mike Frome, who wrote the fine book about the Smokies, *Strangers In High Places*, said that a golden eagle had been sighted in Cataloochee when he visited there in 1974 to protest the building of the major highway into the Valley. Prior to that there had been only two published sightings. A previous golden eagle was seen near Cataloochee, November 3, 1934. And prior to that, Mark had found one killing lambs and caught it in a trap about 1928-29, keeping it in a cage for two years. He said it was a beautiful bird, but, at the time, considered it a bird of prey and dangerous to livestock. The bald eagle has been seen in Cataloochee by Mark, also.

MARK HANNAH: "Assistant Chief Ranger, James B. Light, and I were on special patrol on lower Cataloochee Creek. We were walking up the manway under a dense cover of bushes when we heard something flying overhead. We stopped and there was a large Bald Eagle in the tree fifty or sixty feet above our heads. We both saw it, and it then moved swiftly away. Its head was covered with white feathers."

Six wild turkeys were seen as recently as 1973 at Pretty Hollow Gap, despite the lack of chestnuts since the great blight. The Palmers just about lived on turkey and bear meat, said Turkey George's son. The wild turkey is edible, but can be a little tough though tasty when compared with the soft butterball variety one picks up in the supermarkets these days. Everybody now knows how Turkey George got his name. Yet another story with a folktale quality is told on him.

RAYMOND CALDWELL: "Well, Uncle Turkey was out, and he had this old muzzle-loading gun, and he just had this one bullet. That's the last he had with him. And they was six turkeys, and he knew he had to have those six turkeys. He couldn't think of another way to do it, how he was gonna kill 'em all with that one bullet. They's settin' on a limb. He fired the shot, split the limb, their toes closed back over the limb, and he went and got the turkeys!" (Much laughter over this incredible story.)

Mark Hannah's predilection for tiny detail gives more of a ring of authenticity to his stories.

MARK HANNAH: "I was up on Little Cataloochee, and I saw a little turkey sign up on Long Bunk Mountain. So, I was makin' a little patrol up there, and I went back to the house and got my shotgun. Came back about two or three o'clock in the evenin'. And I couldn't hear a turkey anywhere. I hooted like an owl. Sometimes that'll make 'em gobble... hoot like a hoot owl. That's the way I first got him to gobble, by hooting. But when I came back the second time, there was nuthin' to be heard anywhur."

"I walked up the top along towards Hollow Maple Gap with my gun. And this big turkey jumped out of a hollow snaggy stump, about two or three feet high. But there was ashes in there where there had been a fire sometime. He was dustin' himself in those ashes, and he jumped out of there and started to run from me. And I got down on him with that twelve gauge pump-gun. And I got him."

"He jumped about four feet high and didn't anymore than hit the ground till I had him by the feet. He might have flew off anyway. I'd been trained to get 'em by the feet quick as you could. And he gave me a pretty good time there tryin' to get away."

"I carried him on home. And my father had a word he said: Lawsamighty. Said, 'Lawsamighty, child! That's the biggest turkey that I've ever seen!' Says, 'I've seen my part of 'em!' And that thing's beard measured 11 and 3/4 inches. I still have it at this time. And it was large. I also have the picture of it. It was the biggest turkey that

Daddy'd ever seen. And by far the biggest one I'd ever killed. So... we're all turkey hunters... and bear hunters, too, I guess, when we're raised up in the mountains. It's a pretty good occupation, and a lot of fun. Boy, that is fun!"

Grouse, known locally as pheasant, are also uncommonly good to eat. The hills still echo with their drumming and the sudden explosion of their flight. One nearly startled a hiker to death on the trail above Uncle Steve's place once as it flew out of a clump of ostrich fern by the remains of the old split-rail fencing. But the tenderest little morsels, the bobwhite or quail, though they have been seen at Caldwell Fork at 3,100 feet, are not as plentiful as they were in the '20s before the park took over.

In Cataloochee many a mountain woman took up a shotgun, though, in order to kill the predators which swooped over her henhouse. Hawks and owls preyed on her chickens so she hated them in return. And she knew that special "sound that a rooster makes when a hawk flies over", according to Harold Hannah.

Mark remembers the great horned owl as a particular enemy. One had been catching his chickens and flying away with them. Early one morning, as the owl sat on his barn, Mark's brother shot it. Mark, who was in bed at the time, recalled how he had been awakened by the sound of the owl's falling with a big thump onto the tin roof. Later he had it mounted so he could gaze upon the splendor of his adversary. One hears him often, the great horned owl, late in the night, calling in stentorian whoops across the Cataloochee Divide.

The screech owl, as well, was found at lower altitudes around the chicken yards, while the great barred owl sat amongst the high peaks in company with the peregrine falcon, a bird rather rare in Cataloochee. But, thanks to the former Park Naturalist Arthur Stupka's *Notes on the Birds of Great Smoky Mountains National Park*, we know a great deal about the actual sightings of birds in the Cataloochee area.

The common hawks were the sparrow hawk, Cooper's hawk, red-shouldered, red-tailed, sharp-shinned, and broad-winged. One sees the red-tailed most often along the air currents of the Divide. Both ravens and Cooper's hawks have been sighted at Pin Oak Gap.

Blackbirds, ravens, and crows were all considered crop destroyers. But turkey vultures, while predatory-looking, were actually carrion-eaters, thus were not shot. They are far from as prevalent today in Cataloochee as they were when large numbers of livestock grazed on the high mountain meadows.

At some seasons, Cataloochee is vastly alive with the twittering and calling of birds that are not permanent residents because the valley lies along a high migration route. The author of *Discovering the Appalachians* has a theory about this.

THOMAS CONNALLY: "One reason there is such a large bird population (in the Smokies) is that the range lies at the Southern end of a great migration route which begins in Pennsylvania. The Appalachian range is a natural highway for hawks and eagles especially (because of the) air currents. Air masses strike both sides of the mountain backbone, creating updrafts something like a jet stream. In this powerful updraft, birds save much energy in their southward flight."

However, there are many permanent residents of the valley, some of the more common including the eastern phoebe, blue jay, black-capped chickadee, Carolina chickadee, tufted titmouse, white-breasted nuthatch (often seen along the Cataloochee Divide), brown creeper, kingfisher, winter wren, Carolina wren (found at Pretty Hollow Gap), eastern bluebird, golden-crowned kinglet, starling, (which unfortunately invaded Cataloochee in 1935), cardinal, rufous-sided towhee, slatecolored junco, (locally named the snow-bird, often seen on Hemphill Bald, this most typical bird of the high mountains), field sparrow (observed along the Cataloochee Divide), and the song sparrow (also found around the Hemphill Bald).

Others, like the solitary sandpiper, are scarce transients, recorded only by Richard C. Burns in Cataloochee in 1951, or the horned grebe, seen by Mark in 1940.

Common wintering birds seen here are the white-throated sparrow, purple finch, ruby-crowned kinglet, the hermit thrush, and the American goldfinch. One never tires of watching the goldfinches, like bolts from the blue, dropping in golden swags of flight.

The predominant summer visitors are the entrancing warblers, the identities of which totally confuse the ordinary bird-watcher every year. There are the black and white warbler, blackpoll warbler, worm-eating warbler, golden-winged warbler (seen at Cove Creek Gap and Pin Oak Gap), parula warbler (observed on the Cataloochee Divide), yellow warbler, black-throated blue warbler, black-throated green warbler, Blackburnian Warbler (seen only at the highest altitudes), yellow-throated warbler (seen on Hemphill Bald), chestnut-sided warbler (which often dashes itself to death against windows), prairie warbler, Kentucky warbler, hooded warbler, and the Canada warbler.

Other summer residents in Cataloochee may include the white-eyed vireo, yellow-throated vireo, solitary vireo, red-eyed vireo, yellow-breasted chat, American redstart, oven bird, veery, and the catbird.

Other birds than warblers which can easily be seen in Cataloochee in the summertime are the chipping sparrows (observed on the Cataloochee Divide), the rose-breasted grosbeak, and the red crossbill, which is known by the locals as the saltbird because of its habit of staying by the licklogs where salt was put out for cattle. This bird was a favorite of Tom Alexander's and he frequently recorded having sighted them. The yellow-bellied sapsucker, as well as the Appalachian yellow-bellied sapsucker of the higher altitudes, were seen in the early nineteenth century by Allen Davidson and Ned McFalls when they went to look after the cattle on Mt. Sterling.

ALLEN DAVIDSON: "'What did you shoot at that sapsucker for?', shouted Ned from his ridge, for sap suckers were always 'using' about the licklogs near where we were then. I answered that I had not shot at a sap sucker, but at a deer."

Among the fall immigrants are the bay-breasted and Magnolia warblers, while the Cape May, Tennessee, palm and pine warblers, like the red-winged blackbird and the meadowlark, are seen in both spring and fall flights.

Although they are purportedly uncommon spring migrants and summer residents, several cerulean warblers were seen along the Cataloochee Divide in early July of 1975. Sadly, they had run into windows, killing themselves.

The beautiful indigo bunting has been commonly seen on Mt. Sterling, also, and on Hemphill Bald and in Little Cataloochee in the summer, as well as the colorful scarlet and summer tanagers. The quiet hiker often hears the liquid notes of the wood thrush and the hermit thrust, and the Louisiana water thrush, running over the evening air of summer as a stream burbles over stones, as well as the harsher song of the grackle. Rough-winged swallows and chimney swifts astound watchers with their acrobatics in a valley summer, though there are fewer and fewer chimneys for the swifts to make their homes in now. For summer company, there are also the eastern wood pewee, bluegrey gnatcatcher, acadian flycatcher, and the great-crested fly catcher. The delicate ruby-throated hummingbird is quite amazingly prolific in the area, sending out hoardes of inquisitive little helicopters all over the place. Tom and Judy Alexander loved to see them and were fond of putting out nectar in little vials for their delectation.

The low sweet sound of the mourning dove commonly pervades the morning air of lower Cataloochee, while the whip-poor-will might dominate the lower valley at night, though this bird, with its maddening, repetitive call, is not nearly so prolific here as in warmer climes. The yellow-shafted flicker, which loved to bore holes all over Cataloochee, once gave Cal Messer quite a turn.

MARK HANNAH: "The story I'm about to start now happened on Big Cataloochee. We were over there makin' some music, Cal Messer and I. And while we were messin' around, we went up to the old schoolhouse. They were havin' school on schooldays, but that happened to be on a Saturday, and there were no children there. So, the flickers, or yellow hammers, as the oldtimers called 'em, made nests up in the attic. The holes are still in the building now."

"Anyway, when you'd enter the door and make a little noise, those flickers had a couple of nests up there, and the little ones would make a chattering noise, sounded very much like a rattlesnake. So I heard it and looked back to the truck where Cal was and asked him to come out there and listen. I didn't tell him what it was. When he entered the door, I shook the door a little bit, and those flickers started hollering, the little ones. He listened and started cursing. He said 'Haywood County and North Carolina ought to be sued for damage, lettin' children go to school in a rattlesnake den!'"

Cousins to the flicker and the sapsucker, the hairy and downy woodpeckers, are commonly in evidence here, also, as well as that most marvelous-looking bird of all, the quite prehistoric-appearing, flamboyant pileated woodpecker. The red-headed woodpecker is fairly rare nowadays, having last been seen on Hemphill Bald in 1936. Purple martins and robins have been seen on Ledge Bald.

One of the most feared lords of these mountains, quite apart from the mountain lion and the bear, which reign over the forest, and the hawks and eagles who have dominion in the air, is the timber rattler, who is the undisputed master of all those who crawl close to the ground. Even the panther and the bear give this formidable foe a wide berth. All squirrels, rabbits, weasels, frogs and mice are minions to the revered rattler, for they often end up in his stomach.

One of the surveyors of the North Carolina-Tennessee border had cause to mention King Rattler in his diary of 1799.

JOHN STROTHER: "(We found) a very large rattlebug (which we) attempted to kill, but it was too souple in the heels for us."

Also known locally as a "belltail", the rattlesnake much troubled the great Methodist circuit rider, Bishop Asbury, in 1810, who fervently thanked his Maker when he had safe passage through Cataloochee without being confronted by this hidden emperor of the thickets and stones.

Mark Hannah's leisurely occupation in Cataloochee, much as some people collect stamps or coins, was killing rattlers. He then felt that he was, like St. Patrick in Ireland, delivering the people of evil, though nowadays it is against the law to destroy any kind of animal life in the Park. During his last year as ranger in the valley, he killed twenty-five of them, although the casual hiker seldom, if ever, sees these elusive creatures.

A rattler was quickly dispatched once near Davidson's Gap by what appeared to be a mere tap from a wand held lightly by 'Tot' Henry of Cataloochee Ranch. Arthur Stupka says that in 1952 there was a record of more than fifty of them killed by fishermen in the Cataloochee watershed alone. But within the last year a camper was actually fined by a ranger for endangering the wildlife of Cataloochee by taking the life of a rattler.

The only other contender to the timber rattler's crown is the poisonous northern copperhead who lords it over the lower levels and used to bedevil Cataloochans and their livestock, despite Willis King's contention that it is an uncommon snake in the Smokies. These are fairly common here and love to lie in a warm strawberry patch or blackberry thicket, as berry pickers so well know. Mark says there are more copperheads than rattlesnakes in Cataloochee. His son, Harold, says he still remembers hearing "our faithful dog Gal, that just drifted in and stayed, bark that one special kind of bark that meant a rattler or a copperhead."

Although rattlers are not usually over four feet long, a five footer was killed at the edge of Mt. Sterling Bald at 5,800 feet in 1937. It had just swallowed a squirrel. And another one found in Cataloochee measured out to 67 inches. The higher the elevation, the larger the snake, for some interesting reason. Rattlesnakes swallow their prey whole, so it was noticed from the huge distention, as big around as a man's arm, of one seen near Davidson's Gap in the '60's. A 16 inch long-tailed weasel was once found in the stomach of a rattler killed near Caldwell Fork in July, 1953.

Fortunately, hikers practically never happen upon the poisonous snakes, nor upon the at least twenty-one harmless snakes either, which can be found in Cataloochee and the general Smokies area. More often seen are the tiny ringnecked snake, supposedly the most abundant in the Smokies, the eastern gartersnake, the common watersnake, and the northern black racer. But others that often elude the casual naturalist are the pilot black snake, or black ratsnake, which has been seen at Pin Oak Gap at 4,400 feet... eastern and black kingsnakes, the queen snake, seen on Cataloochee Creek at 2,500 feet, and the corn snake. Neither does one often see the tiny eastern worm snake that Arthur Stupka says is so common, unless it has been mistaken for a fishing worm, nor the ground snake, crowned snake, or the eastern milk snake, a breeding pair of which Willis King discovered on Caldwell Fork once, or the rough green snake, though all are purportedly in the Cataloochee vicinity.

Most mountain men do not stop to think whether a snake is dangerous or not, and will kill almost any on sight. Arthur Stupka says they are also afraid of harmless lizards which they refer to as "scorpions", though the blue-tailed skinks are anything but that. Except for the common northern fence lizard which occasionally runs up as high as 5,188 feet, the skinks generally remain at very low levels in the valley. The most common are the five-lined skink, once found, however, as high as 4,900 feet on the Balsam Mountain, and the broad-headed skink.

Jim Waldroop, then acting ranger in Cataloochee, picked up a small, dark, glistening salamander from the border of Jesse Palmer's millpond one fine October day, but the observer was unable to identify the species before it quickly slithered away. There are at least twenty-seven kinds of salamanders in the Smokies! And all the observer knew at that time is that it was not the giant hellbender, which may be as long as twenty-nine inches, nor was it the red-cheeked or Jordon's salamander, which is entirely confined to the higher altitudes of the Smokies. Arthur Stupka points out that actually very little collecting has been accomplished east of the Balsams which comprises the western boundary of Cataloochee, so the Hellbender has rarely been reported there.

The red-spotted newt, which is a delightful little red eft in its most immature stage, is likely to roam the water courses of Cataloochee, as are the Blue Ridge Mountain salamander, Blue Ridge two-lined salamander, Blue Ridge spring salamander, black-bellied salamander, slimy salamander, and shovel-nosed salamander. The little pygmy salamander has a strangely high range of over 4,000 feet in the spruce-fir forests, like the Jordon's salamander, black-chinned red salamander, and Metcalf's salamander, which is similar to the red-cheeked salamander and has been found on Balsam mountain, Cataloochee Divide, and near Mt. Sterling Ridge by Richard

Highton. The rather rare Midland mud salamander, in larva form, was found in an old spring house at Mt. Sterling by Willis King, who referred to it as an exceptionally large larva of 5 inches. Discovered in Cataloochee Creek by Ronald Brandon and James Huheey, at an elevation of 2,800 feet was the three-lined salamander, at a rather high altitude for this small creature which has only been found on the North Carolina side of the park. Salamander experts go wild when they come to the Smokies because there are so many rare varieties here. It's Salamander Heaven!

There are not nearly so many varieties of toads and frogs in Cataloochee, although it may seem so on a spring night when they begin to orchestrate. One can trace the early spring cries of the northern spring peeper, or Hyla Crucifer, down through the watercourses of West Virginia, Virginia, into the Smokies at Cataloochee. It is one of the most enchanting harbingers of spring, always evocative and poignant. The Upland Chorus Frog is just as likely to call early in a Cataloochee spring, also. The Eastern gray tree frog has been detected as high as 4,888 feet, at Cataloochee Ranch, only a mile from Cataloochee Valley proper. The unmistakable croak of the bullfrog, the great Rana catesbiana (Shaw) surely king of the frogs, if no one else, has been heard, and probably gigged, on Cataloochee Creek at 2,500 feet. Wilfred King has also found an abundance of pickeral frog on Cataloochee Creek. The green frog probably inhabits Cataloochee along its lower levels, as it is found in most watersheds of the park, as is the wood frog, though raccoons, crows, and screech owls, all dearly love them and come down like the Assyrian hoard, killing them by dozens at a time.

Of the two species of toads, the American toad is known to exist here at nearly all elevations, and Willis King has found Fowler's toad at 4,000 feet on Mt. Sterling Ridge, which is quite high for this species. At The Purchase, on the Cataloochee Divide, a watch dog ate a toad and immediately began frothing at the mouth as though rabid. The veterinarian suggested it was because of the American toad's poisonous secretions in its glands.

The large common snapping turtle, an individual to be reckoned with, has been discovered here at 2,600 feet. Even though predators are constantly finding its eggs, the Eastern box turtle seems to be found everywhere, up to 4,000 feet.

But mention Cataloochee Creek to any sportsman, and his eyes will grow wide like flashing green lights registering FISH! FISH! FISH! as if they were the jackpot symbols in a slot machine. Next he will tell you that the mossy green rocks there are the slipperiest in the world. Jarvis Caldwell, who broke his ankle while fishing Cataloochee Creek recently, will confirm this!

Mark Hannah says the rainbow trout are in the lower reaches where Cataloochee Creek runs broad and slowly, while above the falls are the speckled or brook trout. The Creek was first "planted" with rainbow trout about 1910.

The fish are mostly trout of the cold, swift-flowing water variety, though the more sluggish man-made ponds or lakes in Cataloochee may have held other species at one time. Everybody who ever came out of Cataloochee wanted to talk about a prize trout he had caught or knew about. Frank Campbell of Canton wrote about the 27 inch rainbow that Mitch Sutton had caught at the Kerr Place.

FRANK CAMPBELL: "I can surely say one thing about Cataloochee Creek. In my boyhood days, there were more speckled mountain trout in that stream than any place I ever fished. I believe I could have caught in one day more fish than I could carry."

This was undoubtedly true for the speckled and for the rainbow as well, as the fabled Turkey George had once pulled out three hundred and sixty-five rainbow trout in one day, a record that has never been surpassed and which would now be considered a criminal offense! Even Hiram Caldwell could pull them out faster than Taylor Medford, of Iron Duff, could string them.

ELDRIDGE CALDWELL: "(The Medfords) would come over there in the spring and fish... Taylor was the one (my father) played off on... Spring of the year... the busy time of the year. And he (Hiram) told me to get the sheep rounded up; we'd take 'em up there above Uncle Steve Woody's place and turn 'em out, and said 'I'd like to fish a little for these boys.' He knew the stream, the one we call First Cove, so he said, 'Turn the sheep through the cove here. (He was ever one to combine work with play!) Taylor's goin' to carry and I'm goin' to fish!'"

"It was so rough through there, people didn't fish it much. He'd just get a fish up nearly all the time. He told Taylor he'd catch 'im some fish if Taylor could string 'em as fast as he caught 'em. And Taylor said he'd do it. (My father) would git 'em on his hook, throw 'em so hard they'd jerk off the hook. It was all growed up with hemlock, all that deep. Taylor'd get tangled up and fall. (laughs broadly) By the time he'd git up again, my father'd have one on the hook for him to come git. Skinned Taylor all over!"

But Uncle Hiram could be diffident about fishing when he chose to joke with strangers, to his ultimate embarrassment. He was a great one for church, and his home was like a hotel for the elders and clergy that rode into the valley for Sundays and quarterly meetings. Every year or so Palmer Chapel would get a new preacher.

ELDRIDGE CALDWELL: "I'us a-ploughin' and he'us a-hoein' in the cane patch there by the road in the spring. Saw some feller comin' up the creek, fishin' along. He got up even with my father. He come out the creek at the bank, asked him where was a good place to fish. My father said, 'I couldn't tell you. I never been triflin' enough to fish!'"

Later, stunned, Hiram found he had been flippant with his new preacher.

Another avid fisherman was the crippled Major Woody.

RAYMOND CALDWELL: "Major Woody, as I remember him, he could tell the biggest fish stories and always caught, almost caught, the biggest fish that was in the creek. He could move along all right and was an awful good hand to catch rainbow trout. He was a good fisherman, but he always had the fish tale to tell about the big one gettin' away. He used the phrase, 'It was as long as a handsaw.'"

Mark Hannah's good friend and fishing companion from Eastern Carolina corroborated Major's colorful description.

B. H. OATES: "On the board walls of the cabin I observed many low profile drawings of fish. Apparently the people would hold these big fish against the wall and with a piece of black chalk or pencil they marked a line completely around the fish beginning from the head around to the tail and back to the head. The size of these fish were almost unbelievable for a trout, and many of the profiles could not have been completely covered up with a carpenter's handsaw."

Gentle Flora Palmer used to pine for Lost Bottom which was so far back in the mountains that it was hard to find, hence its name. It was here that Glenn Palmer disobeyed his father's orders to collect lost cattle, and caught ninety-seven fish, instead. Flora said the place had no trees, just grass… such a pretty green place. Her face looked wistful as it lit with the remembrance of this small Eden. Cattle ranged over there. It was about one half day's journey over Big Butt Mountain, under which stood Flora's childhood home. Lost Bottom Creek, she said, had beautiful little speckled trout which were above here and the waterfall. The rainbows couldn't get up the falls to eat up the delicate brookies. There's still good fishing there, if one has the inclination to walk that far.

'TINE BENNETT: "Back then we'd git the har (hair) out of a horse's tail, make our fishin' lines. And I'us up there at Uncle 'Tine's, and they had all kinds of speckled trout right up that little creek there."

"Ossie Woody and I used to fish together a lot. What's that youngest boy's name? Jon'than? I used to go in there and stay two or three days at a time with Uncle Steve and Jon'than. He always wore knee pants. And we had a fish over there. We called 'em mullets. You remember them?"

MARK HANNAH: "Yeah, horney-heads. The long nose were called mullets."

'TINE BENNETT: "But we called 'em mullets. And you'd just get out there in the turn of the creek with rock around there, and after awhile, you'd have it plumb full of mullet fish, great ole big things, too, that long. They had a rough scale on 'em, and we'd just take a hand and pick 'em up. But you couldn't pick up a trout fish. He's so slick, he'd just jump out of your hands. What I started to say, me and Jon'than used to get out there, and Ossie, and build us a little rock pen, and go back in an hour maybe twenty-five of them mullets out in there. We'd stop up the hole where the water went through and sink a rock down like that and catch every one of 'em with our hands!"

The little minnow called stoneroller, or "horneyhead" is rarely ever eight inches long, but was widely eaten by the local people. Arthur Stupka says there are over two dozen kinds of minnows in park waters, among them the bright-hued warpaint shiner, the emerald shiner, and the rosy dace... all like some kind of shining sequins in the mountain waters.

Fortunately there are now rules and regulations which govern the watercourses of Cataloochee so that one can't catch or take away, as Turkey George did, 365 fish in a day. 'Fayt Palmer was appointed the first real warden of the area about 1894 by the Love family who owned so much land in there, long before the coming of the park. Then, about 1906, William A. Palmer got someone in the state legislature to pass a law protecting the streams and fish. There was to be no fishing above Turkey George's place. This must have stunned Uncle Turkey, and he undoubtedly paid no attention to it and probably caught those 365 fish in defiance. W. A. Palmer, like his son, Glen, had quite an appetite for fish, but politely wouldn't eat fish at his own table until everyone had had his fill.

About this time, at the turn of the century, the rainbow trout was introduced into the Great Smokies and quickly became the sporting fish of the park. Unfortunately the native speckled trout further upstream are frequently eaten by the rainbow. The brown trout has also been introduced from Europe and, like the rainbow, is not found as far upstream as the little speckled ones that almost bring tears to Mark Hannah's eyes, so dear are they to him.

Although the native trout rarely exceeds twelve inches in length, its flavor was highly prized by Cataloochee herdsmen when they savored them around their campfires in the high mountain balds, bones and all.

By 1976, the new young superintendent of the park told the N. C. National Park, Parkway, and Forests Development Council that fishing for brook trout would be banned in the Great Smokies, as the fish population was now less than fifty percent of what it had been.

BOYD EVISON: "The brook trout is the one native trout of the Great Smokies. In order to preserve it, we should close down all fishing for brook trout."

Allen Davidson's grand-daughter, Elizabeth, used to tell of fishing in Cataloochee Creek with her sister, Virginia, during or just after the first World War. Their father and mother, William and Addie Davidson Williamson, had brought them there to visit the Jarvis Palmers, as the Palmer family had always remained close since their early ties with Addie's father, Allen Davidson. Unbeknownst to their parents, the girls wore the trousers from their brothers' old army uniforms, with big smocks over them. This scandalized the parents and the local people... women in pants! But Elizabeth found them ideal fishing garb. And the voluminous smocks were handy, too, for once she caught a trout in her smock!

That period of 1918-1930, when Jarvis Palmer used to have cabins for fishermen right above his house, was the most abundant fishing time in Cataloochee.

Except for passing references to the ill temper of the yellow jacket, one can touch only fleetingly on the insect life of Cataloochee. However, one really should not ignore the white sphinx moth, maybe the most splendid of them all by the sound of its mysterious name, which is the only pollinator of the beautiful purple rhododendron which abounds on Mt. Sterling.

Consider the tiny gnat. One can scarcely see it and yet it rounds the fishermen up and sends them from the quiet fishing streams to seek the protection of their smoky campfires. Maybe the gnat is the true emperor overall.

What say you to this, Klandaghi? Are you master here, or do you make obeisance, as we humans do, to the whims of the insect world?

EPILOGUE

Palmer's Chapel Church in Big Cataloochee, circa 1930.
Courtesy Great Smoky Mountains National Park Archives.

ONE SUMMER, THERE were nearly a thousand people who streamed in a cavalcade to Cataloochee Homecoming at Palmer Chapel. They sang, as always, "Now Let Us Gather at the River", and ate at the longest picnic table ever seen, under the shade of dark hemlocks and a huge basswood, one of the largest in the Park.

After the service, some of Mark's talented family made music on guitar and banjo. There were his sons, Harold and Lowell, his grandson, red-headed Ronnie Trantham singing his heart out as Sam Smith, his darkly handsome, Cherokee-blooded son-in-law brooded over his guitar.

Behind the musicians, on the other side of the creek, a party of horsemen rode past without a sound, with merely a fleeting glance at the gathering. Something anachronistic about their clothes, their big-brimmed hats and overalls gave them an air of unreality. Yet they seemed quite at home gliding silently by.

Someone photographed this splendid backdrop... the quaint mountain riders behind the earnest musicians. When the developed slides were projected onto the sparkling glass-beaded screen, there was Ronnie singing, Sam playing, Harold and Lowell picking, but no-one in the background.

Running through the slides several times, the photographer could find no clue. Had the woods been too dark? Perhaps the horses had slipped past faster than the camera could catch them? A flickering thought came to mind that the ghostly riders represented Cataloochee As It Was... that they might have been a bit amused, as they rode on past Lucky Button Hole, that everyone was carrying on so about the past... about Them.

THE CATALOOCHEE VALLEY

Nestled deep in the Great Smoky Mountains,
Is a place I once called home,
It's called the Cataloochee Valley,
Where the deer and bears now roam.

It is there I have fond memories,
Of the days so long ago,
Often visiting with my relatives,
At the old country store.

There we had a lot of neighbors,
Always kind and helpful, too,
When came injury or illness,
Each one was there, his share to do.

We had no malls or shopping centers,
No fine clothes with all the frills,
But one thing that was important,
Was our church among the hills.

We gathered there each Sunday,
And sang songs both old and new,
Then an old-fashioned country preacher,
Would bring a message, so loud and true.

Once each year, we meet together,
At the church upon the hill,
There to renew old acquaintance,
And it gives each one a thrill.

In the valley of Cataloochee,
We had a post office, store and mill,
Each one built, owned and operated,
By a man called Uncle Will.

He worked from early morning,
Until very late at night,
Caring for his friends and neighbors,
Seemed to be his greatest delight.

In our peaceful little valley,
We were blessed with neighbors so grand,
The Bennetts, Messers and the Hannahs,
Who lived well from off their land.

Then came the Burgess, Browns, and Woodys,
The Nelsons, Halls, and Conards, too,
Each one working, living, sharing,
With the ones they loved so true.

Just down the road from the church house,
Was the school we all knew well,
Many, many days we spent there,
Learning how to read, write, and spell.

Next came students singing,
"My Country tis of Thee,"
Or perhaps "America,"
The great land of the free.

When the singing ended,
We would bow our heads and pray,
Asking God to guide and help us,
In our work from day to day.

Many memories still linger,
As I think of long ago.
And the quiet little valley,
Where the tall pines grow.

Many a kind word was spoken,
Many lent a helping hand,
While we lived in the Cataloochee Valley,
One of the greatest in the land.

Dedicated to all my loved ones and friends from Cataloochee; especially to my favorite cousins, Verda and Mark Hannah.

Beatrice Burgess Sisk

– Poems from *Smoky Mountain Reflections*, 1989, p. 1.

REFERENCES AND ACKNOWLEDGMENTS

Chapter 1. The Buzzard's Wing

p. 11 So said the Indians about the creation of Cataloochee... Indian legend, p. 239, IV, *Myths of the Cherokee*, James Mooney.

p. 12 "The Devil's Bedchamber", Cherokee legend, p. 50, *Annals of Haywood County*, W.S. Allen, 1935, N.C.

p. 12 "Ga-da-lu-tsi", James Mooney, p. 15, *Great Smoky Mountain Stories*, W. Clark Medford, 1966

p. 13 "Cataluche" etc. *Early History of Haywood County*, W. Clark Medford, p. 81, 1961, pub. by people of county.

p. 13 Hiram Wilburn on Indian trail, folder 5, memo to Ross Eakin, Nov. 24, 1939, Hiram C. Wilburn Collection, MSS 80-17, Western Carolina University Hunter Library Special Collections.

p. 13 Mark Hannah on Indian trail. Elizabeth Powers tape, 1972, Maggie Valley, N.C.

p. 13 Mack Hannah on Indian grave, notebook 7, folder 74, Aug. 23 1939, interview, Hiram C. Wilburn Collection, MSS 80-17, Western Carolina University Hunter Library Special Collections.

p. 14 Flora Palmer Medford, on Indian relics. Elizabeth Powers tape, Iron Duff, 1972

p. 15 Michael Frome on Big Cove, *Strangers in High Places*, Doubleday 1966

p. 15 Allen T. Davidson on Indians, *The Lyceum* magazine, Asheville, N.C. transcript of speech, 1890 or 1891.

p. 16 Ned McFalls and Sam McGaha, p. 336. *History of Western North Carolina*, John Preston Arthur, Asheville, N.C. 1914.

p. 17 Floyd Woody on Indians, Elizabeth Powers tape, Canton, N.C. 1972, June

p. 18 Mark Hannah, on his Cherokee son-in-law. Conversation in the 1970s, Maggie Valley, N.C.

Chapter 2. Paradises: A Point of View

p. 19 Charlie Palmer on Garden of Eden, *Sayings from Old Smoky*, Joseph S. Hall, Cataloochee Press, Asheville, N.C. 1972.

p. 20 Mark Hannah on early hunters, written for Elizabeth Powers, 1970s.

p. 21 Bishop Francis Asbury, on Catahouche, p. 237, *Asbury's Journals*, Nov. 30, 1810 (N.Y. Lane and Scott, 1852)

p. 21 Henry Boehm on Asbury, from *Reminiscences of Henry Boehm*, 1866

p. 22 Mark Hannah on Asbury Crossing, Elizabeth Powers tape, Maggie Valley, May 1972

p. 22 Hiram Wilburn on Davidson Branch, notebook 14, folder 77, pp 23,79, Hiram C. Wilburn Collection, MSS 80-17, Western Carolina University Hunter Library Special Collections.

p. 22 Allen T. Davidson, *The Lyceum* magazine, transcript of speech, Asheville, N.C., 1890 or 91.

p. 23 Asheville Gazette-News of Jan 24, 1905, pp.401–402 from *History of Western North Carolina*, John Preston Arthur, 1914.

Chapter 3. Dirt Captains and Land Pirates

p. 26 Robert Love, "sorrel-topped soap stick", pp. 329–330, *History of Western North Carolina*, John Preston Arthur, 1914.

p. 26 Andrew Jackson on Love's worth, p. 125, *History of Western North Carolina*, John Preston Arthur, 1914.

p. 26 John Strother's diary, *Strother Journal of the State-Line Survey*, 1799, State Archives, Raleigh, N.C.

p. 26 Henry Colwell land entry, p. 47, Early History of Haywood County, W. Clark Medford, 1961.

p. 26 Mitchell Davidson land entry on "old Solomon Messer foundation", *Great Smoky Mountain Stories*. W. Clark Medford, 1966.

p. 27 Reuben Moody's Cataloochee entry, p. 13, *Land o' the Sky*, W. Clark Medford, 1965.

p. 27 Allen T. Davidson's 300 acres entry, p. 47, *Early History of Haywood County*, W. Clark Medford, 1961.

p. 27 Michael Frome on Mark's ancestors, *Strangers in High Places*, Doubleday, 1966.

p. 27 Mark Hannah, his ancestors; early settlement, paper for Elizabeth Powers in the 1970's.

p. 29 Eldridge Caldwell on Levi Caldwell and the Bennetts. Elizabeth Powers tape, Campbell Creek, May 10, 1972.

p. 30 Glenn Palmer on old George Palmer, conversation with Elizabeth Powers and Mark Hannah, Rush Fork Farm, Haywood County, May 10, 1972.

p. 30 Mack Hannah says Jonathan Woody best hunter, Mark Hannah tape for Elizabeth Powers, Maggie Valley, N.C., May 1972.

p. 31 Floyd Woody on the woody clan, Elizabeth Powers tape, Canton, N.C., 1972.

p. 31 Allen T. Davidson on clannishness, *The Lyceum* magazine, transcript of speech, Asheville, N.C., January 1891.

Chapter 4. The Life Line

p. 35 Allen T. Davidson, Cataloochee Trail, *The Lyceum* magazine, transcript of speech, Asheville, N.C. 1890-or 91.

p. 36 W. Clark Medford on the Cataloochee road, *Land o' the Sky*, Waynesville, N.C., 1965.

p. 37 Ocona Lufty toll road, notebook 7, folder 74, Hiram C. Wilburn Collection, MSS 80-17, Western Carolina University Hunter Library Special Collections.

p. 37 Mitchell Sutton on Cataloochee road, notebook 7, folder 74, Hiram C. Wilburn Collection, MSS 80-17, Western Carolina University Hunter Library Special Collections.

p. 37 Interview with Mack Hannah, notebook 7, folder 74, Aug. 23, 1939, Hiram C. Wilburn Collection, MSS 80-17, Western Carolina University Hunter Library Special Collections.

p. 37 Mack Hannah's father's contract for grading the road, notebook 7, folder 76, Hiram C. Wilburn Collection, MSS 80-17, Western Carolina University Hunter Library Special Collections.

p. 37 W. Clark Medford, "a thousand turns", p. 81, *Early History of Haywood County*, Waynesville, N.C. 1961.

Chapter 5. Mt. Sterling: The Last Bastion

p. 39 "A rebellion against rebellion." can't find source, may be Wilma Dykeman in *The French Broad*.

p. 39 Mark Hannah, Civil War vets hiding, Elizabeth Powers tape, May 1972.

p. 39 Allen T. Davidson, letter to wife on Civil War, copy in Elizabeth Powers family files, or in State Archives, Raleigh, N.C.

p. 40 Mark Hannah, Civil War killings, Elizabeth Powers tape, May 1972.

p. 41 Interview with Mitchell Sutton, death of Abraham Hopkins, July 21, 1937, Hiram C. Wilburn Collection, MSS 80-17, Western Carolina University Hunter Library Special Collections.

p. 41 Grooms tune, p. 131, *Early History of Haywood County*, w. Clark Medford, 1961.

p. 42 Interview with Sage Sutton on Grooms' death, Sept. 14, 1937, Hiram C. Wilburn Collection, MSS 80-17, Western Carolina University Hunter Library Special Collections.

p. 42 Interview with Mrs. George Ira McGee on Shelton and Caldwell deaths, notebook 7, folder 74, p. 27, Hiram C. Wilburn Collection, MSS 80-17, Western Carolina University Hunter Library Special Collections.

p. 42, Mark Hannah, Shelton and Caldwell deaths, Elizabeth Powers tape, May 1972.

p. 43 William Holland Thomas, Cherokee battalion, folder 14, Thomas papers, Oct. 17, 1961, WNC University Library, Cullowhee.

p. 43 Interview with Aden Carver, Kirk in Oconaluftee, notebook 7, folder 71, Hiram C. Wilburn Collection, MSS 80-17, Western Carolina University Hunter Library Special Collections.

p. 43 Grandmother Enloe on Col Thomas and the Indians, notebook 7, folder 71, p. 4, Hiram C. Wilburn Collection, MSS 80-17, Western Carolina University Hunter Library Special Collections.

p. 44 Swimmer manuscript, famous Cherokee scouts, edited James Mooney, *19th Annual Report of American Bureau of Ethnology*, Government Printing Office,1897–98.

p. 44 Mark Hannah on Logan Hannah, Elizabeth Powers tape, May 1972.

p. 44 Raymond Caldwell on Mag Mauney Caldwell, Elizabeth Powers tape, 1972.

p. 45 General Theodore F. Davidson, on early Civil War experiences, *Reminiscences and Traditions of Western North Carolina*, read before Pen and Plate Club, Nov. 28, 1928, Asheville, N.C.

p. 46 Interview with Mitchell Sutton on Cataloochee, July 21, 1937, Wilburn papers, notebook 7, folder 74, p. 24, Waynesville Library.

p. 46 "Climbing Bear" and witchcraft, Swimmer manuscript, ed. James Mooney, 19th annual report Bureau of American Ethnology,1897–98.

p. 47 Jarvis Caldwell family on Civil War, Elizabeth Powers tape, Dec. 2, 1971.

p. 48 Interview with Mr. A. M. (Andy) Bennett, on Aunt 'Phronia, Hiram C. Wilburn Collection, MSS 80-17, Western Carolina University Hunter Library Special Collections notebook 7, folder 74, p. 29, Hiram C. Wilburn Collection, MSS 80-17, Western Carolina University Hunter Library Special Collections. Interview Oct. 13, 1937.

p. 48, Mark Hannah, hiding cattle, Elizabeth Powers tape, May 1972.

p. 48 Raymond Caldwell on Granny Pop, Elizabeth Powers tape, Oct. 27, 1972.

p. 49 Colonel Thomas demands Bartlett's scalp, article *Waynesville Mountaineer*, material based on Colonel Stringfield's papers, U. of Western N.C., library, Cullowhee.

Chapter 6. Blockade: Another Rebellion

p. 51 W. Clark Medford, on liquor, *Middle History of Haywood County*, 1968.

p. 51 Raymond Caldwell on liquor, Elizabeth Powers tape, Oct. 27, 1972.

p. 51 Mark Hannah on liquor and sugar, Elizabeth Powers tape, May 1972.

p. 51 Aden Carver on liquor, *Smoky Mountain Folks and their Lore*, Joseph W. Hall, 1960, Great Smoky Mtn. Natural History Assoc.

p. 51 Jarvis Caldwell family on liquor, Elizabeth Powers tape, Dec. 2, 1971.

p. 52 Joseph S. Hall on revenuers, p. 24, *Smoky Mountain Folks and their Lore*, 1960 GSMNHA.

p. 52 Dr. Robert Hilliard Woody on liquor, "Cataloochee Homecoming", *South Atlantic Quarterly*, vol 49, Jan. 1950.

p. 53 'Tine Bennett on liquor, Elizabeth Powers tape, Sylva, N.C. July 27, 1972.

p. 53 Ex-moonshiner, anonymous, on watchers, conversation Elizabeth Powers.

p. 53 Mark Hannah on Braz Whaley, Elizabeth Powers tape, May 1, 1973.

p. 53 Weldon Williamson, former car dealer, conversation Elizabeth Powers, Asheville.

p. 53 Former Hemphill distiller, anonymous, conversation Elizabeth Powers.

p. 53 Raymond Caldwell on stills, Elizabeth Powers tape, Oct. 27, 1972.

p. 54 Pearl Valentine Caldwell on revenuers, Elizabeth Powers tape, Oct. 28, 1972.

p. 54 Vick Smith on Steve Waycaster, notebook 7, folder 74, Hiram C. Wilburn Collection, MSS 80-17, Western Carolina University Hunter Library Special Collections.

p. 54 Raymond Caldwell on malt in mill, Elizabeth Powers tape, Oct. 27, 1972.

p. 55 Eldridge Caldwell on wine, Oct. 28, 1972, Campbell Creek.

p. 55 Mark Hannah on food chopper, Elizabeth Powers tape, May 1972

p. 55 Raymond Caldwell on Major Woody, Elizabeth Powers tape, Oct. 27, 1972

p. 55 Mark Hannah on drink, written for Elizabeth Powers, date?

p. 55 Bascom Lamar Lunsford, on doublings, pp. 157–58, *The King of Madison*, Manly Wade Wellman, UNC Press, 1973.

p. 55 Jim Sutton on Hell's Half Acre, p. 82, *Sayings from Old Smoky*, Joseph S. Hall, Cataloochee Press, Asheville, 1972.

p. 56 Mark Hannah comment on above, date unrecorded, Elizabeth Powers.

p. 56 Anonymous mountain distiller re cap blowing, Elizabeth Powers converse.

p. 56 Glen Messer, helicopter, conversation Elizabeth Powers, Hemphill valley.

p. 57 Mark Hannah on drunken sheriff. Elizabeth Powers tape, July 18, 1973.

p. 57 Zeke story, "awful bad to drink", p. 24, *Smoky Mtn. Folks and their Lore*. Joseph S. Hall, GSMNHA, 1960.

p. 57 Mark Hannah comment on "Zeke" to Elizabeth Powers, date unrecorded.

p. 58 Professor Joseph S. Hall on honest people in Catalooch', p. 24, *Smoky Mountain Folks and their Lore*, GSMNHA, 1960.

p. 58 Paul Messer, Tennessee joke, told to Elizabeth Powers Hemphill Valley, N.C.

Chapter 7. Lost

p. 60 "Lost to time", *Strangers in High Places*, Michael Frome, Doubleday, 1966.

p. 60 "Terrible swift sword", from *The Battle Hymn of the Republic*, Julia Ward Howe.

p. 60 Mark Hannah on church announcement, Elizabeth Powers tape, May 1972.

p. 60 'We wouldn't live out our life much longer", Jackie Turner article, *Waynesville Mountaineer*, Oct. 20, 1971.

p. 60 Jarvis Caldwell on leaving Cataloochee, Elizabeth Powers tape, Dec 2, 1971.

pp. 60–61 Mark Hannah on established prices for Cataloochee, Elizabeth Powers tape, May 1972, plus Jackie Turner article *Waynesville Mountaineer*, Oct. 20, 1971.

p. 61 Aden Carver, "condemned and sold out". p. 29 *Smoky Mtn. Folks and Their Lore*, Joseph S. Hall, 1960, GSMNHA.

p. 61 Steve Woody. "masterest law suit", Sayings from Old Smoky, Joseph S. Hall, Cataloochee Press, Asheville, N.C. 1972.

p. 61 Mark Hannah , horizontal measurement, Elizabeth Powers tape, May 1972.

p. 61 Jarvis Caldwell, possible shoot-out, Elizabeth Powers tape, Dec. 2, 1971.

p. 61 Mark Hannah, first sold property, Elizabeth Powers tape, May 1972.

p. 62 Raymond Caldwell, taking milk cow, Elizabeth Powers tape, Dec 1, 1971.

p. 62 Robert H. Woody on leaving Cataloochee. Elizabeth Powers tape, Durham , Nov, 1971.

p. 62 Horace Kephart on "sulterin'". p. 386, *Our Southern Highlanders,* Macmillan and Co, Publishers, 1929.

p. 62 Docia Styles, p. 54, *Smoky Mountain Folks and Their Lore*, Joseph S. Hall, 1960, GSMNHA.

p. 63 Mark Hannah on Park restrictions, Elizabeth Powers tape, May 1972.

p. 63 Jarvis and Bonnie Caldwell, on Park restrictions, Elizabeth Powers tape, Dec,1971

p. 63 Eldridge Caldwell on Major Woody, Elizabeth Powers tape, Oct. 28, 1972.

p. 63 "Major" complains "Park has rernt". p. 16., *Smoky Mountain Folks and Their Lore*, Joseph S. Hall, 1960, GSMNHA.

p. 64 Anonymous mountain man on new ranger, Elizabeth Powers converse, date unrecorded.

p. 64 Mary Lou Leatherwood Moody, Converse with Elizabeth Powers, Dec., 1971.

p. 64 Mark Hannah "stayed for 31 years", Elizabeth Powers tape, May 1972.

p. 64 Tom Porter recalls. Elizabeth Powers tape, Franklin, 1972, conversation.

p. 65 Mark Hannah on destroying Cataloochee, Jackie Turner article *Waynesville Mountaineer*, Oct. 22, 1971.

p. 65 Needham singled out, letter. Hiram C. Wilburn Collection, MSS 80-17, Western Carolina University Hunter Library Special Collections.

p. 66 Pearl and Eldridge Caldwell on Needham, Elizabeth Powers tape, Oct. 28, 1972.

p. 66 Jarvis Caldwell on how to improve Park, Elizabeth Powers tape, Dec 2, 1971.
pp. 66–67 Floyd woody on how to improve Park, Elizabeth Powers tape, June 24, 1972.
p. 67 Caldwell family on improving Park, Elizabeth Powers tape, Dec. 2, 1971.
p. 67 Mark Hannah on access road, Jackie Turner article, *Waynesville Mountaineer*, Oct. 22, 1971.

Chapter 8. A Rose, a Snake, and a Dove

p. 72 Unknown Tennessee rider, converse EDO, Cataloochee Valley 1972.
p. 72 Asbury story about flatboatmen, *Asbury Journals*.
p. 73 Robert H. Woody on religion, Elizabeth Powers tape, Durham, N.C. Nov. 1971.
p. 73 Horace Kephart on the preacher, p. 341, *Our Southern Highlanders*, Macmillan, 1929.
p. 73 Robert H. Woody on religion.,"Cataloochee Homecoming", *from South Atlantic Quarterly*, vol. 49, Jan. 1950.
p. 74 Floyd Woody, "like to ha' churched me", Mark Hannah tape, Maggie Valley, N.C., Feb. 29, 1976.
p. 74 Jarvis Caldwell on camp meeting. Elizabeth Powers tape, Dec. 2, 1971.
p. 74 Floyd Woody on camp meeting. Elizabeth Powers tape, June 24, 1972.
p. 75 Mark Hannah written comment on Floyd's trick, Elizabeth Powers recv.
p. 75 T.A. Groce, going into Cataloochee, record of Oct. 1909.
p. 75 Hiram Caldwell, to T.A. Groce in above record.
p. 76 Raymond and Jarvis Caldwell on Lizzie Howell Caldwell and Brown Caldwell, Elizabeth Powers tape, Dec. 2 , 1971, Allen's Creek, N.C.
p. 76 "The reformed sinner" may be from Kephart's Highlanders.
p. 77 Floyd Woody on Brown Caldwell, *Sayings from Old Smoky*, by Joseph S. Hall, Cataloochee Press, Asheville, N.C. 1972.
p. 77 Raymond Caldwell on Tom King. Elizabeth Powers tape, Dec 1 1971.
p. 77 Mark Hannah Elizabeth Powers converse, date unrecorded.
p. 77 Robert H. Woody on Noah Conard, Elizabeth Powers tape, Nov. 1971.
p. 77 Flora Messer Morrow on church and funerals. Elizabeth Powers tape, 1973.
p. 78 Mark Hannah Elizabeth Powers tape, May 1972.
p. 78 Mark Hannah, Elizabeth Powers tape, May 1972.
p. 78 Robert H. Woody, "Cataloochee Homecoming", *South Atlantic Quarterly*, vol. 49, Jan, 1950.
p. 79 Mark Hannah, tape Elizabeth Powers, May 1972.
p. 79 Jarvis Caldwell family, Elizabeth Powers tape, Dec. 2, 1971.
p. 79 Flora Palmer Medford, Elizabeth Powers tape, Iron Duff, N.C., Sept. 24, 1972.
p. 79 Robert H. Woody on weddings, "Cataloochee Homecoming", *South Atlantic Quarterly*, vol. 49, Jan. 1950.
p. 79 Jess McGee, interview with Mrs. George Ira McGee, notebook 7, folder 74, p. 28, Hiram C. Wilburn Collection, MSS 80-17, Western Carolina University Hunter Library Special Collections.
p. 80 Flora Messer Morrow, Elizabeth Powers tape, May 6, 1973.
p. 81 Hobert Franklin, on Sutton Sunday school, Mark Hannah tape, Maggie Valley, N.C. Feb. 29, 1976.

References and Acknowledgments 297

Chapter 9. As Cataloochee Goes

p. 84 Colonel Robert Love, letter to William Welch on Andrew Jackson election, Dec. 4, 1828. *Annals of Haywood County*, W.C. Allen, Waynesville. N.C. 1935

p. 84 Interview with Mack Hannah on muster ground, Aug. 23 1939, Hiram C. Wilburn Collection, MSS 80-17, Western Carolina University Hunter Library Special Collections.

p. 84–85 Jarvis and Raymond Caldwell on politics, Elizabeth Powers tape, Dec. 1971

p. 85 Gudger Palmer on William A. Palmer, interview Elizabeth Powers. 197?

p. 86 Tom Porter on politics, interview with Elizabeth Powers and Mark Hannah, Franklin, N.C., 1972.

p. 86 W. Clark Medford, on Cataloochee elections, p. 60, *Great Smoky Mountain Stories*, Waynesville, N.C. 1966.

p. 86 Mark Hannah on voting, Elizabeth Powers tape, May 1972.

Chapter 10. The Long Arm

p. 87 Floyd Woody on youthful pranks. Elizabeth Powers tape, June 24, 1972.

pp. 87–88 Zack Clark shooting, p. 335, *History of Western North Carolina*, John Preston Arthur, Asheville, N.C. 1914.

p. 88 Allen T. Davidson on "Zack" Clark, *The Lyceum* magazine, transcript of speech, Asheville, N.C. 1890 or 91.

p. 88 Mountain lawyers, from "Roamin' the Mountains", John Parris column, *Asheville Citizen-Times*, July 27, 1973, quoting from the above *Lyceum* magazine.

p. 89 Glenn Palmer on "secret lawyer", conversation Elizabeth Powers and Mark Hannah, Rush Fork Farm, Crabtree Bald, Aug. 20, 1972.

p. 89 Mark Hannah comment to Elizabeth Powers on above.

p. 89 Robert H. Woody, "Cataloochee Homecoming", *South Atlantic Quarterly*, vol. 49, Jan, 1950.

p. 89 Anonymous moonshiner, "get caught with a still", Elizabeth Powers converse.

p. 89 Mark Hannah comment to Elizabeth Powers on above.

pp. 89–90 Jarvis and Raymond Caldwell on murder of Rudolph Caldwell, Elizabeth Powers tape, Dec. 2, 1971.

p. 90 Robert Woody on Dude and 'Ras. Elizabeth Powers tape, Nov. 1971, Durham, N.C.

p. 91 Hiram Wilburn on Dude Hannah, notebook 14, folder 77, begin p. 6, Hiram C. Wilburn Collection, MSS 80-17, Western Carolina University Hunter Library Special Collections.

p. 91 Eldridge and Pearl Caldwell on Dude, Elizabeth Powers tape, Oct. 28, 1972.

p. 91 Mark Hannah, Dude and 'Ras court story, Elizabeth Powers converse, date?

p. 91 Eldridge comment on Mark story. Elizabeth Powers tape, May 10, 1972.

p. 91 Joseph S. Hall on "Zeke", p. 24, *Smoky Mountain Folks and Their Lore*, 1960, with GSMNHA.

p. 92 Raymond Caldwell on Tom King, converse with Elizabeth Powers. Xerox of original letter, original written Aug,3, 1933.

p. 93 Mark Hannah on Noah Conard, Elizabeth Powers converse.

p. 93 Cataloochee Wild Man article from *Asheville Citizen-Times*. July 22, 1973, also from John Parris' column, "Roamin' the Mountains" of the same date, called "Legendary Wild Man is for Real".

Chapter 11 The Hickory Stick

p. 96 Jarvis Caldwell on Shanty Branch schoolhouse. Elizabeth Powers tape, 1971.

p. 96 Jonathan Woody on burning of the schoolhouse, article in *Waynesville Mountaineer*, date obliterated.

p. 97 Jarvis Caldwell, rest of the year. Elizabeth Powers tape, Dec. 2, 1971.

p. 97 Mark Hannah, hardships of getting children to school. Elizabeth Powers tape, May, 1972.

p. 97 'Tine Bennett, stopping school for harvest, Elizabeth Powers tape, July 27, 1972, Sylva, N.C.

p. 97 Mark Hannah, same as above.

p. 97 Flora Palmer Medford, early school days, Elizabeth Powers and Mark Hannah converse with her, Iron Duff, Sept. 24, 1972.

p. 98 Robert Palmer, "Boogerman! "Everybody told me this story. Elizabeth Powers.

p. 98 Floyd and Folsom Woody on naughty tricks, Elizabeth Powers tape, 1972.

p. 99 Fred Hannah on schools, converse with Elizabeth Powers and Mark Hannah, Franklin, N.C. 1972.

p. 99 Iva Hannah Bennett on schooling, converse with Elizabeth Powers and Mark Hannah, Iotla Valley, Franklin, N.C. 1972.

p. 99 Robert H. Woody on schooling. "Cataloochee Homecoming", *South Atlantic Quarterly*, vol. 49, Jan. 1950.

p. 99 Tom Porter on 'Lige Messer, conversation with Elizabeth Powers and Mark Hannah, Franklin, N.C., 1972.

p. 100 Robert H. Woody on reading, "Cataloochee Homecoming," *South Atlantic Quarterly* vol. 49, Ja. 1950.

p. 100 Flora Palmer Medford on reading, converse Elizabeth Powers, Sept, 1972.

p. 100 Flora Messer Morrow on teaching. Elizabeth Powers tape, May 6, 1973.

p. 100 Raymond Caldwell on school, Elizabeth Powers tape, Dec. 1971.

p. 101 Gudger Palmer on school, Elizabeth Powers converse, Canton, N.C.

p. 101 Mark Hannah and 'Tine Bennett on school, Elizabeth Powers tape, July, 1972.

p. 102 Flora Messer Morrow on pupils, Elizabeth Powers tape, May 6 , 1973.

p. 102 Mark Hannah, Elizabeth Powers tape, May 1972.

p. 102 Val Hart on last school, from her article "pack Trip Through the Smokies", *National Geographic Magazine*, vol CII, no. 4, Oct., 1972.

Chapter 12. The Best Days of All

p. 103 Eldridge Caldwell, "T'warn't All Hard Work", Elizabeth Powers tape, May, 1972.

p. 103 J. Preston Arthur on the musters, *History of Western North Carolina*, p. 270 and p, 284.

p. 104 Flora Palmer Medford on the muster ground, converse Elizabeth Powers, Sept. 1972.

p. 104 Robert H. Woody, on work parties, "Cataloochee Homecoming", *South Atlantic Quarterly*, vol. 49, Jan. 1950

p. 104 Iva Hannah Bennett on beabbreakings, converse Elizabeth Powers, 1972.
p. 104 Jarvis Caldwell, Elizabeth Powers tape, Dec 2, 1971.
pp. 104–105 Mark Hannah on work party, paper written for Elizabeth Powers.
p. 105 Flora Palmer Medford on Santa Claus, Elizabeth Powers tape, Sept, 1972.
p. 105 Mark Hannah on stolen chicken, Elizabeth Powers tape, May 1972.
pp. 105–106 Eldridge Caldwell on Xmas celebrations, Elizabeth Powers tape, Oct. 1972.
p. 106 Jonathan Woody on Xmas, article, *Waynesville Mountaineer* 1971.
pp. 106–107 Flora Palmer Medford, on holidays. Elizabeth Powers tape, Sept. 24, 1972.
p. 107 Mark Hannah on 4th of July from paper and tape Elizabeth Powers, May 1972.
p. 108 Fred Hannah on Catalooch' celebrations, converse Elizabeth Powers, 1972.
p. 108 Mark Hannah on box suppers, Paper for Elizabeth Powers.
p 108 'Tine Bennett on square dancing. Elizabeth Powers tape, July 27, 1972
p. 109 Eldridge Caldwell on dancing, Elizabeth Powers tape, Oct. 28, 1972
p. 109 Pearl Valentine Caldwell on Mag Mauney, Elizabeth Powers tape, same as above.
p. 109 "patting for dancing" History of Western N.C., I think.
p. 109 Mark Hannah on Rachel Ewart's dancing, written for Elizabeth Powers.
p. 109 Mark Hannah on Ramp convention, written for Elizabeth Powers
p. 110 Robert Woody on dancing Italians, Elizabeth Powers tape, Nov. 1971.
p. 110 Roy Smith on Mark Hannah's dancing, conversation with Elizabeth Powers, Pinch Gut, Hemphill Valley, N.C.
p. 110 Mark Hannah on buckdancing, paper written for Elizabeth Powers.
p. 110 Mark Hannah and 'Tine Bennett on animal fights, Elizabeth Powers tape, 1972.
p. 111 Mark Hannah on toys, Elizabeth Powers tape, May 1972.
p. 111 Robert H. Woody on toys, Elizabeth Powers tape, Nov. 1971.
p. 111 'Tine Bennett and Mark Hannah, toys, Elizabeth Powers tape, July, 1972.
p. 112 Fred Hannah on jumpropes, converse Elizabeth Powers, 1972.
p. 112 Flora Palmer Medford on girls playing ball, Converse Elizabeth Powers, 1972.
p. 112 Floyd Woody on cobbin'. Elizabeth Powers tape, June 24, 1972.
p. 112 Verda Messer Hannah on girls' games, written for Elizabeth Powers.
p. 113 'Tine Bennett on Blind Man's Buff, Elizabeth Powers tape, July 1972.
p. 113 Eldridge Caldwell on riding steers, Elizabeth Powers tape, May 10, 1972.
p. 113 Flora Palmer Medford on Turkey's games, Converse Elizabeth Powers, 1972.
p. 114 Anonymous report, "Woodys bad to git into chickens", Elizabeth Powers tape,'72.
p. 114 Folsom and Floyd Woody on Uncle Andy tricks, Elizabeth Powers tape 1972.
p. 115 Robert H. Woody on tricking Uncle 'Tine, Elizabeth Powers tape, Nov. 1971.
pp. 115–116 Mark Hannah, paper on practical joke, written for Elizabeth Powers.
p. 116 Floyd Woody on blowpipe trick, Elizabeth Powers tape, June 24, 1972.

Chapter 13 Two by Two

p. 119 Mark Hannah, on girls chasing him. paper for Elizabeth Powers.
p. 119 Raymond Caldwell on riding with girls, Elizabeth Powers tape, 1971.
p. 120 Pearl Caldwell on dating Eldridge, Elizabeth Powers tape, Oct. 1972.
p. 120 Robert H. Woody on Italians courting. Elizabeth Powers tape, Nov. 1971.
p. 120 Mary Lou Leatherwood Moody, a 'sweetheart present', Elizabeth Powers converse.
p. 120 Gudger Palmer, "I'll take that one, George" Elizabeth Powers converse.

p. 121 Flora Messer Morrow on courtship. Elizabeth Powers tape, May 1973.
p. 121 Flora Palmer Medford on getting married, Elizabeth Powers converse, Sept 1972.
p. 122 Glenn Palmer on Jesse Palmer's marriage. Converse Elizabeth Powers, Aug 1972.
p. 122 Mark Hannah on courting his wife. Elizabeth Powers tape, May 1972.
p. 122 Flora Messer Morrow on getting permission, Elizabeth Powers tape, May 1973.
p. 122 Pearl Valentine Caldwell on Mitch Sutton, Elizabeth Powers tape Oct. 1972.
p. 123 Robert H. Woody on "charivari", "Cataloochee Homecoming", *South Atlantic Quarterly*, vol, 49 Jan 1950.
p. 123 Mark Hannah on marriage ceremony, written for Elizabeth Powers.
p. 124 Flora Palmer Medford on women's work, Elizabeth Powers converse, Sept, '72.
p. 124 Pearl V. Caldwell on mail carrying. Elizabeth Powers tape, Oct. 1973
p. 125 Mark Hannah on girls carrying mail. Paper for Elizabeth Powers.
p. 125 Mark Hannah on speckled trout, Comment written for Elizabeth Powers.
p. 125 Dr. Nick Medford on "sweetest music". Converse Elizabeth Powers , Oct., 1972.
p. 125 Raymond Caldwell on "our delight" and Hiram's fall from grace, Elizabeth Powers tape, Dec 1, 1971.
p. 126 Jarvis Caldwell on siring of children, Elizabeth Powers tape, Dec 2, 1971.
p. 126 Eldridge Caldwell on Aunt Maria and Dude. Elizabeth Powers tape. Oct. 1972.
p. 127 Judith B. Alexander on Miss Maria. Elizabeth Powers tape, Oct. 31, 1973.
p. 128 Lillian Hannah Stokes on Flora Messer Morrow, Elizabeth Powers converse,
p. 128 Mark Hannah describes Fannie Mack, Elizabeth Powers tape, May 1, 1973.
p. 128 Raymond Caldwell on Aunt Ellender Elizabeth Powers tape, Dec. 2, 1971.
p. 128 Mark Hannah on women riding, paper for Elizabeth Powers.
p. 129 Mark Hannah on Major Woody, converse Elizabeth Powers , 1972.
p 129 Eldridge Caldwell on Steve Woody, Elizabeth Powers tape, Oct 28, 1972.
p. 129 Raymond Caldwell on Steve Woody, Elizabeth Powers tape, Dee 1, 1971.
p. 131 Flora Messer Morrow, 'did a lot of sewing', Elizabeth Powers tape, 1973.
p. 131 Floyd Woody remembers new overalls, Elizabeth Powers tape, June 1972

Chapter 14. Running with the Pack

p. 134 Mark Hannah on his first bearhunt. Paper for Elizabeth Powers.
pp. 135–136 Dr. Nick Medford on etiquette of the hunt. Converse Elizabeth Powers, 1972.
p. 136 Mark Hannah on bearhunts and dogs, Elizabeth Powers tape, May 1972.
p. 136 Dr. Nick Medford on "Alabam", Converse Elizabeth Powers Oct, 1972
p 136 Raymond Caldwell on not having guns, Elizabeth Powers tape, Dec. 1, 1971
p. 136 Mark Hannah on hunting dogs, Elizabeth Powers tape, May 1972.
p. 137 Mark Hannah on "Old Pink", paper written for Elizabeth Powers.
p. 138 Raymond Caldwell on "Honest John" Elizabeth Powers tape, Oct, 27, 1972
p. 138 Jim Gasque, *Hunting and Fishing in the Great Smokies*, Alfred Knopf, 1948.
p. 138 Lee Allen on "Honest John", *Waynesville Mountaineer*, July 1976.
p 138 Turkey George Palmer on bear's skull, as told to Mark Hannah.
p. 139 Will Palmer on hunting Joseph S. Hall recording, Cataloochee 1939, Disc 48, B-l.
p. 139 Mark Hannah's comment on Will Palmer's hunt, written for Elizabeth Powers.
p. 139 Steve Woody on Shanty Mountain hunt, recorded by Joseph S. Hall, Cataloochee Valley, 1939, Disc 12-a.

p. 140 James A. Hannah on Bill Barnes, Box 14, notebook 7, folder 74, p. 1, Hiram C. Wilburn Collection, MSS 80-17, Western Carolina University Hunter Library Special Collections.

p. 141 Major Woody on Tom Barnes, p. 14, Smoky Mountain Folks and Their Ways, Joseph S. Hall, 1960, with GSMNHA.

p. 141 Eldridge Caldwell on Turkey George, Elizabeth Powers tape, Oct. 28, 1972.

p. 142 John Parris, "Turkey George Palmer, a Cataloochee Legend", *Asheville Citizen-Times*, Oct. 24, 1976.

p. 142 Raymond Caldwell on Turkey George, Elizabeth Powers tape, Oct., 1972.

p. 142 Mark Hannah on Turkey George, Elizabeth Powers tape, May 1972.

p. 142 Dr. Nick Medford on Turkey George, converse Elizabeth Powers, Oct. 1972.

p. 142 Robert Palmer on his father, Turkey George, from John Parris article, see above.

p. 143 Will Palmer on Turkey George, Joseph S. Hall recording, Cataloochee Valley, 1939, Disc 48, B-l.

p. 143 Mark Hannah on Steve Woody, Elizabeth Powers tape, May 1972.

p. 143 Dr. Nick Medford on Turkey George, converse Elizabeth Powers, Oct. 1972.

p. 144 Eldridge Caldwell on Uncle Turkey and surveyors, Elizabeth Powers tape, Campbell Creek, Maggie Valley, N.C. Oct. 28, 1972.

Chapter 15 The Blooming of the Beelzebubs

p. 146 Amanda Powers, daughter of Elizabeth Powers, falls in Cataloochee, 1969?

p. 147 W. Clark Medford on Dr, Winton, pp 129–130 *Land o' the Sky*, 1965.

p. 147 Flora Messer Morrow on Daniel J. Cook Elizabeth Powers tape, May, 1973.

p. 147 Mark Hannah on Dr. Kirkpatrick. Elizabeth Powers tape, May 1972.

p. 148 Raymond Caldwell on mailcarriers calling doctor, Elizabeth Powers tape 1972.

p. 148 Dr. Nick Medford on dentistry and Dr. Bob Medford, converse with Elizabeth Powers, Waynesville, N.C., Oct. 25, 1972.

p. 148 Mark Hannah on Dr. MacMahan. Elizabeth Powers tape, May, 1972.

p. 149 Judith Barksdale Alexander on medicine in Cataloochee, Elizabeth Powers tape, Cataloochee Ranch, Fie Top, N.C. oct. 31, 1973.

p. 151 Floyd Woody on Aunt Susie Caldwell, Elizabeth Powers tape, June, 1972.

p. 151 Flora Palmer Medford on grannywomen. Elizabeth Powers tape, Sept, 1972.

p. 151 Mark Hannah, his mother's midwifery, Elizabeth Powers tape, May 1, 1973.

p. 153 Mrs. Fred Hannah on folk remedies, letter to Mark Hannah.

p. 154 Mark Hannah on herbal medicine, Elizabeth Powers tape, May 1, 1973.

p. 154 Balsam poplar info, *Knowing Your Trees*, American Forestry Association, Collingwood and Brush.

p. 154 Miss Janie of Cedar Mountain, article, Adventure Magazine, *Waynesville Mountaineer*, 1973.

p. 155 Flora Palmer Medford on herbal teas. Elizabeth Powers tape and some written for Elizabeth Powers, Sept. 1972.

p. 156 Ross Hutchins on bloodroot, p. 189, *Hidden Valley of the Smokies*, Dodd, Mead 1971.

p. 156 Mark Hannah on his mother's herb doctoring. Elizabeth Powers tape, 1973.

p. 157 John Preston Arthur on milksick, p. 336 *History of Western North Carolina*, Asheville, N.C. 1914.

p. 157 Eldridge Caldwell on flu epidemic, Elizabeth Powers tape, May 10, 1972.
p. 158 Mark Hannah on diphtheria epidemic Elizabeth Powers tape, May 1973.
p. 158 Horace Kephart on halfwits, p. 296 *Our Southern Highlanders*. Macmillan, 1929.
p. 159 Mary Lou Leatherwood Moody on Granny Pop's senility. Converse with Elizabeth Powers, Hazelwood, N.C., Dec. 1971.
p. 159 Flora Palmer Medford on her sister's death. Converse Elizabeth Powers, 1972.
p. 159 Mark Hannah on Rev. Camel's death. Paper for Elizabeth Powers.
p. 161 Eldridge Caldwell on yellow jackets. Elizabeth Powers tape, May, 1972.
p. 161 Jarvis Caldwell on breaking his ankle, converse Elizabeth Powers.
p. 162 Tom Kloss corroborates snake theory, Converse Elizabeth Powers, Cataloochee.
p. 162 Robert Hannah on losing finger to rattler, letter to Mark Hannah.
p. 162 Mark Hannah on snakebites, Elizabeth Powers tape, M y 1972.
p. 162 Jarvis Caldwell on snakebite, Mark Hannah tape, Feb. 29, 1976.
p. 162 Lloyd Caldwell on hog killing Dock Caldwell, Mark Hannah tape, Feb. 29, 1976.
p. 163 Mark Hannah on snake-bitten dog, Elizabeth Powers tape, May 1972.
p. 163 Mildred Bennett Ensley on her husband's attack in Cataloochee, letter to *Waynesville Mountaineer*, 1970s.

Chapter 16 Hiram's Fixation

p. 165 Raymond Caldwell on Hiram's work. Elizabeth Powers tape Dec 1, 1971.
p. 165 Helen Hannah Trantham on Cataloochee work, Letter to Elizabeth Powers.
p. 166 Robert H. Woody on class distinctions, 'Cataloochee Homecoming", *South Atlantic Quarterly*, vol. 49, Jan. 1950.
p. 166 Wait till the sugars are blooming, Glen Messer to Elizabeth Powers.
p. 167 Allen T Davidson, "Low, Dudley, low" *The Lyceum* magazine, transcript of speech, Asheville ,N.C., 1890 or 91.
p. 167 *History of Western North Carolina*, John Preston Arthur.
p. 167 John Preston Arthur on ranging stock, *History of Western North Carolina*, p. 336, 1914.
p. 167 W. Clark Medford on ranging stock, p. 85, *Early History of Haywood County*, 1961.
p. 167 Mark Hannah on domestic animals, Converse Elizabeth Powers.
p. 168 Raymond Caldwell on ranging livestock, Elizabeth Powers tape, Dec, 1971.
p. 168 Hiram Wilburn on Ledge Bald, Notebook 14, Folder 77, beg, p. 6. Hiram C. Wilburn Collection, MSS 80-17, Western Carolina University Hunter Library Special Collections beg, p. 6.
p. 168 Flora Messer Morrow on domestic animals, Elizabeth Powers tape , 1973.
p. 169 T.A. Groce on Cataloochee hogs, recording, "Coming into Cataloochee", Nov. 1909, Jonathan's Creek, N.C.
p. 170 Mark Hannah on raising hogs, paper written for Elizabeth Powers.
p. 171 John Parris on Turkey George and hogs, from "Mightiest of Hunters", *Asheville Citizen-Times*, Oct. 19, 1962.
p. 171 Ernestine Upchurch on wild boars. Elizabeth Powers tape, Oct. 28, 1972.
p. 171 Eldridge Caldwell on chestnuts, hogs, yellow jackets, Elizabeth Powers tape, Campbell Creek, Maggie Valley, N.C. Oct. 28, 1972.

References and Acknowledgments 303

p. 172 Robert H. Woody on bee trees, "Cataloochee Homecoming", *South Atlantic Quarterly*, vol. 49, Jan. 1950.

p. 172 Interview with Neil Sutton, notebook 7, Folder 74, p. 24, Hiram C. Wilburn Collection, MSS 80-17, Western Carolina University Hunter Library Special Collections.

p. 172 Mark Hannah on Neil Sutton, Converse with Elizabeth Powers.

p. 173 Mark Hannah on chickens, Paper written for Elizabeth Powers.

p. 173 Robert H. Woody on tobacco. Elizabeth Powers tape, Durham, N.C. Nov. 1971.

p. 174 Flora Messer Morrow on snuff, Elizabeth Powers tape, May 6, 1973

p. 174 Gudger Palmer on Mollie Runningwolf, Converse Elizabeth Powers, Canton, N.C.

p. 174 Joseph S. Hall on Turkey George and ginseng, pp 20–21, *Smoky Mountain Folks and Their Lore*, 1960, with GSMNHA.

p. 175 'Tine Bennett and Mark Hannah on farming. Elizabeth Powers tape, 1972.

p. 176 Mark Hannah on apple names, converse Elizabeth Powers, Cataloochee Valley.

p. 176 Apple growing in Little Cataloochee. National Park's publication, *Little Cataloochee Historic Structures Report*.

p. 177 Raymond Caldwell on Steve Woody's selling apples, Elizabeth Powers tape 1972.

p. 177 Eldridge Caldwell on storm twisting apple trees, Elizabeth Powers tape, Campbell Creek, Maggie Valley, N.C. Oct. 28, 1972.

Chapter 17 The Compleat Cataloochan

p. 180 Jarvis and Raymond Caldwell on Will Messer, Elizabeth Powers tape 1971.

p. 180 on W.G.B. Messer National Park's publication, *Little Cataloochee Historic Structures Report*.

p. 181 Floyd Burgess on W.G.B. Messer, as told to Mark Hannah.

p. 182 Mark Hannah on little stores, Paper for Elizabeth Powers.

p. 182 W. Clark Medford on the old mail boys. p. 63 *Mountain Times, Mountain People*, 1963.

p. 182 Enos Boyd on Cataloochee mail route, converse Elizabeth Powers.

p. 183 Robert H. Woody on water mill. "Cataloochee Homecoming", from *South Atlantic Quarterly*, vol. 49, Jan. 1950.

p. 183 'Tine Bennett on water wheel, Elizabeth Powers tape, July 1972.

p. 183 Vick Smith on mills, notebook 7, folder 74, pp. 27–28, Hiram C. Wilburn Collection, MSS 80-17, Western Carolina University Hunter Library Special Collections.

p. 184 John Davidson on the Armstrong mill, typescript in possession of Elizabeth Powers, Recollections of Trip to Texas, 1840.

p. 185 Flora Messer Morrow remembers Grandmother Harriet. Elizabeth Powers converse, May 6, 1973.

p. 185 Mark Hannah on Aunt 'Tildy's coverlids, Elizabeth Powers tape May 1972.

p. 185 Judith Barksdale Alexander on Miss Maria's quilts, Elizabeth Powers tape, Cataloochee Ranch, Fie Top. Oct. 31, 1973.

p. 185 Linton Palmer on Miss Maria's bed, converse Elizabeth Powers.

p. 186 Beatrice Burgess Sisk on Daniel Cook, National Park's publication, *Little Cataloochee Historic Structures Report*.

p. 186 Flora Palmer Medford on tanning leather. Paper written for Elizabeth Powers.

p. 186 Mark Hannah comment on above to Elizabeth Powers.

pp. 186–187 Robert H. Woody on home-made items, "Cataloochee Homecoming", *South Atlantic Quarterly*, vol. 49, Jan. 1950.

p. 188 Eldridge Caldwell knew hoofprints, from article on Hiram Caldwell house, *Waynesville Mountaineer*, by Nye, June 1971.

p. 188 Mark Hannah on the flail, Paper written for Elizabeth Powers.

Chapter 18 Shelter

p. 189 Mark Hannah on the Hollow Log Camp, paper written for Elizabeth Powers

p. 190 *Mountain Culture Program* report, Arthur Stupka, Grossman, and Hiram Wilburn, Hiram C. Wilburn Collection, MSS 80-17, Western Carolina University Hunter Library Special Collections.

p. 190 Mark Hannah on Messer apple house. Jackie Turner article in *Waynesville Mountaineer*, Oct. 20,1971.

p. 191 Boyd Evison announces funds for structure repair, *Waynesville Mountaineer*, Jan. 26, 1976.

p. 191 Jarvis Caldwell on building schoolhouse, Elizabeth Powers tape, Dec, 1971.

p. 191 Mark Hannah on building Little Cataloochee Baptist church, paper written for Elizabeth Powers.

p. 192 Flora Palmer Medford on Turkey George house, converse Elizabeth Powers 1972.

p. 192 Eldridge Caldwell on old pioneers' building, Elizabeth Powers tape, '72.

p. 192 Willis King memo to Hiram Wilburn, Hiram C. Wilburn Collection, MSS 80-17, Western Carolina University Hunter Library Special Collections.

p. 192 Eldridge Caldwell on Needham. Elizabeth Powers tape, May 10, 1972.

p. 193 Jarvis Caldwell on old Levi Caldwell house, Elizabeth Powers tape, Dec. 1971.

p. 193 Vick Smith on old Levi Caldwell house, notebook 7, folder 74, pp 27–28, Hiram C. Wilburn Collection, MSS 80-17, Western Carolina University Hunter Library Special Collections.

p. 193 Messer house, National Park's publication, *Little Cataloochee Historic Structures Report*.

p. 194 Robert H. Woody on Uncle 'Tine's house, Elizabeth Powers tape, 1971. And also from "Cataloochee Homecoming" article. S. A. Q.

p. 194 Hiram Wilburn note to John Needham on 'Tine Woody house, folder 2, Hiram C. Wilburn Collection, MSS 80-17, Western Carolina University Hunter Library Special Collections.

p. 194 Robert H. Woody on weatherboarded house, Elizabeth Powers tape, Nov. 1971.

p. 195 'Tine Bennett describes Uncle 'Tine's house. Elizabeth Powers tape, July, 1972.

p. 195 Jim Caldwell house, noted in Wilburn papers, Hiram C. Wilburn Collection, MSS 80-17, Western Carolina University Hunter Library Special Collections.

p. 195 Nye article on Hiram Caldwell house, *Waynesville Mountaineer*, June 23, 1971.

p. 195 Stokey Caldwell, "Cataloochee Kid", converse Elizabeth Powers, Hemphill, NC.

p. 196 Sam Easterby on Hiram Caldwell house, Jackie Turner article, *Waynesville Mountaineer*, Aug. 13, 1973.

p. 196 Linton Palmer on old Palmer house, converse, Elizabeth Powers.

p. 197 W. Clark Medford describes old dogtrot architecture, p. 75, *Early History of Haywood County*, 1961.

p. 197 Mark Hannah on old R John Jackson Hannah house, Elizabeth Powers tape 1972.

p. 197 Daniel Cook, from National Park's publication, *Little Cataloochee Historic Structures Report*.

p. 198 Flora Messer Morrow on Daniel Cook and Jim Hannah house, Elizabeth Powers tape, May 6, 1973.

p. 199 Mark Hannah on remains of Evan Hannah house, Elizabeth Powers tape, May '72.

Chapter 19 Plenty

p. 201, Floyd Woody on plenty to eat, Elizabeth Powers tape, June 24, 1972.

p. 201 Robert H. Woody on good water, Elizabeth Powers tape, Nov, 1971.

p. 201 Mark Hannah on wild game, paper written for Elizabeth Powers.

p. 201 Robert H. Woody on food, '"Cataloochee Homecoming". S.A.Q.

p. 202 Floyd Woody on slim Glenn Palmer, Elizabeth Powers tape, June 24, 1972.

p. 202 Glenn Palmer on eating 47 fish. Elizabeth Powers converse, Aug. 20, 1972

p. 202 'Tine Bennett on Uncle 'Tine's eating habits, July, 1972.

p. 203 Mark Hannah on food at his house, written for Elizabeth Powers.

p. 203 Charlie Palmer reminisces on food, recording of Joseph S. Hall XVIII, 35, Waynesville, N.C. 1962.

p. 204 Pearl and Eldridge Caldwell on berries and wine, Elizabeth Powers tape, Oct. 28, 1972.

p. 205 Turkey George Palmer on canning bear meat, p 21, *Smoky Mountain Folks and Their Lore*. Joseph S. Hall 1960.

p. 205 Mark Hannah on making apple cider, Elizabeth Powers, written for.

p 205 Robert H. Woody on cornbread, Elizabeth Powers tape, Nov. 1971.

p. 205 Flora Palmer Medford on eating habits and recipes, converse with Elizabeth Powers, Iron Duff, N.C. Sept. 24, 1972.

p. 206 John Palmer on Cataloochee food from Adventure Magazine, published by *Waynesville Mountaineer*.

p. 207 "Rattlesnake Patrol Cooks Best Meal", *Waynesville Mountaineer*.

Chapter 20 The Food of Love

p. 209 Mark Hannah, play for the rest of the day, Converse Elizabeth Powers.

p. 209 John Jacob Niles on instrument of the Devil. *The Great Smokies and the Blue Ridge*, ed. Roderick Peattie, Vanguard Press, 1943.

p. 209 "Buckwheat grains", *White Spirituals in the Southern Uplands*, George Pullen Jackson, UNC Press, 1933.

p. 211 Mark Hannah on church singing, Elizabeth Powers tape, May 1972

p. 211 Raymond Caldwell on Aunt Ellender singing. Elizabeth Powers tape, Dec 2, '71.

p. 211 Flora Palmer Medford remembers hymns, Elizabeth Powers converse, Sept 1972.

p. 211 Jarvis and Raymond Caldwell on hymns, Elizabeth Powers tape, Dec 2, 1971.

p. 212 Mark remembers "Rosim the Bow" Elizabeth Powers converse.

p. 212 "Down in the Willow Garden" sung by Wilburn Owen, with his guitar, Oct. 17, 1970.

p. 212 Mark and Fred Hannah on words to songs, Elizabeth Powers converse, & paper.

p. 213 Bascom Lamar Lunsford, more than 300 songs, *The Kingdom of Madison*, Manly Wade Wellman, UNC Press, 1973.

p. 213 Manly Wade Wellman on "Lonesome Laurel", see above.

p. 213 Mark Hannah on songs, Elizabeth Powers converse, and also a paper.

p. 213 Mark Hannah on box supper music. Paper for Elizabeth Powers.

p. 214 Robert H. Woody on Mitch Sutton banjo, Elizabeth Powers tape, Nov. 1971.

p. 214 Eldridge Caldwell on music in Big Cataloochee. Elizabeth Powers tape on Oct 28, 1972.

p. 214 Robert H. Woody on bells, "Cataloochee Homecoming", S.A.Q

p. 214 *Foxfire 3*, on bells, edited by Elliot Wigginton, Rabun Gap. Georgia.

p. 215 Robert H. Woody confesses to photo, Elizabeth Powers letter to.

p. 215 'Tine Bennett on Uncle 'Tine's banjo, Elizabeth Powers tape, July, 1972.

p. 215 Manly Wade Wellman on banjos and fiddles, *The Kingdom of Madison*, UNC Press, 1973.

p. 215 Tom Porter thinks 'Lige educated, converse Elizabeth Powers, 1972.

p. 215 "Bonaparte's Retreat", the Grooms tune, p 151 *Early History of Haywood County*. W. Clark Medford, 1961.

p. 216 Manly Wade Wellman on the bagpipe wail and guitars, *The Kingdom of Madison*, UNC Press, 1973.

p. 216 Mark Hannah on playing with Willie Messer, Elizabeth Powers tape, 1972.

p. 216 Harold Hannah on music in family, letter written to Elizabeth Powers.

p. 217 Samuel Parsons, "Cataloochee Wild Man' song written at Pinch Gut, Hemphill Valley, N.C. Elizabeth Powers tape.

Chapter 21 Tom-Walker-Nation-on-the-Devil!

p. 219 Allen T. Davidson on the Indian tongue. *The Lyceum* magazine, transcript from speech, Asheville, 1890 or 91.

p. 219 Horace Kephart corroborates theory of dialect. *Our Southern Highlanders*, Macmillan, 1929.

p. 219 Judge E.J. Sutherland on surviving Indian words, "Folk Speech on Frying Pan", *Mountain Life and Work* Mag, 1961.

p. 220 Jarvis Caldwell can tell a Cataloochan from his speech. Elizabeth Powers tape, Allen's Creek, Haywood County, N.C. Dec. 2, 1971.

p. 220 Mark and 'Tine Bennett repeat phrases. Elizabeth Powers tape, July 1972.

p. 220 Eldridge Caldwell, prepositions and adverbs, Elizabeth Powers tape 1972.

p. 220 Mark Hannah, prepositions and adverbs, Elizabeth Powers tape May 1972.

p. 220 Dr. Cratis Williams on the 'jutting jaw syndrome' p 5 "Mountain Speech", *Mountain Life and Work* Magazine, 1961.

p. 221 Turkey George Palmer on red fox, quoted by Eldridge Caldwell, Elizabeth Powers tape, Oct. 28, 1972.

pp. 221–223 Some of these are from *Sayings from Old Smoky*, by Joseph S. Hall, Cataloochee Press, 1972, unless otherwise designated.

p. 223 "Dead man" Jarvis Caldwell to Elizabeth Powers tape, Dec. 2 1971.

p. 223 Dick Hughes on owlhead pistol, letter to Elizabeth Powers from Wyoming.
p. 223 "Jarhead" Glen Messer to Elizabeth Powers converse.
p. 223 "Pencil tail" Mark Hannah, Elizabeth Powers converse.
p. 223 Cataloochee nicknames, Mark Hannah, converse Elizabeth Powers.
p. 224 "Little Bluehead", Floyd Woody to Elizabeth Powers tape, June 24, 1972.
p. 224 Turkey George fable, p. 19, Smoky Mountain Folks and Their Lore, Joseph S. Hall, 1960, with GSMNHA.
p. 225 Place names, largely from notebook 14, folder 77, p. 6 onwards, Hiram C. Wilburn Collection, MSS 80-17, Western Carolina University Hunter Library Special Collections.
p. 225 Floyd Woody, tall tales, Mark Hannah tape, Feb 2, 1976
p. 226 "Nice feer'rn" Everett Messer, Cataloochee Divide, Elizabeth Powers converse.
p. 226 Mattie Russell on the Devil, "Devil in the Smokies", *South Atlantic Quarterly*, vol 73, Winter 1974.
p. 226 "Fur" field and "nigh" field, 'Tine Bennett, Tape Elizabeth Powers, July 1972.
p. 226 Jarvis Caldwell on Hosey Mauney and the Devil, Elizabeth Powers tape Allen's Creek, Dec 2, 1971.
p. 227 Raymond Caldwell, planting by the signs, Elizabeth Powers tape, Oct. 1972.
p. 227 Allen T. Davidson on witchcraft in Cataloochee, *The Lyceum* magazine, transcript of speech, Asheville, N.C. 1890-91.
p. 228 "Climbing Bear" tells of witches, Swimmer Manuscript, ed, by James Mooney, 19th annual report, Bureau of American Ethnology, Govt Printing Office, 1897-98.
p. 228 Raymond Caldwell on ghosts, Elizabeth Powers tape Dec 1, 1971.
p. 229 Mark Hannah on ghosts, Elizabeth Powers tape, July 18, 1973.

Chapter 22, Once an Inland Sea

p. 236 "Erosional remnants of roots", Hiram C. Wilburn Collection, MSS 80-17, Western Carolina University Hunter Library Special Collections.
p. 236 Mark Hannah, 'nothing but a bunch of shale', Elizabeth Powers tape 1972.
p. 237 Captain Moore and Captain Harden experience earthquake, *History of North Carolina*, Samuel A'Court Ashe, Vol I, Charles van Noppen, Publisher, pp. 895-898.
p. 237 Caldwell family on Hosey Mauney and the earthquake, Elizabeth Powers tape , Dec. 2, 1971.
p. 238 Mark Hannah on earthquakes of 1914, Elizabeth Powers tape, May 1972.
p. 238 De Soto's men and gold, *History of Western North Carolina*. John Preston Arthur.
p. 238 Mark Hannah on abortive silvermine, Elizabeth Powers tape, May 1972.

Chapter 23, About as Far as New York to California

p. 239 Arnold Guyot calls Luftee Knob, "The Pillar" J.C. Allen, *Annals of Haywood County*.
p. 240 Joseph S. Hall describes Cataloochee, p. 22, *Smoky Mountain Folks and Their Lore*, 1960, with GSMNHA.
p. 241 Mark Hannah on good water, Elizabeth Powers tape May 1972.
p. 241 Mark Hannah on Waterville. Elizabeth Powers tape, May 1972.

Chapter 24, Herrycanes and Sech

p. 244 Colonel John C. Smathers remembers falling stars

p. 245 Mark Hannah on weather folklore, Elizabeth Powers tape, May 1972.

p 245 Donald Culross Peattie describes Smokies, *The Great Smokies and the Blue Ridge*, ed. Roderick Peattie, Vanguard, 1943.

p. 246 Harold Hannah on freak flood, letter to Elizabeth Powers.

p. 246 John. Preston Arthur on "herrycanes", p541. *History of Western North Carolina*, 1914.

p. 247 Eldridge Caldwell on hurricane and Major Woody, Elizabeth Powers tape, May 10, 1972.

p. 248 Eldridge Caldwell on "yarb" doctoring, Elizabeth Powers tape, May 1972.

p. 248 Tom Alexander II, weather article from *Fortune*, reprinted Mar. 10, 1974, *Washington Post*.

p. 248 Robert Henry's weather notes, diary of 1815.

p. 249 Hiram Wilburn's weather notes, Hiram C. Wilburn Collection, MSS 80-17, Western Carolina University Hunter Library Special Collections.

p. 249 Mark Hannah on his father's frozen mustache., paper for Elizabeth Powers.

p. 249 Arthur Stupka's records of the weather, from *The Great Smokies and the Blue Ridge*, ed. Roderick Peattie, Vanguard, 1943.

p. 249 Harold Hannah on stillness of a winter night, letter to Elizabeth Powers.

p. 250 Mark Hannah on Mt. Sterling trip and doctors, EDB tape and paper for Elizabeth Powers.

p. 251 Mark Hannah on Creighton Bennett's water ditch, Elizabeth Powers paper.

p. 251 Tom Alexander on dry season of 1925. Elizabeth Powers converse, Dec. 1971.

p. 252 Eldridge Caldwell on fire of 1925, Elizabeth Powers tape, Oct. 1972.

p. 252 Raymond Caldwell on the big fire, Elizabeth Powers tape, Dec 1 1971.

p. 252 Mark Hannah on fires when he was Ranger in Catalooch', Elizabeth Powers tape May 1972.

p. 252 Harold Hannah on fire towers, letter to Elizabeth Powers.

p. 253 Horace Kephart on native hunters and the weather, *Our Southern Highlanders*, Macmillan, 1929.

Chapter 25 Flora's Ark

p. 255 Charlton Ogburn on foliage of Mt. Sterling, *The Southern Appalachians*, Morrow, 1975.

p. 255 William Bartram on wild strawberries, *The Travels of William Bartram*.

p. 256 Dr. Doris Hammett on wild flowers, *Hiker's Guide to the Smokies*, Sierra Club, 1973, ed. by Dick Murlless and Constance Stallings.

p. 257 Val Hart on autumn flowers, "Pack Trip through the Smokies", *National Geographic* mag., vol CII, no 4, Oct. 1952.

p. 258 Allen T. Davidson, *The Lyceum* magazine, transcript of speech, Asheville, N.C. 1890–91
p. 258 Mark Hannah recalls chestnut blight, Elizabeth Powers converse.
p. 258 Donald Culross Peattie, *The Great Smokies and the Blue Ridge*, ed. Roderick Peattie, Vanguard Press, 1943.
p. 258 Charlton Ogburn calls it the Temperate Zone Tropics, *The Southern Appalachians*, Morrow, 1975.
p. 258 Val Hart on the Cataloochee forests, "Pack Trip through the Smokies", *National Geographic* mag, Oct. 1852.
p. 259 Mark Hannah views decimation of the forests, Elizabeth Powers converse.
p. 259 Mark Hannah on protecting the forests, Jackie Turner article?
p. 260 Dr. Doris Hammett on the big poplars, Hiker's Guide to the Smokies, Sierra Club.
p. 260 Mark Hannah on typical forests of Cataloochee, Elizabeth Powers converse.
p. 261 Tom Alexander on Cataloochee forests, Elizabeth Powers converse, 1971.
p. 262 Joseph S. Hall on Mouse Creek, *Sayings from Old Smoky*. Cataloochee Press, Asheville, N.C. 1972.
p. 262 Robert H. Woody on Italians as loggers, Elizabeth Powers tape, 1971.
p. 263 Eldridge and Pearl Caldwell on shanty cars, The Ledge. Elizabeth Powers tape, Campbell Creek, Oct. 28, 1972.
p. 263 Jarvis Caldwell recollects band mill, Elizabeth Powers tape Dec. 2, 1971.
p. 263 'Tine Bennett and Mark Hannah , timber company head of Catalooch', Elizabeth Powers tape July 27, 1972.
p. 264 William Buckley on superior trees, letter to Doris Hammett, Dec. 8, 1971, TVA staff forester.
p. 264 Hiram Wilburn on largest apple tree, Hiram C. Wilburn Collection, MSS 80-17, Western Carolina University Hunter Library Special Collections.
p. 264 Tom Porter on the smell of Cataloochee, Elizabeth Powers converse , 1972

Chapter 26 Klandaghi and Other Lords

p. 266 Reuben Thwaites on buffalo, his biography of Daniel Boone, pp l7,18.
p. 266 Harold Hannah on panther stories, Letter to Elizabeth Powers.
p. 267 Glen Messer on panther, Elizabeth Powers converse.
p. 267 Panther sighting, article, *Waynesville Mountaineer*, by Jack Horan, 1975.
p. 267 Adeline Howell Davidson recalled panther screams, oral history in Elizabeth Powers family.
p. 268 Thomas Connally on the panther scream, *Discovering the Appalachians*, p. 186, Stackpole Books, 1968.
p. 268 Floyd Woody on Granny Pop and the panther. Elizabeth Powers tape, 1972.
p. 268 Mark Hannah on Wiley Caldwell and the panther, Elizabeth Powers tape, 1972.
p. 269 Boyd Evison on wolves in the Park, 1971. Adventure Magazine, *Waynesville Mountaineer*.
p. 269 Tom Kloos on the Russian boar, Elizabeth Powers converse, Cataloochee Valley.
p. 269 Jonathan Woody on the wolf bounty. Elizabeth Powers converse.
p. 269 Colonel Bryan on the milch cow, *History of Western North Carolina*, J. Preston Arthur, 1914.

p. 269 Turkey George Palmer on wolves, p. 21 *Smoky Mountain Folks and Their Lore*, Joseph S. Hall, 1960, with GSMNHA.

p. 270 Mark Hannah on the chestnut blight and bear travel, Elizabeth Powers tape May, 1972.

p. 270 Mark Hannah on warding off bears, Elizabeth Powers tape, May 1972.

p. 270 Mark Hannah on deer, paper written for Elizabeth Powers.

p. 271 Turkey George acknowledges defeat by deer, p553, *Annals of Haywood County*, W.C. Allen, 1935.

p. 271 Mariella Dumont on shrews, Turkey George Campground, Elizabeth Powers converse, pack trip into Cataloochee.

p. 272 Major Woody on wildcats and coonhunting, p 16, *Smoky Mountain Folks and Their Lore*, Joseph S. Hall 1960.

p. 272 Joseph S. Hall on Major Woody, p. 16, see above.

p. 272 Mark Hannah on Major Woody, Elizabeth Powers converse.

p. 272 Joseph S. Hall on Major Woody and coonhunts, p. 16 see.

p. 272 Raymond Caldwell on possum hunts with Major Woody, Elizabeth Powers tape Hazelwood, N.C. Dec 1, 1971.

p. 273 Mark Hannah on his father's coon hunt. Paper for Elizabeth Powers.

p. 273 'Tine Bennett and Mark Hannah on pistol, Elizabeth Powers tape, 1972

p. 274 Harold Hannah on fox's bark, Letter to Elizabeth Powers.

p. 274 Robert Palmer on squirrels shot by Uncle Turkey, John Parris, "The Mightiest of Hunters", *Asheville Citizen-Times*. Oct. 19, 1962.

p. 274 Glen Messer on squirrel soup. Elizabeth Powers converse.

p. 274 Robert H. Woody on the muzzle-loader, Elizabeth Powers tape, Nov, 1971.

p. 275 Harold Hannah on skunks, Letter to Elizabeth Powers.

p. 275 Floyd Woody on "Polecat John" Elizabeth Powers tape, June 24, 1972.

p. 275 Edwin Way Teale on skunk fumes, *South with the Spring*?

p. 275 Michael Frome on the golden eagle, Elizabeth Powers converse, The Purchase, 1974.

p. 275 Mark Hannah on the golden and bald eagles. Elizabeth Powers tape, May 1972.

p. 276 Raymond Caldwell on Turkey George's 6 turkeys, Elizabeth Powers tape Pinch Gut, Oct. 27, 1972

p. 276 Mark Hannah on his big turkey. Elizabeth Powers tape, May 1972.

p. 277 Harold Hannah on rooster noise. Letter to Elizabeth Powers.

p. 277 Mark Hannah remembers the great horned owl, EDO converse.

p. 277 Bird notes, unless otherwise designated, are based on the observations of Arthur Stupka's book, *Notes on the Birds of the Great Smoky Mountains National Park*. U. of Tenn. Press, 1963, pub. in conjunction with the GSMNHA.

p. 278 Allen T. Davidson on sapsuckers. *The Lyceum* magazine, transcript of speech, Asheville, N.C. 1890–91.

p. 279 Elizabeth Powers sighted cerulean warbler Cataloochee Divide, July 1975.

p. 279 Mark Hannah on Cal Messer and the flickers, Elizabeth Powers tape May 1972.

p. 280 John Strother on the rattlebug, from his *Diary of 1799*- Survey of the N.C.-Tenn. border, State Archives, Raleigh, N.C.

p. 280 Bishop Asbury thanks God for avoiding: rattlers, Asbury's Journals.

- p. 280 Arthur Stupka on rattlers, p. 70, *Amphibians and Reptiles of the Great Smoky Mountains National Park*, by James S. Huheey and Arthur Stupka, U. of Tenn. Press, 1970, in conjunction with GSMNHA.
- p. 280 Willis King on dearth of copperheads p. 5 of above book.
- p. 280 Harold Hannah on snakes. Letter to Elizabeth Powers.
- p. 281 Arthur Stupka and Willis King's observations on amphibians and reptiles constitute the basis of the author's observations on these animals in Cataloochee, unless otherwise designated.
- p. 282 Mark Hannah on trout, Elizabeth Powers converse.
- p. 283 Frank Campbell on trout, Letter to Elizabeth Powers, Oct. 15, 1971.
- p. 283 Eldridge Caldwell on Uncle Hiram's fishing. Elizabeth Powers tape 1972.
- p. 283 Raymond Caldwell on Major Woody's fish stories, EDF tape, Dec.' 1, 1971.
- p. 284 B.H. Gates on Cataloochee fish size. Letter to Mark Hannah.
- p. 284 Flora Palmer Redford on Lost bottom trout, Elizabeth Powers converse, Iron Duff, N.C. Sept. 24, 1972.
- p. 284 'Tine Bennett and Mark Hannah on fishing lines, Elizabeth Powers tape, Sylva, N.C., July 27, 1972.
- p. 284 Arthur Stupka on minnows, p. 53, *Great Smoky Mountains National Park*, a Natural History Handbook, NPS D.C. 1960.
- p. 285 Boyd Evison on brook trout, *Waynesville Mountaineer*, Jan 26, 1976.
- p. 285 Elizabeth W. Dixon on fishing in Cataloochee, oral history in Elizabeth Powers family.

IMAGES FROM THE ORIGINAL 1982 BOOK

Turkey George Palmer

Bear Hunt, Cataloochee circa 1930. Turkey George (cross on chest), Jarvis Caldwell (on horse), Doc Nick Medford (low right)

Weatherboarded log dogtrot house

Palmer's forebay mill

Mag Mauney Caldwell (after leaving Cataloochee)

Uncle Steve Woody

Beech Grove school (John Queen, teacher, top center)

Messer tobacco patch, Little Cataloochee (left to right: Jackie Rakestraw, Myrtle & Willie Messer, Cal Messer (the fiddler))

William G.B. Messer farm, 1916, Little Cataloochee, showing schoolhouse upper left, Braz Whaley house upper right, Messer house lower left

Mack Hannah, father of Mark Hannah, c. 1920, with hunting horn and dogs, Blue and Moove, with coon on knee

ABOUT THE AUTHORS

Mark E. Hannah was born in the Cataloochee Valley in 1906. He married Verda Messer and they raised a family of seven children in their beloved Cataloochee. Mark Hannah was the perfect choice to return to Cataloochee as a ranger after the park was created, to protect the land he loved, and to be a voice of reason to all who still cherished the valley as much as he did.

Mark E. Hannah II is the grandson and namesake of the co-author of this documentary work. Mark has many fond memories of Cataloochee, accompanying Ranger Mark whenever possible on regular rounds, and also a very memorable Christmas Eve trip to Mt. Sterling (see Chapter 24, page 250). Ranger Mark was always committed to documenting Cataloochee history, recording events with his 8 mm camera, and writing poems and telling stories of the events that shaped his years in the Cataloochee Valley.

Elizabeth Dixon Powers was a writer, conservator, and Asheville native whose work reflected a deep connection to the Southern Appalachian landscape. Educated at Wellesley College and the Corcoran Gallery of Art, she published essays including "Cataloochee—A Sense of Place" and authored several unpublished novels. She lived in both South Carolina's Lowcountry and Western North Carolina, where she passed away in 2007.

A native son of the Smokies who grew up in Bryson City and still calls the mountain heartland the home of his heart, **Jim Casada** is a trained historian (Ph. D., Vanderbilt University). After a career as a university professor, he became a full-time freelance writer. He is the author or editor of more than thirty books and has contributed thousands of articles to regional and national magazines. He writes a weekly column for the *Smoky Mountain Times* and is a columnist for *Smoky Mountain Living* and *Carolina Mountain Life*.

www.ingramcontent.com/pod-product-compliance
Lightning Source LLC
Chambersburg PA
CBHW022103150426
43195CB00008B/245